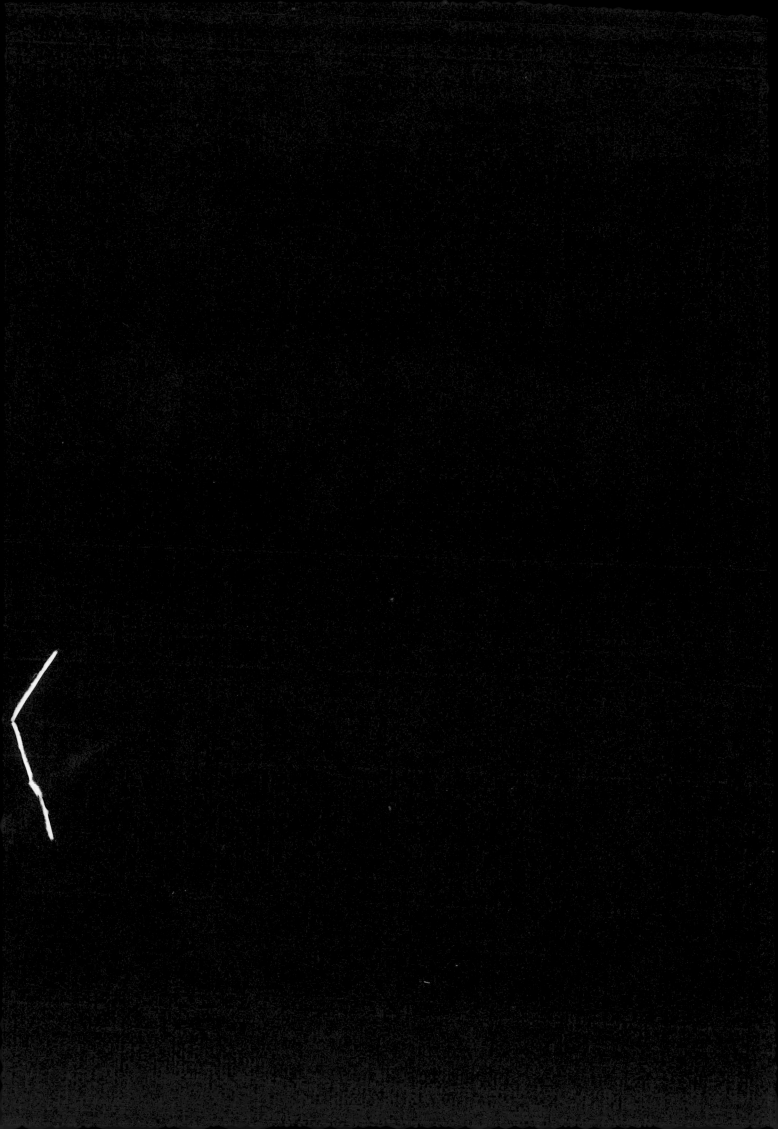

A Pleasure to Cook

Sonia Allison

A Pleasure to Cook

The complete family guide

Elm Tree Books
London

By the same author

The Awful Cook's Book
The Awful Bride's Book
Food for Thought
Dairy Book of Home Cookery
Teach your Mum Sweet & Toffee making
Marmite Guide to Better Cookery
Art of Canned Food Cookery
Horoscope Cook Book
Brighter Budget Cooking
Sauces and Sauce Making
Cake and Cake Decorating
Italian Cooking
Chicken, Turkey, Duck & Game
Barbecue Cook Book
Calorie Counters Cook Book
Cooks' Dictionary
Love of Cooking
The Book of Microwave Cookery
European Cooking
Cut the Cost Cookbook
Sonia Allison's Favourite Recipes
Sonia Allison's Book of Preserving
Cooking in Style
Sonia Allison's Food Processor Cook Book
The Mixer Cookbook
The Bisto Book of Meat Cookery
Lots of Fun to Cook with Rupert
Drinks Dictionary
Sonia Allison's Biscuit Book

First published in Great Britain 1982
by Elm Tree Books/Hamish Hamilton Ltd
Garden House 57–59 Long Acre London WC2E 9JZ

Copyright © 1982 by Sonia Allison
Illustrations copyright © 1982 by Bildstelle Orbis, München

Book design by Malcolm Harvey Young
Line drawings by Beryl Sanders

British Library Cataloguing in Publication Data

Allison, Sonia
 A pleasure to cook.
 1. Cookery
 I. Title
 641.5   TX651
 ISBN 0-241-10843-8

Phototypeset by Oliver Burridge & Company Ltd
Printed in the Netherlands by
Drukkerij de Lange/Van Leer bv

Contents

Acknowledgements

To Conrad Goulden and Anne Engel of Leisure Circle for making *A Pleasure to Cook* happen and to Roger Houghton of Elm Tree Books for being there when it did. To Anne Engel again for her enthusiasm and praise, encouragement, constructive criticism and faith. To my dearly beloved Editor, Connie Austen Smith, for her dedication, immense help, good humour, incredible patience and morale-boosting. To my own marvellous family for their unfailing devotion to my duty. To all, my heartfelt thanks.

Sonia Allison

Introduction

This is a different and rather special cookery book for two reasons.

The first is that it doesn't take for granted that you can already cook. If you can't boil an egg or make a plain white sauce then this book will tell you how. At the same time, it also provides inventive, unusual and tempting recipes to extend the repertoire of the skilled cook and the amateur alike. So this is both an indispensable cook for newly-weds, more experienced cooks *and* a source of new and delicious ideas for special occasions.

Secondly, this book does not assume you will always get it right first time. If, despite repeated efforts, you have never succeeded in making a feather-light sponge or tall, golden and crisp Yorkshire puddings then, in special 'Wrongs and Reasons' sections, Sonia Allison points out where you might have gone wrong and offers practical remedies.

In *A Pleasure to Cook* Sonia Allison has brought together, in one volume, a wealth of cookery knowledge, flair, ingenuity, and experience to make this one of the finest family cookery books available today.

Note

It is very important to remember that measurements in the recipes are given in both metric and imperial and either one or the other should be used when making up a recipe. DO NOT MIX UP the two together when measuring amounts.

The Symbols

At the top of every recipe there are symbols

▲ indicate the comparative difficulty of the recipe from ▲ for easy to ▲▲▲ for complicated.

● indicate the comparative cost of the recipe from ● for reasonable to ●●● for expensive.

Hors d'Oeuvres

Hors d'Oeuvres

Hors d'Oeuvres are intended to set the tone of a good meal and also tempt and tantalize the appetite. Although the choice of a particular savoury or favourite starter dish is very much a personal one, I suggest you serve a cold hors d'oeuvre if the rest of the meal is hot; a hot hors d'oeuvre if the main course and/or dessert are cold. Similarly, if the meal is on the fulsome side, balance it out with a delicate starter; if the meal is light, you can offer something more substantial along the lines of Egg Mayonnaise or Vol-au-Vents.

Colour and texture are also important considerations, and a starter can afford to be vivacious and crisp in character if, for instance, fish in a cream sauce and apple pie are to follow. On the other hand, if the main course is a mixed grill and the dessert fruit salad and ice cream, an acceptable beginning would be either half an avocado pear with French Dressing, a portion of Quiche, or even a simple bowl of spaghetti, elegantly dressed with nothing more complex than some butter and grated Parmesan cheese.

Party Canapés. Clockwise from the foreground: Camembert Rounds; Party Pickle Rolls; Danish Fancies; Tomato Ice Caps; Cheese 'Kebabs'; Brie and Salmon Rolls; Blue Cheese Dates. Centre: Spanish Tapas

10

Party Canapés

ALLOW 2 TO 4 PER PERSON

As these are more suggestions than recipes, it is almost impossible to give exact quantities and I would ask you, therefore, to use your own judgement as far as possible.

Blue Cheese Dates

▲▲●●

Beat together about 3oz (75g) blue vein cheese (such as Danish Blue or Italian Gorgonzola) with sufficient natural yogurt to form a fairly thick cream. Split some dried or fresh dates (skinned if fresh) and remove stones. Pipe cheese mixture into the hollows. Spear a wooden cocktail stick into each then stand, individually, on small lettuce leaves.

Camembert Rounds

▲▲●●●

Cut white bread into rounds with a 2in (5cm) biscuit cutter. Spread with butter. Top with a wedge of Camembert cheese. Garnish with mustard and cress and a gherkin.

Party Pickle Rolls

▲▲●●

Cut brown bread or Pumpernickel into 2in (5cm) rounds with a biscuit cutter. Spread with butter. Top with pickles or chutney and strips of any processed cheese to taste. Garnish each with a gherkin wrapped in ham and spear into bread with a wooden cocktail stick. Add a sprig of parsley.

Danish Fancies

▲▲●●●

Cut brown bread or Pumpernickel into 2in (5cm) rounds with a biscuit cutter. Spread with butter. Top each with a slice of tomato and hard-boiled egg. Garnish with 2 anchovy rolls filled with Danish lumpfish caviar (mock caviar). If liked, add parsley to each.

Tomato Ice Caps

▲▲●●

Hollow out tomato halves and fill with very small dice of potato mixed with homemade or bottled Tartare Sauce (page 176). Garnish each with a radish slice and sprig of parsley, then sprinkle with paprika.

Cheese 'Kebabs'

▲▲▲●●

Mix about 3oz (75g) cream cheese (such as Philadelphia) with 1 grated hard-boiled egg and salt and pepper to taste. Form into balls with damp hands. Toss in dark brown bread-crumbs tossed with paprika. Spear on to toast rounds or biscuits.

Spanish Tapas

▲●●

Cut Cheddar cheese into cubes. Garnish each with 2 stuffed olives speared on to a wooden cocktail stick.

Brie and Salmon Rolls

▲▲●●●

Cut white or brown bread into 2in (5cm) rounds with a biscuit cutter. Spread with butter. Top with squares of Brie cheese wrapped in smoked salmon strips. Garnish with a lemon slice and secure each with a wooden cocktail stick.

Belgium Style Fried Mushrooms

SERVES 4 ▲▲●●●

A light, tempting starter which teams admirably with slices of butter-fried white bread, or toast if preferred.

3oz (75g) butter
1lb (450g) button mushrooms, trimmed
1 tblsp lemon juice
salt and pepper to taste
1 heaped tblsp finely-chopped parsley
4 level tsp finely-grated Cheddar or Gouda cheese

Belgium Style Fried Mushrooms

1 Melt butter in frying pan then heat until sizzling. Add mushrooms. Fry briskly, turning, until all the butter has been absorbed.
2 DO NOT CONTINUE TO COOK UNTIL THE JUICES RUN. Remove from heat. Add lemon juice. Season well to taste. Stir in parsley.
3 Transfer to 4 scallop shells or individual plates and sprinkle with cheese. Alternatively, stand slices of fried bread or toast on to plates and spoon equal amounts of mushrooms over each. Sprinkle with cheese.

Stuffed Eggs

One type of stuffed egg, or a variety as shown in the picture on page 12, is a pretty and appetizing way of starting a summer meal and also makes a welcome contribution to a cold buffet. Allow 3 to 4 filled halves per person as a starter; 1 to 2 if part of a buffet.

VARIATIONS

Seafarer

▲▲●●●

Hard-boil as many eggs as are required. Drain. Crack. Leave to cool completely in a pan of cold water. Shell. Halve lengthwise. Carefully remove yolks and press through a fine mesh sieve directly into a bowl. Mix until creamy with a little Mayonnaise or salad cream. Season. Pipe back into egg white halves. Garnish with 4 peeled prawns and a small sprig of parsley or dill.

Siesta

▲▲●●

Prepare eggs as described in recipe for *Seafarer*. Mix sieved yolks with ½oz (15g) blue vein cheese to every yolk. Beat to a thick cream with Mayonnaise. Work in some chopped stuffed olives. Season. Spoon back into egg white halves. Garnish with slices of stuffed olive and parsley sprigs.

Stuffed Eggs. Left to right: Seafarer; Siesta; Lucullus; Marie-Thérèse; Eggs Tartare

Lucullus

▲▲▲●●

Cook hard-boiled eggs and cool as described in recipe for *Seafarer*. Cut each egg in half centrally. Remove a small sliver from both ends so that the halves stand upright without toppling. Do not remove yolks but top with a covering of Danish lumpfish caviar (mock caviar). Garnish with a rolled anchovy (from a can) and a slice of black olive. Stand on an artichoke heart (also from a can and very well drained). If liked, set some packeted aspic jelly in a shallow dish. Turn out on to a sheet of wet greaseproof paper and chop with a damp knife. Use as an optional extra garnish for the egg halves.

Marie-Thérèse

▲▲●●

Prepare eggs as described in recipe for *Seafarer*. Mix sieved yolks to a thick cream with soured cream and sufficient tomato purée both to flavour and colour the mixture tomato red. Season. Pipe or spoon back into egg white halves. Garnish with canned and well-drained asparagus tips and sprigs of fresh dill or parsley.

Eggs Tartare

▲▲●●

Prepare eggs as described in recipe for *Seafarer*. Mix sieved yolks to a thick cream with bottled or homemade Tartare Sauce (page 176). Add a few finely-chopped anchovies, (from a can) or small flakes of smoked mackerel. Spoon into egg white halves. Stand on lettuce leaves. Garnish with radish slices and a little double cream flavoured with English mustard.

Egg Mayonnaise

ALLOW 2 TO 3 HALVES PER PERSON ▲▲●●

A classical starter which still appeals all over the world, both in the home and restaurants.

Cook hard-boiled eggs and cool as described in recipe for *Seafarer*. Halve lengthwise. Stand 2 or 3 halves, cut sides down, on individual plates lined with lettuce. Coat with Mayonnaise. Drape attractively with canned anchovy fillets then dust very lightly with cayenne pepper (hot) or paprika.

Melon and Cucumber Cocktail

SERVES 6 ▲●●●

A refreshing combination of ingredients blend happily together in this unusual cocktail geared for hot weather eating.

> *1 large cucumber (1lb or 450g)*
> *2 large oranges*
> *6oz (175g) black grapes*
> *½ a Honeydew melon (about 1½lb or 675g)*

> DRESSING
> *5tblsp soured cream*
> *1tblsp lemon juice*
> *2 level tblsp caster sugar*
> *salt and pepper to taste*
> *fresh dill or parsley to garnish*

1 Wash and dry cucumber. Halve lengthwise. Cut into thin slices. Transfer to bowl.
2 Peel oranges, removing all traces of white pith. Cut into thin slices. Separate into triangular-shaped wedges. Add to bowl.

3 Wash and dry grapes. Reserve 12 for decoration. Halve remainder and remove seeds. Add to bowl. Cut melon flesh into small wedges. Add to bowl.

4 For dressing, beat together cream, lemon juice and sugar. Season to taste with salt and pepper. Pour over salad ingredients in bowl.

5 Toss well together. Transfer to cocktail glasses or sundae dishes and garnish each with 2 halved and de-seeded grapes and either a sprig of fresh dill or parsley.

Chicken and Mushroom Vol-au-Vents

SERVES 8 ▲▲▲●●

Make up 8 Vol-au-Vent cases as directed on page 194. Alternatively, thaw and bake 16 frozen puff pastry Vol-au-Vent cases as directed on the packet (small size). Prepare ½pt (275ml) Béchamel Sauce (page 169). Add to it 8oz (225g) cooked and diced chicken and 4oz (100 to 125g) trimmed and sliced button mushrooms. Heat through until bubbling. Spoon into pastry cases and top with lids. Serve straightaway.

Seafood Vol-au-Vents

SERVES 8 ▲▲▲●●

Follow recipe for *Chicken and Mushroom Vol-au-Vents*, adding 12oz (350g) peeled prawns to Béchamel Sauce instead of chicken and mushrooms.

Smoked Haddock Vol-au-Vents

SERVES 8 ▲▲▲●●

Follow recipe for *Chicken and Mushroom Vol-au-Vents*, adding 12oz (350g) cooked and flaked smoked haddock to Béchamel Sauce instead of chicken and mushrooms.

Chicken and Mushroom Vol-au-Vents

Melon and Cucumber Cocktail

13

Pasta with Genoese Pesto

Pasta with Genoese Pesto

SERVES 6 TO 8   ▲●●●

Pesto is a typically Italian condiment which is not only spooned on to any kind of cooked pasta, but also stirred into steaming Minestrone soup to accentuate the flavour. True Pesto is worked in a pestle and mortar (or was before blenders!) and, in its country of origin, is made from an abundance of fresh basil leaves which lend their own particular fragrance to this unique and full-flavoured blend of ingredients. As basil is far less profuse in the cooler climates of the north than in Mediterranean regions, my recipe is a compromise version based on readily-available parsley, perfumed with dried basil and olive oil.

> *2oz (50g) parsley (no stalks), well washed*
> *2 level tsp dried basil*
> *1oz (25g) pine kernels or walnuts*
> *1oz (25g) butter, softened*
> *3oz (75g) grated Parmesan cheese*
> *2tblsp olive oil*
> *4tblsp boiling water*
> *1 level tsp salt*
> *1lb (450g) pasta (flat ribbon noodles or elbow macaroni for instance), freshly cooked*

1 Place parsley, basil, pine kernels or walnuts, butter, cheese, olive oil and water into blender goblet.
2 Run machine until fairly smooth. Spoon out into bowl. Season with salt.
3 Drain pasta. Transfer equal amounts on to 6 or 8 warm plates. Add a teaspoon or two of Pesto to each.

Avocados Exotica

SERVES 4   ▲▲●●●

> *2 large, ripe avocados*
> *2tblsp lemon juice*
> *3oz (75g) Dutch white cabbage*
> *1 medium green pepper (about 4oz or 125g)*
> *8oz (225g) ham*
> *2 medium dessert apples*

Avocados Exotica

DRESSING
2oz (50g) onion
1tblsp salad oil
2 level tsp curry powder
4 rounded tblsp Mayonnaise
1 level tsp mild mustard
salt and pepper to taste

GARNISH
4 canned lychees
4 glacé or maraschino-flavour cherries

1 Halve avocados and remove stones. Carefully scoop flesh into bowl, leaving 'shells' of about $\frac{1}{4}$in (1cm) in thickness.
2 Add lemon juice to bowl and mash avocado flesh coarsely. Shred cabbage finely. Add two-thirds to avocado mixture, reserving last third for garnish.
3 Wash and dry pepper. Halve and remove inside fibres and seeds. Cut flesh into strips. Shred ham. Peel apples and dice. Add pepper, ham and apples to avocado in bowl.
4 To make dressing, peel and grate onion and fry until light gold in the oil. Stir, with curry powder, into the Mayonnaise. Season to taste with mustard and the salt and pepper.
5 Mix two-thirds of the onion Mayonnaise with the avocado mixture, stirring gently. Pile back into avocado shells and transfer to 4 individual plates.
6 Sprinkle with reserved cabbage then top with remainder of Mayonnaise. Garnish with lychees and cherries as shown in the picture.

15

Fantasia Cocktail

½ *level tsp dried tarragon*
¼ *level tsp dried basil*
1 *tblsp wine vinegar*
4oz (125g) *tongue*
4oz (125g) *Gouda or Edam cheese*

DRESSING
4 *rounded tblsp Mayonnaise*
2 *rounded tblsp soured cream*
1 *level tsp prepared English*
   mustard
salt and pepper to taste
1 or 2 *tblsp lemon juice*
water if necessary

1 Wash lettuce heart and shake leaves dry. Use to line 6 to 8 wine-type glasses. Wash and dry tomatoes. Thinly slice. Arrange three-quarters over lettuce. Season with salt and pepper.
2 Add equal amounts of chicken to each glass. Thinly slice cucumber and mushrooms. De-seed pepper and cut into thin strips.
3 Place cucumber, mushrooms and pepper strips into bowl. Add half the parsley or dill, tarragon, basil and vinegar. Season. Toss well. Spoon into glasses.
4 Cut tongue and cheese into strips. Add equal amounts to glasses.
5 To make dressing, beat all ingredients, except water, well together. Thin down to the consistency of pouring cream with water if necessary.
6 Pour into glasses to moisten ingredients. Finally garnish with rest of tomatoes and parsley.

Avocados Vinaigrette

ALLOW ½ AN AVOCADO
PER PERSON   ▲▲●●

Almost a classic Hors d'Oeuvre, all you have to do is halve an avocado lengthwise, remove the stone and stand on 2 individual plates. Brush the flesh with lemon juice to prevent discoloration, then fill cavities with Vinaigrette Dressing (page 180).

Avocados with Prawns

ALLOW ½ AN AVOCADO
PER PERSON   ▲▲●●●

Prepare as *Avocados Vinaigrette*. Fill cavities with peeled prawns or shrimps coated with Mayonnaise (page 175), Cocktail Sauce (page 176), or Thousand Island Dressing (page 176).

Fantasia Cocktail

SERVES 6 TO 8   ▲▲▲●●●

½ *medium round lettuce heart*
8oz (225g) *small and firm*
   tomatoes
salt and pepper to taste
8oz (225g) *cooked chicken, cut*
   into small cubes
8oz (225g) *cucumber, washed and*
   dried
4oz (125g) *button mushrooms,*
   trimmed
4oz (125g) *green pepper, washed*
   and dried
2 *level tblsp chopped parsley or*
   fresh dill (6 sprigs reserved for
   garnish)

Spaghetti Neapolitan

SERVES 4 TO 6   ▲▲●●

Prepare Neapolitan Sauce as directed on page 181. Allow 2 to 3oz spaghetti per person. Bring a large pan of boiling salted water to the boil. Add 2 teaspoons salad oil as this prevents the spaghetti from sticking together. Add spaghetti to pan. Boil about 10 minutes or until spaghetti has reached the 'al dente' stage; tender but still chewy. Drain thoroughly. Tip into a large, warm serving dish. Toss with butter or margarine. Top with Neapolitan Sauce. Serve with grated Parmesan cheese.

Spaghetti Neapolitan

Tuna and Mushroom Cocktail

SERVES 6 ▲▲●●●

1 can (7oz or 198g) tuna, drained
2oz (50g) onion, peeled and grated
4 medium tomatoes, washed and
*   dried*
8oz (225g) button mushrooms,
*   trimmed and sliced*
6oz (175g) ham, cut into strips
4tblsp lemon juice
2tblsp salad oil
1 carton (5 fluid oz or 142ml)
*   soured cream*
2 level tblsp chopped parsley
salt and pepper to taste
6 heaped tsp Tartare Sauce
*   (page 176)*

Fried Scampi

1 Flake tuna in medium-sized bowl.
  Fork in onion. Cut each tomato
  into 8 wedges. Add to bowl with
  mushrooms and three-quarters of
  the ham strips.
2 Beat lemon juice with oil, soured
  cream and parsley. Season with
  salt and pepper. Add to tuna mixture. Toss.
3 Spoon into 6 glasses. Top with remaining ham strips and the Tartare Sauce. Chill lightly before
  serving.

Fried Scampi

SERVES 4 TO 6 ▲▲●●●

1lb (450g) fresh or frozen scampi
*   or peeled prawns*
2 Grade 2 eggs
2tblsp cold milk
about 6 heaped tblsp lightly-toasted
*   breadcrumbs for coating*
deep fat or oil for frying
lemon wedges for garnishing

1 Wash and thoroughly dry scampi
  or prawns. Beat eggs and milk
  well together. Tip breadcrumbs
  on to a piece of foil or greaseproof
  paper.
2 Dip scampi or prawns into egg
  mixture then toss in crumbs.
  Leave to stand for 30 minutes for
  coating to settle and set.
3 Heat oil until hot but not smoking
  or until a cube of bread, dropped
  into the pan, rises to the top at
  once and turns golden in 50
  seconds.
4 Add coated scampi or prawns to
  pan, but only a few at a time to
  prevent the temperature of the oil
  from dropping too rapidly and
  causing sogginess.
5 Fry about 4 to 5 minutes. Lift out
  of pan with a slotted fish slice and
  drain on crumpled paper towels.
6 Transfer to 4 or 6 individual warm
  plates and garnish with lemon.

Fried Scampi Tartare

SERVES 4 TO 6 ▲▲●●●

Prepare exactly as described above,
but accompany the fish with Tartare
Sauce (page 176).

Tuna and Mushroom Cocktail

Mock Fried Scampi

SERVES 4 TO 6 ▲▲●●

Cut 1lb (450g) monk fish into similar-
sized pieces to prawns. Coat and
cook as directed in recipe for *Fried
Scampi*.

Spaghetti Carbonara

SERVES 6 ▲▲●●●

1lb (450g) spaghetti, freshly
*   cooked*
2tsp olive or corn oil
8oz (225g) diced gammon, lightly
*   fried in 1oz (25g) butter or*
*   margarine*
2oz (50g) extra butter
3 Grade 3 eggs
5tblsp double cream
2tblsp milk
salt and pepper to taste
3oz (75g) grated Parmesan cheese

1 Drain spaghetti thoroughly. Return to saucepan. Stand over low
  heat. Toss with oil.
2 Add fried gammon to spaghetti
  with butter. Beat eggs, cream and
  milk well together.
3 Pour over spaghetti then lift up
  and down with 2 spoons until
  eggs are very lightly scrambled.
4 Season to taste with salt and
  pepper and add 2oz (50g) cheese.
  Toss again. Pile on to 6 plates.
  Sprinkle with rest of cheese. Serve
  straightaway.

Mediterranean Salad

SERVES 6 ▲▲●●●

1 round lettuce
2 large tomatoes, each cut into
    8 wedges
1 medium onion, peeled and very
    thinly sliced
2 medium dessert apples, cored
    and sliced
1oz (25g) stuffed olives, sliced

DRESSING
2 rounded tblsp Mayonnaise
2 rounded tblsp soured cream
1 level tblsp chilli sauce or tomato
    ketchup
2tblsp vinegar
salt and pepper to taste

GARNISH
1 can (7oz or 198g) tuna,
    drained and flaked
1 hard-boiled egg, sliced

1 Wash and dry lettuce. Use the
outer leaves to line a glass salad
bowl. Sprinkle with the heart, cut
into shreds.
2 Put tomatoes, onion slices, apples
and olives into basin. Add dressing, made by beating Mayonnaise
with rest of ingredients.
3 Toss well with 2 spoons. Add to
salad bowl. Top with tuna and
slices of egg.

Mediterranean Salad

Below: Spaghetti Carbonara

19

Mixed Hors d'Oeuvre. Left to right, top: Dishes 1, 2, 3, 4 and bottom: Dishes 5, 6, 7

Mixed Hors d'Oeuvre

SERVES 8 ▲▲●●●

A once-upon-a-time favourite both in restaurants and in the home, mixed Hors d'Oeuvre still makes a colourful and appetizing beginning to a fairly formal meal and gives people a wide assortment of 'tasters' from which to choose.

Dish 1
Roll small pieces of melon in Parma ham. Garnish with sliced celery and slices of carrot.

Dish 2
Arrange very thinly-sliced smoked salmon (about 4oz or 125g) on a dish. Garnish with a lemon slice topped with mock caviar, mustard and cress and stuffed olives.

Dish 3
Fill canned artichoke bottoms with Mayonnaise to which chopped parsley has been added. Garnish with black olives and greenery such as curly endive.

Dish 4
Roll up slices of Mortadella sausage and drop a few drained capers into each. Garnish with slices of hard-boiled egg.

Dish 5
Arrange canned artichoke hearts and canned and flaked tuna on a dish. Garnish with beetroot strips and celery leaves.

Dish 6
Arrange asparagus in dish. Coat with French Dressing (page 180). Sprinkle with a band of finely-chopped hard-boiled egg.

Dish 7
Arrange tomato wedges (about 4 medium tomatoes) in a dish. Garnish with onion rings and white cocktail onions. Coat with French Dressing (page 180).

Bean Cocktails

Beans, in all their variety, make inexpensive and appetizing starters which are easy to make and undemanding of difficult-to-find ingredients. Here is a selection of 5 colourful combinations.

Broad Bean and Bacon Cocktail

SERVES 6 ▲▲●●

1lb (450g) broad beans (shelled weight), freshly cooked
6tblsp French Dressing (page 180)
1 small onion, peeled and grated
4oz (125g) streaky bacon, diced and crisply fried

1 Drain beans thoroughly. Put into a bowl and toss with the French Dressing and onion. Cover.
2 Leave in a cool place for 2 hours. Divide equally between 6 glasses. Sprinkle with well-drained bacon.

Green Bean Salad Cocktail

SERVES 6 ▲▲●●

8oz (225g) whole green beans, first broken into short lengths, and freshly cooked
8oz (225g) unpeeled cucumber, washed and thinly sliced
4 medium tomatoes, washed and sliced
6tblsp French Dressing (page 180)
2 level tblsp chopped parsley

1 Drain beans and leave on one side for the time being. Place equal amounts of cucumber and tomato slices into 6 glasses.
2 Top with beans then pour dressing over each. Sprinkle with parsley and chill lightly before serving.

Baked Bean Cocktail

SERVES 4 ▲▲●●

1 medium can baked beans
1 small onion, grated
1tblsp lemon juice
1 garlic clove, peeled and crushed
2 large tomatoes, each cut into
    8 wedges
parsley sprigs for garnishing

1 Mix beans with onion, lemon juice and crushed garlic clove.
2 Divide equally between 4 cocktail glasses. Garnish each with 4 tomato wedges and a sprig of parsley.

Bean Cocktails. Clockwise from bottom left: Broad Bean and Bacon Cocktail; Green Bean Salad Cocktail; Baked Bean Cocktail; Green Bean and Pepper Salad; Hungarian Style Bean Salad

Green Bean and Pepper Salad

SERVES 6 ▲▲●●

12oz (350g) whole green beans, first broken into short lengths, and freshly cooked
1 medium red pepper, de-seeded and coarsely chopped
1 medium onion, peeled and chopped
6tblsp French Dressing (page 180)

1 Toss vegetables with dressing. Divide between 6 glasses. Chill lightly. Serve.

Hungarian Style Bean Salad

SERVES 6 ▲▲●●

8oz (225g) cooked haricot beans
1 large red pepper, de-seeded and cut into thin strips
1 large onion, peeled and grated
4oz (125g) Dutch white cabbage, finely shredded
6tblsp French Dressing (page 180)

1 Toss all ingredients with the dressing. Divide between 6 glasses. Chill lightly. Serve.

Taramosalata

SERVES 8 ▲▲●●●

A beautifully creamy version of a favourite Greek starter, which is served as a dip and eaten with warm Pita bread or, if unavailable, soft bap rolls. A food processor or blender is advisable.

6oz (175g) potatoes (NOT new), freshly boiled
2tblsp boiling water
3tblsp lemon juice
4oz (125g) smoked cod roe (available in jars)
4tblsp olive or other salad oil
1 small garlic clove, peeled and crushed
pepper to taste

1 Place all ingredients into food processor or blender goblet. Run either machine until ingredients form a smooth purée.
2 Spoon into a dish. Serve with bread.

Liver Pâté

▲▲●●●

A fine pâté which I have been making successfully for a number of years. It is fairly rich and a little goes a long way, so I suggest you wrap leftovers securely in cling film and leave in the refrigerator up to 1 week or in the deep freeze up to 3 months.

> 1lb (450g) well-washed pork,
>   lamb or chicken livers or
>   mixture of livers, cut into small
>   pieces
> 3oz (75g) onion, peeled and
>   quartered
> 2oz (50g) plain flour
> 2oz (50g) butter or margarine,
>   melted
> 1 Grade 2 egg, beaten
> 1 carton (5oz or 142ml) double
>   cream
> 1 tblsp cold milk
> ¼ level tsp mixed spice
> 2 level tsp salt (scant measure)
> ¼ level tsp white pepper

1 Mince raw liver and onion together in mincing machine or food processor.
2 Tip into bowl. Beat in rest of ingredients to form a loose mixture which firms up when cooked.
3 Pour into a 2lb (about 1kg) loaf tin, first lined completely with aluminium foil inside and brushed with melted butter or margarine.
4 Cover with a piece of foil (also brushed with melted butter or margarine) and stand tin on a baking tray.
5 Bake 2 hours in moderate oven set to 180°C (350°F), Gas 4. Remove from oven and cool to lukewarm in the tin.
6 Turn out on to a board with the foil still round the sides. Refrigerate until firm and set. Remove foil carefully and cut pâté into slices.
7 Serve on plates lined with lettuce and accompany with freshly-made crisp toast.

Prawn Cocktail

SERVES 4   ▲▲●●●

> 1 lettuce heart from round lettuce,
>   washed and dried
> ¼pt (150ml) Cocktail Sauce
>   (page 176)
> 8oz (225g) peeled prawns
> 4 lemon slices

1 Shred lettuce and divide equally between 4 wine-type glasses.
2 Mix Cocktail Sauce and prawns well together. Spoon into glasses over lettuce. Garnish each with a slice of lemon.

Beef Tartare

SERVES 4   ▲▲●●●

Beef Tartare, said to come from the cuisine of old Russia, is an acquired taste, is very much a luxury for those who enjoy eating raw minced steak, and must be made from top quality, fresh rump or fillet steak.

> 1lb (450g) rump or fillet steak
>   with all fat removed
> salt and pepper to taste
> 4 egg yolks
>
> DISHES OF THE FOLLOWING
> 1 small onion, peeled and grated
> 1 heaped tblsp drained capers,
>   chopped
> 1 heaped tblsp chopped parsley
>
> TO ACCOMPANY
> Worcester sauce
> black pepper, freshly milled

1 Mince meat finely. Season to taste with salt and pepper. Place 4 mounds on to 4 individual plates.
2 Shape into large hamburgers and make a dip in the centre of each. Fill with egg yolks.
3 Serve with dishes of onion, capers and parsley to which people help themselves.
4 To eat, mix meat with remaining ingredients on the plate. Sprinkle to taste with Worcester sauce and the freshly-milled pepper.

Freezer Note
Unless otherwise stated, do not freeze starters which have been prepared ready for eating.

Cocktail Fritters

SERVES 8   ▲▲▲●●

Make up *Savoury Fritter Batter* as directed (page 202) and gently fold in 4oz (125g) chopped chicken or cooked meat, coarsely-flaked canned fish (such as drained tuna), small cubes of hard cheese or sliced green olives. Drop teaspoons of mixture into deep, hot oil and fry about 5 minutes or until Fritters float to the top of the pan and are deep gold and crisp. Remove from pan and drain on kitchen paper. Arrange on serving dish and sprinkle with grated Parmesan Cheese. Serve hot.

Cheese Aigrettes

MAKES ABOUT 20   ▲▲▲●●

> 2oz (50g) Cheddar cheese, finely
>   grated
> Choux Pastry (page 196), freshly
>   made
> deep fat for frying
> extra grated cheese for sprinkling

1 Beat cheese into Choux Pastry then drop teaspoons of mixture into hot oil.
2 Fry until they float to the top and are crisp and golden. Drain on paper towels.
3 Transfer to a serving dish, sprinkle with cheese and serve hot.

Gnocchi Parisienne

SERVES 6   ▲▲▲●●

Make up Choux Pastry as directed (page 196) then stir in 2oz (50g) grated Parmesan cheese. Drop about 20 to 24 teaspoons into a pan of gently simmering salted water. Poach gently about 5 to 7 minutes or until Gnocchi float to the surface. Drain on paper towels. Transfer to an oblong, buttered shallow dish and coat with freshly-made Cheese Sauce (page 169). Sprinkle with 2oz (50g) finely-grated Cheddar cheese or 1oz (25g) grated Parmesan cheese and 1oz (25g) melted butter. Brown under a hot grill.

Hot and Cold Soups

Hot and Cold Soups

Soup can be warming or cooling, dark or light, sweet or tangy, smooth or chunky, sophisticated or basic. It provides endless possibilities for the inventive cook and amid a handful of classics which are established favourites, I have also included some unusual soup recipes for those who, on occasions, appreciate a touch of novelty and welcome the chance to be both experimental and creative.

Cream of Vegetable Soup

SERVES 6 GENEROUSLY ▲▲●●

This is a classic cream soup from which a number of variations stem. It is especially suited to those with blenders, but anyone with patience may prefer to tackle the soup the old-fashioned way and rub the vegetables through a fine mesh sieve. Onion is always included, but the white part of leek (1 large) may be used if a milder flavour is preferred. Although the soup is referred to as 'cream', this describes the texture; cream is only occasionally added:

4oz (125g) onions
1½lb (675g) mixed vegetables
    such as carrots, swede, turnip,
    celery, cauliflower and
    potatoes
2oz (50g) butter or margarine or
    2tblsp salad oil
2pt (1¼ litre) water
2 level tsp salt
white pepper to taste
1 level tblsp cornflour
½pt (275ml) cold milk
chopped parsley for garnishing

1 Peel onions and chop. Peel mixed vegetables. Wash thoroughly and cut into large cubes.
2 Heat butter, margarine or oil in large pan. Add onions and prepared vegetables. Fry gently, with lid on pan, for about 15 to 20 minutes or until pale gold.
3 Add water, salt and pepper. Bring to boil, stirring. Lower heat and cover pan. Simmer gently about ¾ to 1 hour or until vegetables are very soft.
4 Strain liquid into a bowl and leave on one side for time being.
5 Either rub vegetables through sieve directly into saucepan in which soup was cooking or blend, with a little liquid from bowl, to smooth purée in blender goblet. Do this in 2 or 3 batches to prevent machine from overflowing. Tip into pan.
6 Add all remaining liquid to pan. Stir in cornflour, first smoothly mixed with cold milk. Bring to boil, stirring continuously to prevent soup from burning. Simmer 3 or 4 minutes.
7 Adjust seasoning to taste and thin down with a little extra boiling water or hot milk if too thick for personal taste. Ladle into bowls and sprinkle with chopped parsley.

Note The following apply to all soups given below which are variations of the basic recipe.

Flavour Tip
For more piquancy, add a bouquet garni to the vegetables while they are boiling. If preferred, dust servings lightly with nutmeg instead of parsley.

Milk Tip
Any milk may be used but, to reduce richness, try skimmed.

Freezer Tip
Leave soup until completely cold. Pour into container leaving 2in (5cm) headroom to allow for expansion. Cover securely. Freeze up to 3 months. Thaw overnight in the refrigerator or 4 to 5 hours at kitchen temperature before serving.

Indian Style Pea Soup

Cream of Artichoke Soup

SERVES 6 GENEROUSLY ▲▲●●

Make exactly as *Cream of Vegetable Soup*, substituting 2lb (900g) peeled and cut-up Jerusalem artichokes for the mixed vegetables. Add 1 tablespoon lemon juice to the pan with the water as this helps to prevent artichokes from browning.

Cream of Carrot Soup

SERVES 6 GENEROUSLY ▲▲●●

Make exactly as *Cream of Vegetable Soup*, substituting 1½lb (675g) peeled and cut-up carrots for the mixed vegetables. For interesting colour effect, add a few cooked peas to each serving.

Cream of Cauliflower Soup

SERVES 6 GENEROUSLY ▲▲●●

Make exactly as *Cream of Vegetable Soup*, substituting 1½lb (675g) cauliflower florets for the mixed vegetables. You will, for the quantity, probably need 2 cauliflowers or, for ease, use frozen cauliflower florets, straight from frozen. Simmer about 30 minutes.

Cream of Pea Soup

SERVES 6 GENEROUSLY ▲▲●●

Make exactly as *Cream of Vegetable Soup*, but either fry 4oz (125g) chopped-up gammon with the onions or add a ham bone at the same time as the water. Use 1½lb (675g) green peas (shelled weight) instead of mixed vegetables.

Indian Style Pea Soup

SERVES 8 GENEROUSLY

▲▲▲●●

Make exactly as *Cream of Pea Soup*, adding 1 level tablespoon mild curry powder to the fried vegetables. After

Cheese Velouté Soup (page 26)

Cream of Tomato Soup

soup has come to the boil with cornflour and milk mixture, stir in 3 level tablespoons flaked and toasted almonds, 1 rounded tablespoon raisins and 4 tablespoons double cream or thick yogurt.

Cream of Potato Soup

SERVES 6 GENEROUSLY ▲▲●●

Make exactly as *Cream of Vegetable Soup*, but substitute 1½lb (675g) peeled and diced potatoes for the mixed vegetables.

Cream of Tomato Soup

SERVES 6 GENEROUSLY ▲▲●●

Make exactly as *Cream of Vegetable Soup*, but substitute 2lb (900g) cut-up tomatoes for mixed vegetables. Flavour with 2 teaspoons Worcester sauce, 2 teaspoons lemon juice and 2 level teaspoons brown sugar and add with water. Serve with croûtons, made by frying 4 slices diced white bread in 2oz (50g) butter until golden. To heighten colour, add 2 to 3 level tablespoons tubed or canned tomato purée to thickened soup.

Velouté Soups

These are creamy soups made from a roux (see White Sauce section on page 168) of fat and flour, thinned down with stock and enriched with cream. They are quick and easy to prepare and excellent also for using up leftover meat, poultry and vegetables.

Chicken Velouté Soup

SERVES 6 ▲▲●●

1½oz (40g) butter or margarine
1½oz (40g) plain flour
1pt (575ml) chicken stock (either made from simmering giblets in water or from stock cube)
¼ level tsp salt
4oz (125g) cooked chicken, diced or cut into strips
¼pt (150ml) single cream
white pepper to taste
chopped parsley for sprinkling over the top

1 Melt butter or margarine in pan. Stir in flour to form roux. Gradually blend in stock.
2 Cook, stirring continuously, until soup comes to boil and thickens. Season with salt.
3 Add chicken. Cover. Bubble gently 10 minutes. Remove from heat. stir in cream. Season with pepper.
4 Ladle into bowls and sprinkle chopped parsley over each.

Cheese Velouté Soup

SERVES 6 ▲▲●●●

Make exactly as *Chicken Velouté Soup*, adding 3oz (75g) finely-grated Cheddar cheese at same time as cream. Remove from heat, add pepper and stir until cheese completely melts. Place 2 rounded teaspoons chopped parsley or chives (or mixture) into each of 6 soup plates. Ladle soup into each. Add croûtons made from frying 3 slices diced white bread in 1½oz (40g) butter or margarine.

Top: Mushroom Velouté Soup
Centre: with Ham and Cheese
Bottom: with Prawns

Mushroom Velouté Soup

SERVES 6 ▲▲●●●

Make exactly as *Chicken Velouté Soup*, adding 4oz (125g) sliced button mushrooms instead of chicken. Simmer 5 minutes. Sprinkle each portion with parsley.

Mushroom Velouté Soup with Ham and Cheese

SERVES 6 ▲▲●●●

Make exactly as *Mushroom Velouté Soup* but add 4oz (125g) strips of ham with the mushrooms. Sprinkle each portion with 1 heaped teaspoon grated Parmesan cheese. Top with a sprig of parsley.

Mushroom and Prawn Velouté Soup

SERVES 6 ▲▲●●●

Make exactly as *Mushroom Velouté Soup* but add 4oz (125g) prawns with the mushrooms. Sprinkle each portion heavily with chopped parsley.

Mussel Velouté Soup

SERVES 6 ▲▲●●●

Make exactly as *Chicken Velouté Soup*, using fish stock (page 59) instead of chicken and adding 1 level tablespoon tubed or canned tomato purée as soon as soup has come to the boil and thickened. Mix thoroughly until streakiness has disappeared. Stir in cream, pepper and 4oz (125g) mussels (preserved in acid and first well rinsed) instead of chicken. Heat through for 2 minutes. Sprinkle each serving lightly with chopped fresh dill or parsley.

Mussel Velouté Soup

Avocado Velouté Soup (page 28)

Avocado Velouté Soup

SERVES 6 ▲▲▲●●●

Make exactly as *Chicken Velouté Soup* but omit chicken. Instead, blend 1 peeled and cut-up avocado to smooth purée in blender goblet with cream. Stir into soup. Remove from heat. Season with pepper and extra salt if necessary. Peel and slice second ripe avocado. Add 3 or 4 slices to each portion of soup. Serve straightaway and before avocado has a chance to discolour.

Freezer Tip

As most Velouté Soups are quick and fairly uncomplicated to make, there is no advantage in freezing them.

Broths

These fall into a different category altogether and are thick, flavourful and hearty soups, ideally suited to cold weather eating. With the addition of meat or poultry, they are nutritious as well and can be served as a main course. Broths usually contain rice or barley, but these may be omitted if preferred.

Vegetable Broth

SERVES 6 ▲▲●●

> *1 large leek*
> *2 large onions*
> *4 medium carrots*
> *1 small turnip*
> *4oz (125g) swede*
> *4oz (125g) parsnip*
> *2 large celery sticks*
> *2oz (50g) butter or margarine*
> *2pt (1¼ litre) water*
> *3 to 4 level tsp salt*
> *2oz (50g) barley or rice, well washed*

1 Trim leek, leaving on as much green part as possible. Slit almost to top and wash thoroughly. Cut into shreds.
2 Peel onions and slice. Halve each and separate into semi-circular rings. Peel carrots, turnip, swede and parsnip. Cut into strips.
3 Scrub celery. Cut into strips. Heat butter or margarine in large saucepan. Add all prepared vegetables. Stir well to mix.

Vegetable Broth

28

4 Pour water into pan. Add salt and barley or rice. Bring to boil. Lower heat. Cover. Simmer 1¼ to 1½ hours when vegetables and barley should be soft. If rice has been used instead, cooking time can be reduced by ½ hour.

Beef Broth

SERVES 6 ▲▲●●●

Make as *Vegetable Broth*, but slice and dice all vegetables instead of cutting into strips. Add 8oz to 12oz (225 to 350g) 'flash fry' steak, cut into cubes. Simmer 1½ to 1¾ hours.

Scotch Broth

SERVES 6 ▲▲●●●

Make as *Vegetable Broth*, but slice and dice all vegetables instead of cutting into strips. Add 1lb (450g) scrag end neck of lamb. Simmer 1¼ to 1½ hours.

Freezer Tip

Leave any of the Broths to cool completely. Pour into suitable container, leaving 2in (5cm) headroom on top for expansion. Cover securely. Freeze up to 3 months. Thaw completely before reheating; either overnight in the refrigerator or 4 to 5 hours at room temperature.

Minestrone

An Italian version of Broth, many varieties are to be found in Italy although they all share one thing in common — plenty of vegetables and a topping of grated Parmesan cheese.

Beef Broth

Venetian Style Minestrone

SERVES 8 ▲▲●●●

1tblsp olive or corn oil
1 pig's trotter, chopped into small
    pieces
3oz (75g) streaky bacon, chopped
4oz (125g) onion, peeled and
    chopped
8oz (225g) savoy cabbage or
    spring greens, well washed and
    shredded
2¼pt (1¼ litres) water

2 bouquet garni
8oz (225g) tomatoes, skinned and
    coarsely chopped
¼ level tsp dried rosemary
3 to 4 level tsp salt
pepper to taste

ADDITIONS
4oz (125g) cooked rice
6oz (175g) butter-fried chickens'
    livers, cut into small pieces
4 heaped tblsp chopped parsley
grated Parmesan cheese

1 Heat oil in pan. Add trotter, bacon and onion. Fry over medium heat for 10 to 15 minutes or until light gold.
2 Stir in all remaining ingredients. Bring to boil, stirring. Lower heat. Cover. Simmer gently 1½ hours, stirring from time to time.
3 Remove pieces of pig's trotter and cut flesh off bones. Return to Minestrone with rice, liver and half the parsley. Heat through 5 minutes. Remove bouquet garni.
4 Pour into a soup tureen or large dish. Sprinkle with rest of parsley and grated cheese. Serve piping hot.

Minestrone. Left: Venetian Style; Back: Tesino Style; Right: Neapolitan Style

Tesino Style Minestrone

SERVES 8   ▲▲●●●

A more familiar Minestrone, packed with a variety of vegetables and herbs.

>   *2tblsp olive or corn oil*
>   *2oz (50g) streaky bacon, chopped*
>   *3oz (75g) onion, sliced*
>   *12oz (350g) whole green beans,*
>   *fresh or frozen*
>   *10oz (275g) Dutch white cabbage*
>   *10oz (275g) carrots*
>   *10oz (275g) pumpkin flesh or*
>   *marrow, peeled and de-seeded*
>   *12oz (350g) potatoes*
>   *2 leeks*
>   *6 medium celery sticks*
>   *3pt (1¾ litre) stock or water*
>   *1 level tblsp salt*
>   *3 rounded tblsp tubed or canned*
>   *tomato purée*
>   *1 rounded tsp dried basil*
>   *1 level tsp dried marjoram*
>   *4oz (125g) rice or macaroni*
>   *2 heaped tblsp chopped parsley*
>   *grated Parmesan cheese*

1 Heat oil in extra large saucepan. Add bacon and onion. Fry gently, covered, for ¼ hour or until light gold.
2 Meanwhile, top and tail beans, remove stringy sides and break into 2 or 3 pieces.
3 Wash and shred cabbage. Peel carrots and slice. Dice pumpkin flesh or marrow. Peel and wash potatoes then cube.
4 Trim leeks, leaving as much green part as possible. Slit and wash thoroughly. Slice. Scrub celery. Slice.
5 Add all prepared vegetables to pan with stock or water, salt, tomato purée, basil and marjoram.
6 Bring to boil. Stir round. Lower heat. Cover. Add rice or macaroni. Continue to boil gently a further ½ to ¾ hour, keeping pan covered.
7 Ladle into a large soup tureen and sprinkle with parsley. Pass round Parmesan cheese separately.

Vegetarian Tip
Bacon may be completely omitted if preferred.

Neapolitan Style Minestrone

SERVES 6   ▲▲▲●●●

A strongly-flavoured brew that typi-fies Mediterranean cooking. Make only if olives, anchovies and garlic are appreciated.

>   *3tblsp olive oil*
>   *4oz (125g) streaky bacon, chopped*
>   *3oz (75g) onions, peeled and*
>   *chopped*
>   *2 garlic cloves, peeled and chopped*
>   *1 medium green pepper, de-seeded*
>   *and chopped*
>   *8oz (225g) washed courgettes,*
>   *sliced*
>   *1oz (25g) black olives*
>   *2 canned anchovy fillets*
>   *4oz (125g) rice*
>   *1 heaped tsp chopped fresh mint or*
>   *¼ level tsp dried*
>   *3 rounded tblsp tubed or canned*
>   *tomato purée*
>   *1¾pt (1 litre) water*
>   *½ level tsp dried oregano*
>   *½ level tsp dried basil*
>   *grated Parmesan cheese*

1 Heat oil in large saucepan. Add bacon, onions, garlic and green pepper. Cover. Fry 10 minutes over medium heat.

2 Add courgettes, olives, anchovies (without cutting up), rice, mint, tomato purée and water.

3 Bring to boil, stirring. Lower heat. Cover. Simmer 1 hour. Add oregano and basil. Heat through a further 10 minutes.

4 Pour into a soup tureen and serve with a bowl of Parmesan cheese.

Freezer Tip

Any of the Minestrone Soups may be deep frozen up to 1 month. Cheese should always be added afterwards.

French Style Tomato Soup

SERVES 8 TO 10 ▲▲●●

From the area of the Loire, this soup is sometimes served at wedding receptions and is quite quick to make. It is also ideal for summer parties, but does not freeze satisfactorily.

3oz (75g) vermicelli
boiling salted water
2½lb (just over 2kg) ripe tomatoes, blanched and skinned
1 large onion, peeled
1 garlic clove, peeled
2tblsp dripping or oil
2½pt (1¼ litres) chicken or beef stock
salt and pepper to taste
3 rounded tblsp chopped parsley

1 Cook vermicelli in boiling salted water about 7 minutes or until tender. Drain and rinse.

2 Coarsely chop tomatoes. Chop onion. Slice garlic. Heat dripping or oil in large pan. Add onion and garlic. Fry until light gold.

3 Add tomatoes. Fry, turning, 3 minutes. Pour stock into pan. Bring to boil. Lower heat. Add salt and pepper to taste.

4 Cover. Simmer 10 minutes. Add vermicelli. Heat through a further 5 minutes. Stir in parsley. Ladle into bowls.

Brown Onion Soup

SERVES 6 ▲▲●●

The trick with this soup, even if it does not conform strictly to tradition, is to thicken it slightly with flour. The onions are then held in a light suspension and the bread, which sits on top, is less likely to sink. Something else I do of which purists would disapprove. I make my toasted bread separately under the grill and stand 2 slices on top of each bowl. The 'correct' thing to do is to place 2 slices of toast on to each bowl of soup, sprinkle with cheese and then place the bowls in the oven on a tray. It's difficult, it means heating the oven purposely, and is not essential to success – hence my compromise version. The soup is not suitable for freezing.

1½lb (675g) large onions, peeled
2oz (50g) butter, dripping, margarine or oil
2 level tblsp flour
2pt (1¼ litre) boiling water
salt and freshly-milled pepper to taste
12 medium thick slices of French bread
6oz (175g) Gruyère or strong Cheddar cheese, grated

1 Slice onions thinly. Separate slices into rings. Heat fat or oil in large pan until sizzling. Add onions. Cover.

2 Fry over medium heat about 30 minutes or until very soft. Uncover. Continue to fry until dark gold but avoid burning as the flavour will infiltrate the soup and completely spoil it.

3 Stir in flour. Cook 2 minutes. Gradually blend in boiling water. Simmer, stirring continuously, until soup comes to boil and thickens slightly. Bubble gently, uncovered, for about 5 minutes. Season to taste.

4 Meanwhile, toast bread on one side only. Turn over. Sprinkle untoasted sides heavily with cheese. Grill until cheese just begins to melt and brown.

5 Ladle soup into 6 large bowls. Stand 2 slices of cheese toast on each. Serve straightaway.

French Style Tomato Soup

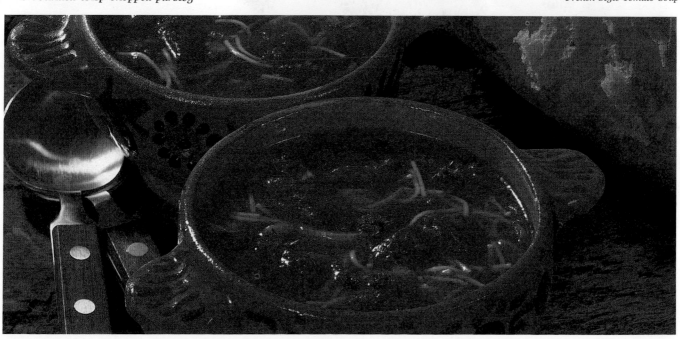

31

Brown Onion Soup (page 31)

Consommé

SERVES 8 ▲▲●●●

Although stock cubes or stock powder – chicken, beef and even vegetable – make a reasonable clear stock that can double as Consommé, the real thing is infinitely superior and, when time permits, well worth the effort. In order to eliminate grease, make the Consommé one day for the next, refrigerate over-

Consommé

night then remove the layer of fat which has risen to the surface and set in a firm layer. Consommé may be used as a base for a vast number of soups featured in the classic French repertoire, and may be served clear with a dash of sherry or port or enhanced either with cooked meat, fish, poultry, eggs, vegetables, cooked pasta, rice or croûtons. It takes well to deep freezing and the meat cooked in the Consommé may be served as

boiled beef for 2 or 3 people with carrots, dumplings and boiled potatoes.

> 8oz (225g) marrow bones
> 2½pt (1½ litres) water
> 12oz (350g) shin of beef, in one
>   piece
> 1 large onion, peeled
> 2 large carrots, peeled
> 2 medium leeks, trimmed but with
>   most of the green left on
> 1 medium parsnip
> 2oz (50g) celeriac or 2 large celery
>   sticks
> 2 level tsp salt
> 1 bay leaf
> 2 cloves
> 4 peppercorns
> 2 juniper berries (optional)
> 1 garlic clove, peeled

1 Put bones into extra large pan. Add water and beef. Bring to boil. Skim off scum as it rises to the top.
2 Add all remaining ingredients. Bring to boil. Lower heat. Simmer very gently for 3 hours. Remove from heat.
3 Take out meat. Use as required. Strain soup into bowl. Cool. Cover. Refrigerate overnight. Remove layer of fat.
4 To serve, reheat until hot, ladle into bowls and add a dash of sherry or port to each. Sprinkle with parsley and serve with bought or homemade cheese biscuits.

Freezer Tip
Freeze up to 3 months.

Pheasant Soup

SERVES 6 TO 8 ▲▲●●●

> remains of 1 pheasant plus carcase
> 3oz (75g) streaky bacon, chopped
> 1oz (25g) lard, dripping or
>   margarine
> 2oz (50g) onion, finely chopped
> 2oz (50g) carrot, peeled and
>   grated
> 1 large celery stick, scrubbed and
>   finely chopped
> 2oz (50g) flour
> 1¾pt (1 litre) water
> 2 level tsp salt
> 4oz (125g) button mushrooms,
>   trimmed and sliced
> 1 wine glass of port
> freshly-milled black pepper to taste
> ¼pt (150ml) double cream
> 2 rounded tblsp chopped parsley

1 Pick pheasant meat off carcase and reserve temporarily with all the bones.
2 Fry bacon by itself until the fat runs. Add fat. Heat until sizzling and bacon browns. Stir in prepared vegetables.

3 Cover. Fry gently 15 minutes or until lightly browned. Uncover. Stir in flour. Gradually blend in water. Add pheasant bones.
4 Season with salt. Bring to boil, stirring. Lower heat. Cover. Simmer 30 minutes.

5 Lift out pheasant bones and discard. Add pheasant meat and mushrooms to soup. Cover. Heat through 10 minutes.
6 Stir in port. Season with pepper. Pour into tureen. Swirl in cream then sprinkle with parsley.

Note Any other game birds may be used if preferred.

Pheasant Soup

33

Bortsch

Bortsch

SERVES 8 GENEROUSLY ▲▲●●●

There are any number of recipes for this classic Russian beetroot soup, but this version is based on one from the Ukraine and has been adapted from a recipe published at the turn of the century.

1lb (450g) shin of beef
2½pt (1¼ litres) water
3 to 4 level tsp salt
1 large onion, peeled and chopped
1lb (450g) cooked beetroots, peeled
2tblsp red wine vinegar or lemon juice
8oz (225g) skinned tomatoes
2 level tblsp tubed or canned tomato purée
8oz (225g) Dutch white cabbage, shredded
4oz (125g) carrots, peeled and sliced
4oz (125g) celery sticks, scrubbed and chopped
1 bayleaf
1 carton (5 fluid oz or 142ml) soured cream
4 heaped tblsp chopped parsley

1 Put beef and water into large pan. Add salt. Bring to boil. Skim. Simmer 1½ hours.
2 Meanwhile, finely chop onions and cut two-thirds beetroots into thin strips. Add to pan with vinegar or lemon juice, tomatoes, purée, cabbage, carrots, celery and bay leaf.

3 Return to boil. Lower heat. Cover. Simmer 30 minutes. Remove meat. Cut up into cubes and return to soup. Remove bay leaf.
4 To heighten colour, grate rest of beetroots and stir into soup. Heat through about 2 minutes. Ladle into bowls. Top each with soured cream and parsley.

Baltic Fish Soup

Baltic Fish Soup

SERVES 6   ▲▲●●●

1tblsp salad oil
2oz (50g) streaky bacon, chopped
1½oz (40g) flour
1pt (575ml) water
1 bouquet garni
2 level tsp salt
2 rounded tsp creamed horseradish
    sauce
8oz (225g) skinned cod fillet, cut
    into cubes
2 large cooked potatoes, cubed
1 carton (5 fluid oz or 142ml)
    soured cream
1 rounded tblsp chopped parsley

1 Heat oil in pan. Add bacon. Fry until crisp and golden. Stir in flour. Cook 2 minutes.
2 Gradually blend in water. Cook, stirring, until soup comes to boil and thickens. Add bouquet garni and salt. Cover. Simmer ¾ hour.
3 Remove bouquet garni and discard. Add horseradish sauce, fish cubes and potatoes to soup. Heat through just long enough to cook fish; about 6 to 8 minutes.
4 Gently stir in cream. Pour into large dish. Sprinkle with parsley.

Note Do not freeze.

Brown Windsor Soup

SERVES 8   ▲▲●●●

Once on every menu in hotels and restaurants, the popularity of this old English soup has waned considerably over the years. All the same, people remember it still and ask for the recipe.

8oz (225g) shin of beef
1lb (450g) beef bones
3pt (1¾ litre) cold water
3 level tsp salt
1tblsp mushroom ketchup
8oz (225g) carrots
8oz (225g) onions
1tsp gravy browning
2 level tsp cornflour
2tblsp cold water

1 Put beef, in one piece, into large pan. Add bones and water. Bring to boil. Remove scum as it rises to top.
2 Add all remaining ingredients except cornflour and water. Cover. Simmer gently 3 hours.

Apricot Soup

3 Remove meat from pan. Stand on plate and shred with 2 forks. Strain liquid into clean pan.
4 Rub carrots and onions through mesh sieve or blend until smooth, with a little liquid from pan, in blender goblet. Return to pan with meat. Bring slowly to boil.
5 Mix cornflour smoothly with water. Add to soup. Cook, stirring all the time, until it comes to boil and thickens.
6 Adjust seasoning. Ladle into soup bowls and serve with cheese biscuits or fingers of brown toast.

Clear Brown Windsor Soup

SERVES 8   ▲▲●●●

Make exactly as *Brown Windsor Soup* but do not add sieved or blended vegetables.

Apricot Soup

SERVES 8 GENEROUSLY
     ▲▲▲●●

An unusual sweet, hot soup that could be served confidently as a prelude to roast duck or pork.

PART 1
1lb (450g) fresh, ripe apricots
½ bottle sweet white wine
¼pt (150ml) water
8oz (225g) caster sugar

PART 2
1¾pt (1 litre) water
3 rounded tblsp fresh white
    breadcrumbs
1 level tsp cinnamon
finely-grated peel of 1 medium
    washed lemon
pinch of salt
2 Grade 3 eggs, separated
3oz (75g) caster sugar
about 12 ratafias or miniature
    macaroons

1 Wash and dry apricots. Slit and remove stones. Put half the stoned apricots into a pan with wine and water. Cook in covered pan until just soft, keeping heat low.
2 Remove from heat. Add half the sugar. Stir over low heat until dissolved. Keep hot temporarily.
3 Place rest of apricots into second pan with water, crumbs, cinnamon, lemon peel and salt. Bring to boil. Lower heat. Cover. Simmer 15 minutes. Cool to lukewarm.

4 Either rub through fine mesh sieve or blend, in 2 or 3 batches, in blender goblet until smooth. Return to pan. Add rest of sugar from Part 1.
5 Stir over low heat until sugar dissolves. Cook gently, uncovered, until mixture thickens and about half the liquid evaporates. This gives a rich and concentrated flavour. Stir frequently.
6 Beat egg yolks with some of this hot apricot mixture. Return to

pan. Remove from heat. Stir well so that egg yolks are dispersed through soup.
7 Add first batch of apricot mixture. Pour into large dish and keep warm. Beat egg whites to stiff snow. Gradually beat in sugar. Continue to beat until thick and peaky.
8 Top soup with mounds of meringue, then sprinkle with ratafias or small macaroons. Serve straightaway.

Note Do not freeze.

Vichyssoise

SERVES 6 TO 8   ▲▲●●●

A classic, chilled soup based on potatoes and leeks.

2 large leeks
1 large onion
2oz (50g) butter or margarine
1½lb (675g) potatoes
¾pt (425ml) chicken stock
½pt (275ml) milk
2 level tsp salt
white pepper to taste
¼pt (150ml) double cream
3 level tblsp scissor-snipped chives or parsley

1 Trim leeks, cutting away all the green part. Slit, wash well and chop. Peel onion and slice.
2 Heat butter or margarine in large pan. Add leeks and onion. Fry gently, with lid on pan, for about ¼ hour, but do not allow to brown.
3 Peel potatoes. Wash and dice. Add to pan with stock, milk and salt. Bring to boil. Lower heat. Cover. Simmer until potatoes are very soft; 30 to 40 minutes.
4 Cool to lukewarm. Either rub through fine mesh sieve or blend, in 3 or 4 batches, in blender goblet until smooth.
5 Pour into bowl. Cover. Chill until ready for serving. Stir in pepper and cream. Adjust seasoning adding, if liked, a dash or two of Tabasco. Sprinkle with chives or parsley. If soup is too thick for personal taste, thin down with a little milk or water before stirring in cream.

Freezer Tip
Vichyssoise may be frozen up to 2 months, but chives or parsley should be omitted and added after soup has thawed.

Vichysoise

Gazpacho

SERVES 6 ▲▲●●●

A Spanish classic, this version is based on the chilled soup from Andalucia.

1 can (about 14oz or 397g)
 tomatoes
1 garlic clove, peeled
¾pt (425ml) tomato juice
3oz (75g) fresh white breadcrumbs
4tblsp olive oil
3tblsp lemon juice
4tblsp cold water
2 level tsp salt
freshly-milled pepper to taste

SIDE BOWLS OF:
½ unpeeled cucumber, washed and
 diced
1 medium onion, peeled and
 chopped
1 medium red or green pepper,
 de-seeded and chopped
3 slices white bread, cut into cubes
 and fried in butter (optional)

1 Rub tomatoes through sieve or blend until smooth in blender goblet. Tip into bowl. Crush garlic and add.
2 Stir in tomato juice, crumbs, oil, lemon juice, water, salt and pepper. Cover. Chill 2 to 3 hours in the refrigerator.
3 To serve, stir round and ladle into dishes. People then add cucumber, onion, pepper and bread cubes according to taste.

Tip
In very hot weather, add 2 ice cubes to each bowl.

Freezer Tip
Freeze tomato mixture only (not accompaniments) up to 3 months. Thaw overnight in the refrigerator.

Chilled Cucumber and Yogurt Soup

SERVES 6 ▲▲●●

1 large cucumber, peeled
½pt (275ml) natural yogurt
1 garlic clove, peeled and chopped
 (optional)
2tblsp lemon juice
2 level tsp salt
½pt (275ml) chilled milk
white pepper to taste

Gazpacho

GARNISH
½ small unpeeled cucumber, washed
 and sliced
parsley

1 Coarsely grate cucumber. Put into bowl with yogurt, garlic, lemon juice, salt and milk.

2 Season to taste with pepper. Cover. Chill at least 4 hours in the refrigerator.
3 To serve, stir round, ladle into bowls and add a few slices of unpeeled cucumber and parsley sprigs to each.

Chilled Cucumber and Yogurt Soup

Lemon Meringue Soup

Lemon Meringue Soup

SERVES 6   ▲▲▲●●●

A novelty soup that can be eaten hot in winter or cold in summer.

    3 large lemons, washed and dried
    ¾pt (425ml) water
    ½pt (275ml) sweet white wine
    8oz (225g) caster sugar
    1oz (25g) cornflour
    2tblsp cold water
    2 Grade 4 eggs, separated

1 Peel lemons thinly. Place peel in pan with water. Bring to boil. Lower heat. Cover. Simmer gently 15 to 20 minutes.
2 Strain into clean saucepan, discarding lemon peel. Add wine to pan with 5oz (150g) sugar. Cook slowly until sugar dissolves.
3 Squeeze lemons and strain. Add juice to pan. Mix cornflour smoothly with water. Add to soup. Cook, stirring, until it comes to boil and thickens.
4 Place egg yolks in cup. Add a few tablespoons of hot soup. Mix well.

Return to pan. Cook until soup just comes up to boil. Take off heat.
5 Pour into bowl. Beat egg whites to stiff snow. Beat in rest of sugar to make a firm meringue. Drop tablespoons on top of soup. Cover so that steam cooks meringue. Serve warm or cold.

Tip
If liked, drop extra lemon slices into soup as an extra flavouring and garnish. Do not freeze.

38

Egg and Cheese Dishes

Egg and Cheese Dishes

Eggs and cheese are highly nutritious and useful protein foods, which lend themselves admirably to a wide variety of appetizing dishes. These range from simple Scrambled Eggs to a culinary masterpiece which has earned for itself worldwide fame and acclaim – the Soufflé. Below are just a taster of recipes which demonstrate the versatility of eggs and cheese as main ingredients and prove how one can create a fantasia of relatively economical meals without fish, poultry and meat.

Scrambled Eggs with Ham

Scrambled Eggs

SERVES 4 ▲▲●

    8 Grade 3 eggs
    2 tblsp milk
    ½ to 1 level tsp salt
    1oz (25g) butter or margarine

1 Beat eggs briskly with a fork to combine yolks and whites.
2 Beat in milk and salt.
3 Melt butter or margarine in saucepan. Swirl round to give base and part of the sides a good coating of fat.
4 Pour in egg mixture. Cook and stir continuously over a low heat until egg mixture is softly set. DO NOT OVERCOOK, as eggs will not only toughen but also separate out into a mass of chunky pieces floating in liquid.
5 Serve as soon as eggs are cooked. If liked, spoon on to toast or fried bread.

40

VARIATIONS

Scrambled Eggs with Ham

SERVES 4 ▲▲●●

Follow recipe for *Scrambled Eggs*, but after pouring egg mixture into pan add 4 to 6oz (125 to 175g) diced ham. Serve each portion topped with scissor-snipped garden chives or chopped parsley.

Scrambled Eggs with Assorted Additions

SERVES 4 ▲▲●●

Follow recipe for *Scrambled Eggs*, but after pouring egg mixture into pan, add either 4 to 6oz (125 to 175g) cold, cooked diced chicken, tongue, corned beef, poultry or roast meat. Alternately, add 4oz (125g) canned and flaked fish (well-drained first), or cooked and flaked smoked haddock or flaked smoked mackerel.

Scrambled Eggs with Fines Herbes

SERVES 4 ▲▲●●

Follow recipe for *Scrambled Eggs*, but after pouring egg mixture into pan, add 1 level tablespoon scissor-snipped chives, 1 level tablespoon finely-chopped parsley, 1 level teaspoon finely-chopped fresh mint and 1 or 2 level tablespoons chopped mustard and cress.

Scrambled Eggs with Cheese

SERVES 4 ▲▲●●

Follow recipe for *Scrambled Eggs*, but after pouring egg mixture into pan, add 2 to 3 oz (50 to 75g) finely-grated Cheddar cheese.

Scrambled Eggs with Curry

SERVES 4 ▲▲●

Follow recipe for *Scrambled Eggs*, but after pouring egg mixture into pan, add 1 to 3 level teaspoons curry powder, depending on strength preferred.

Boiled Eggs

ALLOW 1 TO 2 EGGS
PER PERSON ▲●

'I can't even boil an egg' is not such an unfamiliar cry to cookery writers, so to help those who find boiling eggs problematic, here are some guidelines to follow.

1 Take eggs out of the refrigerator or cold larder some hours before boiling. They are best at kitchen temperature.
2 To prevent eggs cracking in the water, pierce the round end of each carefully with a needle. Alternatively, use a egg piercer, available from hardware shops.
3 To make doubly sure eggs will remain crack-free, add a dash of vinegar or shake of salt to the water. The vinegar will also stop any aluminium pan used for boiling from turning black inside.
4 Lower each egg into pan of water with a tablespoon. DO NOT drop into pan.
5 Ensure that the eggs are completely covered with water, otherwise they will cook unevenly, the yolks tending to fall to one side. Also, stir gently as eggs come to boil to keep yolks in centre.

TO COOK

Cold Water Method
Lower eggs into a pan containing cold water. Bring gently to boil. Lower heat to simmer. For soft-boiled eggs, simmer Grades 1 to 3 for 3 minutes and Grades 4 to 7 for 2 minutes. For eggs with firm whites and soft yolks, simmer Grades 1 to 3 for 4 minutes and Grades 4 to 7 for 3 minutes. For hard-boiled eggs, simmer Grades 1 to 3 for 10 minutes and Grades 4 to 7 for 8 minutes.

Simmering Water Method
Lower eggs into a pan containing gently simmering water. Return to a gentle simmer, as the eggs will cool down the water. For soft-boiled eggs, simmer Grades 1 to 3 for 4 minutes and Grades 4 to 7 for 3 minutes. For eggs with firm whites and soft yolks, simmer Grades 1 to 3 for 6 minutes and Grade 4 to 7 for 5 minutes. For hard-boiled eggs, allow 11 minutes for all sizes.

Note To shell hard-boiled eggs easily, crack the shells as soon as the eggs

Fried Eggs on Mushrooms

are removed from the water to allow steam to escape. Return to pan. Cover with cold water. Drain. Cover with fresh cold water. Leave until eggs are cold, then drain and shell.

To avoid a blue ring forming round the yolks of hard-boiled eggs, do not over-cook in rapidly boiling water and follow the cold water treatment given above.

Coddled Eggs

ALLOW 1 TO 2 EGGS
PER PERSON ▲●

These are lightly-set boiled eggs, requiring the minimum of attention. They are also easy to digest and lovely as a dip for fingers of toast! Place in pan of gently simmering water. Cover securely with lid. Take pan off heat. Leave Grades 1 to 3 for 9 minutes; Grades 4 to 7 for 7 minutes.

Fried Eggs

ALLOW 1 TO 2 EGGS
PER PERSON ▲▲●

Fried Eggs make a tasty snack meal, with or without bacon, at any time of day and may be fried in either butter (which, in my view, imparts the best flavour), margarine, lard, bacon dripping or even oil. Some authorities suggest deep-frying the

eggs, but this can render them greasy and, unless very carefully watched and timed, leathery. I prefer shallow frying, carried out as follows:

1 Melt 2oz (50g) of any of the fats listed above (or the oil) in an 8in (20cm) frying pan. Heat until sizzling.
2 Break first egg into cup. If fresh, tip gently into pan. Repeat with next egg, and so on until you have added no more than 4 eggs in total.
3 Fry until whites are just set. Either baste yolks with hot fat or oil or, for a less greasy result, cover pan with lid or inverted enamel plate. The build-up of steam underneath will cook the top of the eggs and eliminate the need to baste.
4 Lift eggs out of pan with a fish slice and stand on warm plates or freshly-made toast. Serve straight-away. If preferred, serve the eggs with chips and/or baked beans.

Fried Eggs on Mushrooms

ALLOW 1 TO 2 EGGS
PER PERSON ▲▲●●

Follow method for cooking *Fried Eggs* as given above, but instead of hot toast place eggs on a bed of lightly-fried, sliced mushrooms. Garnish with fried tomatoes and chopped parsley.

Poached Eggs

ALLOW 1 TO 2 EGGS
PER PERSON ▲▲●

Lighter, some say, than boiled eggs, poached eggs make an easy-to-digest breakfast, lunch, tea or supper dish and are easy to cook, whether one uses a commercial egg poacher or frying pan. The cooking method is as follows:

1 Pour about ½in (1¼cm) boiling water into a small frying pan. Add ¼ teaspoon vinegar or lemon juice. Bring up to boil then reduce to a slow simmer.
2 Break first egg (any size) on to a saucer. Slip gently into pan. Repeat with second egg if required. Poach gently 2 to 4 minutes (depending on how firm you like the yolks to be).
3 Baste with water from pan to cook top of egg or eggs. Alternatively, cover pan with lid or inverted enamel plate and the build-up of steam underneath will do the same job.
4 Remove each egg from pan with a slotted spoon or fish slice, allowing water to drain away. Serve on buttered toast.

Note
1 To prevent boiling over, do not poach more than 2 eggs at a time.
2 If using a commercial egg poacher, brush the containers with melted butter, margarine or dripping before adding eggs – this time from a cup. The water underneath will cook the eggs but the pan must be kept covered.

Eggs Florentine

SERVES 4 ▲▲●●●

Line a medium-sized, buttered flame-proof dish with hot spinach, allowing 1lb (450g) fresh, or 12oz (350g) frozen or canned. Top with 4 freshly-poached eggs. Coat with Mornay Sauce (page 170) and sprinkle with 2oz (50g) grated Cheddar cheese or 1oz (25g) grated Parmesan. Brown 4 to 5 minutes under hot grill. Serve with toast.

Buck Rarebit

SERVES 4 ▲▲●●●

> 1oz (25g) butter or margarine, melted
> 1 level tsp prepared English mustard
> 6oz (175g) Cheddar cheese, finely grated (or use crumbled Lancashire cheese)
> ½tsp Worcester sauce
> shake of pepper
> 2tblsp milk or single cream
> 4 large slices white or brown bread, toasted on one side only or lightly-toasted on both sides
> 4 freshly-poached eggs

1 Mix butter or margarine with mustard, cheese, Worcester sauce, pepper and milk or cream.
2 Spread equal amounts fairly thickly over untoasted sides of toast, or over any side of the lightly-toasted bread slices.
3 Brown under a hot grill, top with Poached Eggs and serve straight-away.

Welsh Rarebit

SERVES 4 ▲▲●●

Follow recipe for *Buck Rarebit* but do not top the Rarebits with eggs.

Welsh Rarebit with Beer

SERVES 4 ▲▲●●

Follow recipe for *Buck Rarebit* but use 2 tablespoons stout instead of milk. Do not top the Rarebits with eggs.

Baked Eggs

ALLOW 1 TO 2 EGGS
PER PERSON ▲▲●●

Known in France as Oeufs en Cocotte, Baked Eggs can be as simple or as exotic as you like, depending on what is placed underneath the eggs and over the top. Often eggs are placed on a bed of fried mushrooms, coated with cream and baked that way. Occasionally they are dropped into hollows of mashes potatoes to create Egg Nests, which are especially liked by children because they look pretty and inviting. Imagination can run riot, but for every-

day purposes this is how I suggest you go about baking eggs:

1 Choose small cocotte, ramekin or individual heatproof Pyrex glass dishes if you are cooking 1 egg per person; shallow dishes with handles on both sides if you are cooking 2 eggs per person.
2 The latter type of dish should be about 6in (15cm) in diameter and about 2in (5cm) in depth.
3 Brush all dishes used thickly with butter or margarine. Break an egg, or eggs, into a cup then transfer gently to dishes. Dot top with flakes of butter or margarine, and season to taste with salt and pepper.
4 Stand either type of dish in a roasting tin. Pour in sufficient hot water to come half way up the sides. Transfer to moderate oven set to 180° (350°F), Gas 4.
5 Bake between 7 and 10 minutes or until both whites of egg and yolks have set either lightly or firmly, depending on personal taste. Eat with a spoon from the dishes and accompany with bread and butter or toast.

Baked Eggs with Cream

ALLOW 1 TO 2 EGGS
PER PERSON ▲▲●●●

Follow recipe for *Baked Eggs* but instead of butter or margarine, top each egg with a tablespoon of double cream. Season with salt and pepper and bake as directed.

Omelets

ALLOW 2 EGGS PER PERSON

Easy and very quick to produce, omelets make a nutritious and sustaining main course dish whether served absolutely plain or wrapped round assorted fillings. They team well with cooked vegetables or salads, and should be accompanied by either fried potatoes or crusty bread and butter. Experts fold omelets in 3 like an envelope and invert them on to a warm place. I fold mine in half as it is simpler and less likely to cause problems.

Success Tips
1 Make omelets individually, using 2 to 3 eggs.

2 Use a non-stick frying pan (stirring mixture with spatula to prevent surface scratches), or a special shallow omelet pan with solid base and curved sides.

3 All non-stick pans must be treated before use, a technique which is called 'proving'. This helps to stop the egg mixture from sticking but MUST BE CARRIED OUT EVERY TIME if the pan is an all-purpose one and used to fry other foods. Ideally, an omelet pan should be kept for omelets only and wiped with paper towels after use; NEVER wash otherwise it will need 're-proofing'.

4 To 'prove' a pan, melt a walnut-sized knob of butter or lard in the pan. Add about ¼in (½cm) salt. Mix with fat. Heat SLOWLY until hot and salt is just beginning to turn from white to the palest biscuit colour. Draw away from heat. Leave until lukewarm. Tip away salt mixture. Wipe base and sides of pan briskly with paper towels until smooth and shiny.

5 Avoid old frying pans with uneven bases, as no amount of proving will stop the egg mixture from sticking.

6 For 2 or 3 eggs of Grade 3 size, use a pan measuring 6in (15cm) in diameter.

Basic Omelet

SERVES 1   ▲▲●

2 or 3 Grade 3 eggs
2 or 3tsp cold water
salt and white pepper to taste
2 or 3 rounded tsp butter or
*   margarine*
parsley for garnishing

1 Beat eggs until very foamy with water. Season to taste with salt and pepper.

2 Heat butter or margarine in omelet pan until it starts to sizzle. (No fat is necessary in a non-stick pan, although it improves the flavour.)

3 With heat fairly high, pour egg mixture into the middle and quickly tilt pan in all directions until base is completely covered.

4 After about 10 seconds, push edges of omelet inwards towards centre, at the same time gently but quickly circulating pan so

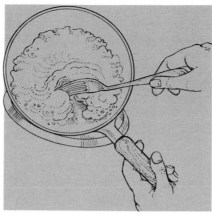

1 Circulate the pan so that the uncooked egg mixture flows into hollows around the edges

that uncooked egg mixture flows into hollows round edges.

5 Cook a further ½ to 1 minute when underside should be set and golden and the top moist but not over-runny. Remove from heat. Loosen edges. Fold omelet carefully in half.

6 Slide on to a warm plate and garnish with parsley. Serve straightaway.

VARIATIONS

Parsley Omelet

SERVES 1   ▲▲●●

Follow recipe for *Basic Omelet*, adding 1 level tablespoon finely-chopped parsley to the egg mixture before frying.

Herb Omelet

SERVES 1   ▲▲●●

This is similar to France's Omelette aux Fines Herbes and is an omelet mixture flavoured with fresh herbs. To make, follow recipe for *Basic Omelet*, but add 2 level teaspoons EACH, chopped parsley, chopped watercress and scissor-snipped chives to the egg mixture before frying.

Omelette

SERVES 1   ▲▲●

This is the French way of spelling omelet, but otherwise is exactly the same as the *Basic Omelet*.

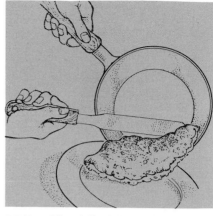

2 Fold carefully in half and slide on to a warm plate

American Style Omelet

SERVES 1   ▲▲●

Follow recipe for *Basic Omelet*, substituting 1 tablespoon milk for the water.

Filled Omelets

▲▲●●●

These are omelets which have HOT fillings added to them BEFORE they are folded. The exception is cheese, and about 1oz (25g) grated Cheddar, Edam, Gouda, Gruyère (or other cheese to taste) should be sprinkled on to the omelet immediately before folding. Other filling suggestions are as follows and are for EACH omelet:

1 1oz (25g) sliced mushrooms, lightly fried in butter or margarine.

2 3oz (75g) blanched and skinned tomatoes, chopped and lightly fried in butter or margarine.

3 2oz (50g) sliced onion, fried until golden in butter, margarine or salad oil.

4 2oz (50g) coarsely-chopped ham or bacon, fried in a little margarine or dripping.

5 About 6 canned asparagus spears, warmed through in a little butter or margarine.

Omelet Arnold Bennett

SERVES 1   ▲▲▲●●

My version of a celebrated and now very fashionable omelet, which makes a most distinguished meal with thin, crisp toast.

Firstly, cook and flake-up 3oz (75g) smoked haddock or cod fillet. Heat gently with 2 tablespoons double cream and 1 level tablespoon grated Parmesan cheese. Pre-heat grill. Make *Basic Omelet* as previously described (page 43). Fill with fish mixture. Fold in half. Slide out on to a shallow heatproof dish. Coat with 2 tablespoons double cream and another level tablespoon of Parmesan. Brown quickly under the grill and serve straightaway.

Omelet Puff

SERVES 2 ▲▲▲●●

More tricky to make than an ordinary omelet, the Omelet Puff has something of the light character of a soufflé.

Swiss Cheese Flan

Choose a 7in (17½cm) double-handed flameproof dish which is shallow rather than deep. Separate 4 Grade 3 eggs. Beat yolks briskly with 4 teaspoons water and salt and pepper to taste. Rinse beaters thoroughly. Pre-heat grill. Whisk egg whites to a stiff snow with about 3 or 4 drops of lemon juice. Fold yolks into whites with a spatula or large metal spoon. When smooth and evenly combined, melt and heat 1oz (25g) butter or margarine in dish, swirling it over sides. Spoon in egg mixture. Cook over moderate heat 2 to 3 minutes or until set and golden underneath. Transfer to grill pan. Cook a further 2 to 3 minutes or until well-puffed and golden. Cut into 2 portions and turn out on to 2 warm plates. Serve with vegetables or salad.

Note Make sure handles can withstand heat without melting.

Soufflé Omelet

SERVES 2 TO 4 ▲▲▲●●

This is a sweet version of the Omelet Puff given above. See page 111 in Dessert section.

Spanish Omelet

SERVES 2 TO 3 ▲▲●●

Known also as Tortilla and an integral part of the Spanish kitchen, this type of omelet is made with potatoes and onion and always left flat for serving. It is usually cooked in a heavy-based and smooth frying pan measuring 7 to 8in (17½ to 20cm) in diameter.

> 1oz (25g) butter or margarine
> 2tsp salad oil
> 1 medium onion, peeled and chopped
> 1 medium cooked potato, diced
> 4 Grade 2 eggs
> 1tblsp cold water
> ½ to 1 level tsp salt
> large pinch of white pepper

1 Heat butter or margarine and oil in pan. Add onion. Fry gently until pale gold.
2 Stir in potato. Fry 5 minutes, turning. Beat eggs briskly with rest of ingredients.
3 Pour into pan over vegetables. Cook about 3 to 4 minutes or until base is firm and golden. Transfer pan to pre-heated hot grill and leave 2 to 3 minutes or until top is set.
4 Cut into 2 or 3 portions and transfer to individual plates. Serve straightaway with fried or grilled tomatoes.

Spanish Omelet with Mixed Vegetables

SERVES 2 TO 3 ▲▲●●

Follow recipe for *Spanish Omelet* but add 1 small and diced-up green pepper and 2 skinned and coarsely-chopped tomatoes with the potatoes. Fry an extra 2 minutes before adding the egg mixture.

Swiss Cheese Flan

SERVES 4 GENEROUSLY AS A
MAIN COURSE AND UP TO 8
AS A STARTER ▲▲▲●●●

*Shortcrust Pastry made with 8oz
(225g) flour (page 186)*

FILLING
*3oz (75g) Gruyère cheese, finely
  grated
3oz (75g) Emmental cheese,
  finely grated
¼pt (150ml) whipping cream
¼pt (150ml) milk
3 Grade 2 eggs, separated
½ level tsp salt
¼ level tsp white pepper
¼ level tsp grated nutmeg*

1 Place a 10in (25cm) flan ring on
large, buttered baking tray. Brush
inside of flan ring with melted
butter.
2 Roll out pastry fairly thinly. Use
to line flan ring. Cover base thickly
with cheese.
3 Whisk cream smoothly with milk,
egg yolks, salt and pepper. In
separate bowl, beat whites to a
stiff snow. Using a metal spoon or
spatula, fold yolk mixture into
whites.
4 When completely smooth, spoon
into flan case over cheese. Sprinkle
with nutmeg.
5 Bake 35 minutes in moderately
hot oven preheated to 190°C
(375°F), Gas 5. Remove from
oven and lift off flan ring. Cut flan
into portions and serve hot.

Quiche Lorraine

SERVES 4 AS A MAIN COURSE
AND 6 AS A STARTER ▲▲▲●●●

This is a classic Quiche from Lorraine
in France, and contains no cheese. It
is, in essence, a baked egg custard
flan with the addition of bacon.

*Shortcrust Pastry made with 6oz
(175g) flour (page 186)*

FILLING
*4 to 5oz (100 to 125g) streaky
  bacon, unsmoked for preference
¼pt (150ml) milk
¼pt (150ml) whipping
  cream* } *heated until
  lukewarm*
*3 Grade 3 eggs
salt and pepper to taste
¼ level tsp grated nutmeg*

Quiche Lorraine

1 Roll out pastry fairly thinly and
use to line an 8in (20cm) flan ring
standing on lightly-greased baking tray. Alternatively, use pastry
to line an 8in (20cm) sandwich
tin and stand on tray. Leave aside
in the cool temporarily.
2 De-rind bacon and cut into thinnish strips. Fry gently, without
additional fat, until lightly cooked;
about 3 to 4 minutes.
3 Remove from heat. Cool. Spread
over base of pastry case. Beat next
5 ingredients well together. Strain
into pastry case through a fine
mesh sieve.
4 Sprinkle top with nutmeg. Bake
¼ hour in moderately hot oven set
to 200°C (400°F), Gas 6. Reduce
temperature to cool 160°C
(325°F), Gas 3 and continue to
bake a further 30 to 40 minutes
or until filling is golden and feels
firm when lightly pressed.
5 Remove from oven. Lift off flan
ring. Cool Quiche to lukewarm.
Cut into portions and serve.

Prawn Quiche

SERVES 4 AS A MAIN COURSE
AND 6 AS A STARTER ▲▲▲●●●

Follow recipe for *Quiche Lorraine* but
use 3oz (75g) peeled prawns instead
of bacon. Sprinkle top with 1oz (25g)
finely-grated Cheddar cheese instead
of nutmeg.

Fried Onion Quiche

SERVES 4 AS A MAIN COURSE
AND 6 AS A STARTER ▲▲▲●●●

Follow recipe for *Quiche Lorraine* but
use 3oz (75g) butter-fried, sliced
onions instead of bacon. Sprinkle top
with 1oz (25g) finely-grated Cheddar
cheese instead of nutmeg.

Spinach Quiche

SERVES 4 AS A MAIN COURSE
AND 6 AS A STARTER ▲▲▲●●●

Follow recipe for *Quiche Lorraine* but
use 6oz (175g) chopped and frozen
spinach (thawed completely) instead
of bacon. Fry it lightly in 2oz (50g)
butter or margarine and leave until
cold. Spread over base of flan. Beat
eggs with cream only and OMIT
MILK altogether. Pour into flan case
over spinach. Sprinkle top with 1oz
(25g) finely-grated Cheddar cheese
and ¼ level teaspoon nutmeg.

Tomato and Ham Quiche

SERVES 4 AS A MAIN COURSE
AND 6 AS A STARTER ▲▲▲●●●

Follow recipe for *Quiche Lorraine* but
use 2oz (50g) skinned and sliced
tomatoes and 2oz (50g) chopped
ham instead of bacon. Sprinkle top
with 1oz (25g) finely-grated Cheddar
cheese instead of nutmeg.

Egg and Bacon Pie

Macaroni Cheese with Tomato

SERVES 4 ▲▲●●

Follow recipe for *Macaroni Cheese* but add 4oz (125g) skinned and coarsely-chopped tomatoes to the sauce at the same time as the macaroni.

Macaroni Cheese with Bacon

SERVES 4 ▲▲●●●

Follow recipe for *Macaroni Cheese* but add 4oz (125g) chopped and fried lean bacon to the sauce at the same time as the macaroni.

Cheese, Onion and Potato Pie

SERVES 4 ▲▲●●

> 1lb (450g) potatoes, weighed
>   AFTER *peeling*
> 8oz (225g) onions, weighed
>   AFTER *peeling*
> 6oz (175g) Cheddar, Gouda or
>   Edam cheese, finely grated
> salt and pepper to taste
> ½pt (275ml) warm milk
> 1oz (25g) butter or margarine

1 Rinse potatoes, slice thinly and wipe dry in clean teatowel. Slice onions thinly and separate slices into rings.
2 Fill a 3 to 3½pt (about 1¾ to 2 litre) buttered heatproof dish with alternate layers of potatoes, onions and two-thirds of the cheese. Begin and end with potatoes and sprinkle salt and pepper between layers.
3 Pour milk gently down side of dish then sprinkle rest of cheese on top. Dot with butter or margarine. Cover with lid or foil.
4 Bake 1 hour in moderate oven set to 180°C (350°F), Gas 4. Uncover. Return to oven for further ¾ to 1 hour or until potatoes are soft and top is dark gold. Serve hot with vegetables to taste or salad.

Freezer Tip
The pie may be deep frozen up to 3 months. It should be thawed about 4 hours at kitchen temperature and reheated before serving.

Egg and Bacon Pie

SERVES 4 TO 6 ▲▲▲●●

> Shortcrust Pastry made with 8oz
>   (225g) flour (page 186)
>
> FILLING
> 6oz (175g) streaky bacon,
>   de-rinded and cut into strips
> 4 Grade 3 eggs
> 1 rounded tblsp chopped parsley
> salt and pepper to taste
>
> GLAZE
> beaten egg

1 Divide pastry into 2 pieces, one slightly larger than the other. Roll out large piece and use to line base and sides of a 7in (17½cm) ungreased sandwich tin.
2 Cover base with bacon. Break eggs, one by one, into a cup then slide into pie on top of bacon. Sprinkle with parsley. Season to taste with salt (not too much in case the bacon is salty) and pepper.
3 Moisten edges of lining pastry with water. Cover with lid, rolled from rest of pastry. Press edges well together to seal. Make 2 slits in the top to allow steam to escape.
4 Brush top with beaten egg. Bake 45 minutes in moderately hot oven set to 200°C (400°F), Gas 6. Remove from oven. If serving hot,

cut into 4 or 6 wedges and serve straightaway. If serving cold, cool off in tin before cutting. Accompany with salad if cold; cooked vegetables if hot.

Macaroni Cheese

SERVES 4 ▲▲●●

> 3oz (75g) elbow macaroni
> boiling salted water
> ½pt (275ml) Basic White Pouring
>   Sauce (page 168), freshly made
> 6oz (175g) Cheddar cheese, grated
> ½ level tsp prepared mustard
> salt and pepper to taste

1 Cook macaroni in boiling salted water for about ¼ hour or until just tender. Keep pan covered throughout and avoid over-cooking as macaroni will become 'slushy'.
2 Drain. Leave on one side temporarily. Add 4oz (125g) cheese to sauce with mustard. Stir until cheese has melted. Season to taste.
3 Stir in macaroni. Transfer mixture to 1½pt (¾ litre) buttered heatproof dish. Sprinkle rest of cheese on top. Reheat and brown for 20 minutes in hot oven set to 220°C (425°F), Gas 7. Serve with green vegetables.

Neapolitan Pizza

MAKES 2 (EACH SUFFICIENT
FOR 4 SERVINGS)   ▲▲▲●●●

As Pizzas freeze so well, it is worth
making two from 1lb (450g) white
bread dough and keeping one in
reserve.

> Pizza Pastry (page 241), already
> risen and 'knocked-back'

TOPPING
12oz (350g) onions, chopped
2 to 4 medium garlic cloves,
  crushed
3tblsp salad oil (or olive oil if
  preferred)
6 level tblsp tubed or canned
  tomato purée
2 level tsp dried basil
2 level tblsp chopped parsley
3 level tsp caster sugar
2lb (1kg) blanched and skinned
  tomatoes, sliced
1 level tsp salt
1lb (450g) Mozzarella cheese
  (usually sold in packets)
2 cans (each about 1¾oz or 50g)
  anchovies in oil
24 black olives

1 Divide Pizza Pastry into 2 equal
   portions. Roll each out thinly into
   a 10in (25cm) circle. Stand on 2
   large and very well-greased baking trays. Alternatively, roll out to
   fit 2 × 12in (30cm) well-greased,
   round Pizza tins.
2 Fry onions and garlic fairly briskly
   in the oil until pale and gold. Stir
   in purée, basil, parsley and sugar.
   Warm through. Remove from
   heat.
3 Spread equal amounts over Pizzas
   to within ½in (1¼cm) of edges.
   Leave in a warm place until
   double in thickness. Top with
   tomato slices then sprinkle each
   Pizza with salt.
4 Slice Mozzarella cheese very
   thinly. Place on top of tomatoes.
   Decorate Pizzas with criss-cross
   strips of anchovies then add olives
   to taste. Trickle anchovy oil over
   each.
5 Bake both Pizzas for 40 minutes
   in moderately hot oven set to
   200°C (400°F), Gas 6. Remove
   from oven. Cut into portions and
   serve while hot.

Freezer Tip
Leave Pizza (or portions) until completely cold. Fast-freeze, uncovered,
until hard. Wrap and seal securely.

Macaroni Cheese with Tomato

Freeze up to 6 months. Thaw 3 to 4
hours at kitchen temperature. Reheat before serving.

Tuna Pizza

MAKES 2 (EACH SUFFICIENT
FOR 4 SERVINGS)   ▲▲▲●●●

Make exactly as *Neapolitan Pizza* but
use only 1½lb (¾kg) tomatoes for both
Pizzas. Top with 2 cans (each about
7oz or 200g) drained and flaked tuna
BEFORE covering with cheese. Omit
anchovies. Use green stuffed olives
instead of black. Trickle tuna oil over
each before baking.

Sausage Pizza

MAKES 2 (EACH SUFFICIENT
FOR 4 SERVINGS)   ▲▲▲●●●

Make exactly as *Neapolitan Pizza* but
use only 1½lb (¾kg) tomatoes for both
Pizzas. Top with 8oz (225g) VERY
THINLY-SLICED salami or garlic
sausage BEFORE covering with
cheese. Omit anchovies and olives.
Garnish each with a criss-cross of
canned red pimiento (red pepper)
and stud with about 2 tablespoons
drained capers.

Cheese, Onion and Potato Pie

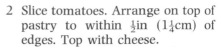

Puff Pastry Pizza

Individual Pizzas

MAKES 8 ▲▲▲●●

Follow recipe for any of the Pizzas given above but first divide dough into 8 equal pieces. Roll each into a 6in (15cm) round then cover as directed, but treating each Pizza individually. Place on 2 baking trays and, after rising, bake 25 to 30 minutes in hot oven set to 230°C (450°F), Gas 8. Eat hot and/or cool and freeze.

Puff Pastry Pizza

SERVES 6 ▲▲●●●

A richer-than-usual Pizza but quick to make with frozen puff pastry. If serving as a cocktail snack, cut into

'Pizza' Toasts

slim wedges and allow one Pizza for 12 servings.

1 packet (about 13oz or 370g) frozen puff pastry, thawed

TOPPING
4 tomatoes, skinned and sliced
4oz (125g) sliced processed cheese or sliced Mozzarella cheese
5 or 6 canned sardines or 2 canned pilchards
12 stuffed green olives, halved
2 level tblsp drained capers
1 can (about 7oz or 200g) tuna
1 level tsp dried oregano, basil or marjoram

1 Roll out pastry thinly into a 10in (25cm) round. Place on wet baking tray. (See Rough Puff Pastry Baking Tip on page 191.)

2 Slice tomatoes. Arrange on top of pastry to within ½in (1¼cm) of edges. Top with cheese.

3 Decorate with whole sardines or halved pilchards, the olives, capers and drained and flaked tuna.

4 Sprinkle with herbs and trickle tuna oil over the top. Bake ¾ hour in hot oven set to 220°C (425°F), Gas 7. Cut into portions and serve straightaway.

Scone-Based Pizza

SERVES 4 ▲▲●●●

Another short-cut style Pizza which is an invaluable and fast standby recipe if there is no time for bread dough. Make up recipe for Plain Scones (page 198). Roll out into an 8in (20cm) round. Stand on baking tray. Cover with any of the Pizza toppings previously given. Bake 30 to 40 minutes in hot oven set to 220°C (425°F), Gas 7. Cut into portions and serve straightaway.

'Pizza' Toasts

SERVES 4 ▲▲●●●

A total compromise where authentic Pizza is concerned, but an easy lunch or supper dish that is both filling and attractive.

3oz (75g) trimmed and sliced mushrooms
1oz (25g) butter
4 slices lean ham (each about 1oz or 25g), cut into fairly narrow strips
4 large tomatoes
4 slices bread, toasted on one side only
4 slices packeted processed cheese, each slice halved
4 rounded tsp scissor-snipped fresh chives

1 Fry mushrooms gently in the butter for 3 or 4 minutes. Add ham. Fry a further 2 to 3 minutes, turning.

2 Slice tomatoes fairly thickly. Cover untoasted sides of bread with the fried mushrooms and ham mixture. Add tomato slices.

3 Top each with 2 half slices of cheese. Cook under a hot grill until cheese begins to melt. Remove from grill. Sprinkle with chives. Serve straightaway.

Snack Toasts

'Things' on or in between toast always go down well, and are ideal for those who enjoy TV or fireside snacks or just the pleasure of an easily-prepared meal.

Salami Toasts

SERVES 4   ▲▲●●●

4 large slices white or brown bread
butter or margarine
4 slices Emmental cheese (about
  1oz or 25g each)
12 very thin slices salami
1 small cored green pepper,
  de-seeded and cut into rings
4 egg yolks
salt and pepper to taste
2 level tsp chopped parsley

1 Toast bread on one side only. Spread untoasted sides with butter or margarine.

Snack Toasts. Top left: Salami Toasts; Bottom left: Banana Cheese Toasts; Top centre: Toasted Cheese and Bacon Sandwiches; Bottom centre: New Orleans Toasts; Right: Cheese and Tomato Fancy Egg Toasts

2 Top each with a slice of cheese, 3 slices salami and 2 green pepper rings. Add an egg yolk to each.
3 Cook under moderate grill for 8 to 10 minutes. Serve straightaway.

Banana Cheese Toasts

SERVES 4   ▲▲●●●

4 slices white or brown bread
butter or margarine
2 large or 4 small bananas
6oz (175g) mild Cheddar cheese,
  grated
4 medium tomatoes, skinned and
  coarsely chopped
4 rounded tsp chopped parsley

1 Toast bread on one side only. Spread untoasted sides with butter or margarine.
2 Slice bananas. Place equal amounts on to buttered sides of toast. Sprinkle with cheese. Top with tomato.
3 Heat through about 5 minutes under hot grill. Sprinkle with parsley before serving.

Toasted Cheese and Bacon Sandwiches

SERVES 1   ▲●●

LIGHTLY toast 2 large slices bread. Spread 1 slice with butter or margarine. Cover with 2oz (50g) coarsely-chopped and lightly-fried bacon and 1½oz (40g) grated Cheddar cheese. Stand under hot grill until cheese just melts. Remove from grill. Cover with second slice of toast, first spread with butter or margarine. Garnish with parsley. Serve straightaway.

New Orleans Toasts

SERVES 4   ▲▲●●

4 slices white or brown bread
1 medium onion, peeled
1 medium green pepper, cored and
  de-seeded
2oz (50g) butter or margarine
4 slices ham, halved (about 4 to
  6oz or 125 to 175g)
4oz Cheddar cheese, finely grated
mustard and cress or rape and
  cress for garnishing

1 Toast bread on one side only. Leave on one side temporarily.
2 Thinly slice onion. Cut pepper into strips. Heat butter or margarine in small pan. Add prepared vegetables. Fry gently, with lid on pan, for 10 minutes.
3 Spoon equal amounts on to untoasted sides of toast. Add 2 half slices of ham to each then sprinkle with 1oz (25g) cheese.
4 Heat under a hot grill until cheese just begins to melt. Garnish with cress before serving.

Cheese and Tomato Fancy Egg Toasts

SERVES 4 ▲▲▲●●

4 slices white or brown bread
Mayonnaise
4 slices ham (about 4oz or 125g)
4 medium tomatoes, sliced
4 slices processed cheese, each cut into 2 triangles
4tblsp tomato ketchup
4 freshly fried or poached eggs (pages 41–2)
4 rounded tsp scissor-snipped chives

1 Toast bread on 1 side only. Spread untoasted sides thinly with Mayonnaise. Cover with ham then top with tomatoes.
2 Arrange 2 triangles of cheese on each. Heat under a hot grill until melted.
3 Coat the centres with tomato ketchup. Add an egg to each. Sprinkle with chives. Serve straightaway.

Roman Gnocchi

SERVES 4 AS A MAIN COURSE
AND 8 AS A STARTER ▲▲●●●

Delicious as a dish in its own right, Gnocchi also makes an excellent accompaniment to roast lamb or beef braised in wine.

1pt (575ml) milk
5oz (150g) semolina
1 level tsp salt
2oz (50g) butter or margarine
3oz (75g) grated Parmesan cheese
$\frac{1}{4}$ level tsp ground nutmeg
1 level tsp prepared English mustard
1 Grade 2 egg, well beaten

TOPPING
1 extra oz (25g) butter, melted

1 Pour milk into saucepan. Add semolina and salt. Cook, stirring over medium heat, until mixture comes to the boil and thickens. Simmer 2 minutes.
2 Beat in butter or margarine, 2oz (50g) cheese, nutmeg, mustard and egg. Return to low heat. Cook and stir a further 2 to 3 minutes.
3 Spread evenly into oiled Swiss roll tin measuring 12 by 8in (30 by 20cm). Leave until cold. Cover. Refrigerate until cold and firm.
4 Cut into rounds with a 1in (2½cm) biscuit cutter dipped in water. Arrange trimmings in buttered heatproof dish (about 1½pt or $\frac{7}{8}$ litre capacity).

Roman Gnocchi

5 Top with overlapping rings of Gnocchi rounds. Sprinkle with rest of cheese. Coat with butter. Reheat and brown 20 minutes in hot oven set to 220°C (425°F), Gas 7. Spoon out of dish and serve with grilled tomatoes or leaf spinach.

Scotch Eggs

MAKES 6 ▲▲▲●●

Appetizing hot or cold, Scotch Eggs are part of the British way of life and make a convenient lunch or supper snack at any time of the year. For picnics, they should be carried whole and cut on the spot; otherwise they should be halved before serving and placed on plates with the cut sides uppermost. They team especially well with salads and pickles.

6 Grade 3 hard-boiled eggs (method, page 41)
about 6tsp plain flour
1lb (450g) pork or beef sausage meat
1 level tsp powder mustard

COATING
2 Grade 3 eggs
1tblsp cold water or milk
2oz (50g) fresh white breadcrumbs

FOR FRYING
deep fat or oil

1 Shell eggs and coat all over lightly with flour. Mix sausage meat with mustard by kneading both together.
2 Divide sausage meat into 6 equal portions. Flatten each and wrap evenly round eggs, making sure there are no thin patches.
3 Beat eggs and water or milk well together in deep plate. Add Scotch Eggs and toss over and over until completely coated.
4 Transfer, one by one, to sheet of greaseproof paper covered with breadcrumbs. Coat each egg completely with crumbs.
5 Leave to stand 30 minutes for coating to settle and set. Lift up each egg, shake off surplus crumbs, then carefully lower in pan of deep, hot fat or oil with spoon.
6 Fry about 8 to 10 minutes to cook sausage meat. Lift out of pan and drain on crumpled paper towels. Cut in half before serving.

Fondue Neuchâtel

Fondue Neuchâtel

SERVES 6　　　▲▲▲●●●

Steeped in tradition, Fondue eating is an aged Swiss ritual although whether this type of cheese dip — which is exactly what a Fondue is — originated in Switzerland is arguable in that Holland, too, has had its own version for a very long time. Be that as it may, it should be made in what is known as a 'caquelon'; a heavy-based and relatively shallow flameproof casserole which sits, ultimately, over a spirit stove on the table. Fondue sets are readily available but, in their absence, any flameproof casserole, over any form of table heater, may be used. The true Swiss Fondue is made from a mixture of Gruyère and Emmental cheese, supplemented with wine,

Kirsch and cornflour, and eaten with small cubes of crusty French bread speared on to forks (there are even special elongated Fondue forks to go with the Fondue sets) which are twirled round in the cheese mixture. The cheese-coated bread cube is then lifted out of the dish and eaten. Custom has it that if a lady drops the bread cube into the Fondue, she has to pay a forfeit by kissing one of the gentlemen. If a gentleman errs in the same way, he has to treat all the guests to a bottle of wine. If the same person drops the bread twice, he or she has to give the next Fondue party!

A Fondue party is a pleasantly informal way of entertaining, but to avoid accidents, no more than six people should be gathered round one Fondue pot. In true traditional style, a small glass of chilled Kirsch (or either the clear French spirit Mirabelle or Balkan plum brandy) should be thrown back halfway through the meal. This is known as the 'coup de milieu'. Tea without milk is the best drink to accompany a Fondue but white wine is also acceptable, though less kind to the digestion!

1 large garlic clove, peeled and
　halved
12oz (350g) Gruyère cheese,
　grated
12oz (350g) Emmental cheese,
　grated
½pt (275ml) dry white wine
　(Moselle or Rhine)
1 level tblsp cornflour
1 liqueur glass Kirsch (or other
　clear spirit such as Mirabelle or
　Balkan plum brandy)
2tsp lemon juice
freshly-milled black pepper
¼ level tsp nutmeg

1 Press cut clove of garlic over base and sides of heatproof Fondue dish. Add both cheeses and the wine.
2 Cook gently, over low heat, until cheeses have melted. Mix cornflour smoothly with Kirsch (or other spirit). Add to Fondue with lemon juice.
3 Bring to boil, stirring. Season to taste with pepper and nutmeg. When mixture has thickened smoothly and is bubbling, transfer to spirit stove on the table. Place Fondue forks and cubes of bread nearby.

51

Normandy Style Fondue

SERVES 6 ▲▲▲●●

A fake really, but quite delicious!

Follow recipe for *Fondue Neuchâtel*, but use grated Cheddar cheese instead of the Swiss cheeses and substitute dry cider for wine. Mix cornflour with a liqueur glass of Calvados (apple brandy from France) instead of Kirsch etc.

English Fondue

SERVES 6 ▲▲▲●●

Another contradiction, but more economical than the Swiss version.

Follow recipe for *Fondue Neuchâtel*, but use grated Cheshire cheese instead of the Swiss cheeses and substitute pale ale for wine. Mix cornflour with 1 level teaspoon powder mustard, 1 teaspoon Worcester sauce and 4 tablespoons milk instead of Kirsch etc.

Dutch Cheese Dip

SERVES 6 ▲▲▲●●

Follow recipe for *Fondue Neuchâtel*, but use grated Gouda cheese instead of the Swiss cheeses and substitute milk for wine. Mix cornflour with 4 tablespoons cold water instead of Kirsch etc.

Success Tips

1 If Fondue becomes very thick and tacky at the table, add a pinch or two of soda bicarbonate.
2 Do not freeze leftovers but store, covered, in the refrigerator up to 3 weeks. Spread over toast and grill to give a speedy Cheese Toast.

Cheese Soufflé

SERVES 4 AS A MAIN COURSE
AND 8 AS A STARTER ▲▲▲●●

Soufflés and champagne have much in common. They both bubble with lightness, carry impressive crowns and tempt the appetite with their distinctive subtlety of flavour and delicate golden hue. Contrary to what most people have been led to believe, Soufflés are relatively simple to make and depend almost entirely

for their success on:

1 Correct proportion of ingredients to size of dish.
2 Careful and unhurried mixing, and the incorporation of air from beaten egg whites.
3 Not opening the oven door at any stage while the Soufflé is baking as it would undoubtedly collapse.
4 Eating the Soufflé as soon as it comes out of the oven and before it has a chance of sinking down on itself – which it does very quickly indeed.

The recipe below is for a classic Cheese Soufflé. Variations follow.

> 2oz (50g) butter or margarine
> 2oz (50g) plain flour
> ½pt (275ml) milk, heated till hot but not boiling
> 4 Grade 3 eggs
> 6oz (175g) Cheddar cheese, very finely grated
> ¼ level tsp salt
> 1 level tsp powder mustard
> ½tsp lemon juice

1 Choose a glass or pottery Soufflé dish with ridged sides of 2½pt (1½ litre) capacity. It should also measure 7½in (about 19cm) across the top, 6½in (about 16½cm) across the base and 3in (7½cm) in depth. Brush inside with melted butter or margarine.
2 In order to support the Soufflé as it rises, wrap a strip of Bakewell non-stick parchment paper, or greaseproof paper, round the OUTSIDE of the dish, making sure that it stands at least 4in (10cm) above top edge. Hold in place by tying with string or holding the ends with sticky tape. Even a heavy elastic band can be used. Brush inside of the greaseproof paper only with melted butter or margarine. The parchment paper requires no greasing. Preheat oven to moderately hot, 190°C (375°F), Gas 5.
3 Melt butter or margarine in saucepan. Stir in flour to form a roux. Cook 1 minute. Keeping heat low, gradually add milk. Cook, stirring non-stop, until mixture comes to the boil and thickens.
4 Still stirring, continue to cook until it forms a ball in the centre of the pan, leaving sides clean. Take pan off heat.
5 Separate eggs by adding yolks to saucepan and pouring whites into

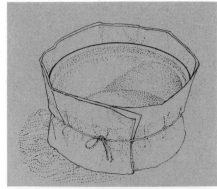

1 The paper, wrapped carefully around the outside of the soufflé dish and held in place with string

2 Fold the beaten whites into the cheese mixture

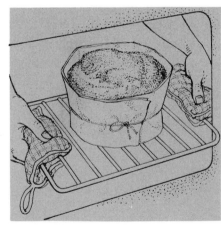

3 Remove the cooked soufflé from the oven

clean, dry bowl. Beat yolks into roux mixture, followed by cheese, salt and mustard.
6 Whip whites and lemon juice together until mixture looks like a huge puff of white cloud. Stop at this stage otherwise the whites will lose their power of aeration, break up and look like a mass of cottonwool balls.
7 Using a large metal spoon or spatula, carefully and gently (no

need to hurry) fold whites into cheese mixture. When absolutely smooth and evenly combined, pour into prepared Soufflé dish. Stand on baking tray. Put into centre of oven and bake undisturbed, with no shelf above, for 45 minutes. Take out of oven, remove strip of paper and serve Soufflé straightaway, while it is still tall and golden. Accompany with a green salad.

VARIATIONS

Seafood Soufflé

SERVES 4 AS A MAIN COURSE AND 8 AS A STARTER ▲▲▲●●

Follow recipe for *Cheese Soufflé* but omit cheese and add instead 6oz (175g) finely-flaked canned tuna or pink salmon, mashed dressed crab, cooked and mashed smoked haddock fillet or very finely-chopped peeled prawns.

Poultry Soufflé

SERVES 4 AS A MAIN COURSE AND 8 AS A STARTER ▲▲▲●●

Follow recipe for *Cheese Soufflé* but omit cheese and add instead 6oz (175g) finely-minced, cooked poultry.

Ham Soufflé

SERVES 4 AS A MAIN COURSE AND 8 AS A STARTER ▲▲▲●●

Follow recipe for *Cheese Soufflé* but omit cheese and add instead 6oz (175g) finely-minced ham.

Asparagus Soufflé

SERVES 4 AS A MAIN COURSE AND 8 AS A STARTER ▲▲▲●●

Follow recipe for *Cheese Soufflé* but omit cheese and add instead 6oz (175g) canned asparagus (drained weight), very finely chopped.

Fish

Fish

Fish is a first-class, body-building protein food and comes from the sea, lakes, rivers, streams, ponds and brooks. There are four basic types: white fish such as cod, plaice, haddock, coley and sole; oily fish which include deeper-coloured salmon, herring, mackerel and eel; molluscs which cover clams, oysters, scallops and mussels; shellfish (technically crustacea) in the form of lobster, crab, crawfish, prawns of all types and shrimps. The odd man out here is eel – which has no ventral fins – but is still categorized as a fish.

Nutritionally, fish is low in carbohydrates and calories and therefore highly regarded by slimmers. It has important trace elements (minerals) such as potassium, phosphorus, sodium, iodine and fluorine from sea fish. Canned pilchards, herring and sardines – where very often the bones are eaten as well – are an excellent source of calcium. All fish contain vitamins of the B group but oily fish, additionally, contain vitamins A and D. White fish is light and easy to digest but oily fish, with natural oil distributed throughout its flesh, is richer and therefore somewhat more filling. Because fish, weight for weight, is less satisfying than meat, allow 8oz (225g) fish with bone per serving, and 6oz (175g) fillets. Freshwater fish, which sometimes cause confusion, do NOT come from salty sea water but live in rivers, lakes and streams. They include salmon, trout, carp (very popular in central Europe) and bream.

CHOOSING FRESH FISH

With fewer and fewer 'wet' fish shops about, more and more people depend on frozen fish which is always impeccably fresh and fine-tasting. In fact, white fish is one of the few foods that is as good frozen as it is fresh, and you can rest assured it has not been left standing about to go stale; fish is cleaned and frozen as soon as it is caught and should reach you in top condition. The oily fish tend to dry out and frozen salmon, for instance, is never quite the same as fresh. Those who still have access to a local fishmonger and are able to buy fish 'from the slab' should make sure the body is rigid, the tail firm, the eyes bulging and not sunken, gills reddish and scales plentiful and glistening with all the colours of an opal. The skin of flat fish should be smooth and un-wrinkled and spots on plaice a healthy, bright orange. In short, if fish looks sprightly this is as good a guarantee of freshness as any. Most of the popular fish are available all the year round but salmon, salmon trout and crustacea are at their peak during summer. The season for molluscs is autumn and winter, and some authorities maintain that these should be eaten only when there is an 'r' in the month. Some people who live at the coast are less cautious and certainly eat mussels until May, although most fish restaurants stop serving them at the end of April.

CARE OF FISH

Fresh fish does not improve if left to stand about in a warm or humid atmos-phere and should therefore be unwrapped, washed briefly under COLD water (never hot as the delicate flakes could start cooking and molluscs open up), put on a plate and refrigerated until needed. It should, whenever possible, be bought and eaten on the same day, but will still be satisfactory after 12 hours refrigeration. Some frozen fish, such as fillets, can be cooked from frozen but please be guided in this by packet directions.

CUTS

FILLETS Slices of fish cut away from the bone.

STEAKS AND CUTLETS Slices taken from the middle of what I call 'round' fish such as cod and haddock.

TRIMMINGS These include head and bones and make excellent fish stock.

TAIL END Exactly what it says. A triangular-shaped piece of fish with the tail end still attached. Because it is less fleshy than middle cuts, it is relatively inexpensive and a tail end of salmon, once cooked and flaked, makes an excellent fish salad.

BASIC COOKING METHODS

Baked Fish

▲●●

This is an excellent way of cooking fish for maximum flavour. Choose whole fish (cleaned but with heads left on), cutlets, steaks, thick fillets and even a well-scaled and trimmed tail end. Wash fish briefly and dry with paper towels. Season inside and out. Transfer to a baking tin or dish brushed with melted butter or mar-garine. Brush thickly with more melted butter or margarine then cover tin or dish with double thick-ness of foil. Set the oven to 180°C (350°F), Gas 4 and bake whole fish 12 minutes per 1lb (450g), steaks and cutlets 15 to 20 minutes accord-ing to thickness, fillets 10 to 15 minutes and tail end 10 minutes. Serve with any of the sauces recom-mended for fish (see Sauce section, page 168) and accompany with boiled or creamed potatoes and 2 or 3 other cooked vegetables to taste.

Foil-Baked Fish

▲●●

Also known as Fish 'en Papillote', this method of cooking is an excellent way of preserving flavour and moist-ure and creates no mess. Choose fish as given for Baked Fish above. Stand on a piece of well-greased foil, treat-ing fillets, cutlets and steaks indi-vidually. Brush seasoned fish with more melted butter or margarine and, for increased flavour, add a tiny piece of dried bay leaf, a thin slice of washed lemon, one or two pepper-corns (it makes no odds whether black or white) and a sprig of parsley to each. Wrap securely and bake for times given under Baked Fish. For traditional French style 'en Papil-lote', wrap the fish in a double thick-ness of greased, greaseproof paper instead of foil.

Fried Fish (1)

SERVES 4   ▲▲●● or ●●●

Wash and dry 8 fillets of plaice or skinned sole (lemon, Dover or witch). Season. Dust lightly with 1½ level tablespoons flour. Dip in 1 Grade 2 egg beaten with 2 teaspoons water. Coat all over with lightly-toasted breadcrumbs. Fry in about 1in (2½cm) hot fat or oil for 6 to 7 minutes, turning once or twice. Drain on paper towels. Serve traditionally with lemon wedges and Tartare Sauce (page 176). Accompany with chips or fried (sauté) potato rounds. Alternatively, serve garnished with fried banana slices and glacé cherries and accompany with Savoury Rice (below).

Cooking Tip
Start by standing plaice fillets in pan with flesh sides down.

Savoury Rice

▲▲●●

1oz (25g) butter or margarine or 1tblsp salad oil
1 medium onion, peeled and finely-chopped
8oz (225g) easy-cook, long grain rice
½ level tsp turmeric (bright yellow powder used in pickles and Indian dishes)
1 bouquet garni
1pt (575ml) boiling water
2 level tsp salt

1 Heat butter, margarine or oil in heavy-based pan until sizzling. Add onion. Fry over medium heat until a warm gold.
2 Stir in rice. Fry, turning, a further 2 minutes. Add all remaining ingredients.
3 Bring to boil. Stir round twice. Lower heat. Cover. Cook 20 to 25 minutes or until rice grains are separate and fluffy and have absorbed all the liquid.
4 Remove bouquet garni and 'fluff' rice by gently stirring with a fork.

Fried Fish (2)

SERVES 4   ▲▲●● or ●●●

Wash and dry 8 fillets of fish. Dip fish in Coating Batter (page 202) and fry

Fried Fish (1)

in hot, deep fat or oil for 5 to 6 minutes, depending on thickness. Remove from pan with a slatted metal fish slice (plastic would melt) and drain on crumpled paper towels. Accompany with chips.

Frying Tip
To see if fat or oil is the correct temperature (neither too cold nor too hot), drop a cube of white bread into the pan. If it sinks to the bottom, rises to the top immediately and turns golden brown in 50 seconds, then you can start adding the fish, but ONLY 2 pieces at a time. If you add too many all at once, the temperature of the fat or oil will fall and the fried fish will turn out greasy and soggy.

Grilled Fish

Grilled Fish

ALLOW 1 CUTLET, STEAK,
SMALL WHOLE FISH OR
THICK FILLET PER PERSON
▲▲●● or ●●●

Choose steaks or cutlets of cod, coley, haddock or salmon; gutted and cleaned herring, mackerel, trout (as in the picture), small plaice or sole, whiting or red mullet; thickish fillets of plaice, sole, cod or haddock. Wash fish and wipe dry with paper towels. Make 3 diagonal cuts on both sides of whole fish so that grill heat can penetrate more easily. Melt

a fairly comfortable piece (about 1 to 2oz or 25 to 50g) of butter or margarine and leave aside for the moment. Season fish with salt and pepper inside and out. Stand grill rack in grill pan and brush with melted butter or margarine. Arrange fish on rack. Brush with more butter or margarine. Grill 5 to 7 minutes. Turn over with 2 spoons or tongs to prevent breaking up the flesh. Brush with rest of melted butter or margarine. Grill a further 5 to 7 minutes, depending on thickness. Serve hot and coat with grill pan juices. Garnish with lemon slices. If preferred, accompany with any of the sauces recommended for fish in the Sauce section (page 168).

Grilled Salmon Maître d'Hôtel

SERVES 4 ▲▲●●●

   4 salmon cutlets or steaks
   1oz (25g) melted butter
   2 rounded tblsp fresh breadcrumbs
   Maître d'Hôtel Butter (page 178)
   lemon wedges and parsley for
      garnishing

1 Brush salmon with melted butter and grill as directed in recipe for Grilled Fish. After turning, brush with more butter and sprinkle with crumbs.

Make 3 diagonal cuts on both sides of whole fish

2 Grill a further 5 to 7 minutes. Transfer to 4 warm plates and accompany with Maître d'Hôtel Butter. Garnish with lemon and parsley.

Poached Fish

ALLOW EITHER 2 FILLETS,
1 STEAK OR CUTLET PER
PERSON ▲▲●● or ●●●

This is one of the most popular ways of cooking fish in that it is relatively easy, economical (unless wine is used as the cooking liquid!) and delicate. The liquid should barely cover the fish and may be water, milk, fish stock (see below), wine or even cider. The fish should be lightly sprinkled with salt and the heat kept fairly low, so that the liquid bubbles at a very slow pace. If it boils vigorously, the fish will fall to pieces and taste uninteresting. Keep the pan uncovered, and to save disturbing the fish while it is cooking, baste every so often with the hot liquid. This not only moistens the fish but stops the top from drying out. For fillets, allow about 10 minutes poaching time per pound (450g); for steaks and cutlets, about 2 minutes longer. Serve with any suitable sauce from the Sauce section (page 168) made, if liked, with liquid in which fish was poached.

Grilled Salmon Maître d'Hôtel

Oven-Poached Fish

▲▲●● or ●●●

With large fish kettles of old not so much in evidence, the best way of poaching a whole fish (salmon or salmon trout) is to place it lengthwise or diagonally into a roasting tin. Add sufficient water to come half way up the sides of the fish, sprinkle with salt, then cover tin with foil. Cook in oven set to 190°C (375°F), Gas 5, allowing 20 minutes per pound (450g). Drain thoroughly and carefully and serve with a suitable sauce from the Sauce section (page 168) made, if liked, with liquid in which fish was poached.

Fish Stock

MAKES ABOUT 1¾PT (1 LITRE)

▲▲●●

8oz (225g) onions, peeled and quartered
4oz (125g) carrots, peeled and cut into thick slices
1 bouquet garni
3 level tsp salt
1½lb (675g) fish trimmings
1¾pt (1 litre) cold water

1 Place all ingredients into a pan. Bring to boil, stirring. Lower heat. Cover.
2 Simmer gently for 1 hour. Strain. Use as required.

Poached Halibut

Poached Fish

Court Bouillon

MAKES ABOUT 1¾PT (1 LITRE)

▲▲●●

This is a deeper-flavoured version of Fish Stock and commonly used in France. To make, follow recipe for *Fish Stock* but use half water and half dry white wine. Include also 1 level teaspoon peppercorns, 2 well-scrubbed and broken celery sticks and ½ teacup well-washed parsley. If you like the taste of nutmeg, add 1 or 2 sprinklings or a small blade of costly mace.

Freezer Tip
Either the Fish Stock or Court Bouillon may be deep frozen up to 3 months, but must be strained first or flavours will intensify.

Poached Halibut

SERVES 4   ▲▲●●

Poach a 2lb (900g) piece of halibut in Court Bouillon as directed in recipe for Poached Fish. Add 1 sliced-up lemon and 1 very thinly sliced onion. Serve with Hollandaise Sauce (page 174) or any other sauce to taste. (See Sauce section, page 168.)

Poached Trout with Normandy Sauce

with butter or margarine; 1oz (25g) to every 4 pieces. The plate should then be stood on top of a saucepan containing gently simmering water, covered with a second plate (inverted) or suitably-sized lid. The fish should then be steamed until the flesh looks creamy and no longer translucent. It should be served coated with juices from the plate and accompanied with cream potatoes and green vegetables to taste.

Note The only whole fish suitable for steaming are whiting, but these should be gutted, cleaned thoroughly, boned and beheaded. They should be opened out on the plate, skin side down, and only one fish cooked at a time.

Poached Trout with Normandy Sauce

SERVES 4 ▲▲▲●●●

Poach 4 medium-sized, cleaned trout in Court Bouillon as previously described under Oven-Poached Fish (page 59). Remove from pan and stand on a clean tea towel. Strip off skin, leaving on heads and tails. Sprinkle with chopped parsley and coat with Normandy Sauce (page 170). Accompany with boiled potatoes and freshly-cooked baby peas and carrots tossed in butter.

Steamed Fish

▲●● or ●●●

This is considered one of the most delicate ways of cooking fish and steamed whiting, cod or plaice are certainly easy to digest and creamy in texture. Fillets are the best 'cut' and should be washed briefly, wiped dry with paper towels and transferred to an enamel plate, lightly-brushed with butter or margarine. The fillets should be coated with 2 teaspoons milk per fillet and dotted

Poached Sole with Curry Cream Sauce

SERVES 4 ▲▲▲●●●

4 medium-size Dover or lemon
  soles, skinned
Court Bouillon or Fish Stock
½pt (275ml) Béchamel Sauce,
  freshly made (page 169)
2 to 3 level tsp Madras ⎫
  curry powder   ⎪
2tblsp boiling water   ⎬ mixed
4tblsp double cream   ⎪
2tsp lemon juice   ⎭
1 egg yolk
2 bananas, halved lengthwise
1oz (25g) butter
2tblsp mango chutney for garnish

1 Poach soles in Court Bouillon or Fish Stock as previously described under Oven-Poached Fish (page 59).
2 Meanwhile, stand Béchamel Sauce over low heat and gently whisk in curry powder mixed with water, double cream and lemon juice.
3 Bring just up to boil. Remove from heat. Beat in egg yolk. Cover temporarily.
4 Fry bananas gently in butter. Lift fish gently out of liquid and drain on a clean tea towel. Transfer to a warm serving dish.
5 Coat with half the sauce then top with fried bananas and chutney. Serve rest of sauce separately and accompany with freshly-cooked rice, a mixed salad and half moons made from Puff Pastry (page 193).

Poached Sole with Curry Cream Sauce

Flemish Style Cod Casserole

SERVES 4 TO 5 ▲▲●●

1½lb (675g) cod fillet, cut into 2in (5cm) cubes

2 whole lemons (small), well washed and dried

6oz (175g) onions, peeled and very finely chopped

2 rounded tblsp parsley, finely chopped

2 rounded tblsp dill or chives, finely chopped

2 level tsp salt

¼pt (150ml) dry white wine

6 rounded tblsp breadcrumbs, lightly toasted

2oz (50g) butter or margarine, melted

1 Wash fish cubes and wipe dry with paper towels. Transfer to a well-buttered, fairly shallow oven-proof dish.

2 Cut lemons into very thin slices. Place on top of cod then cover with the chopped onions, followed by parsley and either dill or chives.

3 Sprinkle with salt and gently pour wine into dish. Coat thickly with breadcrumbs then moisten with melted butter or margarine.

4 Bake 30 minutes in oven set to 220°C (425°F), Gas 7. Serve from the dish and accompany with boiled potatoes and a lettuce salad tossed with French Dressing (page 180).

Flemish Style Cod Casserole

1 Heat half the butter or margarine in saucepan. Add onion. Fry gently, with lid on pan, until very pale gold.

2 Add cod fillets and fry fairly briskly for 4 minutes, turning once. Remove to plate temporarily.

3 Melt rest of butter in pan. Heat until sizzling. Stir in well-dried spinach. Fry, turning, 10 minutes over low heat. Keep pan covered throughout.

4 Spread onion, butter and spinach mixture evenly over base of heat-proof dish.

5 Top with fish fillets, season with salt and nutmeg if used, then arrange a band of tomatoes along the centre.

6 Sprinkle with grated cheese and bake, uncovered, in oven set to 220°C (425°F), Gas 7. Allow 20 to 25 minutes and accompany with creamed potatoes or freshly-cooked macaroni.

Cheesy Baked Tomato Cod on Spinach

Cheesy Baked Tomato Cod on Spinach

SERVES 4 ▲▲●●●

3oz (75g) butter or margarine

1 medium onion, peeled and finely chopped

4 fillets of cod, each about 6oz (175g) in weight

2lb (900g) leaf spinach, very well-washed, drained and cut into shreds

1 level tsp salt

¼ level tsp nutmeg (optional)

4 medium tomatoes, washed and sliced

4oz (100 to 125g) Cheddar cheese, finely grated

Fish Cakes

Fish Cakes

SERVES 4 ▲▲●●

1lb (450g) potatoes
8oz (225g) cooked and flaked fish
or 1 medium can pink salmon or
tuna, well-drained and flaked
½oz (15g) butter or margarine,
melted
¼ level tsp onion powder
1 level tsp powder mustard
salt and pepper to taste
milk for mixing if necessary
2 Grade 3 eggs, well beaten
4 heaped tblsp toasted breadcrumbs
2in (5cm) hot fat or oil for frying

GARNISH
lemon slices
fresh parsley or dill

1 Peel potatoes and wash. Cook in boiling salted water until soft. Drain. Mash finely.
2 Stir in fish, butter or margarine, onion and mustard powder, salt and pepper to taste and sufficient milk (if necessary) to bind mixture together. Depending on the potatoes themselves, and the type of fish, the mixture might hold without additional liquid.
3 Leave until cold. Divide equally into 8 or 10 pieces. Shape each piece into a round cake. Coat with egg. Toss in crumbs. Leave to stand 10 minutes for crumb coating to harden.

4 Fry in hot fat or oil until golden brown and crisp on both sides, turning once. Drain on paper towels. Serve straightaway, garnished with lemon and parsley.

Plaice Meunière

SERVES 4 ▲▲●●●

8 medium-sized fillets of plaice
salt and pepper
flour
4oz (125g) butter
1tsp salad oil
1tblsp lemon juice
1 rounded tblsp chopped parsley

1 Wash and paper-dry fillets. Season on both sides with salt and pepper. Coat with flour.
2 Heat half the butter with oil until sizzling. Add fish fillets, 2 at a time. Fry 5 minutes over medium heat, turning once.
3 Remove to a warm serving plate. Add rest of butter to pan. Fry gently until it just begins to turn light brown.
4 Stir in lemon juice and parsley and spoon over fish. Serve straightaway with plain boiled potatoes and cooked vegetables to taste.

Cooking Tip
For a less rich dish, use 3oz (75g) butter instead of 4oz (125g). Fry the fish in 2oz (50g) as directed above, then add rest of butter to pan.

Sole Meunière

SERVES 4 ▲▲●●●

Follow recipe for *Plaice Meunière*, using sole fillets instead of plaice.

Soused Herring

SERVES 4 ▲▲●●

A tangy, traditionally British dish that makes delicious summer eating.

4 large herring, cleaned and boned
1 large onion
1 level tblsp pickling spice
1 medium bay leaf, divided into 4
pieces
¼pt (150ml) malt vinegar or lemon
juice
4tblsp boiling water
2 level tsp caster sugar
1 level tsp salt

1 Wash and dry herrings. With skin sides outside, roll up each herring from head end to tail.
2 Arrange in a 1½pt (1 litre) heatproof dish. Peel and slice onions and separate slices into rings. Place amid the herrings.
3 Sprinkle with spice and bay leaf. Mix last 4 ingredients together. Pour over herrings.
4 Cover dish with lid or foil. Cook 1½ hours in oven set to 150°C (300°F), Gas 2. Remove from oven and leave to cool in the liquor.
5 Chill for 1 to 2 hours in the refrigerator before serving. Accompany with bread and butter.

Kedgeree

SERVES 8 ▲▲●●

Another popular British speciality that was once part of breakfast during the Edwardian period. Now it makes an excellent lunch or supper dish.

4oz (125g) butter or margarine
8oz (225g) smoked haddock,
cooked and flaked (all skin and
bones removed)
6oz (175g) fresh cod or haddock,
cooked and flaked
1lb (450g) cooked weight long
grain Indian rice (about 6oz or
175g raw)
2 Grade 4 eggs, hard-boiled and
chopped
¼pt (150ml) single cream

*1 level tblsp curry powder
(optional)
salt and pepper to taste
1 rounded tblsp chopped parsley*

1 Melt butter or margarine in saucepan. Stir in fish, rice, 1 chopped egg, cream and curry powder if used.
2 Season to taste with salt and pepper. Heat through over low heat, keeping pan uncovered, until mixture is piping hot.
3 Stir frequently with a fork to keep rice separate. Pile into a warm dish and sprinkle with second egg and parsley.

Poached Finnan Haddock

SERVES 4 ▲▲●●

Poach 1lb (450g) smoked haddock as directed in recipe for Poached Fish (page 58), using milk only. Serve hot topped with pieces of butter or poached eggs (1 egg per person).

Skate with Lemon Butter Sauce

SERVES 4 ▲▲●●

Although skate is most frequently eaten deep fried, it is excellent if simmered as given below and then coated with melted butter and lemon juice. Where fresh skate is available, ask the fishmonger to give you the 'wings' (which are actually the fins) which look somewhat like fans.

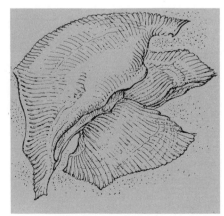

1 The fins of skate look like 'wings'

Make sure the skate is very fresh and, if possible, buy and cook on the same day.

*4 'wings' of skate, each about 8oz (225g) in weight
Fish Stock (page 59) or water to cover
2tblsp malt vinegar (which reduces the slight taste of ammonia)
2 to 3 level tsp salt*

TO SERVE
*2oz (50g) butter, melted
1tblsp lemon juice
1 level tblsp finely-chopped parsley*

1 Place skate in pan with all remaining ingredients. Slowly bring to boil. Lower heat.
2 Cover pan. Simmer very gently for 25 to 30 minutes. Drain. Arrange on a warm serving dish.
3 Heat butter until it sizzles and browns lightly. Stir in lemon juice. Pour over skate. Sprinkle with parsley.

Baked Stuffed Fish

SERVES 8 ▲▲●●

Choose a suitable stuffing from the Stuffing section (page 234) and pack into the cavity of a whole, cleaned haddock or small cod weighing about 2lb (900g). Bake as directed in recipe for Baked Fish (page 56).

Baked Stuffed Cutlets

SERVES 4 ▲▲●●

Choose a suitable stuffing from the Stuffing section (page 234) and pack into 4 cod or haddock cutlets so that the two flaps on each cutlet wrap round the stuffing. Place in greased tin and bake as directed in recipe for Baked Fish (page 56).

Trout with Almonds

SERVES 4 ▲▲●●

One of the great fish classics of all time, this is easier to make at home now that trout are farmed commercially and readily available frozen. The art of presentation lies in being very generous with the almonds.

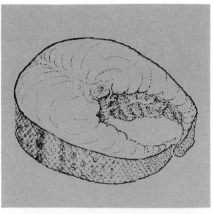

1 Stuff the cutlet . . .

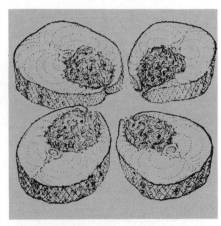

2 so that the two flaps on each cutlet wrap around the stuffing

*4 medium trout, cleaned (do not remove heads)
salt and pepper
flour for coating (about 3 level tsp per trout)
4oz (125g) butter
2tsp salad oil
4 to 5oz (125 to 150g) flaked almonds
2tblsp lemon juice*

1 Wash and dry trout. Season inside and out with salt and pepper. Coat with flour.
2 Heat 2oz (50g) butter and oil in heavy frying pan. Add trout, two at a time, and fry gently for 10 minutes, turning once. Remove to warm serving dish or individual warm plates.
3 Add rest of butter and almonds to pan. Fry over medium heat until almonds turn a light gold.
4 Stir in lemon juice. Heat through. Pour pan juices over trout then top with almonds.

Fish Kebabs

BASTE
4tblsp salad oil
2tblsp sweet sherry
1 level tsp salt
freshly-ground pepper

TO ACCOMPANY
¼pt (150ml) yogurt
¼pt (150ml) double cream
1 level tsp salt
¼ level tsp dried mint
1 level tblsp chopped parsley
freshly-cooked rice

1 Cut haddock into ½in (1¼cm) wide strips by about 4in (10cm) in length. Place in glass or pottery bowl. Add lemon juice, oil and garlic. Stir round. Cover. Leave to stand ½ hour.
2 Take fish out of bowl. Roll up strips and thread directly on to skewers alternately with tomatoes and onions.
3 Stand in grill pan. Beat oil with sherry, salt and pepper. Brush over kebabs. Grill 10 minutes, turning 2 or 3 times and brushing heavily with the sherry mixture each time.
4 Transfer to 8 warm dinner plates. Accompany with a sauce made from yogurt mixed with cream, salt, mint and parsley. Serve with a separate bowl of rice.

Cooking Time
Treated this way, the onions will remain crisp. If softer onions are preferred, simmer, whole, in boiling salted water for 5 minutes. Drain, rinse and cut into quarters.

Oatmeal Herrings

SERVES 4   ▲▲●●

A Scottish classic, these oatmeal-coated and fried herrings are a highly-esteemed dish and are particularly tasty if fried in bacon dripping.

4 cleaned and boned herring
salt and pepper to taste
1 Grade 3 egg
2tblsp milk
4 heaped tblsp rolled oats, crushed with a rolling pin to coarse crumbs
about 3in (7½cm) melted bacon dripping or margarine for frying

1 Wash and dry fish. Sprinkle inside and out with salt and pepper.
2 Dip in egg beaten with milk. Coat with oats which have been sprinkled on a piece of grease-proof paper.
3 Fry in hot dripping or margarine for 8 minutes, turning once. Remove from pan and drain on crumpled kitchen paper. Serve hot.

Fish Kebabs

SERVES 8   ▲▲●●●

Oriental in character, these make an interesting dish for entertaining and are fairly quick to prepare and cook.

2lb (900g) fresh haddock fillet, skinned
4tblsp lemon juice
1tblsp salad oil
1 garlic clove, peeled and chopped
8 small tomatoes, quartered
4 small onions, peeled and quartered

Salmon Mayonnaise

SERVES 8 TO 10   ▲▲●●●

Choose a whole salmon weighing 4 to 5lb (2 to 2¼kg) with head. Slit, gut, wash thoroughly and remove head. Poach as directed in recipe for Oven-Poached Fish (page 59), using water or Court Bouillon. Remove tin from oven and leave fish to cool to luke-warm in the cooking liquor. Lift out of pan on to a plate. Cover. Leave until cold. Carefully remove skin, taking care not to disturb the salmon flesh. Using two fish slices, lift whole salmon on to an oblong or oval serving dish. Garnish with a line of peeled and very thinly-sliced cucumber running from head end to tail. Accompany with Mayonnaise and salad.

Salmon Trout Mayonnaise

SERVES 8 TO 10 ▲▲●●●

Follow recipe for *Salmon Mayonnaise*, using a salmon trout instead.

'Wrapped' Salmon

SERVES 8 TO 10 ▲●●●

Because salmon can sometimes be dry if poached, this method of cooking helps the fish to keep its moisture more or less intact, and is especially recommended for whole frozen salmon. Wash and dry fish, making sure it has completely defrosted if frozen. Stand on a double thickness of foil which has been heavily brushed with melted butter. Brush fish, inside and out, with more butter, then sprinkle with salt and pepper to taste. Wrap closely in foil. Place in large roasting tin and cook in oven set to 190°C (375°F), Gas 5, allowing 10 minutes per pound (450g). Unwrap, remove skin and serve salmon with new boiled potatoes tossed in butter, garden peas, Hollandaise Sauce (page 174) and a dish of very thinly-sliced cucumber. If to be served cold, leave until lukewarm in the foil, unwrap and remove skin. Transfer to a serving dish. Cover. Refrigerate until cold. Garnish as Salmon Mayonnaise (page 64) and serve with Mayonnaise and salad.

Seafood Cider 'Casserole'

SERVES 6 TO 8 ▲▲●●●

4tblsp salad oil
3 large, skinned tomatoes, quartered
1 large onion, peeled and finely chopped
1 garlic clove, peeled and finely chopped
¼pt (150ml) cider
1¼lb (675g) haddock fillet, cut into 2in (5cm) cubes
1 bay leaf
1 small jar (about 5oz or 150g) mussels in vinegar, drained
8oz (225g) peeled prawns
1 level tsp salt
white pepper to taste
4 drops Tabasco

Seafood Cider 'Casserole'

1 carton (5 fluid oz or 142ml) soured cream
4tblsp French Calvados (apple brandy) or brandy
2 egg yolks
2 rounded tblsp chopped parsley

1 Heat salad oil in pan. Add tomatoes, onion and garlic. Cover pan. Fry over low heat for 10 minutes.
2 Pour in cider and slowly bring to boil. Add fish cubes and bay leaf. Cover pan. Simmer gently 8 minutes. Gently stir in mussels, prawns, salt, pepper and Tabasco.
3 Cover. Simmer very gently for 5 minutes. Remove from heat.
4 Beat together cream with Calvados or brandy and the egg yolks. Carefully stir into fish mixture, taking care not to break up cubes of fish.
5 Transfer to a warm serving dish and sprinkle with parsley. Serve straightaway with slices of crusty French bread.

Provence Scampi or Prawns

SERVES 4 ▲▲●●●

An extravagant speciality from the Mediterranean, usually served on a bed of buttered rice.

2tblsp salad oil (olive if preferred)
1 small onion, peeled and chopped
1 garlic clove, peeled and crushed
1lb (450g) ripe tomatoes, blanched and chopped
2 level tblsp tubed or canned tomato purée
1 level tsp salt
2 level tsp caster sugar
4tblsp dry white wine
1lb (450g) peeled scampi or prawns
2 heaped tblsp chopped parsley

1 Heat oil in large pan. Add onion and garlic. Fry gently, uncovered, until pale gold.
2 Add tomatoes, purée, salt, sugar and wine. Bring to boil, stirring. Lower heat. Cover pan. Simmer gently for 30 minutes.
3 Add scampi or prawns. Mix well. Cover pan. Cook until fish are hot, about 5 minutes over medium heat. Serve on rice and sprinkle with parsley.

Choosing Tip

Scampi is an Italian term to describe members of the crustacea family which, in the United Kingdom, are more likely to be Dublin Bay prawns, resembling lobsters in miniature. Although associated with Irish waters (hence the name), similar prawns are also found in Scotland.

Scallops in Mustard Sauce

SERVES 4 TO 6 ▲▲●●●

Wash and dry 8 scallops with their orange roes. Place in saucepan. Cover with cold water and add 1 teaspoon salt. Bring to boil. Lower heat. Cover. Simmer 6 minutes. Drain, reserving ¼pt (150ml) water. Make up Mustard Sauce (page 170) using half fish water and half milk. Cut up scallops. Add to sauce with orange roes. Heat until just hot. Adjust seasoning to taste. Serve with creamed potatoes or buttered rice.

Scallops Béchamel with Mushrooms

SERVES 4 TO 6 ▲▲▲●●

Cook 8 scallops and roes as directed in recipe for Scallops in Mustard Sauce, but do NOT retain the water. Cut up scallops and reserve temporarily with orange roes. Make a Béchamel Sauce as directed (page 169). Add 4oz (125g) butter-fried mushrooms and the scallops with roes. Heat through gently. Transfer to 4 or 6 buttered heatproof dishes. Sprinkle with grated cheese, allowing about 2oz (50g) Parmesan or 3oz (75g) Cheddar. Brown briefly under a hot grill. Serve with toast.

Dressed Crab

ALLOW 1 SMALL PER SERVING; 1 MEDIUM PER 2 SERVINGS
▲▲▲●●

Although some fishmongers still dress crabs and display them in their windows, many people living at the coast probably undertake the job themselves. For novices who would like the basic technique, here is how to go about it. Stand the crab on its back. Break off legs and claws by twisting. Separate body from shell by pushing upwards from tail flap. Remove the stomach bag — located below the head — from the shell, plus the feathery gills as these are *inedible*. Any green matter should also be removed and disposed of. Take out the soft, brown pulpy meat with a spoon and transfer to a basin. Cover and leave on one side temporarily. Crack

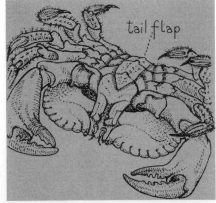

1 Whole crab

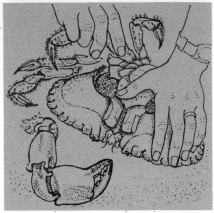

2 Stand the crab on its back and break off legs and claws by twisting

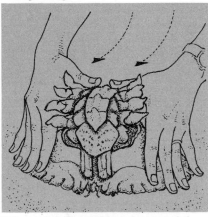

3 Separate body from shell by pushing upwards from tail flap

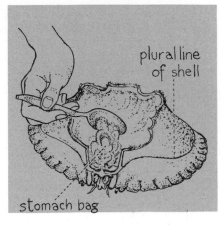

4 Remove stomach bag and discard

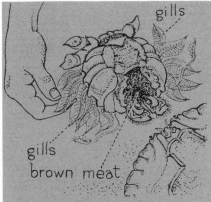

5 Remove the gills which are inedible and spoon brown meat into a basin

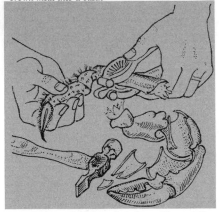

6 Crack large and medium-sized claws with a small hammer or nut cracker

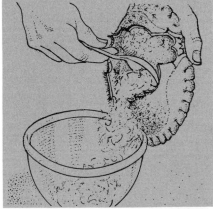

7 Remove all white meat from the body and spoon into a basin

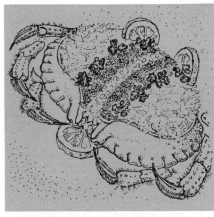

8 Clean shell then arrange crab mixtures as shown with brown meat in the middle and white meat either side. Garnish with chopped egg and parsley

large and medium-sized claws with a small hammer or nut cracker and remove the white flesh. Put into second basin with white meat from body. Wash shell thoroughly and wipe dry. Using a fork, mix brown crab meat with 1 heaped tablespoon soft brown breadcrumbs, ½ level teaspoon prepared English mustard, ½ teaspoon Worcester sauce, a large pinch of cayenne pepper, 1 tablespoon single cream or top of the milk and 2 or 3 teaspoons lemon juice. Spoon, in a wide band, into centre of cleaned shell. Arrange white meat on either side. Garnish with lines of chopped hard-boiled egg and chopped parsley. Accompany with Mayonnaise and salad.

Moules Marinière

SERVES 4 ▲▲▲●●

2¼ to 3 quarts mussels (about 3 litres)
2oz (50g) butter
4 shallots or small onions, peeled and finely chopped
1 garlic clove, peeled and crushed
¼pt (150ml) dry white wine
4tblsp water
1 bouquet garni
3 rounded tblsp fresh white breadcrumbs
2 rounded tblsp chopped parsley
freshly-milled pepper

1 Scrub mussels thoroughly under cold, running water to remove weedy bits from the sides. Tip into a clean colander and rinse again thoroughly to remove grit.
2 Lift out and throw away any mussels which have opened. Melt butter in a pan. Add shallots or onions and garlic. Fry gently until a very light gold.
3 Pour in wine and add bouquet garni. Bring to boil. Lower heat. Cover. Simmer 6 or 7 minutes. Add mussels.
4 Increase heat. Cook mussels briskly until shells open. This should take about 6 to 8 minutes and it is advisable to shake the pan all the time for even heat distribution. Remove bouquet garni.
5 Stir in breadcrumbs. Ladle mussels and liquor from pan into 4 deep soup plates. Sprinkle with parsley and serve straightaway with spoons and forks.

Tip

The 'beard', surrounding the lower shell of each mussel should be removed by the person eating the dish and discarded. Finger bowls containing cold water and a slice of lemon should be provided, as some people pick up the mussel shells to drink the liquor.

Lobster Mayonnaise

ALLOW ½ PER PERSON ▲▲▲●●

An expensive luxury, Lobster Mayonnaise is one of the highlights of summer eating and is very much a special occasion dish.

Scallops Béchamel with Mushrooms

To cook a live lobster, check shell for holes. If any are visible, literally stuff with bread to act as wedges. Plunge lobster into a pan of boiling water, head first. Keep pan covered until lobster stops wriggling, and you can only tell by lifting the lid and having a look every so often. Uncover. Lower heat. Simmer 12 minutes per lb (450g). Cool in the cooking liquor. Lift out of pan with tongs. Knock a hole in the shell near the head and leave to stand so that excess liquid trickles out. When completely cold, split body through shell (2 halves). Remove sac in the head which is inedible and also dark intestine which can be seen lying along the tail. Arrange on plates, cut sides up. Accompany with Mayonnaise and salad.

Oysters

ALLOW 6 TO 12 PER PERSON

▲▲▲●●

A seasonal luxury, highly esteemed by gastronomes and eaten — or swallowed – with tremendous relish. Oysters are always accompanied by dry white wine; NEVER spirits.

Choose oysters which are rotund and with shells tightly closed. Opening requires skill, but this can be carried out fairly competently in the following way:

1 Insert a knife through the hinge of the oyster.
2 Sever the ligament which joins the oyster to its flat, top shell.
3 Now serve the oyster, in its own liquor, in the deep half shell.
4 To eat (or swallow) sprinkle with lemon juice (if you look closely, you will see that fresh oysters shrink very slightly) and a few drops of Tabasco.

Poached Oysters

ALLOW 6 TO 12 PER PERSON

▲▲▲●●

Many recipes call for cooked oysters, and this is the method. Open oysters and tip liquor from shells into pan. Add oysters. Cook gently until the edges just begin to curl. This takes a few minutes and oysters should not be allowed to overcook or they will toughen.

Angels on Horseback

ALLOW 2 TO 3 PER PERSON
AS A COCKTAIL SNACK

▲▲▲●●

Wrap halved rashers of bacon round shelled, uncooked oysters. Spear on to cocktail sticks. Grill until bacon is crisp, turning once or twice. Serve hot.

Freezing Tips

In general, few *cooked* fish dishes freeze very successfully except fish cakes, pastry fish pies and other made-up dishes where flaked fish forms an integral part of the dish; for instance, Kedgeree. Fresh fish, conversely, takes very well to freezing, and below is a brief and simple guide to freezing and storage times.

FILLETS (THIN) Rinse under cold water and leave wet. Stack one on top of the other in groups of 4, interleaving each with freezer layer tissue for ease of separation. Overwrap. Seal. Label.

FILLETS (THICK) Wrap individually and seal. Transfer 4 to 6 pieces (depending on number in family) to a polythene bag. Seal and label.

WHOLE FISH (LARGE AND SMALL) Clean and gut. Wash thoroughly. Leave wet and fast freeze, uncovered, until hard. Double wrap. Seal and label.

Storage

WHITE FISH 3 months

OILY FISH 2 months

COOKED DISHES 2 months

SHELLFISH Not at all. This is best left to commercial freezer companies who deal with freshly-caught fish and freeze it at sea.

Meat and Offal

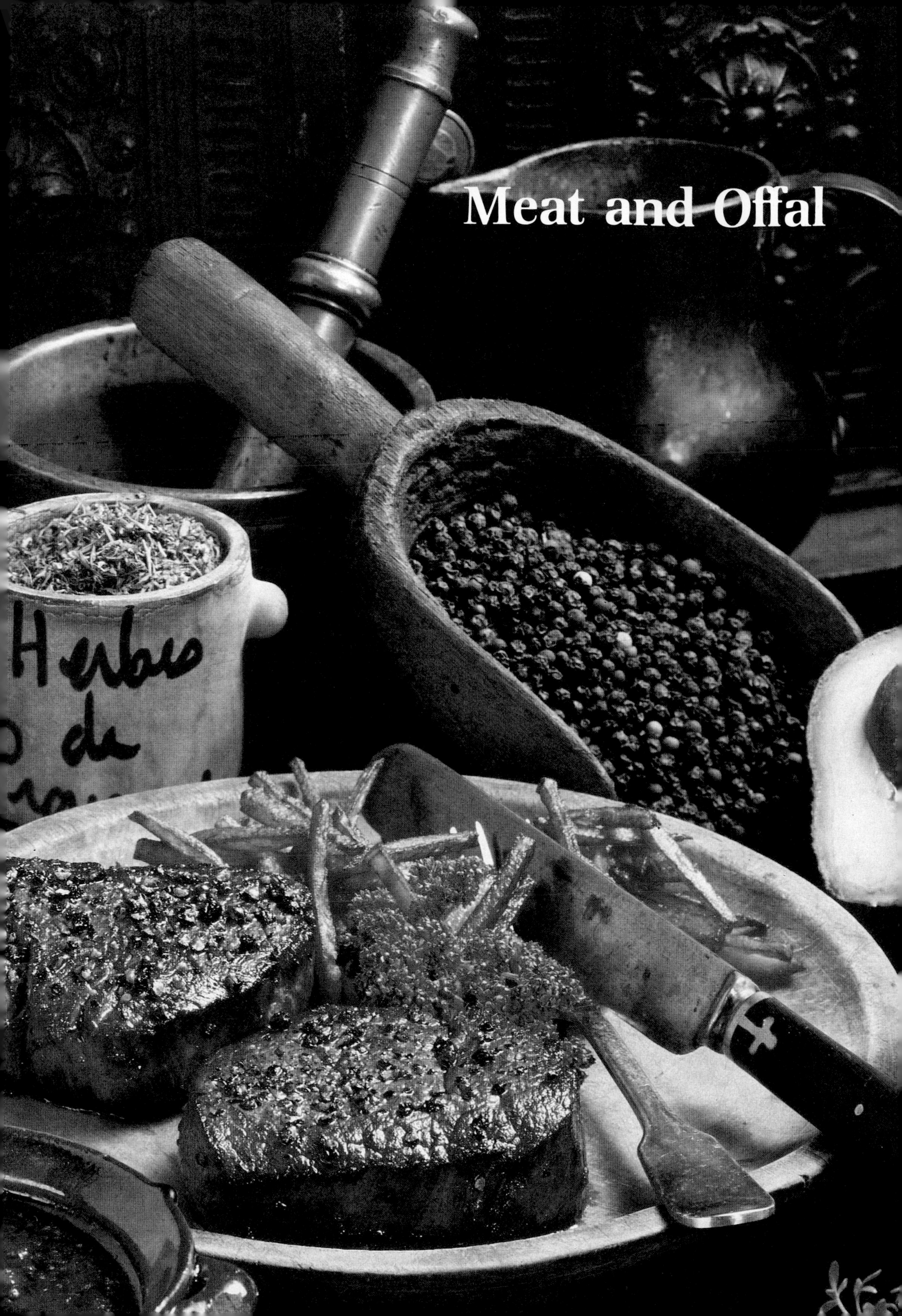

Meat and Offal

Meat and offal between them hold more appeal than any other protein food and certainly there is an enormous choice of cuts and types for every style of meal, be it a basic and economical lamb stew or a lavish and wine-laced Boeuf Bourguignonne. Although prices worldwide have made meat more of a luxury and less of an everyday occurrence than it used to be, it is still eaten at some stage by many people during the course of a week and often at weekends as well, and the variety of recipes in this section are intended to suit every occasion from a family evening meal to a special dish for entertaining.

For guidance, I have listed below the different kinds of cooking methods for beef, lamb, pork, bacon and veal and suggested the most suitable cuts for each method.

Beef

Roasting top rump, topside, foreribs, sirloin and fillet. Also silverside but this needs slow roasting as it is a tougher cut than the others.
Grilling and Frying rump, sirloin and fillet.
Stewing leg or shin, clod, neck, chuck, blade and flank.
Pot Roasting and Braising top rump, topside, flank, brisket, chuck, blade and ribs.
Boiling brisket and silverside.

Lamb

Roasting leg, loin, chump, shoulder, best end neck and breast.
Grilling and Frying loin and chump.
Stewing scrag and middle neck.
Pot Roasting and Braising shoulder and middle neck.
Boiling leg to replace leg of mutton which is hard to find.

Pork

Roasting leg, chump, loin with kidney attached, belly, hand and spring, blade bone and spare ribs.
Grilling and Frying chump chops, loin chops, spare rib chops, slices of belly.
Stewing belly, hand and spring, and bladebone.
Pot Roasting and Braising bladebone, spare rib and belly.

Bacon

Grilling and Frying back and streaky rashers, bacon chops, gammon steaks and gammon rashers.
Stewing collar, slipper and hock.
Pot Roasting and Braising as stewing cuts.
Boiling middle and corner gammon, gammon hock, slipper, collar and joints of back.

Veal

Roasting boned breast, shoulder (boned or unboned), loin and leg.
Grilling and Frying chops, and thinly-beaten cutlets and fillets cut from the leg.
Stewing knuckle, shoulder, breast.
Pot Roasting and Braising shoulder (boned or unboned), leg, and boned and rolled breast.
Boiling veal is not usually boiled.

Offal

Roasting lambs' and calves' hearts.
Grilling and Frying lambs' and calves' kidneys, lambs' and calves' liver (the latter is very expensive).
Stewing calves' and ox heart, oxtail, kidneys from all animals, lambs', pigs' and ox liver, sweetbreads.
Pot Roasting and Braising as stewing cuts.
Boiling dressed tripe and tongues (either fresh or pickled).

Other Offal

1 Brains are very delicate and poached in the same way as fish.
2 Lambs' sweetbreads are often gently simmered, coated with egg and breadcrumbs and then fried in butter or margarine and a few teaspoons salad oil.

BEEF

Roast Beef

ALLOW 8 TO 12oz (225 TO 350G) BEEF ON THE BONE PER PERSON; 6 TO 8oz (175 TO 225G) BEEF OFF THE BONE PER PERSON ▲●●●

Wash beef under cold, running water and dry with paper towels. Stand in roasting tin. Brush with a little melted dripping, butter or margarine. Place in oven set to 220°C (425°F), Gas 7. Reduce temperature to 180°C (350°F), Gas 4. Continue to roast, allowing 20 minutes per pound (450g) and 20 minutes over. For well-done meat, allow an extra 5 minutes per pound (450g); for under-done meat, allow 5 minutes per pound (450g) less. Leave to stand for 5 minutes before carving. Accompany with Gravy (page 172), Horseradish Sauce (page 183), English mustard, Yorkshire Pudding (see below), roast potatoes, boiled potatoes and seasonal vegetables to taste.

Yorkshire Pudding

SERVES 4 TO 6 ▲▲●●

4oz (125g) plain flour
1 level tsp salt
1 Grade 3 egg
½pt (275ml) cold milk or use half milk and half water for lighter batter
2tsp salad oil or melted margarine
2oz (50g) extra dripping or melted margarine

1 Sift flour and salt into bowl. Make well in centre. Drop in whole egg (broken into a cup first to make sure it is fresh) then gradually beat to a batter with half the milk or milk and water.
2 Continue beating until batter is smooth and bubbles rise to the surface. Gently beat in rest of liquid with salad oil or melted margarine. Cover. Refrigerate 1 hour.
3 Heat dripping or margarine in 10 by 12in (25 by 30cm) roasting tin until very hot. Pour in batter. Place tin in oven set to 200°C (400°F), Gas 6. Bake 40 minutes to 1 hour or until well-puffed and golden. Serve straightaway.

Miniature Yorkshires

MAKES 12 ▲▲●●

Make up half the batter but omit fat or oil. Divide equally between 12 well-greased bun tins. Bake until well risen and golden, allowing about 25 minutes in oven set to 220°C (425°F), Gas 7.

Beef Stew and Dumplings

SERVES 4 ▲▲●●

1½lb (675g) stewing steak, as lean as possible
1oz (25g) margarine or dripping
4oz (125g) onions, peeled and chopped
4oz (125g) carrots, peeled and sliced
4oz (125g) parsnip or swede, peeled and diced (optional)
1½oz (40g) flour
1pt (575ml) water
1¼ level tsp salt
white pepper to taste
bouquet garni (optional)

Dumplings

▲▲●●

4oz (125g) self-raising flour
pinch salt
1oz (50g) packeted suet, finely shredded
about 4tblsp cold water to mix

1 Cut beef into cubes. Wash and paper-dry. Heat margarine or dripping in saucepan. Add onions, carrots and parsnip or swede if included.
2 Fry gently until golden brown. Move vegetables to edge of pan. Add beef, a few cubes at a time. Fry until well sealed and golden. Sprinkle flour over meat and vegetables. Mix in well.
3 Add water gradually. Bring to boil, stirring. Season with salt and pepper. Add bouquet garni if used. Lower heat and cover. Simmer gently for 1½ to 2 hours or until meat is tender. Stir occasionally to prevent sticking. Remove bouquet garni.
4 About 30 minutes before meat is ready, make Dumplings. Sift flour and salt into bowl. Toss in suet. Mix to soft dough with water.

5 With floured hands, shape into 8 small dumplings. Drop gently on top of stew. Cover with lid. Cook a further 20 minutes or until well-risen and at least double their original size.
6 Serve stew and dumplings straightaway and accompany with boiled potatoes and seasonal vegetables to taste.

Success Tip
The stew tends to stick less if thickened just before the Dumplings are added or, if stew is cooked without Dumplings, at the end of the cooking time. To do this, omit the flour at the beginning and simmer beef in water with vegetables and seasonings. Just before serving, mix 2 level tablespoons cornflour with 3 tablespoons cold water. Add to stew. Bubble gently until thickened, stirring.

Beef Stew

Beef Stew Variations

SERVES 4 ▲▲●●

Instead of water, use beer, dry cider or tomato juice for cooking.

Sea Pie

SERVES 4 ▲▲●●

Follow recipe for *Beef Stew and Dumplings* but instead of turning the suet mixture into dumplings, roll into a round a little smaller than the top of the saucepan. Place carefully on top of meat mixture and cover with lid. Simmer a further 30 minutes. Cut pastry into 4 portions (triangles) and serve with portions of stewed beef.

Beef Pie

Beef Crumble

SERVES 4 ▲▲●●

Make *Beef Stew* (page 71) exactly as directed but omit Dumplings. Leave until cold. Place in 2pt (1¼ litre) greased pie dish. Sprinkle thickly with Crumble made by sifting 6oz (175g) flour, ½ level teaspoon salt and 1 level teaspoon powder mustard into a bowl, and rubbing in 3oz (75g) butter or margarine.

Beef Pie

SERVES 4 ▲▲▲●●●

Make *Beef Stew* exactly as directed (page 71) but omit Dumplings. Leave

until cold. Place in 1pt (575ml) pie dish with rim, doming meat mixture up in the centre. Make up 6oz (175g) Shortcrust Pastry using 6oz (175g) flour (page 186). Roll out about 1½in (4cm) larger all the way round than top of pie dish. Dampen rim of pie dish with water then line with pastry strips, cut from trimmings. Dampen trimmings with more water then cover with lid of pastry, pressing edges well together to seal. Brush with beaten egg. Decorate with pastry cut-outs and brush with more egg. Make a hole in the top to allow steam to escape. Bake 30 to 40 minutes (or until golden brown) in

oven set to 220°C (425°F), Gas 7. Serve with boiled potatoes and seasonal green vegetables to taste.

Steak and Kidney Pie

SERVES 4 ▲▲▲●●●

Make as *Beef Pie* but when stewing meat, reduce quantity by 6oz (175g) and add the equivalent amount of diced ox kidney.

Pastry Variation

If preferred, top Beef or Steak and Kidney Pie with 8oz homemade (225g) Rough Puff or Flaky Pastry (pages 190–192) or 1 small packet defrosted frozen puff pastry.

Steak Pie on a Plate

SERVES 4 TO 6 ▲▲▲●●●

Make *Beef Stew* exactly as directed but omit Dumplings. Make up 8oz (225g) Shortcrust Pastry with 8oz (225g) flour (page 186). Roll out just over half and use to line an 8in (20cm) well-greased, heatproof plate. Top with COLD beef mixture, doming it up in centre. Dampen edges with water then cover with lid, rolled from rest of pastry. Make a slit in the top to allow steam to escape then brush with beaten egg. Bake 30 to 40 minutes (or until golden) in oven set to 220°C (425°F), Gas 7. Serve with boiled potatoes and seasonal vegetables.

1 Line the rim of the pie dish with pastry strips, cut from trimmings

2 Cover with a lid of pastry and press edges together

3 Trim off surplus pastry

Boiled Beef

SERVES 4 TO 6 ▲●●

3lb (1½kg) salted silverside or
  rolled brisket
cold water
1 bouquet garni
1 large onion, peeled and left whole
1 large celery stalk, scrubbed and
  broken into 4 pieces
1 large carrot, peeled and left whole

1 Soak beef overnight in cold water.
  Rinse. Put into large saucepan.
  Cover with fresh water. Bring to
  boil. Drain. Repeat twice more to
  reduce excess saltiness.
2 Cover again with cold water.
  Bring to boil. Skim. Add bouquet
  garni, and vegetables. Cover. Simmer gently 2 to 2½ hours or until
  meat is tender.
3 Lift meat out of pan. Carve into
  slices and serve with Horseradish
  Sauce (page 183) and boiled
  potatoes.

Boiled Beef

Boiled Beef and Carrots

SERVES 4 TO 6 ▲▲●●

Follow recipe for *Boiled Beef* (page
73) but omit whole carrot. When
meat is almost cooked, add 8oz
(225g) peeled and sliced carrots and
continue to simmer for a further 30
minutes. Carve meat and surround
with carrots. If liked, accompany
with Dumplings (page 71) simmered
separately in water.

Steak and Kidney Pudding

SERVES 4 TO 6 ▲▲▲●●●

Suet Crust Pastry (page 189)
1lb (450g) stewing steak
6oz (175g) ox kidney
1 slightly rounded tblsp flour
1 level tsp salt
pepper to taste
4oz (125g) onion, peeled and
  chopped
4tblsp water or brown ale

1 Roll out two-thirds of the pastry
  on floured surface and use to line
  a well-greased 1½pt (just under 1
  litre) china-type pudding basin.
  Avoid light-weight plastic as it
  could lose its shape.

2 Wash and dry steak and kidney.
  Cut into small cubes. Mix flour
  with salt and pepper and tip onto
  a plate. Add steak and kidney.
  Toss over and over until the pieces
  are well coated. Mix with onion.
3 Transfer to pastry-lined basin with
  any left-over flour. Pour in water
  or ale. Dampen edges of lining
  pastry with water then cover with
  lid, rolled from rest of pastry.
4 Cover securely with greased,
  greaseproof paper topped with a
  piece of foil. Cook 3½ hours in pan

of gently boiling water, keeping
lid on pan throughout.
5 Top up with extra boiling water
  now and then to prevent pan boiling dry. When Pudding is ready,
  take out of saucepan and remove
  covering. Wipe sides dry and tie a
  clean linen table napkin round
  outside of basin.
6 To serve, spoon portions out of
  the basin and accompany with
  boiled potatoes and seasonal vegetables to taste.

1 Line a pudding basin with pastry

2 After filling, cover with a lid, rolled from the rest of the pastry

73

American Ranch Steak

Cornish Style Pasties

MAKES 4 ▲▲▲●●

Shortcrust Pastry made with 8oz (225g) flour (page 186)

FILLING
4oz (125g) ox liver
8oz (225g) frying steak
3oz (75g) onion, peeled and chopped
4oz (125g) potato, peeled and diced
salt and pepper to taste
4tsp cold water
beaten egg for brushing

1 Divide pastry into 4 equal pieces and roll each out into a 6in (15cm) round. Leave aside temporarily.
2 Wash liver and steak and dry with paper towels. Cut into tiny cubes. Mix with onion and potato.
3 Place equal amounts of filling on to centres of pastry rounds. Sprinkle each with salt and pepper and 1 teaspoon water. Moisten edges with water then bring up

towards the centre, forming a 'seam' across the centre of each pastry.
4 Press edges well together to seal and press into flutes. Stand Pasties on greased baking tray and brush with egg. Bake $\frac{1}{4}$ hour in oven set to 220°C (425°F), Gas 7. Reduce temperature to 160°C (325°F), Gas 3 and continue to bake a further $\frac{3}{4}$ hour. Serve hot or cold.

1 Press edges of the pastry well together to seal and press into flutes

Beef Pot Roast

SERVES 4 TO 5 ▲▲●●

$2\frac{1}{2}$lb (just over 1kg) beef for pot roasting, in one piece
2oz (50g) margarine or dripping
6oz (175g) onions, peeled and sliced
4oz (125g) carrots, peeled and sliced
4 medium celery stalks, scrubbed and sliced
$\frac{1}{2}$pt (275ml) boiling water
1 level tblsp tomato purée
1 level tblsp mushroom ketchup
1 level tsp salt
pepper to taste

1 Wash and dry beef. Heat margarine or dripping in sturdy pan. Add beef. Fry fairly briskly until well sealed and brown all over. Remove to plate temporarily.
2 Add vegetables to remaining fat in pan. Fry until a warm gold. Move to edges of pan. Stand beef in centre.
3 Mix water thoroughly with rest of ingredients. Pour into pan over beef. Bring to boil. Lower heat. Cover.
4 Simmer gently 2 hours, turning meat twice or 3 times. Carve into slices and serve with vegetables from pan and any remaining pan juices.

Flavour Tip
A crushed clove of garlic and bay leaf may be added for increased flavour. For a luxury touch, red wine may replace water.

Grilled Steak

ALLOW 6 TO 8OZ (175 TO 225G) PER PERSON ▲●●●

Choose steaks (page 70) which are thick as opposed to thin as these tend to remain moist and tender. Wash and dry with paper towels. Stand in grill pan brushed with melted butter or margarine. Brush steaks with more melted butter or margarine. Grill 1 minute. Turn over. Brush again with melted butter or margarine. Grill a further 2 to 3 minutes per side for rare steaks, 4 to 5 minutes per side for medium steaks and 6 to 7 minutes for well done steaks. Sprinkle with salt and pepper before serving. Top with Savoury Butter pats (page 178).

French Style Pepper Steaks

American Ranch Steak

▲▲●●●

Cook steak (preferably thick rump) exactly as directed above and serve in individual dishes with 2 or 3 rashers of grilled bacon and freshly-heated baked beans.

Fried Steak

ALLOW 6 TO 8oz (175 TO 225G) PER PERSON ▲●●●

Choose same cuts as for Grilled Steak (page 70). Wash and dry each piece. Melt 1oz (25g) butter or margarine in heavy-based frying pan. Add steak or steaks. Fry for length of time given for grilling, turning 4 times. Sprinkle with salt and pepper before serving. Top with Savoury Butter pats (page 178).

French Style Pepper Steaks

SERVES 4 ▲▲▲●●●

4 fillet steaks, each 1in (2½cm) thick
3 level tblsp black peppercorns, coarsely crushed or ground out of pepper mill
2oz (50g) butter
2tsp salad oil
salt
6tblsp brandy
3tblsp boiling water
1 level tsp mixed herbs
2tsp Worcester sauce
¼tsp Soy sauce
¼pt (150ml) double cream (optional)

1 Wash and dry steaks. Press crushed peppers on to both sides of each, using the flat or your hands. Transfer to plate. Cover. Leave to stand ½ hour.

2 Heat butter and oil in pan. Add steaks. Fry 5 minutes, turning once. (They should be rare but if preferred, cook as directed for well-done steaks under Grilled Steak on page 74.)

3 Sprinkle with salt. Pour brandy into pan over steaks. Flame. As soon as flames have subsided, remove steaks to a warm plate and keep hot.

4 Add water, herbs and Worcester and Soy sauces to pan. Swirl round. Heat through until very hot. Pour over steaks. For a richer sauce, stir in cream. Heat until hot. Pour over steaks. Accompany with thin chips and garnish with parsley.

Variation
If preferred, heat cream separately and pour into serving dish. Decorate with slices of avocado brushed with lemon.

Cheeseburgers

Beef Stroganov

SERVES 4 ▲▲▲●●●

1lb (450g) fillet or rump steak
3oz (75g) butter
1tsp salad oil
2oz (50g) onion, peeled and grated
12oz (350g) button mushrooms and stalks, trimmed and thinly sliced
1 level tsp salt
white pepper to taste
4tblsp dry white wine
2 level tsp tomato purée
¼pt (150ml) double cream
1 level tblsp pickled cucumber, finely chopped

1 Wash and dry steak and cut into strips about three times the size of a matchstick. Leave aside temporarily.
2 Heat butter and oil in heavy-based frying pan until sizzling. Add onion. Fry gently until soft but still white, keeping pan half covered.
3 Add steak and fry 4 minutes over a slightly increased heat. Remove to plate with slotted spoon. Reserve.
4 Add mushrooms to rest of butter in pan. Fry fairly briskly for 4 minutes, turning all the time. Replace steak and mix in well.
5 Add salt, pepper, wine, purée, cream and pickled cucumber. Stir round. Bring just up to the boil. Remove from heat. Serve straightaway with freshly-cooked rice. Accompany with seasonal vegetables to taste or a salad.

Chili Con Carne

SERVES 6 ▲▲●●

2oz (50g) margarine or dripping
8oz (225g) onions, peeled and chopped
1 garlic clove, peeled and crushed
1lb (450g) minced raw beef
1 can (about 1lb or 450g) peeled tomatoes
½pt (275ml) water
¼ to ½ level tsp cayenne pepper (very fiery, so be careful)
1½ to 2 level tsp salt
1 can (about 1lb or 450g) red kidney beans, drained and rinsed
1tsp Worcester sauce

1 Heat margarine or dripping in heavy-based pan. Add onions and garlic. Fry gently until deep gold.
2 Add meat. Increase heat. Stir until well-browned and crumbly. Add tomatoes, water, cayenne pepper and salt.
3 Bring to boil, stirring. Lower heat. Cover. Simmer gently for 1 to 1½ hours or until meat is very soft. Uncover. Continue to cook until most of the liquid has evaporated, stirring from time to time.
4 Add kidney beans and Worcester sauce. Mix in gently. Heat mixture through until piping hot. Serve with rice.

Warning
Cooked red kidney beans are not poisonous and those from a can are completely safe. If you would prefer to use dried kidney beans, soak overnight in water to cover. Drain. Boil fairly vigorously for at least ½ hour. Reduce heat. Cover. Simmer until tender.

Hamburgers

SERVES 4 ▲●●

1lb (450g) raw minced beef
3oz (75g) onion, peeled and grated
3oz (75g) fresh white or brown breadcrumbs
1 Grade 2 egg, lightly beaten
½ to 1 level tsp salt
1 level tsp anchovy essence (optional)

1 Knead all ingredients well together. Divide equally into 8 pieces.
2 Shape each into a round hamburger. Stand in greased grill pan. Grill 7 minutes. Turn over. Grill a further 7 minutes.
3 Serve straightaway with chips or baked jacket potatoes and either cooked vegetables or a mixed salad.

Cheeseburgers

SERVES 4 ▲▲●●

Place cooked *Hamburgers* (see above) inside toasted buns spread lightly with mustard and topped with halved tomatoes grilled with strips of processed cheese. Serve on lettuce and garnish with parsley.

Novelty Cheeseburgers

SERVES 4 ▲▲●●

Make *Hamburgers* exactly as directed above. Cut 2oz (50g) Cheddar cheese into 8 cubes. Enclose 1 cube in each Hamburger before grilling so that it starts to melt as the Hamburgers are being cooked.

Fondue Bourguignonne

FOR SERVINGS, SEE BELOW
▲▲▲●●●

Fondue Bourguignonne is one of the all-time great meat specialities and is basically a luxury, do-it-yourself meal prepared in deep pans over spirit stoves at the table. (One for every 4 persons to prevent accidents.) Special Fondue sets are available, including long-handled forks, and these are a practical investment

Fondue Bourguignonne

Fondue Chinoise

if you enjoy this fairly informal – if somewhat expensive – way of entertaining.

The technique is to provide diners with a selection of accompaniments to include sauces, pickles, salads, condiments, crusty French bread, sometimes chips and cubes of rump or fillet steak; at least 4oz (125g) per person. The Fondue pan (or pans) is half-filled with oil which is then heated and placed over a spirit stove – usually the base of the Fondue pot. Diners then help themselves to selected accompaniments, which they put on to their dinner plates, and also take some chunks of bread or chips. They then spear a cube of steak on to their Fondue fork and hold it in the hot oil, allowing about $1\frac{1}{2}$ to $2\frac{1}{2}$ minutes, depending on whether they like it pink or well done. The meat is then taken off the Fondue fork, picked up with a dinner fork and dipped in the sauces etc on the plate. It is eaten with chosen accompaniments and the whole exercise is repeated with the next cube of steak.

To get off to a good start, prepare the sauces first, either choosing some of the Mayonnaise variations (pages 175–6) or making sauces from the following:

1 1 carton (5oz or 142ml) natural yogurt mixed with 1 medium peeled and crushed garlic clove, 1 level teaspoon mint sauce and salt to taste.

2 1 carton (5oz or 142ml) soured cream mixed with one finely-mashed small avocado, 1 level teaspoon curry powder and 2 teaspoons lemon juice.

For the rest of the accompaniments, arrange the following (or a selection) in small dishes:

1 Canned artichoke hearts moistended with French Dressing.
2 Canned palm hearts and black olives coated with lemon juice.
3 Cubes of cooked carrot soaked in French Dressing.
4 Sliced gherkins.
5 Continental sweet-sour fruits (available from speciality food shops).
6 Prepared mustard.
7 Mango chutney.
8 Bowl or bowls of mixed salad.
9 Pickled mushrooms mixed with stuffed olives.
10 Mixed pickles in vinegar.

The essential drink? Burgundy.

Fondue Chinoise

SERVES 6   ▲▲▲●●●

This is the Chinese version of the Fondue Bourguignonne but instead of oil, an assortment of meats, prawns and vegetables are simmered in rich stock and, at the very end, everyone mixes his or her bowl of egg yolk with Soy sauce and remaining stock and drinks it as soup – a kind of reverse course meal!

3 cans concentrated consommé
3 cans water
6 egg yolks
6tblsp Soy sauce
8oz (225g) deep-frozen turkey breasts, cut into thin slivers and thawed
8oz (225g) deep-frozen fillet steak, cut into thin slivers and thawed
8oz (225g) deep-frozen pork fillet, cut into thin slivers and thawed
8oz (225g) chicken livers, thawed if frozen and well washed
8oz (225g) peeled prawns, thawed if frozen and rinsed
8oz (225g) button mushrooms, trimmed and sliced
1 small can bamboo shoots
8oz (225g) fresh bean sprouts
2 leeks, trimmed and slit

1 Pour consommé and water into a pan and heat until boiling. Pour into 2 deep Fondue pans. Stand on spirit stoves already on the table.

2 Place egg yolks in 6 individual soup bowls and pour 1 tablespoon Soy sauce into each. Leave beside peoples' plates.

3 Arrange well-dried and cut-up turkey breast, steak, pork fillet, livers, prawns and mushrooms in separate dishes. Cut drained bamboo shoots into strips and put on to another dish with washed and dried bean sprouts.

4 Wash leeks very thoroughly. Cut into rings (discarding most of the green parts) and place in dish. Spoon coarsely-milled black pepper, paprika and cayenne into small bowls.

5 Stand all the dishes and bowls on the table and then proceed as for the Fondue Bourguignonne (above), spearing meat and chosen vegetables into the hot consommé and cooking to suit personal taste.

6 Season with selected condiments, choosing from the peppers plus tomato ketchup, Worcester sauce etc. Finally, spoon remaining consommé into the soup bowls, mix with the egg yolk and Soy sauce and drink from the bowls.

Success Tips

1 To make the dish more substantial, serve with freshly-cooked noodles tossed with butter.
2 If the meat is sliced while still partially frozen, the slices will be thinner.
3 Offer guests a choice of long fondue forks or chopsticks.

Boeuf Bourguignonne

SERVES 6 ▲▲▲●●●

2oz (50g) butter or margarine
2tsp salad oil
8oz (225g) onions, peeled and
  chopped
1 garlic clove, peeled and crushed
8oz (225g) gammon, chopped
2lb (900g) braising steak, cubed
2 level tblsp flour
½pt (275ml) Burgundy
¼pt (150ml) hot water
1 bouquet garni
1 level tsp salt
pepper to taste
12 shallots or small onions, peeled
6oz (175g) button mushrooms,
  trimmed but left whole
2 heaped tblsp finely-chopped
  parsley

1 Heat butter or margarine and salad oil in pan. Add onions and garlic. Fry gently until golden brown. Add gammon and steak. Fry a further ¼ hour over high heat, turning.
2 Stir in flour then gradually blend in Burgundy and water. Cook, stirring, until mixture comes to boil and thickens. Add bouquet garni and salt and pepper to taste.
3 Cover. Simmer gently 1½ hours, stirring. Mix in shallots or onions. Cover. Continue to simmer a further ½ hour. Remove bouquet garni.
4 Add mushrooms. Cook 10 minutes. Stir in parsley. Serve with boiled potatoes and seasonal vegetables to taste.

LAMB

Roast Lamb

ALLOW 6 TO 8OZ (175 TO 225G) RAW WEIGHT WITH BONE PER PERSON; 4 TO 6OZ (125 TO 175G) WITHOUT BONE PER PERSON ▲●●

Wash lamb and dry with paper towels. Place joint in roasting tin or, if very fatty (breast for instance), stand on rack in tin so that meat is not forced to sit in a pool of its own fat. Brush with melted butter or margarine ONLY if joint is very lean. Otherwise place in oven set to 220°C (425°F), Gas 7. Reduce at once to 180°C (350°F), Gas 4. Roast for 25 minutes per pound (450g) and 25 minutes over. Do not baste unless the joint was marinated and you decide to use this liquid to coat the lamb while it is roasting. Remove to board or dish and carve fairly thickly into slices, sections or cutlets (depending on cut). Accompany with Gravy (page 172), Mint Sauce (page 184), Onion Sauce (page 170), redcurrant jelly, roast and boiled potatoes, small carrots tossed in butter and garden peas.

Italian Style Roast Lamb

ALLOW SAME QUANTITIES AS ROAST LAMB ABOVE ▲▲●●●

Choose leg. Roast as above but sprinkle lamb with 1 level teaspoon dried rosemary before placing in oven. Baste with ¼pt (150ml) red Chianti mixed with 1 peeled and crushed garlic clove.

Stewed Lamb

SERVES 4 ▲▲●●

2lb (900g) scrag end neck of lamb
2 level tblsp flour
1 level tsp salt
pepper to taste
2oz (50g) margarine or dripping
6oz (175g) onions, peeled and
  chopped

2 medium celery stalks, scrubbed
  and sliced
2 medium carrots, peeled and sliced
1oz (25g) pearl barley, washed
¾pt (425ml) water

1 Wash and dry lamb then coat with flour, first seasoned with salt and pepper.
2 Heat margarine or dripping in heavy pan. Add flour-coated lamb, a few pieces at a time. Fry until well browned. Remove to plate temporarily.
3 Add onions, celery and carrots to remaining fat in pan. Fry gently until light gold. Stir in barley and water then replace lamb.
4 Bring to boil, stirring. Lower heat. Cover. Simmer 1½ hours, stirring from time to time to prevent sticking. Accompany with freshly-boiled vegetables.

Mid-European Lamb Casserole

SERVES 4 ▲▲●●

12 oz (350g) diced lamb shoulder
  (boned weight)
¾pt (425ml) water
6 peppercorns
1 large onion, peeled but left whole
12oz (350g) potatoes, peeled and
  diced
12oz (350g) carrots, peeled and
  fairly thickly sliced
12oz (350g) kohlrabi, peeled and
  diced
1 large slit leek, well washed and
  cut into fairly wide slices
2 level tsp salt
½ level tsp caraway seeds (optional)
2 rounded tblsp chopped parsley
extra parsley for garnish

1 Place lamb, water, peppercorns and onion in saucepan. Bring to boil. Skim. Lower heat. Cover. Simmer ¾ hour.
2 Add vegetables, salt, caraway seeds if used and chopped parsley. Bring to boil again. Lower heat. Cover. Continue to simmer a further ½ hour or until vegetables are tender.
3 Garnish with parsley and serve from the pot. Extra vegetables are unnecessary, though sprouts team very well with the casserole.

79

Italian Style Roast Lamb (page 79)

2 Turn. Continue to grill a further 6 minutes, turning twice and brushing with butter or margarine.

3 Transfer to warm dinner plates and top with pats of Savoury Butter. Garnish with watercress.

Lamb and Coconut Curry

SERVES 4 TO 6 ▲▲▲●●

1½lb (675g) lamb shoulder, cubed (boned weight)
2oz (50g) unsalted butter
2tsp salad oil
12oz (350g) onions, peeled and chopped
2 garlic cloves, peeled and chopped
1 to 2 level tblsp mild curry powder
1 level tblsp tomato purée
1 rounded tsp mint sauce
½pt (275ml) water
1 level tblsp desiccated coconut
¼ level tsp cinnamon
¼ level tsp cumin seeds
1 small bay leaf
2 large tomatoes, skinned and chopped
2 level tsp salt

SIDE DISHES OR SAMBALS OF:
natural yogurt
mango chutney
4oz (125g) cottage cheese mixed with diced banana
sliced onions sprinkled with a little turmeric
lime pickle

1 Wash and dry lamb with paper towels. Heat butter and oil in large pan. Add onions and garlic. Fry to a rich brown.

2 Move to edges of pan. Add lamb to centre, a few cubes at a time. Fry until well-sealed and brown. Add curry powder, tomato purée and mint sauce. Cook, stirring, 5 minutes.

3 Stir in rest of ingredients. Slowly bring to boil, stirring. Lower heat. Cover. Simmer 1½ hours. Cool. Refrigerate. Leave overnight. covered.

4 Next day, remove layer of fat from top and bubble gently for 30 minutes before serving. Serve with freshly-cooked Bashati Rice and the suggested Sambals.

Lancashire Style Hot Pot

SERVES 4 ▲▲●●

1½lb (675g) best end neck of lamb cutlets
3 lambs' kidneys
1lb (450g) potatoes, peeled and thinly sliced
8oz (225g) onions, peeled and thinly sliced
salt and pepper to taste
½pt (275ml) beef stock (made from cube and water)
1oz (25g) margarine, melted

1 Wash cutlets and wipe dry with paper towels. Remove as much excess fat as possible. Remove outer skin of kidneys then cut each into thin slices.

2 Arrange half the potatoes and onions in 3pt (1½ litre) greased casserole. Place cutlets and kidney slices on top. Season well with salt and pepper.

3 Cover with rest of potatoes and onions, finishing with an overlapping layer of potatoes. Season again. Pour stock into dish then trickle margarine over top.

4 Cover with lid or foil. Bake 1½ hours in oven set to 180°C (350°F), Gas 4. Uncover. Continue to bake a further 30 to 40 minutes or until top is golden brown.

Tip
To keep to an old tradition, add 8 shelled oysters with the kidneys!

Grilled Lamb Chops

SERVES 4 ▲▲●●●

8 loin or 4 chump chops
1oz (25g) melted butter or margarine
Savoury Butter to taste (page 178)
watercress

1 Wash and dry chops. Place in greased grill pan. Brush with butter or margarine. Stand under hot grill. Cook 1 minute. Turn. Cook 1 minute.

Moussaka

SERVES 4   ▲▲▲●●

1lb (450g) unpeeled aubergines
salt
4tblsp salad oil
8oz (225g) onions, thinly sliced
2 garlic cloves, peeled and crushed
12oz (350g) cold roast lamb,
   minced
2oz (50g) fresh white breadcrumbs
1 level tblsp tomato purée
¼pt (150ml) tomato juice
½pt (275ml) Cheese Sauce (page
   169)
1 Grade 2 egg, beaten
2oz (50g) Cheddar cheese, grated

1 Top and tail aubergines. Cut into ½in (1¼cm) thick slices. Place, in a single layer, on large board or platter. Sprinkle heavily with salt and leave ½ hour. (This draws out a certain amount of moisture and prevents aubergines from absorbing too much oil.)

2 Turn slices over. Sprinkle again with salt. Leave ½ hour. Rinse under cold water. Gently squeeze dry in clean cloth. Heat oil in frying pan. Add aubergine slices. Fry briskly on both sides until golden. Remove to plate temporarily.

3 Add onions and garlic to remaining oil in pan. Fry to a warm gold. Add lamb, crumbs, purée and juice. Mix well.

4 Line a 3pt (1¾ litre) greased casserole with half the aubergine slices. Spread with meat mixture. Cover with rest of aubergine slices.

5 While sauce is still in its saucepan, whisk in the beaten egg. Pour over the Moussaka and sprinkle with cheese. Cover with lid or foil. Cook ¾ hour in oven set to 180°C (350°F), Gas 4. Uncover. Continue to cook 15 to 25 minutes or until top is golden and crusty.

Shepherd's Pie

SERVES 4   ▲▲●●

12oz (350g) cold, minced lamb
   (leftovers from cooked joint)
½pt (275ml) Gravy (page 172)
1 to 1½lb (450 to 675g) freshly-
   boiled potatoes
1 to 2oz (25 to 50g) butter or
   margarine
4 to 6tblsp hot milk
salt and pepper to taste

1 Combine lamb and gravy and place in 2pt (1¼ litre) greased pie dish.

2 Mash drained potatoes over low heat (in saucepan in which they were cooked) until fluffy, then cream with butter, milk and seasoning to taste.

3 Swirl over meat mixture. Reheat and brown for 30 to 40 minutes in oven set to 220°C (425°F), Gas 7. Serve with seasonal vegetables.

Mid-European Lamb Casserole (page 79)

Boiled Lamb with Caper Sauce

1 Fill a large saucepan with alternate layers of potatoes, onions,
and lamb, sprinkling salt and
pepper between layers.
2 Pour stock into pan and gently
bring to boil. Cover. Lower heat.
Simmer about 1½ hours or until
ingredients literally fall to pieces.
3 Pile on to 4 warm plates and
sprinkle with parsley. Serve while
still very hot.

Boiled Lamb with Caper Sauce

SERVES 6 TO 8 ▲▲●●●

In the absence of mutton, which is
now no longer easy to find, I suggest
a leg of lamb be substituted and the
best to choose is frozen from New
Zealand.

*3lb (1½kg) leg of frozen lamb,
completely thawed*
water
1 level tsp salt
1 large onion, peeled but left whole
*2 large carrots, peeled but left
whole*
1 small turnip, peeled and diced
*4oz (125g) swede or parsnip,
peeled and diced*
*½pt (275ml) Caper Sauce (page
169)*
*boiled potatoes or Dumplings (page
71) sprinkled with fried
breadcrumbs*

1 Wash lamb and place in large
saucepan. Add cold water to cover
and the salt. Bring to boil and
skim. Lower heat and cover. Simmer ¼ hour. Add prepared vegetables.
2 Simmer 25 minutes per pound
(450g) and 25 minutes over or
until lamb is very tender. Lift out
of pan and transfer to warm dish.
3 Surround with vegetables, carve
into slices and serve with the
Caper Sauce and either potatoes
or Dumplings.

Carving Tip
If butcher bones and ties joint, it will
be easier to slice.

Irish Stew

SERVES 4 ▲▲●●

*2lb (900g) potatoes, peeled and
sliced*
*12oz (350g) onions, peeled and
sliced*
*2lb (900g) middle neck of lamb
cutlets, washed and dried*
1 level tsp salt
freshly-milled pepper to taste
*¾pt (425ml) boiling stock (use
chicken cube and water)*
chopped parsley for garnishing

PORK

Roast Pork

ALLOW 8 TO 12oz (225 TO
350G) PORK WITH BONE PER
PERSON; 4 TO 6oz (125 TO
175G) PORK WITHOUT BONE
PER PERSON ▲●●

Wash joint and dry with paper
towels. Score fat and rind for traditional crackling. Stand in roasting
tin. Brush rind lightly with salad oil
then sprinkle liberally with salt. Place
in oven set to 230°C (450°F), Gas 8.
Reduce to 180°C (350°F), Gas 4.
Roast for ½ hour per pound (450g)
and ½ hour over. Carve into slices
and serve with Gravy (page 172),
Apple Sauce (page 184), Sage and
Onion Stuffing (page 235) (baked
separately or in balls round the joint),
and assorted vegetables to include
roast and boiled potatoes.

Glazed Roast Pork

ALLOWANCES AS ABOVE ▲▲●●

Remove skin from joint so that an
exposed layer of fat is uppermost.
Stand in roasting tin. Brush with
baste made from 1 tablespoon Soy
sauce, 2 tablespoon chicken stock,
1 tablespoon clear honey, 1 tablespoon dark brown sugar (soft variety), 2 tablespoons olive oil, 1 level
teaspoon salt and 1 tablespoon
bottled sweet-sour sauce (available
from leading supermarkets and
oriental shops). Roast as above,
brushing with the baste fairly frequently. Serve with freshly-cooked
rice and fried or grilled mushrooms.

82

Glazed Roast Pork

Sweet-Sour
Pineapple Pork

SERVES 4 ▲▲●●●

1oz (25g) butter or margarine
8oz (225g) onions, peeled and
chopped
1 garlic clove, peeled and crushed
4 spare rib of pork chops, washed
and paper-dried
2tblsp mushroom ketchup
3tblsp malt vinegar
1 can (12oz or 350g) pineapple
cubes with syrup
½ to 1 level tsp salt
1 level tblsp cornflour
2tblsp cold water

1 Melt butter or margarine in large frying pan. Add onions and garlic. Fry gently until pale gold. Move to one side of pan.
2 Add chops, two at a time. Fry on both sides until golden, turning twice. Spread the four chops and onions etc in a single layer over base of pan.
3 Coat with mushroom ketchup, vinegar and syrup from can of pineapple. Top with pineapple cubes and sprinkle with salt.
4 Cover. Simmer gently for 40 minutes. Mix cornflour smoothly with cold water. Pour into pan over chops. Cook, uncovered, until liquid comes to boil and thickens.
5 Transfer to 4 warm plates and accompany with freshly-boiled rice or noodles.

Grilled Pork Chops

SERVES 4 ▲▲●●●

4 pork loin chops, each 4 to 6oz
(125 to 175g)
melted butter or margarine for
brushing
Savoury Butter to taste (page 178)

1 Wash and dry chops with paper towels. Stand in greased grill pan. Brush with melted butter or margarine. Grill 7 to 9 minutes, according to thickness.
2 Turn over. Brush with more butter or margarine. Continue to grill a further 7 to 9 minutes or until completely cooked through.
3 Serve each with pat of Savoury Butter. If liked, garnish with watercress and accompany with fried potatoes and seasonal vegetables.

Pork Pie

SERVES 6 ▲▲▲●●●

Hot Water Crust Pastry (page 195)
1lb (450g) hand and spring of
    pork, diced (boned weight)
2oz (50g) onion, peeled and grated
1 level tsp dried sage
pinch of nutmeg
⅛ level tsp pepper
8tblsp water
1 Grade 4 egg, beaten (for
    brushing)
2 scant level tsp gelatine

1 Roll out two-thirds of FRESHLY MADE and warm pastry. Working fairly quickly and using lightly floured hands, mould round OUTSIDE of well-greased 6in (15cm) round cake tin. Keep rest of pastry covered and warm.
2 Turn over on to greased baking tray (hollow side of cake tin now facing) and tie a wide band of greaseproof paper temporarily

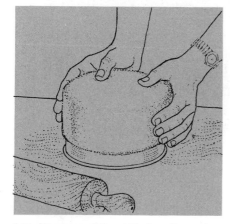

1 Mould pastry round the outside of a well-greased round cake tin

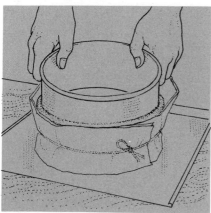

2 Tie a wide band of greaseproof paper around pastry. Carefully remove the cake tin, leaving a shell of crust

round pastry. Very carefully remove cake tin, leaving a shell of crust ready for filling.
3 Mix pork with onion, sage, nutmeg, pepper and half the water. Spoon into pastry case. Dampen edges with water. Cover with lid, rolled from rest of pastry. Press edges well together to seal.
4 Remove strip of paper from sides. Brush pie all over with beaten egg and make a smallish hole in the centre to allow steam to escape. Decorate with leaves, cut from trimmings, and brush with more egg.
5 Bake ¼ hour in oven set to 200°C (400°F), Gas 6. Reduce temperature to 180°C (350°F), Gas 4. Continue to bake for 1¾ hours. Remove from oven.
6 Soften gelatine in rest of water. Heat gently to dissolve but do not boil. Funnel into pie through hole. Leave until cold. Refrigerate a few hours before cutting.

Festive Ham

SERVES UP TO 10 ▲▲▲●●●

1 × 4lb (2kg) piece of corner or
    middle cut of gammon, boned
    and tied
water for boiling

GLAZE
3oz (75g) soft brown sugar (dark
    variety)
1 rounded tsp black treacle or
    molasses
2 level tsp powder mustard
2oz (50g) butter
2tblsp orange juice
1tsp cider or red wine vinegar
pinch of ground allspice

DECORATION
cloves
2 sliced oranges
glacé cherries

1 Place gammon in large saucepan. Cover with cold water. Slowly bring to boil. Drain. Repeat twice more to remove excess salt. Cover with fresh water. Bring to boil. Lower heat. Cover. Simmer 2½ hours.
2 Drain. Stand joint in roasting tin. Strip off skin. Score fat into diamond design with sharp knife. Heat all glaze ingredients gently together until butter melts. Brush over fat. Stud with cloves.

3 Bake about 30 to 40 minutes – or until fat is golden and gleaming – in oven set to 180°C (350°F), Gas 5. Brush frequently with leftover glaze.
4 Cool completely. Before serving, decorate as shown with orange slices and cherries, held in place with cocktail sticks. Carve fairly thinly.

Fruited Gammon with Corn Fritters

SERVES 4 ▲▲▲●●●

4 gammon steaks, each 6oz
    (175g), rinds removed
2oz (50g) butter or margarine,
    melted
4 canned pineapple rings, very well
    drained

Corn Fritters

MAKES 16

4oz (125g) self-raising flour
½ level tsp salt
¼ level tsp powder mustard
2 Grade 3 eggs, well beaten
2tblsp cold milk
8 heaped tblsp cooked sweetcorn
deep oil for frying

1 Snip fat all the way round gammon to stop steaks from curling up as they cook. Stand in greased grill pan. Brush with ½oz (15g) butter or margarine. Grill 5 to 7 minutes, depending on thickness.
2 Turn over. Brush with more butter or margarine. Grill a further 5 to 7 minutes. Transfer to 4 warm plates and top with pineapple rings, first fried in remaining butter or margarine until golden on both sides. Accompany with Corn Fritters, made as follows:
3 Sift flour, salt and mustard into bowl. Mix to thick batter with eggs and milk. Stir in corn. Heat oil until hot and sizzling. Drop in 16 tablespoons of batter, a few at a time.
4 Fry until puffy and golden brown. Allow 5 to 6 minutes and, if necessary, turn over with a spoon although if the oil is deep enough, the fritters will roll over by themselves. Lift out and drain on paper towels. Serve while still very hot.

Speed Tip
Make up the Fritter Batter a little
ahead of time and fry the Fritters
while the gammon is grilling.

Sausage Rolls

MAKES 8 LARGE ROLLS OR
12 COCKTAIL SIZE   ▲▲●●

   *1 small packet puff pastry, thawed
      if frozen* OR
   *1 small packet frozen shortcrust,
      also thawed* OR
   *8oz (225g) Shortcrust Pastry
      (page 186) made with 8oz
      (225g) plain flour*
   *8oz (225g) sausage meat (pork or
      beef)*
   beaten egg for brushing

1 Roll out pastry thinly into an
   oblong of 8in (20cm) in width.
   Cut into 2 strips.
2 With floured hands, divide sausage meat into 2 equal-sized pieces
   and roll each into an 8in (20cm)
   length. Stand both lengths on to
   pieces of pastry.
3 Moisten edges of pastry with
   water. Fold in half over sausage
   meat. Press edges well together to
   seal. You should now have two
   large sausage rolls with sausage
   meat completely enclosed.
4 Cut each into either 4 or 6 pieces
   (to make individual rolls) and
   transfer to greased tray. Brush
   with beaten egg.
5 Bake $\frac{1}{4}$ hour in oven set to 220°C
   (425°F), Gas 7 for puff pastry or
   $\frac{1}{4}$ hour at 200°C (400°F), Gas 6
   for shortcrust. Reduce temperature and continue to bake a

Festive Ham

further 12 to 15 minutes at 180°C
(350°F), Gas 4. When crisp and
well browned, remove to cooling
rack. Store, covered, in the refrigerator unless eaten hot or
warm.

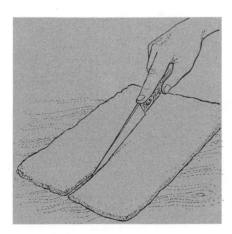

*1 Roll out pastry into an oblong 8in (20cm) in
width. Cut into 2 strips*

*2 Place rolls of sausage meat on to the pieces of
pastry*

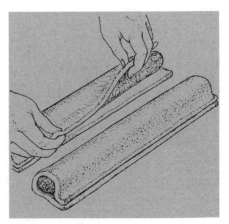

*3 Moisten edges of the pastry with water. Fold in
half over the sausage meat. Press edges well together
to seal*

85

Veal Goulash

VEAL

Roast Veal

ALLOW 8 TO 12OZ (225 TO 350G) VEAL ON THE BONE PER PERSON; 4 TO 6OZ (125 TO 175G) BONED VEAL PER PERSON ▲●●●

Stand tied joint in roasting tin and coat heavily with melted butter or margarine as veal is a dry meat and needs moistening. If liked, cover with rashers of streaky bacon but this is an optional extra. Place joint in oven set to 230°C (450°F), Gas 8. Reduce temperature to 180°C (350°F), Gas 4. Roast 30 minutes per pound (450g) and 30 minutes over as veal should be well cooked; it is indigestible if underdone. Leave 10 minutes before carving then serve with Gravy (page 172) grilled or roast bacon rolls (made from streaky bacon rashers and served with wooden cocktail sticks as plastic ones would melt), lemon wedges, roast and boiled potatoes and seasonal vegetables to taste.

Veal Goulash

SERVES 4 ▲▲●●●

1½lb (675g) stewing veal, diced (boned weight)
2oz (50g) lard or margarine (Hungarians would use only lard)
8oz (225g) onions, peeled and grated
2 level tblsp paprika
4 medium-sized green peppers
8oz (225g) tomatoes, blanched and skinned
1 level tsp salt
large pinch cayenne pepper

1 Wash veal and dry with paper towels. Heat lard or margarine in heavy-based saucepan. Add onions. Fry until light gold.
2 Add veal cubes, a few at a time, and fry briskly until well sealed and golden. Stir in paprika and leave over low heat.

3 Wash and de-seed peppers. Cut flesh into strips. Add to pan. Continue to fry over fairly high heat for 10 minutes, stirring constantly.
4 Chop tomatoes and add to pan with salt and cayenne pepper. Lower heat and cover. Simmer very slowly ¾ to 1 hour or until veal is very tender.
5 Stir from time to time and add a very little boiling water only if you must; a traditional Goulash should literally cook in its own juices.
6 Serve very hot with small pasta shells. Extra cooked vegetables are not usually served and pearl barley may be substituted for the pasta.

Italian Style Scaloppine with Lemon

SERVES 4 ▲▲●●●

4 slices of veal fillet, each 6oz (175g)
salt and white pepper
2tblsp flour
2½oz (65g) butter
2tsp olive or salad oil
¼pt (150ml) chicken stock, made from cube and water
1 wine glass white Chianti
1tblsp lemon juice
4 fairly thick slices of unpeeled lemon

GARNISH
extra slices of lemon
1 level tblsp chopped parsley
parsley sprigs

1 Wash and dry veal with paper towels. Sprinkle with salt and pepper then dust with flour.
2 Heat butter and oil in large frying pan. Add veal fillets. Fry 3 minutes per side over brisk heat. Remove to plate temporarily.
3 Add stock, wine and lemon juice to remaining butter and oil in pan. Bring to a gentle boil. Replace veal and top each with a lemon slice.
4 Cover. Simmer 12 to 17 minutes or until each piece of veal is cooked through. Transfer meat to a warm dish and keep hot. Boil pan juices fast until reduced by about one-third.

5 Pour over veal. Sprinkle with parsley and finally garnish with extra lemon slices and sprigs of parsley. Serve with fried potatoes and a mixed salad.

Wiener Schnitzel

SERVES 4   ▲▲▲●●●

4 escalopes of veal (fillet), each 6oz (175g)
salt and pepper
1½ level tblsp flour
2 Grade 4 eggs, beaten
8 heaped tblsp lightly-toasted breadcrumbs (homemade for preference and not the garish golden ones)
at least 3in (7½cm) of oil for frying

GARNISH
2 Grade 2 eggs, hard-boiled and shelled
4 slices lemon
4 anchovies, rolled
4 level tsp chopped parsley
2 level tsp small capers, drained

1 Ask butcher to beat veal until paper thin. Wash and dry. Snip round edges of each to prevent escalopes from curling up as they fry.
2 Sprinkle with salt and pepper then dust with flour. Beat eggs until foamy. Tip crumbs on to large sheet of greaseproof paper or foil.
3 Dip escalopes first into eggs then coat well with crumbs. Shake each one to remove excess crumbs then leave 30 minutes for coating to settle. Check for thin patches and fill in by dabbing with egg and pressing on more crumbs.
4 Heat oil in large frying pan until hot (see Fried Fish, page 57). Add coated escalopes, one at a time, and fry 8 to 10 minutes. There should be sufficient room in the pan for veal to float about.
5 Lift out of pan and drain on paper towels. Repeat, frying rest of escalopes. Place on large platter lined with a paper doyley.
6 Garnish centre of each with a slice of egg, a slice of lemon, 1 anchovy roll, 1 teaspoon parsley and 1 teaspoon capers. Separate whites from yolks of eggs and chop each individually. Sprinkle bands of chopped yolk and white over each escalope. Serve with fried potatoes and a green salad.

Italian Style Scaloppine with Lemon

Kebab Assortment

ALLOW 1 PER PERSON

Creamy Veal Kebabs

SERVES 4   ▲▲▲●●●

1½lb (675g) leg of veal, boned weight
8oz (225g) onions, peeled and grated
1 garlic clove, peeled and crushed
1 carton (5oz or 142ml) soured cream
1 bay leaf, crumbled
3 or 4 grindings black pepper
1 level tsp salt

1 Wash and dry veal and cut into 1in (2½cm) cubes. In enamel or glass dish, combine onions with garlic, soured cream, bay leaf, pepper and salt.
2 Add meat cubes and toss over and over in the cream mixture. Cover. Refrigerate 6 hours. Before serving, thread meat on to 4 skewers.
3 Place in buttered grill pan. Grill under high heat about ¼ hour, turning 2 or 3 times and spooning over the cream and onion mixture. Serve with rice and accompany with salad.

Kebab Assortment. Right: Creamy Veal Kebabs; Centre: Prune and Pineapple Lamb Kebabs; Left: Minted Yogurt Kebabs

Fried Liver with Orange

Prune and Pineapple Lamb Kebabs

SERVES 4 ▲▲▲●●

8 stoned prunes
4tblsp dry red wine
2 canned pineapple rings, well
    drained
1tblsp white rum
1lb (450g) pork fillet
8 cocktail sausages

BASTE
3tblsp salad oil
1 level tsp French mustard
1 level tsp paprika
1 level tsp salt
1½tblsp wine or cider vinegar

1 Soak prunes overnight in the red wine, keeping dish or bowl covered. About 1 hour before serving, stand pineapple on plate and trickle over the rum.
2 Wash and dry pork and cut into 1in (2½cm) cubes. Remove prunes from wine. Cut each pineapple ring into 8 pieces.
3 Thread all ingredients alternately on to 4 skewers. Stand in greased grill pan. Beat all baste ingredients well together.
4 Brush over kebabs. Grill 25 to 30 minutes or until cooked through, turning at least 4 times and brushing with baste every time. Serve with Greek style Pitta or sesame seed bread.

Minted Yogurt Kebabs

SERVES 4 ▲▲▲●●

1lb (450g) lamb fillet, cut from leg
    (boned weight)
1 carton (5oz or 142ml) natural
    yogurt
1 level tsp mint sauce
1 level tsp salt
1 garlic clove, peeled and crushed
1tblsp salad oil

1 Wash and dry lamb and cut into 1in (2½cm) cubes.
2 Beat yogurt in bowl with all remaining ingredients. Add lamb. Toss over and over. Cover. Refrigerate overnight or 8 hours during the day.
3 Before serving, thread meat on to 4 skewers and stand in greased grill pan. Grill about 12 minutes, turning 3 or 4 times. Serve with rice.

Serving Tip
All Kebabs may be accompanied by a mixed salad.

OFFAL

Egg and Crumbed Liver

SERVES 4 ▲▲●●

Coat 1 lb (450g) lamb or pork liver (4 pieces) with flour, beaten egg and crumbs exactly as for the Wiener Schnitzel (page 87). Fry 6 to 8 minutes, turning twice. Drain on paper towels and serve hot with chips and seasonal vegetables to taste.

Fried Liver with Orange

SERVES 4 ▲▲●●●

Prepare exactly as directed for *Egg and Crumbed Liver* above. Serve garnished with peeled slices of orange.

Grilled Liver

SERVES 4 ▲●●

Wash and dry 1lb (450g) lamb or pork liver (4 pieces). Stand in greased grill pan. Brush with 1oz (25g) melted butter or margarine. Grill 2 to 3 minutes. Turn over. Brush with more butter or margarine. Grill a further 2 to 3 minutes. Serve straightaway, garnished with watercress.

Stewed Liver

SERVES 4 ▲▲●●

Follow recipe for *Beef Stew* (page 71), substituting 1 to 1½lb (450 to 675g) ox liver for the beef. Simmer about 1 to 1¼ hours when liver should be tender.

Tripe and Onions

SERVES 4 ▲▲●●

2lb (900g) dressed tripe
8oz (225g) onions
¾pt (425ml) milk
1 level tsp salt
2 level tblsp cornflour
4tblsp cold water
white pepper to taste

1 Wash tripe thoroughly and cut into finger-length strips or into 2in (5cm) squares.
2 Place in large saucepan. Peel and slice onions. Add to pan with milk and salt. Bring to boil, stirring. Lower heat. Cover.
3 Simmer gently for 1 hour or until tripe is very soft. Mix cornflour

smoothly with water. Add to tripe mixture. Cook, stirring, until liquid comes to boil and thickens.

4 Continue to cook for 5 minutes then season with pepper. Serve on toast or accompany with creamed potatoes.

Stuffed Hearts

SERVES 4 ▲▲●●

4 calves' hearts
stuffing to taste (see Stuffings section page 234)
2oz (50g) butter or margarine, melted
4tblsp stock
salt and pepper to taste

1 Soak hearts for ½ hour in cold, salted water. Drain and rinse. Remove fat and tubes. Cut through membranes to make 1 cavity in each heart.

2 Fill with stuffing. Transfer to heat-proof dish. Coat with butter or margarine and the stock. Sprinkle with salt and pepper to taste.

3 Cover with lid or foil and cook 1½ hours in oven set to 160°C (325°F), Gas 3. Serve with pan juices and accompany with creamed potatoes, redcurrant jelly or cranberry sauce and seasonal vegetables to taste.

Tongue in Madeira Sauce

SERVES 8 ▲▲▲●●●

1 fresh ox tongue weighing 3lb (1¼kg)
cold water
8oz (225g) onions, peeled but left whole
2 large carrots, peeled but left whole
2 large celery stalks, well washed and scrubbed
1 bouquet garni
2 level tsp salt
Madeira Sauce (page 173)
4oz (125g butter-fried mushroom slices)
tiny Dumplings (page 71) optional fried mushroom slices

1 Remove excess tubes and fat from root end of tongue and discard. Place tongue in large bowl. Cover

Tongue in Madeira Sauce

with cold water and leave to soak 2 to 3 hours, covered.

2 Drain and rinse. Transfer to large saucepan. Cover with cold water. Bring to boil. Skim. Add all remaining ingredients except last 3. Reboil. Lower heat. Cover. Simmer 3½ to 4 hours or until very tender. Remove bouquet garni.

3 Drain tongue, stand on board and strip off skin. Cut into slices. Transfer to dish. Surround with Madeira Sauce first heated through with mushrooms. Add dumplings (if made). Serve with creamed potatoes and seasonal vegetables to taste.

Kidneys Flambé

SERVES 4 ▲▲▲●●●

1lb (450g) calves' kidneys
½pt (275ml) cold milk
salt and pepper
paprika
2tsp salad oil
½oz (40g) butter or margarine
2oz (50g) onion, peeled and chopped
4oz (125g) button mushrooms, sliced
2 heaped tblsp chopped parsley
¼ wine glass brandy
¼ wine glass dry sherry
1 carton (5oz or 142ml) soured cream
1 level tsp prepared English mustard
1 large tomato, washed and dried

1 Cut kidneys into slices and rinse under cold, running water. Soak in cold milk for ½ hour. Drain and

dry. Sprinkle with salt, pepper and paprika.

2 Heat salad oil with butter or margarine until sizzling. Add kidney slices and fry 6 minutes, turning twice. Remove to plate for time being.

3 Add onion, mushrooms and half the parsley to remaining oil mixture in pan. Fry gently ¼ hour. Replace kidneys and mix in well. Add the brandy, warm through and flame.

4 Beat sherry with soured cream and mustard. Add to pan. Stir well to mix. Heat through without boiling. Sprinkle rest of parsley on top, then garnish with wedges of tomato. Serve with small pasta such as macaroni or shells.

Stewed Kidneys

SERVES 4 ▲▲●●

Make as *Beef Stew* (page 71), substituting 1lb (450g) well-washed ox kidney for the beef. Simmer only 1 hour.

Kidneys in Red Wine

SERVES 4 ▲▲●●●

Make as *Beef Stew* (page 71), substituting 1lb (450g) well-washed ox kidney for the beef. Add dry red wine instead of water. Simmer only 1 hour.

89

Kidneys Flambé (page 89)

Oxtail Stew

SERVES 4   ▲▲●●

   *3lb (1½kg) oxtail, divided into
     joints
   1oz (25g) margarine or dripping
   8oz (225g) onions, peeled and
     chopped
   1 large carrot, peeled and sliced
   1 small turnip, peeled and diced
   1 large celery stalk, well washed
     and broken into large pieces
   1 bouquet garni
   ¾pt (425ml) cold water
   2 to 3 level tsp salt
   2 level tblsp cornflour
   3tblsp cold water
   1tblsp malt vinegar
   2 heaped tblsp chopped parsley*

1 Wash oxtail and dry with paper
   towels. Melt margarine or dripping in large pan. Add oxtail. Fry
briskly until brown. Remove to
plate temporarily.
2 Add vegetables to remaining fat
   in pan. Fry 20 minutes or until
   golden brown. Replace oxtail.
   Add bouquet garni, water and
   salt. Bring to boil and skim.
3 Lower heat and cover. Simmer
   very slowly for 3 hours or until
   tender. Cool. Refrigerate, covered,
   overnight. Before serving, remove
   hard layer of fat from the top.
4 Bring slowly to boil then stir in
   cornflour mixed smoothly with
   water. Cook until mixture thickens
   and clears. Stir in vinegar and
   parsley, and adjust seasoning to
   taste.
5 Remove bouquet garni bag and
   serve oxtail with boiled potatoes
   and seasonal green vegetables.

Fried Sweetbreads

SERVES 4   ▲▲▲●●

Soak 1lb (450g) calves' sweetbreads
in lukewarm, salted water for 2
hours. Drain. Transfer to saucepan.
Cover with cold water and add 3
teaspoons lemon juice. Slowly bring
to boil and simmer 5 minutes. Drain
and rinse. Leave in bowl of cold
water until cool. Drain and remove
parts which look like skin and gristle.
Simmer sweetbreads 20 minutes in
milk to which 1 level teaspoon of
salt has been added. Cool in the milk.
Lift out and wipe dry. Coat with
flour, egg and crumbs exactly as
directed for Wiener Schnitzel (page
87). Fry until crisp in 2oz (50g)
butter or margarine to which 2 teaspoons salad oil have been added.

Poultry and Game

Poultry and Game

Game has its seasons (which I shall come to later) but chicken and turkey are with us all the year round, providing a very popular, high-protein food at reasonable cost. The versatility of poultry is legion and moving away from the traditional roast bird, which one might have at weekends and over the Easter and Christmas holidays, chicken and turkey can be dressed up in so many different guises that whole books have been devoted to this one subject alone.

The main advantage of poultry is its complete adaptability, appetizing flavour and contrasting meat; breast and wings for those who enjoy light, white meat (and indeed for slimmers as this part of the bird has fewer calories), and legs and thigh for others who favour darker meat with its more concentrated flavour. From a very simple style of preparation and cooking (the roast I mentioned earlier), poultry can be lifted high into the realms of haute cuisine and this, I believe, is what makes it so appealing to everyone; to children who often prefer their portions left undisguised – except for crumbed and fried chicken which is an eternal favourite – and everyone else who may opt for a Chinese speciality, an oriental style curry, a colourful Goulash from central Europe, a cream and cider concoction from Normandy or an exotic American style salad crammed with fruit, nuts and mayonnaise. Thanks, in the main, to the breeders, what was once a luxury food is now a much more down-to-earth proposition with no problems whatever regarding availability whether the choice is farm fresh or frozen. And this applies equally to what I term 'cultivated' ducks (as apposed to wild ducks belonging to game) which are bred for freezing and sold all the year round via supermarkets and freezer centres.

GUIDELINES

Frozen poultry does need somewhat more care and attention than fresh and below are some tips which are worth heeding to stave off problems.

Roast Chicken garnished with Ham and Mushroom Tarts

1 Defrost ANY KIND of poultry and duck COMPLETELY before cooking, allowing a minimum of 2 to 3 hours per pound (450g) at kitchen temperature and 6 to 7 hours per pound (450g) in the refrigerator. The latter method is the most hygienic and also the most economical, in that the icy bird lowers the temperature inside the cabinet and consequently less power is needed.

2 Leave the wrapper on the bird but slit it at one end. Also remove the giblet bag as soon as it 'yields' as this enables the bird to defrost more quickly.

3 Rinse fresh or defrosted bird inside and out under cold, running water but DO NOT wipe dry with a cloth as this spreads harmful germs. Instead, pat dry with paper towels and throw away immediately.

4 DO NOT STUFF bird ahead of time but immediately before roasting. Again this has to do with the build-up of germs. For the same reason, large birds should be stuffed at the neck end only and the body cavity left empty so that oven heat is able to penetrate right through to the centre of the bird.

5 As a general rule, allow 2 to 3oz (50 to 75g) raw weight of stuffing per pound (450g) of poultry. For convenience, stuffings may be prepared in advance and left, covered, in the refrigerator until ready for use.

6 DO NOT slow roast a large bird overnight in a cool oven. The heat will not be powerful enough to kill off germs which can cause food poisoning at worst, or severe stomach upsets at best. 'Old-fashioned' poultry was reared differently and the bacteria problem gave less cause for concern.

7 When choosing poultry, allow the following amounts of raw weight per person:

12oz (350g) chicken, turkey and capon (a neutered cock bird)
1lb (450g) duck and goose
1 whole poussin (a 6 to 8-week old chicken)
½ a spring chicken (a 2½ to 3lb or 1kg bird which is between 2 and 4 months old)
12oz (350g) boiling fowl

8 A large, roast bird benefits if left to stand at least 10 minutes before being carved. This enables the flesh to 'firm-up' and prevents unnecessary crumbling, especially of the breast.

9 Leftover, cold poultry should ALWAYS be well wrapped to prevent dryness and stored in the refrigerator. In case the following factor has caused an element of worry and doubt in the past, made-up dishes from cooked and left-over frozen birds may be re-frozen quite satisfactorily up to 6 months.

Roasting Times

CHICKEN Allow 25 minutes per pound (450g) for all weights

TURKEY Allow 25 minutes per pound (450g) for small birds weighing up to 12lb (5½kg)
Allow 20 minutes per pound (450g) for medium birds weighing up to 16lb (7¼kg)
Allow 18 minutes per pound (450g) for large birds weighing up to 25lb (11¼kg)

Success Tips

1 If foil-wrapped, allow an extra 2 minutes per pound (450g) and, to brown bird, peel back foil for last ½ hour for chickens; for last 50 minutes for small and medium turkeys; for 1 to 1½ hours for large turkeys.
2 ALWAYS calculate time AFTER stuffings have been placed in bird.

DUCK Allow 30 minutes per pound (450g) for all weights. DO NOT FOIL-WRAP as this will inhibit skin from browning and make it rubbery.

Oven Temperatures
See individual recipes.

Roast Chicken or Capon

▲▲●●

Stand washed and dried chicken in roasting tin. Brush all over with 1oz (25g) melted butter or margarine, or cover breast with streaky bacon rashers. Alternatively, wrap in greased foil. Place in hot oven set to 225°C (425°F), Gas 7. Reduce temperature straightaway to 180°C (325°F), Gas 4. Roast as given under Roasting Times. Serve with Gravy (see below) roast and boiled potatoes, chipolata sausages, bacon rolls (optional), Bread Sauce (page 183) and seasonal cooked vegetables. It is not obligatory to serve ALL the accompaniments and for the sake of time and economy, compromise with a selection.

Gravy

Pour away all but about 2 tablespoons dripping from roasting tin. Return tin to low heat. Stir in 1 level tablespoon cornflour. Gradually work in ½ pint (275ml) water. Cook, stirring until gravy comes to boil and thickens. Simmer 1 minute. Season. For special occasions, add 3 teaspoons medium sherry, port, Marsala or Madeira. Also gravy browning, if liked, to heighten colour.

Economy Tip
Keep liquid that is poured off. Cover and leave to cool. Store in the refrigerator. Remove layer of fat that has risen to top and keep stock underneath as a basis for soups, sauces or stews.

Garnish Tip
For a complete change of style, garnish chicken with baked tartlet cases filled with chopped mushrooms and ham in a cream sauce.

Roast Turkey

▲▲●●

Roast exactly as *Chicken* (above), working to times previously given.

Roast Turkey

Crumbed and Fried Chicken

1 Wash and dry chicken joints. Stand in greased grill pan, skin sides down. Place under high heat.
2 Brush with melted fat and sprinkle with salt and pepper. Grill 10 minutes. Turn over. Brush with more fat and sprinkle with salt and pepper. Grill 10 minutes. Repeat once or twice more, depending on size of joints and thickness of flesh.
3 Remove from grill pan and transfer to 4 warm dinner plates. Garnish with watercress and lemon. Serve hot with pasta, rice or fried potatoes. Accompany with cooked vegetables to taste or a mixed salad.

Crumbed and Fried Chicken

SERVES 4 ▲▲▲●●

4 large chicken joints
2 rounded tblsp flour, well seasoned with salt and pepper
2 Grade 2 eggs
1 tblsp salad oil
1 tblsp cold milk
8 heaped tsp lightly-toasted or golden breadcrumbs
a deep pan of oil or melted dripping, no more than half full to prevent spillage

GARNISH
fried parsley
lemon slices

1 Wash and dry chicken. Coat each piece all over with the seasoned flour.
2 In deep enamel plate or fairly large, shallow dish, beat together eggs, oil and milk. Tip breadcrumbs on to large sheet of foil or greaseproof paper.
3 Lift up each piece of chicken and shake off surplus flour. Dip in beaten egg mixture then toss in crumbs, making sure they form an even layer and there are no 'bald' patches on pieces of chicken as these would cause spluttering.
4 Leave chicken to stand in the cool for at least 30 minutes to give coating a chance to settle and set. Before cooking, heat oil or dripping until a haze (not smoke) can be seen rising from the surface.

To test if temperature is correct, drop a smallish cube of bread into pan. If oil or dripping is ready the cube will sink to bottom, rise to the top straightaway and turn brown in 50 seconds.
5 Add chicken to pan, one piece at a time to prevent cooling down the oil or fat too quickly. Fry fairly gently for 20 to 30 minutes, depending on the size of the chicken.
6 The joints should float about in the pan but, to ensure even browning, turn once or twice with tongs or 2 spoons. Avoid 'stabbing' chicken with prongs of a fork as juices will run out and make the flesh dry.
7 When chicken is ready, lift out of pan and drain on kitchen paper towels. Drop a handful of parsley into the pan. Leave ½ minute. Lift out and drain.
8 Arrange chicken on a plate. Garnish with parsley and lemon. Accompany with Tomato Sauce (page 182), a mixed salad and either chips or baked jacket potatoes.

Grilled Chicken

SERVES 4 ▲▲●●

4 medium chicken joints
1½oz (40g) melted butter or margarine
salt and pepper

GARNISH
watercress sprays
lemon wedges

Devilled Grilled Chicken

SERVES 4 ▲▲●●

Before grilling, coat chicken joints with 2 level tablespoons flour seasoned with 2 to 3 level teaspoons curry powder, 1 level teaspoon mustard and generous pinch of cayenne pepper. Gently pour half butter or margarine over joints rather than brush.

Chicken Chow Mein

SERVES 4 TO 6 ▲▲▲●●

An Americanized Chinese style dish which is an excellent way of using up leftover cooked chicken or turkey.

1 small green pepper
1 small red pepper
½pt (275ml) water
2oz (50g) onion
2 tblsp salad oil
2 large celery stalks
½oz (15g) flour
½pt (275ml) hot chicken stock
2 tblsp Soy sauce
4oz (125g) button mushrooms, trimmed and sliced
8oz (225g) leftover chicken or turkey, cut into strips
freshly-cooked ribbon noodles, drained
3oz (75g) fried onions
1oz (25g) salted almonds

94

1 Wash and dry peppers. Halve and remove seeds. Cut into strips. Simmer 5 minutes in the water. Drain.
2 Peel onion and chop. Fry in the hot oil gently until pale gold. Wash and dry celery. Thinly slice. Add to pan. Fry a further 1 minute, turning.
3 Sprinkle flour over vegetables then blend in chicken stock. Cook, stirring, until mixture boils. Add Soy sauce, two-thirds of pepper strips, sliced mushrooms and chicken. Cover. Simmer $\frac{1}{4}$ hour.
4 Arrange noodles on serving dish. Top with rest of pepper strips then pile with fried onions and almonds. Serve with separate dish of freshly-cooked rice or noodles.

Coq au Vin

SERVES 6 ▲▲▲●●●

1 oven-ready chicken weighing 4lb (just under 2kg)
salt and pepper
4 slightly rounded tblsp flour
2oz (50g) butter, margarine or bacon dripping
2tsp salad oil
6oz (175g) onions, peeled and chopped
1 garlic clove, peeled and crushed
3oz (75g) gammon, chopped
12 small onions (pickling type) or shallots
1 heaped tblsp chopped parsley
1 bouquet garni
$\frac{3}{4}$pt (425ml) Burgundy or other dry red wine
6oz (175g) button mushrooms, trimmed
extra salt and pepper to taste

GARNISH
6 triangles of fried bread
parsley sprigs

1 Cut chicken into 6 pieces then wash and dry with paper towels. Sprinkle all over with salt and pepper. Coat with flour. Heat fat and oil in large, heavy-based pan.
2 As soon as it sizzles, add chicken. Fry briskly, turning twice, until well browned. Remove to plate. Leave on one side temporarily.
3 Add chopped onions, garlic and gammon to remaining fat etc in pan. Fry until golden. Replace chicken joints. Add whole onions or shallots, parsley, bouquet garni and Burgundy or other wine.

Devilled Grilled Chicken

4 Bring to boil. Skim. Lower heat. Cover. Simmer gently 1 hour. Stir occasionally. Add whole mushrooms. Mix in well. Cover again. Cook a further $\frac{1}{4}$ hour. Remove bouquet garni and adjust seasoning to taste.

5 Transfer to serving dish. Garnish with fried bread and parsley sprigs. Accompany with whole boiled potatoes and cooked vegetables to taste.

Chicken Chow Mein

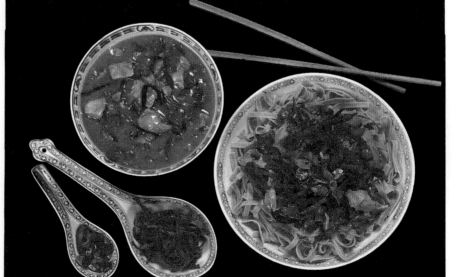

Coq au Vin (page 95)

(page 93). Keep hot. In large pan, melt 2oz (50g) butter, margarine or dripping and heat until sizzling. Add 1lb (450g) parboiled and diced potatoes, 8oz (225g) peeled and coarsely chopped onions and 6oz (175g) cubed streaky bacon. Fry until golden. Stand the two hot chickens on top and sprinkle with freshly-milled black or white pepper. Garnish with parsley sprigs and accompany with extra potatoes, boiled in their skins. A mixed salad makes a refreshing accompaniment.

Chicken Maryland

SERVES 4   ▲▲▲●●●

Prepare exactly as *Fried Chicken* (page 94). Accompany with Corn Fritters (page 84) and small whole bananas fried finally in butter or margarine until golden brown.

Peasant Chicken

SERVES 8   ▲▲●●●

Roast 2 by 3lb oven-ready chickens (just under 1½kg each) exactly as given in recipe for *Roast Chicken*

Oriental Mandarin Chicken with Almonds

SERVES 8   ▲▲▲●●●

2oz (50g) raisins
1 wine glass Madeira
2 oven-ready chickens each 3lb or
    just under 1½kg
salt and pepper to taste
2 level tsp paprika
4tblsp salad oil
1 can mandarin oranges
1 garlic clove
¼pt (150ml) hot chicken stock
1 level tblsp cornflour
1tblsp water
1tblsp Soy sauce
½ level tsp ground ginger
¼pt (150ml) whipping or double
    cream
1oz (25g) butter
2oz (50g) almond flakes

1 Tip raisins into small bowl. Add Madeira and leave to soak for 30 minutes.
2 Cut each chicken into 4 portions. Rinse under cold water. Dry with paper towels. Sprinkle all over with salt, pepper and paprika. Leave on one side for the time being.
3 Heat oil in large, wide and heavy-based pan. As soon as it sizzles, begin to add pieces of chicken. Fry until crisp and golden, allowing 10 minutes for the 8 pieces.
4 Drain mandarins. Reserve fruit. Pour syrup over chicken. Add peeled and crushed garlic clove with the stock. Bring slowly to boil. Lower heat. Cover. Simmer ¾ hour. Add raisins and Madeira and continue to cook a further 5 minutes.

Peasant Chicken

5 Lift chicken portions out of pan on to a warm serving dish. Keep hot. Mix cornflour smoothly with water and Soy sauce. Add to pan with ginger.

6 Bring to boil, stirring continually. Simmer 2 minutes. Add the cream. Bubble very gently. Melt butter in small pan. Add almonds. Fry very slowly until pale gold. Remove from heat.

7 Stir reserved mandarins into sauce then pour over chicken. Sprinkle with almonds and serve with rice or noodles. The most appropriate vegetable is either Chinese leaves (cooked) or Mange Tout (see pages 217–218).

Oriental Mandarin Chicken with Almonds

Spanish Paella

SERVES 4 ▲▲▲●●●

4 medium joints roasting chicken
2oz (50g) butter
1tblsp olive or salad oil
6oz (175g) onion, peeled and chopped
1 garlic clove, peeled and crushed
4oz (125g) garlic sausage or Spanish Chorizo sausage
8oz (225g) long grain rice (easy cook, American)
¼ level tsp saffron strands
1pt (575ml) hot chicken stock
1 small green pepper, de-seeded and coarsely chopped
1 level tsp salt
6oz (175g) cooked peas, fresh or frozen
4oz (125g) peeled prawns
4oz (125g) cooked lobster or white crab meat, fresh or frozen

GARNISH
12 fresh mussels
8 unpeeled prawns

1 Divide chicken into 8 pieces. Wash and dry with paper towels. Heat butter and oil in large frying pan.

2 Add chicken joints. Fry on both sides until golden brown and crisp. Remove to a large plate temporarily. Add onion and garlic to remaining butter and oil in pan. Fry gently until light gold.

3 Slice sausage fairly thickly. Add to pan with rice and saffron. Mix in well. Cover with stock. Bring to boil, stirring. Add chopped pepper.

4 Cover securely. Simmer 10 minutes. Stir round. Season with salt. Transfer to heatproof dish that is large enough to take all the ingredients in a single layer.

5 Stand chicken joints on top, skin sides uppermost. Cover with lid or foil. Cook 45 minutes in oven set to 180°C (350°F), Gas 4.

6 Uncover. Sprinkle with peas and prawns then add pieces of lobster or crab meat. Cover again. Return to oven. Cook a further 15 minutes or a little longer until chicken is tender and cooked through.

7 About 10 minutes before serving, wash and scrub mussels under cold running water. Tip into pan with about 2 tablespoons water. Shake over brisk heat until shells open.

8 Remove Paella from oven. Uncover. Top with mussels and unpeeled prawns and serve while still very hot.

Roast Duck

SERVES 4 ▲▲●●●

1 × 4lb (2kg) oven-ready duck, thawed if frozen and giblet bag removed
Sage and Onion Stuffing or other stuffing if preferred (pages 234–237)
salt

ACCOMPANIMENTS
Gravy (page 93)
Apple Sauce (page 184)
red cabbage, optional (page 212)
roast and boiled potatoes
cooked peas or French beans

1 Wash and dry duck under cold, running water. Wipe dry with paper towels. Prick skin all over with a fork so that fat runs freely. Stuff with selected stuffing or leave empty.

2 Stand on grid in roasting tin. Sprinkle with salt. Roast 30 minutes per pound (450g) in oven set to 200°C (400°F), Gas 6. This higher than usual temperature produces deliciously crisp skin, soft meat and minimal fat on bird itself.

3 Make gravy with 2 tablespoons of residual duck fat as described on page 93. Cut duck into 4 portions with poultry shears (which is much easier than carving) and serve with suggested accompaniments.

Roast Goose ▲▲●●●

Roast exactly as Duck, allowing 12oz (350g) raw weight per person. Stuff, if liked, with cut-up cooking apples (well washed and dried) to absorb grease. Serve with exactly the same accompaniments. If preferred, leave unstuffed.

Spanish Paella (page 97)

Gingered Goose

SERVES 10 ▲▲▲●●●

1 × 7½ to 8lb (3½ to 4kg) goose
salt
1 level tsp ground ginger
1 level tsp garlic granules
1 jar (12oz or 350g) preserved
    ginger in syrup, drained

1 Wash and dry goose. Sprinkle with salt, ginger and garlic granules.
2 Stand on rack in roasting tin. Roast exactly as directed in recipe for Roast Goose (page 97), coating from time to time with ginger syrup.
3 Garnish with pieces of preserved ginger and serve with 1lb (450g) freshly-boiled rice forked with 2oz (50g) butter and 3oz (75g) raisins soaked in 4 tablespoons dry sherry.

Old English Duck

SERVES 4 ▲▲▲●●●

Roast a 4lb (2kg) duckling exactly as directed on page 97. Transfer to dish and keep hot. To make sauce, pour off all but 2 tablespoons fat from roasting tin. Stand tin over medium heat. Stir in 2 level tablespoons cornflour then blend in ¾pt (425ml) hot water, 1 tablespoon mushroom ketchup, 1 rounded tablespoon redcurrant jelly and ½ level teaspoon salt. Bring to boil, stirring continuously. Pour in 2 tablespoons Madeira or port. Reheat until bubbling and simmer about 2 minutes more or until every particle of redcurrant jelly has melted. Pour over duck and serve straightaway.

Gingered Goose

Duck with Orange Sauce

SERVES 4 ▲▲▲●●●

Roast a 4lb (2kg) duckling exactly as directed on page 97. Meanwhile, wash and dry 2 medium oranges. Coarsely grate off peel then halve fruit and squeeze out juice. Peel 2 more medium oranges, removing all traces of pith. Slice thinly then cut each slice in half. When duck is ready, remove from oven and transfer to dish. Keep hot. Pour off all but 2 tablespoons fat from roasting tin. Stand tin over medium heat. Stir in 2 level tablespoons flour. Cook 3 minutes. Gradually blend in ½pt (250ml) hot water, the grated orange peel and juice, 1 rounded tablespoon redcurrant jelly, 1 wine glass of dry sherry and salt and pepper to taste. Bring to boil, stirring constantly. Simmer 2 minutes. Stir in orange slices. Divide duck into 4 pieces with poultry shears. Transfer to serving dish and coat with sauce. Accompany with either baby new potatoes tossed in butter or Duchesse potatoes and a selection of seasonal vegetables.

Chinese Fruited Duck

SERVES 4 ▲▲▲●●●

Roast a 4lb (2kg) duck exactly as directed on page 97, but instead of sprinkling with salt, brush skin with 2 tablespoons of Soy sauce mixed with 1 crushed garlic clove. Keep duck hot, make gravy as directed on page 93 and leave in pan. Transfer duck to dish and decorate with 2 unpeeled and sliced oranges, 1 can drained mandarin oranges (reserve syrup and 1 tablespoon mandarins) and ½ a sliced banana brushed with lemon juice. Garnish with parsley and 2 glacé cherries. Slice other half of banana and add to gravy with reserved mandarins and thin strips of orange peel. Reheat briefly until hot. Serve with the duck.

Salmi of Duck

SERVES 6 ▲▲▲●●●

1 × 4lb (2kg) duck
¾pt (425ml) Madeira Sauce (page 173), freshly made
4oz (125g) button mushrooms
1 carton (5oz or 142ml) soured cream
salt and pepper to taste
parsley for garnishing
triangles of butter-fried bread to accompany

1 Roast duck exactly as directed in recipe for *Roast Duck* (page 97), allowing only 1 hour. Remove from oven and cut meat away from bones. (A slow task and not very easy; a sharp knife is therefore a great help.)
2 Keep Madeira Sauce in saucepan and stand over medium heat. Add duck pieces. Bring gently to boil. Lower heat and cover. Simmer over lowish heat for 1 hour. Add mushrooms and mix in well. Cover pan. Simmer a further 10 minutes.
3 Spoon soured cream into pan. Blend in thoroughly, making sure all traces of streakiness disappear. Adjust seasoning to taste and transfer to warm serving dish. Garnish with parsley and accompany with fried bread.

Chinese Fruited Duck

1 Heat butter or margarine and salad oil in pan until sizzling. Add green and red peppers and fry until pale gold.
2 Add mushrooms and fry a further 2 minutes. Stir in flour then gradually blend in stock or water and milk. Cook, stirring, until sauce comes to the boil and thickens.

3 Add poultry or duck. Mix in well. Cover pan. Bubble gently for 20 minutes, stirring from time to time. Beat cream with egg yolks and lemon juice.
4 Pour into poultry mixture, blending well. Reheat 5 minutes. Season to taste with salt and pepper and serve with freshly-cooked rice.

Salmi of Duck

Poultry à la King

SERVES 4 ▲▲▲●●●

2oz (50g) butter or margarine
2tsp salad oil
1 small green pepper, de-seeded and chopped
1 small red pepper, de-seeded and chopped
4oz (125g) button mushrooms and stalks, trimmed and sliced
1oz (25g) flour
¼pt (150ml) poultry stock or water
¼pt (150ml) milk
12oz (350g) cold cooked poultry or duck, diced
1 carton (5oz or 142ml) soured cream
yolks of 2 Grade 3 eggs
2tblsp fresh lemon juice, strained
salt and pepper to taste

GAME

Game comprises wild birds and animals which are generally in season during the autumn and winter months. Each variety has its own season (see below) and for a traditional 'gamey' flavour the birds etc should be hung in a cool pantry or larder for the number of days indicated. If the weather is warm for the time of year, less time need be allowed. Conversely if the weather is cold, 1 or 2 days longer may be advisable. There is no close season for rabbit or pigeon. Although there is no close season for hare, it should not be eaten when in kindle and so its sale is prohibited between March and July.

Type of Game	When in Season	Approximate days to allow for hanging
Snipe	Aug 12 to Jan 31	4 to 7
Grouse	Aug 12 to Dec 10	4 to 5
Partridge	Sept 1 to Feb 1	5 to 8
Pheasant	Oct 1 to Feb 1	5 to 8
Woodcock	Oct 1 to Jan 31	4 to 5
Pigeon	All year	2 to 3 (optional)
Hare	not sold between March and July	7 to 8

RABBIT 3 to 4 (optional)

Pigeon and rabbit are usually sold and eaten unhung but this is a matter of personal taste and preference. It is not obligatory to hang *any* game but is customary in Great Britain. If liked, hang for 2 to 3 days.

WATER GAME

These comprise mallard, teal and widgeon which are in season from September 1 to February 20 (inland season ends on January 21). They should be hung about 2 to 3 days.

Casseroled Rabbit

Casseroled Rabbit

SERVES 8 ▲▲●●

3lb (1½kg) rabbit joints
2 rounded tblsp flour
3 medium carrots
2 medium onions
1 large trimmed leek, well washed
salt and pepper to taste
½pt (275ml) chicken stock (use
*   cube and water)*
6oz (175g) trimmed button
*   mushrooms and stalks, left*
*   whole*
8oz (225g) frozen peas, defrosted
about 1 rounded tblsp chopped
*   parsley*
extra parsley sprigs for garnishing

1 Wash and dry rabbit joints and coat with flour. Leave on one side temporarily.
2 Peel and thinly slice carrots and onions. Shred leek. Mix vegetables together and use to cover base of large heatproof casserole, first well greased with butter or margarine.
3 Sprinkle with salt and pepper. Top with rabbit and season again. Pour chicken stock gently into dish then cover with lid or foil. Cook 1½ hours in oven set to 180°C (350°F), Gas 4.
4 Uncover. Stir in mushrooms and peas. Leave uncovered then return to oven and cook a further ½ hour. Sprinkle with parsley, garnish with one or two parsley sprigs and serve with boiled potatoes.

Roast Rabbit

SERVES 4 ▲▲●●●

1 whole, young rabbit, medium
*   size*
2oz (50g) butter or margarine,
*   melted*
6 rashers streaky bacon

ACCOMPANIMENTS
Gravy
Cranberry Sauce (page 183) packed
*   into canned pear halves (well*
*   drained)*
boiled potatoes
roast potatoes
seasonal vegetables to taste

1 Wash and dry rabbit. Stand in roasting tin and brush all over with melted butter or margarine. Drape bacon rashers over rabbit. Brush with more butter.

Normandy Style Pheasant (page 102)

2 Place in oven set to 280°C (450°F), Gas 8 and roast 15 minutes. Reduce temperature to 190°C (375°F), Gas 5 and roast for 15 minutes to every 1lb (450g) of rabbit. Baste often to prevent dryness.
3 Divide into portions and serve with suggested accompaniments. If liked, top each portion with a wedge of lemon.

Rabbit Pie with Vegetables

SERVES 6 ▲▲▲●●

1 whole young rabbit, medium size
1oz (25g) butter or margarine
3oz (75g) streaky bacon, chopped
6oz (175g) potatoes, peeled and
*   diced*
6oz (175g) carrots, peeled
3 slim leeks, washed and trimmed
*   then sliced*
¼ level tsp finely-grated lemon peel
½ level tsp marjoram
1 level tblsp chopped parsley
stock made from chicken cube and
*   water*
Shortcrust Pastry made with 8oz
*   (225g) flour (page 186)*
beaten egg for brushing

1 Divide rabbit into neat joints. Wash and dry. Heat butter or margarine in saucepan. Add bacon. Fry until crisp. Add rabbit joints, 2 at a time. Fry until golden. Remove to plate temporarily.
2 Add prepared vegetables to remaining butter etc in pan. Fry until golden. Transfer rabbit and vegetables to a 2pt (just over 1 litre) pie dish with rim.
3 Sprinkle with lemon peel, marjoram and parsley then pour in sufficient stock to come half way up sides. Roll out pastry at least 1in (2½cm) wider all the way round than the top of dish.
4 Moisten rim with water. Line with a strip of pastry cut from trimmings. Moisten strip with more water then cover with rolled out lid. Press edges well together to seal. Make 2 slits in top to allow steam to escape.
5 Brush with egg to glaze. Decorate with leaves cut from trimmings and brush with more egg. Bake 20 minutes in hot oven set to 220°C (425°F), Gas 7. Reduce to 160°C (325°F), Gas 3. Continue to bake a further 1½ hours.

101

'Jugged' Hare

SERVES 4 TO 6   ▲▲▲●●●

*1 prepared hare, jointed and with
    blood reserved for sauce
    (optional)*
2oz (50g) butter
2tsp salad oil
*6oz (175g) onions, peeled and
    chopped*
*6oz (175g) carrots, peeled and
    chopped*
*2 medium-sized celery stalks,
    scrubbed and washed*
1½pt (⅞ litre) water
2 level tsp salt
2 bouquet garni
1 bay leaf
3 level tblsp flour
6tblsp cold water
1 rounded tblsp redcurrant jelly

1 Wash and dry hare joints with
paper towels. Heat butter and oil
in large pan until sizzling. Add
onions, carrots and celery. Fry
gently until light gold.
2 Move to edges of pan. Add hare
joints, 2 pieces at a time. Fry until
well sealed and brown.
3 Pour water into pan. Season with
salt. Add bouquet garni and bay
leaf. Bring to boil. Skim. Lower
heat. Cover. Simmer very gently
until hare is soft, allowing up to
about 2 hours.
4 Lift hare out of pan on to a dish
and keep hot. Strain gravy into a
clean pan. Mix flour smoothly
with water. Add to gravy. Cook,
stirring continuously, until it
comes to the boil and thickens.
Whisk in reserved blood (optional).
5 Add redcurrant jelly and leave to
simmer over low heat until
melted. Adjust seasoning to taste.
Pour gravy over hare. Serve with
extra redcurrant jelly, boiled potatoes and seasonal vegetables to
taste.

Traditional Note Jugged Hare should,
traditionally, be served surrounded
by Forcemeat Balls made by mixing
together 4oz (125g) fresh white
breadcrumbs, 2oz (50g) finely-
shredded suet, 1 level teaspoon
mixed herbs, ½ level teaspoon grated
lemon peel and ½ level teaspoon salt
and binding with milk. They should
be shaped into 12 balls and fried
until crisp in a mixture of lard and
bacon dripping.

Roast Pheasant

SERVES 4   ▲▲▲●●●

*1 ready-prepared pheasant, plucked
    and drawn*
2oz (50g) frying steak, in 1 piece
4 to 5 rashers streaky bacon
*2oz (50g) butter or margarine,
    melted*
flour

GARNISH
watercress
tail feathers

TO ACCOMPANY
*2oz (50g) butter-fried brown
    breadcrumbs*
Bread Sauce (page 83)
Gravy (page 93)
very thin chips or potato crisps

1 Wash and dry pheasant. Place
steak inside body cavity to keep
pheasant moist and succulent.
Stand bird in roasting tin.
2 Cover completely with bacon
rashers. Baste with one-third of
the butter. Roast ½ hour in oven
set to 200°C (400°F), Gas 6.
3 Remove rashers. 'Froth' breast by
pouring over remaining butter
and sprinkling with flour. Return
to oven and continue to roast for
a further 25 minutes.
4 Remove to serving dish. Garnish
vent end with watercress and tail
feathers, and serve with the listed
accompaniments and either
seasonal green vegetables or a
mixed salad.

Normandy Style Pheasant

SERVES 4

Follow directions for *Roast Pheasant*
above but baste with 5 tablespoons
dry cider in addition to butter. Instead of listed accompaniments,
serve with Gravy plus butter-fried
apple pieces (use dessert apples) and
boiled chestnuts also fried in butter.
Include also boiled potatoes and
salad.

Roast Partridge

SERVES 4   ▲▲▲●●●

Follow exact directions for *Roast
Pheasant* above, but use 2 birds,
and stuff each with 1oz (25g) butter
or margarine instead of steak. Garnish with watercress but no feathers.

Roast Grouse

SERVES 4   ▲▲▲●◑●

Treat exactly as *Roast Partridge*
above. If liked, add Cranberry Sauce
(page 183) to the list of accompaniments.

Roast Pigeons

SERVES 4

Allow 4 pigeons, 1 per person. Wash
and dry. Stuff each with ½oz (15g)
butter or margarine. Stand in roasting tin. Baste heavily with more
melted butter or margarine. Roast
30 minutes in oven set to 200°C
(400°F), Gas 6, basting frequently.
Serve each on a slice of butter-fried
bread and garnish with watercress.
Accompany with Gravy (page 93)
flavoured with a little sherry or port,
thin chips and seasonal vegetables
or a green salad.

Hot and Cold
Puddings and Desserts

Hot and Cold Puddings and Desserts

Although some always opt for cheese and biscuits at the end of a meal, the great majority still prefer a dessert which is sweet rather than savoury, and it is for those people I now present a hot and cold assortment of old and new favourites ranging from creamy Rice Pudding to the glories of Profiteroles.

Rice Pudding

SERVES 4 ▲●

2oz (50g) round grain pudding rice
1pt (575ml) hot milk
1oz (25g) caster sugar
1 × 2in (5cm) strip of washed
  lemon peel minus pith
  grated nutmeg for sprinkling
  over top
½oz (15g) butter or margarine,
  melted

1 Wash and drain rice. Tip into 1½pt (¾ litre) buttered pie dish such as Pyrex. Add milk and sugar. Stir round. Leave to soak 45 minutes for rice to soften partially.
2 Drop lemon peel on top then sprinkle with nutmeg. Trickle with melted butter or margarine.
3 Cook 2 to 2½ hours in centre of oven set to 150°C (300°F), Gas 2. Stir in skin during first 1¼ hours of cooking as this enriches the pudding and turns it a creamy-golden colour. Remove from oven. Serve hot or cold.

Variations

If preferred, use barley, flaked rice, tapioca or elbow macaroni.

Semolina Pudding

SERVES 4 ▲●

1pt (575ml) cold milk
1½oz (40g) semolina
1oz (25g) caster sugar
½oz (15g) butter or margarine
¼tsp vanilla essence or 1 level tsp
  finely-grated lemon peel
  (optional)

1 Pour milk into pan. Sprinkle in semolina. Cook, stirring continuously, until mixture comes to boil and thickens.
2 Add sugar and butter or margarine. Continue to stir over low heat for about 5 minutes or until pudding is piping hot.
3 Gently whisk in vanilla or lemon peel. Spoon pudding into 4 dishes. Serve straightaway.

Semolina Whip

Sago Pudding

SERVES 4 ▲●

Make exactly as *Semolina Pudding*, substituting sago for semolina.

Semolina Whip

SERVES 4 ▲▲●●

Make *Semolina Pudding* exactly as directed. Remove from heat. Beat in 2 egg yolks from Grade 3 eggs. Beat 2 egg whites with few drops of lemon juice to a very stiff snow. Gently fold into semolina mixture with a metal spoon. Divide between 4 to 6 dishes. Refrigerate until very cold. Before serving, decorate top with some whipped cream and canned fruit such as cherries.

Bread and Butter Pudding

SERVES 4 ▲▲●●

4 large slices white bread, crusts
  removed (from cut loaf)
2oz (50g) butter
2oz (50g) currants
2oz (50g) caster sugar
2 Grade 2 eggs
1pt (575ml) warm milk

1 Spread bread slices thickly with butter then cut into fingers. Arrange half in 1½pt (⅞ litre) buttered pie dish. Sprinkle with all the fruit and half the sugar.
2 Top with rest of bread fingers, buttered sides uppermost. Beat eggs and milk well together. Strain into dish over bread.
3 Sprinkle rest of sugar on top. Leave pudding to stand about 30 minutes so that bread absorbs some of the milk and egg mixture.
4 Afterwards bake ¾ to 1 hour in oven set to 160°C (325°F), Gas 3. When ready the top should be brown and crusty and the pudding itself well puffed.
5 Remove from oven (pudding will quickly sink back on itself) and spoon out on to plates. Serve straightaway.

Apple Charlotte

SERVES 4 ▲▲●●

1lb (450g) cooking apples
4oz (125g) caster sugar
4oz (125g) fresh white
breadcrumbs
finely-grated peel of medium
washed and dried lemon
4oz (125g) butter, melted

1 Peel, core and slice apples. Toss together sugar, crumbs and lemon peel.
2 Fill a buttered 2pt (1¼ litre) heat-proof dish with alternate layers of apple slices and crumb mixture, beginning with apples and ending with crumbs and sprinkling butter between layers.
3 Bake 1 hour in oven set to 190°C (375°F), Gas 5. By this time, the apples should be tender and the top golden brown.
4 Remove from oven and spoon on to plates. Serve with cream or custard.

Plain Sponge Pudding

SERVES 4 TO 6 ▲▲●●

6oz (175g) self-raising flour
½ level tsp salt
3oz (75g) butter or margarine
(kitchen temperature)
3oz (75g) caster sugar
1 Grade 2 egg
½tsp vanilla essence
6tblsp cold milk for mixing

1 Well grease a 2pt (1¼ litre) pudding basin. Cut and grease a round of foil to go over top of basin and act as a lid.
2 Sift flour and salt into bowl. Rub in butter or margarine finely. Toss in sugar. Using a fork, mix to a softish batter with unbeaten egg, essence and milk.
3 Stir briskly without beating then spoon pudding mixture into basin. Cover with round of greased foil and tie on with thin string or thick thread.
4 Place in large saucepan then add sufficient boiling water to come half way up sides of basin. Cover with lid and cook steadily for 1¾ to 2 hours when pudding should be well risen and firm.

5 Replenish boiling water in pan every now and then to keep up the level. When pudding is ready, carefully lift out with hands protected by oven gloves. Wipe sides dry with clean teatowel.
6 Turn pudding out on to a warm dish, cut into portions and transfer to plates. Coat with sauce to taste (see Sauce section on page 168) or serve with cream or custard.

VARIATIONS

Jam or Syrup Pudding

SERVES 4 TO 6 ▲▲●●

Follow recipe for *Plain Sponge Pudding* but add 2 rounded tablespoons jam or golden syrup to basin before spooning in pudding mixture.

Chocolate Pudding

SERVES 4 ▲▲●●

Follow recipe for *Plain Sponge Pudding* but use 5oz (150g) self-raising flour and 1oz (25g) cocoa powder. Increase vanilla essence to 1 teaspoon. If liked, use soft brown sugar instead of caster. Serve with Chocolate Sauce (page 184) or single cream.

Lemon or Orange Pudding

SERVES 4 ▲▲●●

Follow recipe for *Plain Sponge Pudding* but add the finely-grated peel of 1 washed and dried lemon or orange at the same time as the sugar.

Baked Plain Pudding

SERVES 4 ▲▲●●

Make up *Plain Sponge Pudding* as directed above but spread into 2pt (1¼ litre) well-buttered dish. Bake 50 minutes to 1 hour in oven set to 180°C (350°F), Gas 4. Turn out on to a warm dish. Cut into portions and serve with suitable sauce to taste (see Sauce section on page 168) or with cream or custard.

Flavour Tip
This baked version is delicious if 2 level teaspoons ginger and 1 level teaspoon cinnamon are sifted with

the flour and salt, and the vanilla is omitted. After turning out, one of the most companiable sauces is lightly-sweetened stewed apple, heated until bubbling with a small knob of butter or margarine.

Rich Sponge Pudding

SERVES 4 TO 6 ▲▲●●

4oz (125g) self-raising flour
4oz (125g) butter or margarine
(kitchen temperature)
4oz (125g) caster sugar
¼tsp vanilla essence or 1 level tsp
orange or lemon rind
2 Grade 2 eggs
2tblsp cold milk

1 Well grease (melted butter is best) a 2pt (1¼ litre) pudding basin. Cut and grease a round of foil to go over top of basin and act as lid.
2 Sift flour on to plate. Place butter or margarine with sugar and essence or peel into bowl and cream until light and fluffy in texture, pale in colour and the consistency of whipped cream. Do this with either the back of a wooden spoon or electric beaters.
3 Break 1 egg into cup and check for freshness. Add to creamed mixture with 1 slightly rounded tablespoon flour. Beat in well. Repeat with second egg and another tablespoon flour.
4 Using a spoon, fold in rest of flour alternately with milk. When smooth and evenly combined, transfer to basin.
5 Cover with round of greased foil and tie on with thin string or thick thread. Place in large saucepan then add sufficient boiling water to come half way up sides of basin.
6 Cover with lid and cook steadily for 1¾ to 2 hours when pudding should be well risen and firm. Replenish boiling water in pan every now and then to keep up the level.
7 When pudding is ready, carefully lift out of pan with hands protected by oven gloves. Wipe sides of basin dry with clean teatowel.
8 Turn out on to a warm dish, cut into portions and transfer to plates. Serve with cream, custard or sauce to taste (see Sauce section on page 168).

105

VARIATIONS

Jam or Syrup Pudding

SERVES 4 TO 6 ▲▲●●●

Follow recipe for *Rich Sponge Pudding* but add 2 rounded tablespoons jam or golden syrup to basin before spooning in pudding mixture.

Sultana Pudding

SERVES 4 TO 6 ▲▲●●●

Follow recipe for *Rich Sponge Pudding* but add 2oz (50g) sultanas (or cur-

rants if preferred) at the same time as vanilla essence or grated peel.

Baked Rich Sponge Pudding

SERVES 4 TO 6 ▲▲●●●

Make up *Rich Sponge Pudding* as directed (page 105) then smooth into a 2pt (1¼ litre) buttered pie dish. Bake ¾ to 1 hour in oven set to 180°C (350°F), Gas 4, when pudding should be well risen and golden. Turn out on to a warm dish. Serve with sauce accompaniments as steamed version.

College Pudding

Steamed Suet Pudding

SERVES 4 TO 6 ▲▲●●

4oz (125g) plain flour
¼ level tsp salt
1½ level tsp baking powder
4oz (125g) fresh white breadcrumbs
3oz (75g) packeted suet, finely shredded
3oz (75g) caster sugar
2 Grade 3 eggs
½tsp vanilla essence
about 5tblsp cold milk to mix

1 Well grease a 2pt (1¼ litre) pudding basin. Cut and grease a round of foil to go over top of basin and act as lid.
2 Sift flour, salt and baking powder into bowl. Toss in crumbs, suet and sugar.
3 Break eggs into cup and check for freshness. Add to dry ingredients with vanilla and milk. Fork-stir briskly to form a slack dough which drops off the fork when you lift it out of the bowl.
4 Transfer to prepared basin. Cover with round of greased foil and tie on with thin string or thick thread. Place in large saucepan and add sufficient boiling water to come half way up sides of basin.
5 Cover with lid and cook steadily for 3 hours when pudding should be well risen and firm. Replenish boiling water every now and then to keep up the level.
6 When pudding is ready, carefully lift out of pan with hands protected by oven gloves. Wipe sides of basin clean with clean tea-towel.
7 Turn out on to warm dish, cut into portions and transfer to plates. Serve with custard.

Tip
If preferred, cook in conventional steamer.

VARIATIONS

Jam, Syrup or Marmalade Pudding

SERVES 4 TO 6 ▲▲●●●

Follow recipe for *Steamed Suet Pudding* but add 2 rounded tablespoons jam, syrup or marmalade to basin before spooning in pudding mixture.

College Pudding

SERVES 4 TO 6 ▲▲▲●●

Follow recipe for *Steamed Suet Pudding* but sift dry ingredients with 1 level teaspoon mixed spice and use half caster and half soft brown sugar (light variety). Add 4oz (125g) sultanas or raisins (or mixture) and 1 level teaspoon finely-grated lemon peel at the same time as the sugar.

Steamed Fruit Pudding

SERVES 4 ▲▲●●

1½lb (675g) fruits suitable for stewing (choice to taste and according to season)
1 rounded tblsp fresh white or brown breadcrumbs
5oz (150g) granulated or demerara sugar
1tblsp water
Suet Crust Pastry (page 189)

1 Trim and prepare fruit according to type. Toss with crumbs, sugar and water.
2 Roll out just under three-quarters of the pastry and press over sides and base of well-greased, 2pt (1¼ litre) basin to form an even lining.
3 Fill with fruit mixture. Dampen edges of lining pastry with water. Cover with lid, rolled from rest of pastry. Pinch edges well together to seal.
4 Cover with foil and cook 3 hours as for *Steamed Suet Pudding* (page 106).

Christmas Pudding

MAKES 2 PUDDINGS, EACH ENOUGH FOR 8 PERSONS

▲▲▲●●

4oz (125g) plain flour
1 level tsp allspice
½ level tsp cinnamon
8oz (225g) fresh white breadcrumbs
12oz (350g) suet, finely shredded
8oz (225g) soft brown sugar (dark variety) or molasses sugar
12oz (350g) sultanas
8oz (225g) currants
4oz (125g) seedless raisins

Christmas Pudding. Photograph by Brown and Polson Cornflour

2oz (50g) mixed chopped peel
2oz (50g) blanched and lightly-toasted almonds or walnuts, chopped but not too finely
finely-grated peel of 1 small lemon
4 Grade 2 eggs, well beaten
4tblsp brandy, whisky or rum
¼pt (150ml) milk or stout

1 Well grease 2 × 2pt (1¼ litre) pudding basins. Cut and grease 2 rounds of foil to go over top of basin and act as lids.
2 Sift flour, allspice and cinnamon into bowl. Toss in crumbs, suet, sugar, fruits, chopped peel, nuts and grated lemon peel.
3 Fork in eggs, spirit and either milk or stout. Mix thoroughly. Divide between the prepared basins. Cover with clean teatowel and leave in the kitchen overnight.

4 Next day, cover with rounds of foil and tie on with thin string or thick thread. Cook as given for *Steamed Suet Pudding* (page 106), allowing 6 hours.
5 When ready, cool to lukewarm then turn out of basin. Wrap in greaseproof paper when completely cold then overwrap with foil. Store in the cool until needed.
6 Before serving, re-cook each pudding for 2 hours in greased basin. Turn out, coat with warm brandy or rum (about 3 to 4 tablespoons) and ignite. Add a seasonal decoration. Serve with Simple White Pouring Sauce (page 168), made with cornflour, sweetened with sugar and flavoured with the squeezed juice of ½ orange and shreds of peel.

Puffy Jam Turnovers

Mince Pies

MAKES 12 ▲▲●●

*Shortcrust Pastry made with 8oz
(225g) flour (page 186)
12oz (350g) mincemeat
1oz (25g) chopped walnuts or
almonds (optional)
½tsp almond essence
beaten egg for brushing
icing sugar*

1 Roll out pastry thinly. Cut into 12 rounds with 3½in (9cm) cutter. Gather up trimmings, re-roll and cut into further 12 rounds with 2½in (6cm) cutter.
2 Use larger rounds to line 12 deep bun tins. Mix mincemeat with rest of ingredients. Spoon equal amounts into each.
3 Cover with lids by pressing them gently on to pies (no need to damp and seal). Brush lightly with egg. Bake until warm gold and slightly risen; about 20 to 25 minutes in oven set to 220°C (425°F), Gas 7.
4 Leave to cool slightly then carefully remove from tins. Dredge icing sugar through a fine mesh sieve over each. Eat warm with either whipped cream, White Sauce (page 168) flavoured with spirit or sherry and sweetened with sugar, ice cream or custard.

Tip
Store remainders in airtight tin. Reheat briefly before serving. Mince Pies will keep several weeks and also take quite happily to deep-freezing. Therefore you can batch bake.

Puffy Jam Turnovers

MAKES 12 ▲▲●● or ●●●

*homemade Flaky or Rough Puff
Pastry (pages 190–192) or
1 large packet frozen puff
pastry, defrosted
about 12tsp firm jam or
redcurrant jelly
beaten egg for brushing
icing sugar*

1 Roll out pastry fairly thinly (slightly thicker if homemade). Cut into 12 × 3in (7½cm) squares. Dampen edges with brush dipped in water.
2 Place a teaspoon of jam on to each square and fold over to form triangles. Pinch edges well together to seal then transfer to 1 or 2 wetted baking trays.
3 Brush only top with egg (if you brush the joined edges the pastry will be unable to puff) then bake

20 to 25 minutes in oven set to 220°C (425°F), Gas 7.
4 Transfer to a wire rack and dredge with icing sugar through a fine mesh sieve. Eat while still warm and coat with single cream or Custard Sauce (see page 176).

Jam Tart

SERVES 4 TO 6 ▲▲●●

*Shortcrust Pastry made with 6oz
(175g) flour (page 186)
2tblsp firm jam*

1 Roll out pastry thinly and use to line an 8in (20cm) greased heat-proof plate (not too deep). Trim away surplus from edges.
2 Spread jam over centre, making sure edges are left completely clear. Dampen edges with brush dipped in water.
3 Gather up trimmings and re-roll thinly. Cut into strips. Arrange in criss-cross fashion over top of pie, pressing ends of each strip well on pastry rim.
4 Bake 30 to 35 minutes in oven set to 200°C (400°F), Gas 6 or until pastry is a warm brown colour. Serve warm with cream or custard.

VARIATIONS

Lemon Curd Tart

SERVES 4 TO 6 ▲▲●●

Make exactly as *Jam Tart* but use lemon curd instead of jam.

Treacle Tart

SERVES 4 TO 6 ▲▲▲●●

Make exactly as *Jam Tart* but use the following mixture instead of jam: 2 level tablespoons fresh white breadcrumbs mixed with 1½ level tablespoons black treacle, 1½ level tablespoons golden syrup, ½ level teaspoon finely-grated lemon peel and 2 level teaspoons lemon juice.

Custard Tart

SERVES 4 TO 6 ▲▲●●●

Roll out pastry as for *Jam Tart* opposite and use to line an 8in (20cm) deepish greased plate; an enamel one is excellent. Fill with ¼ pint (150ml) warm milk beaten with 2 Grade 2 eggs, 2 Grade 2 egg yolks and 2oz (50g) caster sugar. Sprinkle lightly with nutmeg. Stand on baking tray then place in oven set to 220°C (425°F), Gas 7. Bake 15 minutes. Reduce temperature to 180°C (350°F), Gas 4. Continue to bake a further 30 to 40 minutes or until pastry is lightly browned and custard feels firm and set when lightly pressed with finger. Remove from oven and serve warm.

Fruit Crumble

SERVES 4 ▲▲●●

1lb (450g) mixture of redcurrants, raspberries and gooseberries
4 to 6oz (125 to 175g) caster sugar, according to sweetness of fruit
2tblsp water

TOPPING
6oz (175g) plain flour
¼ level tsp mixed spice or finely-grated lemon peel (optional)
3oz (75g) butter or margarine
3oz (75g) caster or soft brown sugar (light variety)

1 Prepare fruit according to type. Arrange in layers, with sugar between, in greased 2pt (1¼ litre) dish. Add water.
2 To make crumble, sift flour and spice or lemon peel into bowl. Rub in butter or margarine finely. Toss in sugar. Sprinkle thickly over fruit then press down lightly with fork.
3 Bake 15 minutes in oven set to 190°C (375°F), Gas 5. Reduce temperature to 180°C (350°F), Gas 4. Continue to bake a further 40 to 45 minutes or until top is golden brown.
4 Spoon out on to plates and serve with cream or custard.

Variation Tip
If preferred, use 1lb (450g) peeled, cored and sliced cooking apples instead of combination above. Or cut-up rhubarb.

Fruit Fritters

SERVES 4 TO 6 ▲▲●●

1lb (450g) cooking apples
Sweet Fritter Batter (page 202)
a pan of deep oil for frying
caster or icing sugar for sprinkling over the top

1 Peel apples and remove centre cores. Cut each apple into about 4 or 5 slices.
2 Coat with batter and fry in hot oil for about 3 to 4 minutes or until golden.
3 Lift out of pan, drain on crumpled kitchen paper and sprinkle with caster or sifted icing sugar. Serve hot.

Fruit Crumble

Variation Tip
Use fresh or canned pineapple rings (the latter well drained first) or quartered bananas instead of apples.

Raspberry Pie

SERVES 6 ▲▲▲●●

1½lb (675g) raspberries
Shortcrust Pastry made with 8oz (225g) flour (page 186)
4oz (125g) caster sugar
beaten egg for brushing
extra caster sugar or icing sugar for top

1 Gently wash raspberries and remove stalks if necessary. Cut pastry into 2 pieces, one a little longer than the other.
2 Roll out the small piece and use to line a deep 8in (20cm) heatproof plate, first lightly buttered. Fill with alternate layers of fruit and sugar, beginning and ending with fruit.
3 Dampen edges of pastry with brushed dipped in water then cover with lid, rolled and cut from second piece of pastry.
4 Pinch edges of pastry well together to seal then make hole or slit in top to allow steam to escape. Brush with egg and stand on baking tray.
5 Bake 45 to 50 minutes in oven set to 200°C (400°F), Gas 6. The pastry should, at this stage, be golden brown and crusty.
6 Remove from oven and dust top with sugar. Cut into portions and serve warm with whipped cream.

Raspberry Pie (page 109)

Pie on a Plate

SERVES 6 ▲▲▲●●●

Follow recipe for *Raspberry Pie* (page 109) but use 1lb (450g) cooking apples, gooseberries, rhubarb, currants, apricots, plums, greengages, strawberries or mixture of fruit. Line a FLAT 8in (20cm) buttered heat-proof plate with the smaller half of pastry. Fill centre with alternate layers of fruit and sugar, beginning and ending with fruit. Finish as for Raspberry Pie but bake 20 minutes in oven set to 220°C (425°F), Gas 7. Reduce temperature to 180°C (350°F), Gas 4 and continue to bake a further 40 to 45 minutes or until golden brown. Note that juices build up inside the pie so when you cut into it, be prepared for a flow of liquid.

Deep Dish Fruit Pie

SERVES 6

Fill a 2pt (1¼ litre) rimmed pie dish with alternate layers of 2lb (900g) prepared fruit (apples, gooseberries, cut-up rhubarb, stemmed currants etc) and 8oz (225g) granulated sugar, doming up the filling in the centre. Have ready Shortcrust Pastry made with 8oz (225g) flour (page 186). Roll out until 1½in (4cm) larger all the way round than top of dish. Dampen rim of dish with brush dipped in water. Line with strips of pastry cut from trimmings. Dampen strips then cover with lid. Make 2

holes or slits in top to allow steam to escape then brush with beaten egg. Stand on baking tray. Bake 20 minutes in oven set to 220°C (425°F), Gas 7. Reduce temperature to 180°C (350°F), Gas 4. Continue to bake a further 45 to 50 minutes or until pastry is golden brown and fruit is cooked through. Serve hot with cream or custard.

Apple Strudel

SERVES 10 ▲▲▲●●●

Strudel Pastry (page 194)
4oz (125g) butter or margarine, melted
2 rounded tblsp lightly-toasted breadcrumbs
3 rounded tblsp ground almonds
2lb (900g) peeled cooking apples, cored and thinly sliced
2 level tsp cinnamon
3oz (75g) caster sugar
2oz (50g) flaked almonds, lightly toasted and coarsely crushed
4oz (125g) raisins
icing sugar

1 Roll out pastry as directed and fold over edges. Brush all over with melted butter or margarine then sprinkle with half the crumbs and almonds.

2 Cover with apples, leaving edges clear. Sprinkle with two-thirds of remaining butter or margarine, the rest of crumbs and ground almonds, cinnamon, sugar, flaked almonds and raisins.

3 Fold edges again over filling to make a kind of double hem, then,

with the aid of the cloth on which it is sitting, roll up the Strudel and slide straight on to a well-buttered baking tray.

4 Brush with rest of butter or margarine. Bake until golden brown and crisp-looking; about 35 to 45 minutes in oven set to 190°C (375°F), Gas 5. Cool to lukewarm on tray.

5 Sift icing sugar heavily over top then cut into pieces. Serve with whipped cream.

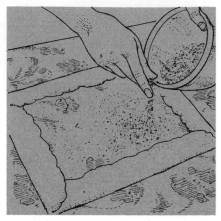

1 Roll out the pastry until the pattern of the cloth underneath shows through. Fold the edges to form a hem

2 Cover pastry with filling, leaving edges clear. Fold edges again to make a double hem

3 Using the cloth roll up and slide straight on to a buttered baking tray

Cream Cheese Strudel

SERVES 10 ▲▲▲●●

Make exactly as *Apple Strudel* but change the filling thus: sprinkle rolled pastry with 2 rounded tablespoons toasted crumbs. Mix 1lb (450g) curd or sieved cottage cheese with 2 Grade 2 egg yolks, 2oz (50g) melted butter or margarine, 1 level tablespoon cornflour, 3oz (75g) caster sugar, 1 teaspoon vanilla essence, 1 level teaspoon finely-grated lemon peel and 3oz (75g) seedless raisins. Spread over pastry, leaving edges clear. Fold edges over filling to make double hem then roll up and proceed as for Apple Strudel, brushing the Strudel before baking with 1½oz (40g) melted butter or margarine.

Vanilla Soufflé

SERVES 4 TO 6 ▲▲▲●●

2oz (50g) butter or margarine
2oz (50g) plain flour
½pt (275ml) warm milk
2oz (50g) caster sugar
1tsp vanilla essence
4 Grade 3 eggs, separated (room temperature)

1 Well-grease (preferably with butter) a 2½pt (1½ litre), straight-sided glass, pottery or china soufflé dish, usually with ridged sides.
2 Melt butter or margarine in saucepan. Stir in plain flour to make roux (see White Sauce section on page 168). Gradually blend in warm milk.
3 Cook, stirring or whisking continually, until sauce comes to boil and thickens sufficiently to leave sides of pan clean and form itself into a ball.
4 Cool slightly. Beat in sugar, essence and egg yolks. In separate clean and dry bowl, beat whites to a stiff and peaky snow.
5 Beat 3 heaped tablespoons of beaten whites into sauce mixture to loosen it slightly. Using a large metal spoon and working slowly, fold in rest of whites by cutting deeply into mixture and tossing it over on itself so that the whites gradually become incorporated. DO NOT BEAT.

Cream Cheese Strudel

6 When smooth and evenly combined, spoon into prepared dish. Place into oven set to 190°C (375°F), Gas 5. Bake 45 minutes WITHOUT OPENING OVEN DOOR.
7 Remove from oven and serve straightaway as a Soufflé quickly sinks down on to itself and loses its beautiful appearance.

VARIATIONS

ALL SERVE THE SAME NUMBER AND HAVE SAME SYMBOL GRADINGS

Coffee Soufflé

Follow directions for *Vanilla Soufflé* but dissolve 3 to 4 heaped teaspoons instant coffee powder in the milk. Omit vanilla.

Chocolate Soufflé

Follow directions for *Vanilla Soufflé* but mix milk smoothly with 1 level tablespoon cocoa powder before bringing to boil, stirring continuously, and leaving until lukewarm. Include vanilla.

Orange or Lemon Soufflé

Follow directions for *Vanilla Soufflé* but add 1 level teaspoon finely-grated orange or lemon peel instead of vanilla.

Raspberry Soufflé

Follow directions for *Vanilla Soufflé* but add 4 rounded tablespoons finely-crushed raspberries with the vanilla.

Soufflé Omelet

SERVES 4 ▲▲▲●●

6 Grade 3 eggs
1½oz (40g) caster sugar
1tsp vanilla essence
1½tsp lemon juice
1½oz (40g) unsalted butter
3 heaped tblsp apricot jam
2tsp water } *warmed through together*
caster sugar

1 Separate eggs. Beat yolks to a thick, creamy paste with sugar and essence. In separate bowl — which must be dry and clean — whip egg whites and lemon juice to stiff snow.
2 Using a large metal spoon, gently fold whipped whites into egg yolk mixture until all traces of streakiness have disappeared.
3 Sizzle half the butter in 2 × 6in (15cm) omelet pans with heat-resistant handles. Spoon one quarter of the egg mixture into each. Cook 3 minutes over medium heat.
4 Stand beneath preheated grill and leave to cook until golden and puffy; about 3 minutes. Tip out on to greaseproof paper sprinkled heavily with caster sugar.
5 Score a central line down each with knife. Spread one half with jam then fold each omelet in half. Repeat with rest of egg mixture (making total of 4 separate omelets) and serve straightaway.
6 Crushed berry fruit mixed with orange-flavoured liqueur such as Grand Marnier or Cointreau, apple purée or gooseberry purée also make excellent toppings for Soufflé Omelets.

Cooking Tip
If preferred, make one omelet in a 10in (25cm) pan and cut into portions.

Raspberry Soufflé

Soufflé Omelet (page 111)

Traditional Pancakes

MAKES 6   ▲▲●●

4oz (125g) plain flour
pinch salt
1 Grade 3 egg
½pt (275ml) cold milk (skimmed
  for lighter result)
2tsp melted butter, margarine or
  salad oil
about ½oz (15g) melted lard or
  white cooking fat for brushing
caster sugar for greaseproof paper
juice of 1 large lemon or bottled
  lemon juice

1 Sift flour and salt into bowl. Beat to smooth and thickish batter with whole egg and half the milk. Continue to beat until bubbles rise to the surface.

2 Gently stir in rest of milk and the melted fat or oil which gives pancakes a velvety texture. Cover batter. Leave to stand in a cool place for at least 1 hour. This resting time softens the flour and gives the pancakes more stretchability.

3 Before cooking, brush an 8in (20cm) heavy-based frying pan with melted lard or fat. Heat until very hot. Stir batter gently round.

4 Pour about 3 tablespoons batter into pan then tilt quickly in all directions until base is completely covered. Cook until underside is golden. Turn or toss over.

5 Cook second side until golden. Turn out on to sugared greaseproof paper. Sprinkle with lemon juice and roll up by slipping edge

of pancake nearest to you between prongs of fork and then turning fork over and over.

6 Slide fork out of pancake, slip on to a plate and serve straightaway. Repeat with rest of batter mixture.

Guidelines

(1) To keep pancakes warm as each is being cooked, stand one on top of the other on a plate resting over a pan of gently boiling water. Cover with lid.

(2) To store pancakes for a day or two, stand one on top of the other in an airtight tin with greaseproof paper between each. Reheat, minus paper, on a plate over a pan of boiling water.

(3) To freeze, arrange unfilled pancakes in a stack with freezer film between each. Wrap and seal securely. Label. Leave a maximum of 3 months. Thaw about 2 hours at kitchen temperature. Reheat over hot water.

Crèpes Suzette

SERVES 6   ▲▲▲●●

6 cooked pancakes (see above)
10 cubes of sugar
2 medium oranges, washed and
  dried
1 medium lemon, washed and dried
4oz (125g) unsalted butter
2 level tblsp caster sugar
1 liqueur glass orange flavour
  liqueur
1 liqueur glass brandy

1 Either roll up pancakes or fold each up like an envelope. Rub

cubes of sugar against oranges so that they absorb the aroma of the peel.

2 Halve fruit and squeeze out the juice. Strain into a large frying pan. Add sugar cubes, butter and caster sugar. Heat slowly until butter has melted. Pour in orange liqueur.

3 Add pancakes, baste with pan juices and heat through until hot. Warm brandy in separate pan. Pour over pancakes and ignite. Take to table while still flaming. Serve when flames have subsided.

Baked Egg Custard

SERVES 4 TO 6   ▲▲●●

2 Grade 2 eggs
2 Grade 2 egg yolks
1pt (575ml) milk, brought to boil
  then cooled to lukewarm
2 level tblsp caster sugar
1tsp vanilla essence (optional)
grated nutmeg

1 Beat whole eggs, yolks, milk, sugar and essence well together.

2 Strain into 1½pt (⅞ litre) buttered pie dish. Sprinkle a little nutmeg on top. Stand on baking tray.

3 Stand in roasting tin containing sufficient warm water to reach half way up sides of dish.

4 Bake until firm and set; ¾ to 1 hour in oven set to 160°C (325°F), Gas 3. Remove dish from tin of water and wipe sides dry. Serve warm with stewed fruit.

Crème Caramel

SERVES 8   ▲▲▲●●

Melt slowly 2oz (50g) granulated sugar in 2 tablespoons cold water. Cover pan until mixture just comes up to boil. Uncover. Continue to boil until mixture turns a dark golden colour. Stir in 1 tablespoon hot water. Pour into 6in (15cm) buttered cake tin and move tin round until base is completely covered with caramel. Make custard as above, using 1 extra egg yolk and half milk and half single cream. Bake as directed, allowing 1¼ to 1½ hours. Cool. Refrigerate overnight. Turn out into a dish as the caramel will have melted and turned into a thin sauce. Spoon portions on to individual plates.

Beignets

SERVES 6 ▲▲▲●●●

deep pan of oil for frying
Choux Pastry (page 196)
caster sugar
4oz (125g) plum jam
4tblsp water

1 Heat oil until hot. Carefully drop in 6 to 8 teaspoons of Choux Pastry, giving them adequate room to float about.
2 Fry about 7 to 8 minutes, turning them over with a spoon from time to time. Lift out of pan. Drain on paper towels.
3 Arrange on a warm dish and sprinkle with sugar. Repeat until all the pastry has been used up. Serve while still hot.
4 Accompany with jam sauce made by slowly heating together the jam and water.

Profiteroles

SERVES 4 TO 6 ▲▲▲●●●

Choux Pastry (page 196)
½pt (275ml) double cream
2tblsp cold milk
2 level tblsp caster sugar
Chocolate Sauce (see Sauce section on page 184)

1 Using a teaspoon, spoon 20 equal amounts of mixture on to well-greased baking tray, leaving room between each as they puff up and spread slightly. Alternatively, pipe small mounds of mixture on to tray.
2 Bake until deep gold and well risen, allowing 25 minutes in oven set to 220°C (425°F), Gas 7. Remove from oven and leave to stand 5 minutes.
3 Make a small slit in the side of each. Return to oven and leave 7 minutes, with heat switched off and door open, to dry out.
4 Cool on a wire rack. When completely cold and 1 or 2 hours before serving, whip cream, milk and sugar together until thick. Cut each puff in half then sandwich together with cream.
5 Arrange in a dish in pyramid fashion and coat gently with Chocolate Sauce, making sure it is the right consistency to flow down the sides. Refrigerate about 1 hour before serving.

Crêpes Suzette

Gâteau St Honoré

SERVES 8 GENEROUSLY

▲▲▲●●●

Flan Pastry (page 187)
Choux Pastry (page 196)
½pt (275ml) double cream
5tblsp single cream
4 slightly-rounded tblsp caster sugar
6 slightly-rounded tblsp apricot jam
2tblsp water
¼tsp almond essence (optional)
5 glacé cherries, halved

1 Roll out pastry into an 8in (20cm) round using a plate as a guide. Transfer carefully to greased baking tray. Set oven to 220°C (425°F), Gas 7.
2 Prick pastry all over with fork. Dampen a 1in (2½cm) border with brush dipped in water.
3 Using an icing bag and ½in (1¼cm) plain icing tube, pipe a ring of Choux Pastry round dampened pastry border.

4 Pipe 10 mounds of remaining Choux Pastry on to second greased tray. Stand tray with pastry towards top of oven and Choux mounds in centre. Bake 15 minutes. Reverse trays. Reduce temperature to 190°C (375°F), Gas 5. Bake a further 20 minutes.
5 Remove from oven and leave 5 minutes. Treat the small puffs as Profiteroles above. Cool pastry with Choux ring and puffs on wire rack.
6 About 2 hours before serving, whip creams and sugar together until thick. Leave in the refrigerator for the moment.
7 Heat jam, water and essence gently together until jam has completely melted. Stand pastry base on serving dish and pile about two-thirds cream mixture in middle. Brush Choux ring thickly with jam.
8 Split puffs in half. Sandwich together with remaining cream. Place side by side on top of ring. Brush thickly with more jam then top each with a half cherry. Chill ½ hour before serving.

113

Baked Apples

Baked Apples

SERVES 4 ▲▲●●

4 Bramley apples (the best as they
  'puff' up of their own accord)
4tsp golden or maple syrup, honey
  or raspberry jam
½ to 1 level tsp finely-grated
  orange or lemon rind
4tblsp warm water
2 level tblsp caster sugar
1oz (25g) butter or margarine

1 Wash and dry apples and remove
  stalks. Cut out cores without
  going right through the apples or
  filling will fall out; in other words,
  leave a reasonably thick base on
  each.

2 Using a sharp knife, score a line
  round each apple, about one-
  third of the way down. For a more
  unconventional effect, score each
  apple downwards into 4 sections.
3 Stand in dish. Mix syrup, honey
  or jam with rind. Spoon into apple
  cavities. Spoon water into dish
  with 1½ level tablespoons sugar.
4 Top each apple with a piece of
  butter then bake about 45 minutes
  in oven set to 180°C (350°F), Gas
  4. When ready, they should look
  soft and puffy. Baste 2 or 3 times.
5 Sprinkle with rest of sugar then
  spoon out of dish on to warm
  plates. Add a little cooking liquid
  to each.

Raspberry and Cream Babas

Rum Babas

MAKES 12 ▲▲▲●●●

YEAST BATTER
2 level tsp dried yeast or ½oz (15g)
  fresh yeast
5tblsp milk, a little warmer than
  blood heat
1oz (25g) strong plain white flour
1 level tsp caster sugar

REMAINING INGREDIENTS
5oz (150g) strong plain white
  flour
⅛ level tsp salt
1 level tblsp caster sugar
3oz (75g) butter
3 Grade 3 eggs, well beaten

1 Brush 12 Baba moulds or 3in
  (7½cm) individual ring tins with
  lard or white cooking fat. Dust
  very lightly with flour.
2 For batter, stir yeast into milk and,
  if using dried yeast, stand 5
  minutes. Stir in flour and sugar.
  Leave in a warm place 20 to 25
  minutes or until mixture froths
  up.
3 In separate bowl, mix together
  flour, salt and sugar. Rub in butter
  finely. Stir, with eggs, into yeast
  batter mixture. Beat briskly for 5
  minutes.
4 Half fill prepared tins with mixture. Cover with sheets of greased
  greaseproof paper and leave in a
  warm place to rise until mixture
  comes two-thirds of the way up
  each tin; about 25 to 30 minutes.
5 Bake 10 to 15 minutes in oven set
  to 200°C (400°F), Gas 6, when
  Babas should be well risen and
  golden brown. Leave in tins 5
  minutes then turn out on to a
  large wire rack or racks with
  plates underneath.
6 Prick Babas all over with a fork
  then soak with syrup made by
  heating ¼ pint (150ml) water with
  4oz (125g) caster sugar, finely-
  grated peel of ½ a washed and
  dried lemon, and 6 tablespoons
  rum.
7 Stir over low heat until sugar dissolves but do not allow syrup to
  boil. Spoon over Babas until they
  are moist right through. Leave
  until cold then brush with melted
  apricot jam for a golden glaze.
8 Before serving, pipe each with a
  ring of whipped cream (allowing
  about ½ pint or 275ml), then
  decorate with halved glacé cherries and pieces of angelica.

Raspberry and Cream Babas

MAKES 12 ▲▲▲●●●

Make *Babas* as above. Stand on dish and fill with about 1lb (450g) fresh raspberries. Decorate as shown with whipped cream, allowing about ½ pint or 275ml.

Savarin

SERVES 8 ▲▲▲●●●

Choose an 8in (20cm) Savarin tin which is a fluted ring mould with a rounded base as can be seen in the picture. Grease with melted white cooking fat or unsalted butter and dust with flour. Make up *Rum Baba* mixture as given previously (page 114). Spoon into tin. Cover with greased greaseproof paper and leave to rise in a warm place about 45 to 55 minutes or until mixture almost reaches top of tin. Bake 20 to 25 minutes in oven set to 200°C (400°F), Gas 6. Leave in tin 5 minutes then turn out on to a wire rack with a plate underneath. Prick all over and moisten with same syrup as Rum Babas. Brush with melted apricot jam. If liked, leave plain, except for a border of whipped cream. Alternatively, coat top with thick Chocolate Sauce (page 184) or fill centre with canned fruit. Decorate with slivers of pistachio nuts.

Savarin

3 Using a large metal spoon, fold in rest of sugar alternately with cornflour. When thoroughly mixed, pipe 16 circular whirls on to prepared trays. If preferred, spoon ovals of mixture on to trays using a tablespoon dipped in hot water.
4 Bake until a very pale creamy colour, allowing 1½ to 1¾ hours in oven set to 110°C (225°F), Gas ¼. Remove from oven and leave to cool down for about 10 minutes.
5 Lift off trays carefully then return to trays upside down. Leave to

dry out a further 30 minutes in oven with heat switched off. Cool on a wire rack. Store in an airtight tin when completely cold.
6 Before serving, whip ½pt (275ml) double cream with 2 tablespoons cold milk and 1 level tablespoon caster sugar until thick. Sandwich meringues together in pairs with cream, and arrange on dish.

Tip
Do not make Meringues in stormy weather as whites will not stiffen satisfactorily.

Chocolate Meringues (page 116)

Cream Meringue

MAKES 8 PAIRS ▲▲▲●●●

whites of 3 Grade 3 eggs
squeeze of lemon juice
7½oz (215g) caster sugar
3 level tsp cornflour

1 Brush 2 baking trays with oil. Line with either foil, greaseproof paper or non-stick parchment paper. Under no circumstances oil or grease foil on paper as meringues will stick.
2 Tip whites into a clean and dry bowl. Add a squeeze of lemon. Whisk until very stiff. Add three-quarters of the sugar in a steady stream and continue to whisk until meringue is VERY THICK and stands up in peaks when beaters are lifted out of bowl.

115

Fruit and Cream Meringues

Chocolate Meringues

MAKES 8 PAIRS ▲▲▲●●●

Make Meringues exactly as described under *Cream Meringues* (page 115). When completely cold, brush flat sides of each with 4oz (125g) melted plain chocolate and leave until set. Before serving, sandwich together with whipped cream then decorate top of each with a whirl of cream and ½ a glacé cherry.

Fruit and Cream Meringues

MAKES 8 LARGE ▲▲▲●●●

Make meringue mixture exactly as described under *Cream Meringues* (page 115) but pipe 8 large rounds of mixture on to prepared trays. Bake at same temperature but allow ¼

Rhubarb Meringue

hour longer. When completely cold, pile with ½pt (275ml) double cream, whipped until thick with 2 tablespoons cold milk and 1 level tablespoon caster sugar. Stud with canned mandarins and halved glacé cherries.

Rhubarb Meringue

SERVES 4 ▲▲●●

1½lb (675g) trimmed rhubarb,
   cut into 1in (2½cm) lengths
8oz (225g) caster sugar
finely-grated peel of ½ a washed
   and dried lemon
large pinch of cinnamon

MERINGUE
whites of 2 Grade 3 eggs
squeeze of lemon juice
5oz (150g) caster sugar
2oz (50g) flaked almonds

1 Place rhubarb into pan with sugar, lemon peel and cinnamon. Slowly bring to boil. Simmer gently, uncovered, for 3 to 5 minutes or until fruit is just tender; do not overcook or it will fall to pieces.
2 Place rhubarb and syrup into heatproof dish. Make up meringue as directed in recipe for *Cream Meringues* (page 115). Pile on top of rhubarb, leaving a border of rhubarb uncovered.
3 Scatter meringue with almonds then bake ¾ hour in oven set to 140°C (275°F), Gas 1. Spoon on to plates and serve hot.

Semolina Pear 'Cream'

SERVES 5 ▲▲●●

Make up *Semolina Pudding* as directed on page 104. Spread over shallowish plate. Top with 5 ripe pear halves (use Comice for preference) as shown in the picture, brushed with a little lemon juice. Fill centre of each with a de-seeded grape topped with red jam. Stud sections in between pears with about 4 to 6oz (125 to 175g) de-seeded black grapes. Chill lightly before serving.

Poached Pears with Blackberries

SERVES 4 ▲▲●●

8oz (225g) blackberries
2 rounded tblsp caster sugar
4 ripe dessert pears, Comice for
   preference
juice of 1 medium lemon
½pt (275ml) sweet wine
6tblsp water
3 rounded tblsp caster sugar
¼tsp vanilla essence

1 Wash blackberries gently under cold, running water. Shake dry in colander and leave to drain for ¼ hour. Afterwards tip into bowl and toss with the 2 tablespoons sugar.
2 Peel pears, halve and carefully scoop out cores. Brush all over with lemon juice. Leave aside temporarily.
3 Pour lemon juice into shallow pan with wine, water and sugar. Stir over gentle heat until sugar dis-

solves. Add pears and vanilla. Poach, covered, for 15 minutes.

4 Remove pears to serving dish. Fill centres with blackberries then pile remainder in centre. Coat with syrup in which pears were poached. Chill before serving.

Fruit Tarts

MAKES 10 TO 12 ▲▲▲●●●

Roll out Flan Pastry (page 187) thinly and cut into 10 to 12 rounds with a 3in (7½cm) fluted biscuit cutter. Use to line 10 or 12 bun tins. Cover inside of each with round of foil to prevent pastry from rising as it bakes. Bake 10 minutes in oven set to 200°C (400°F), Gas 6. Remove foil. Return tartlet cases to oven and continue to bake until warm gold; another 10 to 12 minutes. Carefully remove to wire rack and leave until cold. About 1 hour before serving, whip ¼pt (15ml) double cream until thick with 1 level tablespoon caster sugar and 1 tablespoon milk. Spoon equal amounts into tartlets. Top each with a border of well-drained canned mandarins then fill centres with fresh raspberries as shown in the picture overleaf.

Summer Fruit Salad

SERVES 6 ▲▲●●●

12oz (350g) strawberries, hulled
    and washed
8 fresh, ripe figs or canned figs if
    preferred
1 medium-sized orange
1 red-skinned dessert apple
8oz (225g) black grapes
juice of 1 medium lemon
4 rounded tblsp icing sugar, sifted
4tblsp sweet sherry

1 Slice strawberries. Wash and dry fresh figs or well drain canned figs and cut each into quarters.

2 Peel orange, removing all traces of pith, and cut out segments of flesh from between membranes with sharp knife.

3 Wash and dry apple but do not peel. Cut into quarters and remove core. Slice thinly. Halve grapes and remove seeds.

4 Tip all fruit into large bowl and toss gently with lemon juice, sugar and sherry. Cover. Refrigerate 2 to 3 hours.

Semolina Pear 'Cream'

5 Transfer to bowl and serve with whipped cream or ice cream and sweet biscuits.

Fruit Fool

SERVES 4 GENEROUSLY ▲▲●●●

1¼lb (575g) gooseberries, apples or
    rhubarb or mixture
3tblsp water
6oz (175g) caster sugar
¾pt (425ml) freshly-made custard,
    covered with round of damp
    greaseproof paper
¼pt (150ml) double cream
2 heaped tsp chopped nuts for
    decoration

1 Prepare fruit according to type. Place in saucepan. Add water. Bring to boil. Lower heat. Cover. Simmer until fruit is soft and pulpy.

2 Beat until smooth then stir in sugar. Leave until cold. When custard is cold, remove greaseproof paper and skin will come away with it.

3 Fold fruit smoothly into custard. Whip cream until thick and whisk two-thirds into fruit mixture.

4 Transfer to serving dishes or glasses. Decorate with remaining cream then sprinkle with nuts. Refrigerate 1 hour before serving.

Poached Pears with Blackberries

117

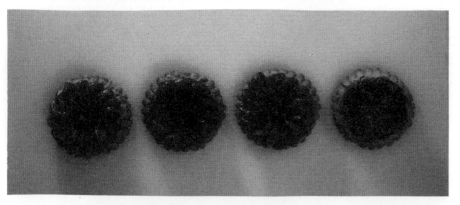

Fruit Tarts (page 117)

Gooseberry Cream Flan

SERVES 10 ▲●●●

1 shop-bought flan case measuring
    about 10 to 12in (20 to 25cm)
2 × 1lb cans gooseberries
½pt (275ml) double cream
2tblsp milk
1tblsp caster sugar
3 level tblsp raspberry or apricot
    jam
1oz (25g) flaked and toasted
    almonds

Fruit Fool (page 117)

1 Stand flan case on large plate or
   dish. Drain gooseberries. Moisten
   flan with some of the syrup.
2 Whip cream, milk and sugar together until thick. Spread jam
   over base of flan case. Fill with
   gooseberries.
3 Pipe cream in a border round
   edge then sprinkle with almonds.
   Refrigerate about ½ hour before
   serving.

Tip

Reserve syrup for fruit salads, fruit
drinks or milk shakes.

Lemon Mousse

SERVES 6 TO 8 ▲▲▲●●

6 level tsp gelatine
6tblsp cold water
4 Grade 2 eggs, separated
4oz (125g) caster sugar
finely-grated peel and juice of
    1 large lemon, washed and dried
½pt (275ml) double cream

DECORATION
about ¼pt (150ml) extra double
    cream
1oz (25g) chopped walnuts

1 Wash and dry a 1½pt (⅞ litre)
   straight-sided soufflé dish. Tie a
   folded strip of greaseproof or non-
   stick parchment paper round outside, making sure it protrudes 3in
   (7½cm) above top edge of dish as
   this has to support the Mousse
   mixture. Brush inside of strip
   lightly with salad oil (greaseproof
   paper only).
2 Tip gelatine into a saucepan. Add
   water. Leave 3 minutes to soften.
   Stand over minimal heat. Stir
   until melted. Leave on one side for
   time being.

3 Whisk egg yolks and sugar together until very thick, pale in
   colour and almost paste-like.
   Whisk in melted gelatine, lemon
   peel and lemon juice. Leave in the
   cool until just beginning to thicken
   and set.
4 Beat egg whites to a stiff snow.
   Whip cream until thick. Fold
   alternately into gelatine mixture.
   When smooth and evenly combined (and all traces of streakiness have disappeared), pour into
   prepared dish, allowing Mousse
   to reach almost to top of paper
   band.
5 Refrigerate until firm and set.
   Very carefully remove paper then
   decorate top of Mousse with
   whipped cream and walnuts.
   Spoon on to plates.

Orange Mousse

SERVES 6 TO 8 ▲▲▲●●

Make exactly as directed for *Lemon
Mousse* but substitute 2 medium
oranges for the lemon. Spoon into 6
or 8 glasses and leave in refrigerator
until set. Before serving, sprinkle with
chopped pistachio or walnuts and
decorate with fresh orange slices.

Berry Fruit Mousse

SERVES 6 TO 8 ▲▲▲●●

Make exactly as directed for *Lemon
Mousse* but omit lemons and instead
add ½pt (275ml) very finely-crushed
raspberries or strawberries. Pour
into a soufflé dish or divide between
6 to 8 dishes.

Chocolate Mousse

SERVES 4 ▲▲▲●●

4oz (125g) plain chocolate
1oz (25g) butter
1tsp hot water
4 Grade 2 eggs, separated (kitchen
    temperature)
4tblsp double cream, whipped until
    thick
small pieces of extra plain chocolate
    for decoration

1 Break up chocolate and put, with
   pieces of butter, into basin standing over saucepan of hot, but not
   boiling water.

2 Leave until melted, stirring once or twice. Blend in water then beat in egg yolks.

3 Whisk egg whites to stiff snow. Beat about one quarter into chocolate mixture. Fold in remaining beaten whites with a large metal spoon.

4 When smoothly combined, transfer to 4 individual dishes. Refrigerate at least 4 hours. Decorate with cream and nuts before serving.

Chilled Mandarin Cheesecake

SERVES ABOUT 10   ▲▲▲●●●

BASE
4oz (125g) butter or margarine
8oz (225g) digestive biscuits, crushed
4 level tsp gelatine
1 can mandarin oranges, drained
1lb (900g) curd cheese or cottage cheese, rubbed through a fine mesh sieve
¼pt (150ml) double cream
2 Grade 3 eggs, separated
4oz (125g) caster sugar
finely-grated peel and juice of 1 medium lemon, washed and dried

DECORATION
reserved mandarin oranges
1oz (25g) plain chocolate, grated

1 Brush an 8in (20cm) spring clip tin (flat base with hinged sides) with a thin layer of melted unsalted butter.

2 Heat butter or margarine in pan. Add biscuits. Stir well to mix. Press thickly over base of tin.

3 Soften gelatine in 4 tablespoons mandarin syrup. Reserve 10 mandarins for decoration. Coarsely chop remainder. Tip gelatine and syrup mixture into saucepan and melt over low heat.

4 Place cheese into a bowl and beat in gelatine mixture. Stir in mandarins. Whip cream until thick and fold into cheese with egg yolks, sugar and grated peel and juice of lemon.

5 Leave until just beginning to thicken and set then fold in egg whites, beaten to a stiff snow. When smoothly combined, pour into prepared tin.

6 Refrigerate until firm and set. To unmould before serving, dip tin into hot water and hold for 5 seconds. This melts outside of mixture very slightly and enables sides of tin to be unclipped easily without dragging. If sides remain obstinate, dip tin in hot water for

another 5 seconds or so. Wipe dry. Leave cake on base.

7 Decorate top with reserved mandarins and grated chocolate then cut into portions with a knife dipped in hot water. Store leftovers in the refrigerator.

Summer Fruit Salad (page 117)

Gooseberry Cream Flan (page 118)

Pour into pan. Cook, stirring, until mixture comes to boil and thickens.

5 Simmer 2 minutes. Beat in egg yolks with butter or margarine. Pour into pastry case.

6 To make meringue, beat egg whites to a stiff snow. Gradually beat in sugar and continue beating until mixture is thick, white, glossy and feels heavy on the beaters.

7 Pile over pie, spreading meringue to edges of pastry. Stand on baking tray and bake for about $1\frac{1}{2}$ to 2 hours in oven set to 110°C (225°F), Gas $\frac{1}{4}$. It is essential that the meringue cooks slowly and dries out, otherwise it will 'weep' on standing. Serve pie very cold.

Summer Pudding

SERVES 6 ▲▲●●●

$1\frac{1}{2}$lb (675g) assorted berry fruits, fresh or frozen
4tblsp water
4oz (125g) caster sugar
6 large slices white bread, de-crusted
whipped cream to serve

1 Prepare fruit according to type if fresh and rinse. Tip into pan. If using frozen fruit, partially defrost and transfer to saucepan.

2 Add water. Bring to boil. Cover. Lower heat and simmer about 20 minutes or until soft and slightly pulpy. Tip in sugar and stir until dissolved.

3 Cut bread into fingers and use between a third and a half to line base and sides of a 2pt (1 litre) pudding basin.

4 Add half the fruit and top with some more bread. Fill with rest of fruit, cover with remaining bread fingers and weigh down with a saucer or plate and heavy garden stone.

5 Refrigerate overnight. Before serving, turn out into a dish and spoon portions on to plates. Serve with cream.

Baked Cheesecake

SERVES 10 ▲▲▲●●

biscuit base as given for Chilled Mandarin Cheesecake (page 119)
$1\frac{1}{2}$lb (675g) curd cheese or cottage cheese, rubbed through fine mesh sieve
6oz (175g) caster sugar
3 Grade 2 eggs
4oz (125g) butter, melted
1oz (25g) cornflour
1 level tsp vanilla essence
finely-grated peel and juice of 1 medium washed and dried lemon

1 Brush an 8in (20cm) spring clip tin (flat base with hinged sides) with a thin layer of melted unsalted butter.

2 Place cheese in large bowl then beat in all remaining ingredients. When smoothly mixed and even in texture, pour into tin.

3 Bake $1\frac{1}{4}$ hours in oven set to 150°C (300°F), Gas 3. Switch off oven heat, leave door open and allow cake to cool down for $\frac{1}{2}$ hour.

4 Remove from oven and leave until cold. Refrigerate overnight and unclip sides before cutting into wedges and serving.

Lemon Meringue Pie

SERVES 6 ▲▲▲●●

Shortcrust Pastry made with 6oz (175g) flour (page 186)
2 level tblsp cornflour
4 level tblsp caster sugar
finely-grated peel and strained juice of 3 medium-sized lemons, washed and dried
$\frac{1}{4}$pt (150ml) water
2 Grade 3 eggs, separated
2 rounded tsp butter or margarine
4oz (125g) extra caster sugar

1 Roll out pastry and use to line an 8in (20cm) greased sandwich tin or flan ring resting on greased baking tray.

2 Line base and sides with foil to prevent pastry from rising as it cooks. Bake 15 minutes in oven set to 220°C (425°F), Gas 7. Remove foil carefully. Return pastry case to oven for another 15 to 20 minutes or until golden brown and crisp-looking.

3 Remove from oven. Cool to lukewarm. Remove from tin or lift off flan ring. Transfer to a wire rack and leave till completely cold.

4 For filling, mix cornflour, sugar and lemon peel to a smooth paste with the lemon juice and water.

Trifle

SERVES 6 TO 8 ▲▲●●●

Much has been written about trifles and many recipes are to be found in assorted cook books. Yet few give the old English version which is nothing more than cake, jam, sherry, custard sauce, cream and a scattering of hundreds and thousands for decoration.

You can, if you like, use a homemade, jam-filled sponge sandwich (page 143), and break it into smallish pieces. Alternatively, buy 8 trifle sponge cakes, split each and sandwich together with raspberry jam. Cut into cubes. Place sponge sandwich or sponge cakes into mixing bowl. Moisten with sweet sherry then combine with homemade Egg Custard Sauce (page 176) or 1 pint (575ml) custard made with powder, milk and sugar. Toss over and over then transfer to glass serving dish. Cool. Whip ½ pint (275ml) double cream until thick with 4 level tablespoons caster sugar and 2 tablespoons milk. Pile over Trifle then sprinkle with hundreds and thousands.

Syllabub

SERVES 6 ▲▲●●●

¼pt (150ml) sweet white wine or cider
finely-grated peel and juice of 1 medium lemon
3oz (75g) caster sugar
½pt (275ml) double cream, taken from refrigerator

1 Pour wine or cider into bowl. Add lemon peel and juice and the sugar. Cover. Leave to stand at kitchen temperature for 4 hours.
2 Add cream and beat until mixture thickens and is softly stiff. Spoon into 6 wine-type glasses and refrigerate at least 6 to 8 hours before serving.

Ice Cream

I am not sure how many people actually go to the bother of making their own ice cream these days but for those who still do or would like to have a try, the recipe which follows gives superb results and is a personal favourite of my own family. The secret of its success lies in the addition of soured cream.

Vanilla Ice Cream

SERVES 8 TO 10 ▲▲▲●●●

½pt (275ml) double cream
½pt (275ml) single cream
1 carton (142ml or 5oz) soured cream
4 Grade 2 eggs
6oz (175g) caster sugar
2tsp vanilla essence

1 Beat double and single creams together until thick. Whisk in soured cream.
2 Separate eggs, putting whites into one bowl and yolks into another.
3 Beat whites to a stiff snow. Add half the sugar and continue beating until meringue is very thick and peaky.
4 Add rest of sugar to yolks. Beat until mixture lightens considerably in colour and forms a thick paste.

5 Using a large metal spoon, fold beaten whites and yolks alternately into whipped creams. Flavour by stirring in vanilla then transfer to an oblong dish which is suitable for the deep freeze.
6 Cover securely then freeze about 6 hours or until firm. Scoop into bowls or dishes and add a wafer to each.

To Vary

1 Use any other flavouring essence to taste such as almonds or rum.
2 Fold in grated chocolate for chocolate speckle.
3 Fold in chopped dried fruits and nuts for tutti-frutti.
4 Ripple in brightly-coloured liqueur such as Creme de Menthe (peppermint) or Cherry Brandy.

Orange Mousse (page 118)

121

Chocolate Mousse (page 118)

Fresh Fruit Ice

SERVES 8 ▲▲●●●

This is best homemade and is not too difficult to cope with.

> ½pt (275ml) fruit purée, made
>   from soft berry fruits
> 2 level tblsp golden syrup, melted
> 2 rounded tblsp caster sugar
> ½pt (275ml) double cream

1 Mix fruit purée with syrup and sugar.
2 Whip cream until thick and combine with fruit.
3 Pour into dish. Cover. Freeze 6 to 8 hours or until firm. Scoop into dishes to serve, and decorate with mint leaves.

Poires Belle Hélène

SERVES 4 ▲●●●

Place 2 or 3 scoops of vanilla ice cream into each of 4 sundae glasses. Top each with 2 canned pear halves, first well drained. Coat with hot Chocolate Sauce (page 184).

Peach Melba

SERVES 4 ▲▲●●

Make a raspberry purée by rubbing 8oz (225g) fresh or frozen raspberries through a sieve and sweetening to taste with icing sugar. Alternatively, blend raspberries and sugar (about 2oz or 50g caster) to smooth purée in blender goblet. Place 2 or 3 scoops of vanilla ice cream into each of 4 sundae glasses. Top each with a well-drained canned peach half then coat with raspberry purée.

Lemon Sorbet

SERVES ABOUT 8 ▲▲▲●●

> 9oz (250g) caster sugar
> ¾pt (425ml) water
> 3 large lemons
> 2 egg whites from Grade 2 eggs

1 Put sugar and water into saucepan. Wash and dry lemons. Peel thinly then add rind to pan. Warm gently, over medium heat, until sugar melts. Stir from time to time.

2 Squeeze lemons and strain juice into pan. Leave until completely cold. Remove lemon peel. Transfer mixture to shallow dish. Cover. Freeze until half-set.

3 Beat egg whites to a stiff snow. Beat lemon mixture until completely smooth then fold into whites with a large metal spoon.

4 Return to an oblong container. Cover securely. Freeze until firm. Scoop into small dishes to serve.

Orange Sorbet

SERVES ABOUT 8   ▲▲▲●●

Make exactly as *Lemon Sorbet* but omit lemons completely and use orange juice instead of water and the finely-grated peel of 1 medium washed and dried orange. If juice is unsweetened, keep amount of sugar the same. If already sweetened, use 6oz (175g) sugar.

Baked Alaska

SERVES 6   ▲▲●●●

Also known as Omelette Soufflé Suprème and Norwegian Omelet, Baked Alaska can be made as follows:

Stand a single layer of sponge cake or Victoria Sandwich Cake (page 00) on a heatproof plate. Moisten with sherry, port or fruit juice. Top with scoops of ice cream (flavour to taste). Coat COMPLETELY with meringue, made as directed for Lemon Meringue Pie (page 120). 'Flash' bake for 3 to 4 minutes in oven set to 230°C (450°F), Gas 8. DO NOT overcook or ice cream will melt; the meringue should be flecked with gold and this happens fairly quickly in a hot oven.

To Vary
Stud meringue with pieces of glacé fruits before baking.

Chilled Mandarin Cheesecake (page 119)

123

Sweetmeats

Sweetmeats

Making sweets at home is a non-routine, non-tedious way of creating all manner of attractive treats which can be enjoyed by one's own family or given away as seasonal gifts to appreciative friends. Over the years I have been asked many times for confectionery recipes by those who prefer home-made varieties to shop-bought, and by others who are often involved in producing truffles, toffees, fudge and the like for fêtes, bazaars, school open-days and bring-and-buy sales. In answer to all those requests, here is a mixed bag of sweetmeats with something in it for everyone — even simple, uncooked confections for children to make by themselves.

GUIDELINES

1 When making sweets which require boiling, choose a sturdy, deep saucepan in preference to a shallow one. Also make sure the base is strong, heavy and flat to prevent the sugar from catching and burning.
2 NEVER stir hot sugar mixtures with metal spoons as the handles will become uncomfortably hot. Avoid plastic implements as they will melt and/or become misshapen in the heat. Use a long wooden spoon for stirring whenever possible, or a spatula made from rubber and fitted to a wooden handle.
3 One of the most important rules is to grease a tin for toffee or fudge etc BEFORE starting to make the sweets. This is because any of these types of mixtures, with a high sugar content, sets quickly and may be difficult to spread smoothly if left to stand while a tin is being prepared.
4 Keep children well away from pans of boiling toffee etc and make sure the handle is facing towards the back of the cooker to prevent knocking it accidentally and causing the pan to topple. It is worth noting that syrup burns are very dangerous.
5 Spillage can cause an unpleasant mess which is extremely difficult to clean. Therefore watch the contents of the pan carefully to prevent boiling over.
6 In the past, sweet-making enthusiasts always invested in a sugar thermometer which registered the temperature of the boiling mixture. This, in turn, told one if the sweets had cooked for the required amount of time to set satisfactorily, and was an accurate gauge which eliminated guess work and doubt. However, in the absence of these somewhat costly thermometers, the following tests are reliable enough.

Soft Ball
This is a test for fudges and some other types of sweets. Pour a little of the boiling mixture into a cup of cold water. If it forms a soft ball which flattens between the fingers, then the mixture has cooked for long enough. (On sugar thermometer, 238°F to 240°F or 115°C.)

Hard but Malleable Ball
This is a test for soft toffees and caramels. Pour a little of the boiling mixture into a cup of cold water. If it forms a hard but malleable ball, then the mixture has cooked for long enough. (On sugar thermometer, 250°F or 121°C.)

Hard Threads Which Are Flexible
This is a test for hardish caramels. Pour a little of the boiling mixture into a cup of cold water. If it forms hard threads which bend without snapping, then the mixture has cooked for long enough. (On sugar thermometer, 280°F or 138°C.)

Hard Threads Which Are Brittle
This is a test for hard toffees, butterscotch and some caramels. Pour a little of the boiling mixture into a cup of cold water. If it forms hard threads which are brittle and crackly, then the mixture has cooked for long enough. (On sugar thermometer, 300°F or 149°C.)

TRUFFLES

A favourite with almost everyone, these are a delicious chocolate confection which requires no cooking at all. There are many kinds, but I shall begin with a basic recipe and simple variations.

Chocolate Vanilla Truffles

MAKES ABOUT 30   ▲▲●●●

12oz (350g) plain chocolate, broken into pieces
2oz (50g) butter
2 egg yolks (from Grade 3 eggs)
1tsp vanilla essence
4oz (125g) icing sugar, sifted

DECORATION
extra sifted icing sugar
sifted cocoa powder

1 Place chocolate and butter in basin standing over pan of hot, but not boiling, water. Leave up to 30 minutes or until both chocolate and butter have melted, stirring once or twice.
2 Remove basin from pan and wipe sides dry. Beat in egg yolks, essence and sugar. Leave until cold then refrigerate until mixture becomes firm but not hard.
3 Shape half the mixture into 15 logs; the other half into marbles. Coat some in icing sugar and the remainder in cocoa powder.
4 Transfer to paper sweet cases (optional) and store in the refrigerator up to 1 week or a cold larder up to about 4 days.

Chocolate Rum Truffles

MAKES ABOUT 30   ▲▲●●●

Follow recipe for *Chocolate Vanilla Truffles* but beat in 1 tablespoon dark rum instead of the vanilla. Coat truffles in chocolate vermicelli instead of sugar and/or cocoa.

Tip To help the chocolate vermicelli to stick, coat truffles first in a little lightly-beaten egg white.

Chocolate Whisky Truffles

MAKES ABOUT 30 ▲▲●●●

Follow recipe for *Chocolate Vanilla Truffles* but beat in 1 tablespoon whisky instead of the vanilla. Coat truffles in desiccated coconut instead of sugar and/or cocoa.

Chocolate Brandy Truffles

MAKES ABOUT 30 ▲▲●●●

Follow recipe for *Chocolate Vanilla Truffles* but beat in 1 tablespoon brandy instead of the vanilla. Coat truffles in finely-chopped hazelnuts or walnuts instead of sugar and/or cocoa.

Mocha Truffles

MAKES ABOUT 30 ▲▲●●●

Follow recipe for *Chocolate Vanilla Truffles* but beat in 3 level teaspoons instant coffee powder instead of the vanilla. Coat truffles in cocoa powder only.

Chocolate Almond Truffles

MAKES 24 ▲▲●●●

4oz (125g) plain chocolate, broken into pieces
2oz (50g) butter
2tblsp double cream
2 egg yolks (from Grade 3 eggs)
2oz (50g) ground almonds
6oz (175g) icing sugar, sifted

DECORATION
cocoa powder

1 Place chocolate and butter in basin standing over pan of hot, but not boiling, water. Leave up to 30 minutes or until both chocolate and butter have melted, stirring once or twice. Remove basin from pan and wipe sides dry.
2 Beat cream, egg yolks, almonds and sugar into chocolate mixture. Leave until cold then refrigerate until firm but not hard.
3 Shape into 24 balls and coat with cocoa powder. Transfer to paper sweet cases (optional) and store up to 1 week in the refrigerator or 2 to 3 days in a cold larder.

Chocolate Vanilla Truffles

Economical Chocolate Truffles

MAKES 24 ▲▲●●●

Follow recipe for *Chocolate Almond Truffles* but substitute cake crumbs for almonds.

Peppermint Creams

MAKES ABOUT 40 ▲▲●●●

1lb (450g) icing sugar
1tsp peppermint essence
2oz (50g) butter, melted
2tblsp double cream, heated to lukewarm
extra sifted icing sugar for rolling out

1 Sift icing sugar into bowl. Add essence, butter and cream.
2 Mix well to form a stiff paste, working in a little extra sifted icing sugar if mixture remains on sticky side.
3 Turn out on to surface dusted with icing sugar. Roll out to $\frac{1}{4}$in ($\frac{3}{4}$cm) in thickness. Cut into rounds with a 1in (2$\frac{1}{2}$cm) biscuit cutter, re-rolling and re-cutting trimmings to give the full amount.
4 Transfer to a tray or board lined with foil and leave until set. Store in the cool.

Chocolate Rum Truffles

Chocolate Peppermint Creams

MAKES ABOUT 40　▲▲●●

Follow recipe for *Peppermint Creams* but when set, brush tops with 3 to 4oz (75 to 100g) melted plain chocolate. Use a pastry brush and leave until set before eating.

Rose Creams

MAKES ABOUT 40　▲▲●●

Follow recipe for *Peppermint Creams* but use 1 teaspoon rose essence instead of peppermint. Also work in sufficient red colouring to tint mixture pale pink.

Left: Economical Chocolate Truffles (page 127); Right: Raisin Corn Crunchies (page 130); Centre: Marzipan Cherry 'Wafers' (page 131)

Lemon or Orange Creams

MAKES ABOUT 40　▲▲●●

Follow recipe for *Peppermint Creams* but add the very finely-grated peel of 1 lemon or small orange instead of peppermint essence. Also work in sufficient yellow or orange colouring to tint the mixture pale lemon or orange.

'Pistachio' Creams

MAKES ABOUT 40　▲▲●●

Follow recipe for *Peppermint Creams* but use 1 teaspoon almond or ratafia essence instead of peppermint. Also work in sufficient green colouring to tint the mixture light green.

Chocolate Marshmallows

MAKES 8OZ (225G)　▲●●●

4oz (125g) plain chocolate
½oz (15g) butter
4oz (125g) marshmallows

1 Break up chocolate and place, with butter, in basin standing over pan of hot, but not boiling, water. Leave about 30 minutes until melted, stirring once or twice.
2 Take a marshmallow and spear on to a wooden cocktail stick. Swirl around in the melted chocolate until completely coated.
3 Lift out and stand on a piece of greaseproof paper or foil. Leave until chocolate has set before eating.

Tip For parties, slide a glacé cherry on to each stick before serving the Chocolate Marshmallows.

Uncooked Chocolate Fudge

MAKES ABOUT 30 PIECES

▲▲●●●

4oz (125g) plain chocolate
3oz (75g) butter
1 Grade 3 egg, beaten
2tblsp sweetened condensed milk
1tsp vanilla essence
1lb (450g) icing sugar, sifted

1 Break up chocolate and place, with pieces of butter, in basin standing over pan of gently simmering water. Leave until both have melted, stirring once or twice.
2 Remove basin from pan and work in the egg, condensed milk, essence and icing sugar.
3 When smooth and evenly combined, spread into buttered tin measuring about 11 by 7in (27½ by 17½cm). Leave in a cool place until firm.
4 Cut into about 30 squares and store in an airtight tin in a cool place.

Uncooked Chocolate Nut Fudge

MAKES ABOUT 30 PIECES

▲▲●●●

Follow recipe for Uncooked Chocolate Fudge but work in 2 to 3oz (50 to 75g) coarsely-chopped hazelnuts at the same time as all the other ingredients.

Uncooked Chocolate Fruit and Nut Fudge

MAKES ABOUT 30 PIECES

▲▲●●●

Follow recipe for Uncooked Chocolate Fudge but work in 2oz (50g) EACH, sultanas and coarsely-chopped unsalted peanuts at the same time as all the other ingredients.

Uncooked Chocolate and Ginger Fudge

MAKES ABOUT 30 PIECES

▲▲●●●

Follow recipe for Uncooked Chocolate Fudge but work in 4oz (125g) coarsely-chopped, preserved ginger (in syrup) at the same time as all the other ingredients.

Vanilla Fudge

MAKES ABOUT 25 TO 30 PIECES

▲▲▲●●

1lb (450g) granulated sugar
2oz (50g) butter or margarine
¼pt (150ml) single cream or unsweetened evaporated milk (canned)
2tsp vanilla essence

1 Brush a 6in (15cm) square tin or small roasting tin with butter. Place all ingredients into heavy-based saucepan.
2 Heat gently, stirring continuously, until sugar dissolves and butter melts.
3 Increase heat slightly and boil mixture, uncovered, about 15 to 20 minutes or until it reaches the soft ball stage (page 126). Stir frequently to prevent sticking.
4 Take pan off heat. Cool fudge mixture for 15 minutes. Beat steadily until it loses its shine and is thick and creamy.
5 Spread evenly into tin. Cut into squares when cold. Store in an airtight tin.

Chocolate Fudge

MAKES ABOUT 25 TO 30 PIECES

▲▲▲●●

Follow recipe for Vanilla Fudge but melt 2oz (50g) plain chocolate in the milk with the sugar and butter or margarine. Also add, at the same time as the essence, 1 level tablespoon sifted cocoa powder.

Cherry Nut Fudge

MAKES ABOUT 25 TO 30 PIECES

▲▲▲●●

Follow recipe for Vanilla Fudge. After mixture has cooled for 15 minutes, add 2oz (50g) EACH, coarsely-chopped glacé cherries and walnuts. Beat etc as directed.

Coffee Fudge

MAKES ABOUT 25 TO 30 PIECES

▲▲▲●●

Follow recipe for Vanilla Fudge but add 1 level tablespoon instant coffee powder or granules instead of vanilla.

Peppermint Lumps

MAKES ABOUT 12oz (350G)

▲▲●●

1oz (25g) butter
4 level tblsp caster sugar
2 level tblsp golden syrup
½tsp peppermint essence
3½oz (90g) instant dried, low-fat skimmed milk granules
sifted icing sugar

1 Place butter, sugar and syrup into heavy-based saucepan.
2 Stir over low heat until butter melts. Increase heat and boil fairly briskly for 2 minutes ONLY when a little of the mixture, dropped into a cup of cold water, forms a soft ball (page 126).
3 Remove from heat. Add essence. Stir in milk granules and spoon on to plate. Leave until cool enough to handle, then shape into 4in (10cm) lengths.
4 Roll in sifted icing sugar then cut into ½in (1¼cm) pieces with sharp knife. Store in an airtight tin when cold.

Tips
1 To measure syrup easily, use metal spoon and dip in boiling water before spooning syrup out of tin or jar.
2 Do NOT allow mixture to cool off too much as it will be impossible to cut.

Milky Vanilla Candies

MAKES 18

▲●●

1oz (25g) butter or margarine
2 level tblsp golden syrup
1oz (25g) soft brown sugar
1tsp vanilla essence
3½oz (90g) instant dried, low-fat skimmed milk granules
drinking chocolate for coating

1 Place butter or margarine, syrup and sugar into heavy-based pan. Leave over low heat until butter melts, stirring.
2 Take pan off heat. Add essence. Stir in milk granules. Mix in well with wooden spoon.
3 When cool enough to handle, roll into 18 balls between hands. Toss in drinking chocolate, tipped on to greaseproof paper or foil.
4 Leave 1 hour before eating. Store in an airtight tin when cold.

129

Milky Peppermint Candies

MAKES 18   ▲▲●●

Follow recipe for *Milky Vanilla Candies*, but use ½ teaspoon almond essence instead of vanilla.

Milky Orange Candies

MAKES 18   ▲▲●●

Follow recipe for *Milky Vanilla Candies*, but add 1 level teaspoon finely-grated orange peel instead of vanilla.

Raisin Corn Crunchies

MAKES 16 TO 18   ▲▲●●●

1oz (25g) unsalted peanuts
6oz (175g) plain chocolate, broken into pieces
½oz (15g) butter
6oz (175g) seedless raisins
2 heaped tblsp cornflakes, slightly crushed

1 Coarsely chop nuts. Put chocolate and butter into basin standing over pan of hot, but not boiling, water. Leave until melted, stirring once or twice.
2 Remove basin from pan and wipe sides dry. Stir peanuts, raisins and cornflakes into chocolate mixture.
3 Using 2 teaspoons, place 16 to 18 neat little mounds of mixture on to a piece of greaseproof paper or foil.
4 Leave in the cool until set. Store in the refrigerator.

Marzipan Toffee Apricots

MAKES 20   ▲▲▲●●

20 large, dried apricots (plump and soft)
4oz (125g) marzipan (shop-bought)
8oz (225g) caster sugar
2tblsp cold water

1 Well wash apricots and dry thoroughly. Cut each in half.
2 Cut marzipan into 20 equal-sized pieces. Use to sandwich apricot halves together. Secure by spearing with wooden cocktail sticks.

130

3 Tip sugar into pan. Add water. Stir over low heat until melted. Bring to the boil. Cover for 1 minute. Uncover. Boil fairly briskly until sugar turns a warm gold and forms into brittle threads (page 126) when a little of the mixture is poured into a cup of cold water. Remove pan from heat.
4 Quickly swirl apricots round in the syrup. Lift out on to a piece of aluminium foil. Leave until cold and set before eating. Store in a dry place to prevent the toffee from becoming sticky.

Marzipan Toffee Apricots

Toffee

MAKES ABOUT 1 LB (450G)   ▲▲▲▲●●

4oz (125g) golden syrup
4tblsp water
2oz (50g) butter
1lb (450g) caster sugar
2tsp light malt vinegar

1 Brush an 8 by 6in tin (22½ by 17½cm) with melted butter or margarine.
2 Pour syrup and water into a heavy-based, deep pan. Add butter, sugar and vinegar. Stir until butter and sugar have melted.
3 Bring to boil. Cover for 30 seconds as this helps to prevent crystallization. Uncover. Increase heat slightly.
4 Boil toffee fairly briskly, uncovered, for about 12 to 18 minutes or until a little of the mixture forms hard threads which are flexible (page 126) when a little of the mixture is poured into a cup of cold water. Remove from heat.
5 Pour into prepared tin and leave until set. Tip out on to a board and break into pieces with a small hammer.

Brazil Nut Toffee

MAKES ABOUT 1¼ LB (550G)   ▲▲▲●●●

Follow recipe for *Toffee* but stir in 4oz (125g) coarsely-chopped Brazil nuts immediately after removing from heat.

Treacle Toffee

MAKES ABOUT 1¼ LB (550G)   ▲▲▲●●●

Follow recipe for *Toffee* but add 4oz (125g) black treacle in addition to syrup. Increase water to 8 tablespoons. Use soft brown sugar instead of caster. Reduce vinegar to 1 teaspoon.

Butterscotch

MAKES ABOUT 1 LB 2OZ (500G)   ▲▲●●●

¼pt (150ml) water
1lb (450g) demerara sugar
3oz (75g) butter

1 Well butter a 6in (10cm) square tin. Place all ingredients into a large, heavy-based pan.
2 Cook over low heat, stirring, until sugar dissolves and butter melts. Bring to a gentle boil. Cover for 1 minute to prevent crystallization. Uncover. Increase heat slightly.
3 Boil butterscotch fairly briskly, uncovered, for about 12 to 15 minutes or until a little of the mixture forms hard threads which are brittle (page 126).
4 Pour carefully into prepared tin. When almost set, mark into bars with a knife dipped in butter.
5 Break when hard and wrap each bar separately in aluminium foil.

Honeycomb

MAKES ABOUT 8OZ (225G) ▲▲●●

3 level tblsp clear honey
5 level tblsp caster sugar
4tblsp hot water
½oz (15g) butter
½tsp EACH, vinegar and soda bicarbonate

1 Place all ingredients, except soda bicarbonate, into a heavy saucepan.
2 Stir over a low heat until sugar and honey dissolve and butter melts.
3 Bring slowly to boil. Cover for 30 seconds to prevent crystallization. Uncover. Increase heat slightly.
4 Boil honeycomb, uncovered and without stirring, for about 5 to 7 minutes or until a little of the mixture forms hard, brittle threads when dropped into a cup of cold water (page 126). Meanwhile, butter a small tin.
5 Take off heat. Stir in soda bicarbonate when mixture will immediately foam up in the pan.
6 Pour into prepared tin and leave until set. Break up and eat. Do not keep, as honeycomb rapidly becomes sticky.

Peanut Toffee Crunch

MAKES ABOUT 50 PIECES ▲▲●●

10oz (275g) soft brown sugar (dark variety)
6oz (175g) golden syrup
¼pt (150ml) warm water
2oz (50g) butter or margarine
1tsp vanilla essence
8oz (225g) unsalted peanuts, coarsely chopped

1 Brush a 7in (17½cm) square tin with butter or margarine. Place all ingredients, except peanuts, into a fairly deep and heavy-based pan.
2 Cook over medium heat, stirring, until sugar dissolves and butter melts. Bring to boil. Cover for 30 seconds to prevent crystallization. Uncover.
3 Boil steadily about 12 to 15 minutes or until a little of the mixture forms hard, brittle threads when dropped into a cup of cold water (page 126).
4 Stir in nuts then pour toffee into prepared tin. Leave until hard then break into pieces with a small hammer. Store in an airtight container.

Praline

▲▲●●

To make, crush up as much *Peanut Toffee Crunch* as you think you will need for a recipe such as homemade ice cream. For a luxury touch, use hazelnuts instead of peanuts.

Caramels

MAKES ABOUT 36 ▲▲●●

4oz (125g) soft brown sugar, light variety
4oz (125g) soft brown sugar, dark variety
2oz (50g) golden syrup
4tblsp single cream
2oz (50g) butter
1tsp vanilla essence

1 Brush a 6in (15cm) square tin with melted butter or margarine.
2 Place all ingredients into a tall and heavy-based pan. Stir over low heat until sugars have dissolved. Bring to the boil. Cover for 30 seconds to prevent crystallization. Uncover.
3 Boil steadily, stirring frequently, for about 15 minutes or until a little of the mixture forms a hard but malleable ball (page 126) when dropped into a cup of cold water.

4 Pour into prepared tin and leave until set. Turn out of tin on to a board and cut or saw into squares. Wrap each in cellophane paper or cling film.

Coconut Ice

MAKES ABOUT 40 PIECES ▲▲▲●●

¼pt (150ml) milk
1lb (450g) caster sugar
6oz (175g) desiccated coconut
1½tsp vanilla essence
red food colouring

1 Brush an 8in (20cm) square tin with melted butter. Place milk and sugar into a sturdy saucepan. Stir over low heat until sugar dissolves. Bring to the boil. Cover for 30 seconds to prevent crystallization. Uncover.
2 Boil steadily for 7 to 10 minutes or until a small amount of mixture forms a soft ball (page 126) when dropped into a cup of cold water.
3 Take pan off heat. Stir in coconut and essence. Cool 5 minutes. Beat briskly until mixture is fairly thick and creamy.
4 Spread half into prepared tin. Tint rest of coconut ice pale pink with a few drops of food colouring. Spread over white portion in tin.
5 Leave in the cold until firm and set. Cut into squares. Store in an airtight tin.

Marzipan Cherry 'Wafers'

MAKES 20 ▲●●●

4oz (125g) ground almonds
2oz (50g) icing sugar, sifted
2oz (50g) caster sugar
½tsp almond essence
¼tsp vanilla essence
1 egg yolk
10 glacé cherries, halved

1 Tip all ingredients into a bowl, except cherries. Knead together with fingers to form a pliable but non-sticky paste.
2 Turn out on to a surface dusted with sifted icing sugar. Shape into 20 marbles with sugared hands.
3 Flatten slightly then place half a cherry on each. Leave in the cool until firm before eating. Store in an airtight tin.

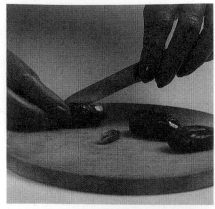

1 Stone dates

2 Fill each with a whole blanched almond

3 Enclose each date with marzipan

4 Dip end of each date in melted chocolate

Marzipan and Almond Chocolate Dates

MAKES ABOUT 1LB (450G)

▲▲▲●●●

Make up marzipan exactly as given in the recipe for *Marzipan Cherry 'Wafers'*. Stone 8oz (225g) dates. Fill each with a whole, blanched almond, using a total of about 3oz (75g). Roll out marzipan fairly thinly. Cut into squares large enough to wrap round each date and enclose it completely. Melt 4oz (125g) plain chocolate in basin over hot water. Dip end of each date into melted chocolate as shown in the photograph. Leave to set on greaseproof paper or foil.

Marzipan and Almond Chocolate Dates

Teatime Assortment

Teatime Assortment

Home baking always brings pleasing rewards and what can equal the delicious flavour and welcoming aroma of freshly-made cakes, pastries and biscuits? I know not everyone feels confident when it comes to turning out a feather-light sponge, a well-risen Madeira and costly Almond Macaroons so I hope the guidelines and recipes which follow will dispel some of the worries and provide enough inspiration to get you started on traditional teatime favourites and special occasion treats such as the ever popular éclairs, meringues, white-iced Christmas Cake and crisp, melt-in-the-mouth, buttery shortbreads.

GUIDELINES

Plain Cakes

These are cakes made by the rubbing-in method and the proportion is up to half fat to flour; for example 3 to 4oz (75 to 125g) fat to every 8oz (225g) flour. The fat is rubbed into the sifted flour etc until the mixture looks like a mass of fine breadcrumbs (see Shortcrust Pastry on page 186), sugar is then added and so are either dried fruits, nuts, coconut etc. The cake is then stirred briskly to a thickish consistency with unbeaten eggs and either milk (the most usual) or fruit juice (occasionally). The flour may be self-raising or plain but if the latter is used, 2 level teaspoons baking powder should be sifted with every 8oz (225g) flour. The term 'plain' may be misleading to some of you because, with their assorted additions, most of these cakes are anything but. However, 'plain' in this case refers only to the ratio of fat to flour and is one of those technical terms cookery writers have grown up with and continue to use! Typical cakes under this category are Family or Everyday Fruit Cake and Rock Buns.

Rich Cakes

These are cakes made by the creaming method in which the chosen fat and sugar are beaten together until they form a light, soft and fluffy mixture not unlike whipped cream in colour and appearance. A wooden spoon, electric beaters or a work-top mixer may be used for this operation. Whole eggs at kitchen temperature are then beaten in, followed by any additions listed in the recipe. Sifted dry ingredients are folded in last with a large metal spoon or plastic spatula. The proportion of fat to flour is anything from half to equal; 4 to 8oz (125 to 225g) fat to every 8oz (225g) flour. Again, plain or self-raising flour may be used but please refer to individual recipes for the amount of baking powder to add with plain flour as the quantity decreases as the ratio of fat increases. Typical examples of rich cakes are Victoria Sandwich, Madeira, Fairy and Christmas.

Sponge Cakes

These are fatless cakes made only from 3 ingredients; eggs, sugar and flour in the ratio of one, one and one upwards. This means 1 Grade 3 egg is used to every 1oz (25g) caster sugar and 1oz (25g) flour and so on. The flour may be either plain or self-raising if the mixture is baked in shallow sandwich tins, but MUST be plain if baked in a deep tin to prevent the cake from rising up too much initially and then sinking in the middle. Sponge cakes are made by what is called the whisking method in which the egg or eggs and sugar are beaten together until they thicken considerably and billow like clouds; 1 Grade 3 egg and 1oz (25g) caster sugar will, if beaten long enough, bulk up to 6 fluid oz (175g) so the usual 3 egg sponge mixture for 2 × 7in (or 17½cm) sandwich tins will produce quite a bowlful of thick froth before the flour is added. Sponge cakes are light and airy but, because of their lack of fat, stale quickly and are best eaten freshly made. They make an excellent base for trifles and fancy layered cakes filled and covered with cream or butter cream.

'Melted' Method Cakes

These are moist, spicy, dark-coloured cakes which improve with keeping and should be left a minimum of 1 day before cutting. Ingredient combinations tend to vary from one cookery writer to another but the basic technique of making remains the same; the fat, syrup and/or treacle plus fat are always melted slowly together before being combined with the eggs and dry ingredients. A typical example of a cake made by the melting method is Gingerbread.

All-Together Cakes

Also known as easy-mix cakes, these are quick and simple to make in that all the ingredients are put into a bowl and beaten together for 2 to 3 minutes until well blended. The ingredients are similar to those used for Rich Cakes but up to 1 level teaspoon of baking powder is added to every 4oz (125g) self-raising flour in order to give the cakes the necessary 'lift'. As with other cakes in this group, the amount of baking powder is decreased as the proportions of fat and eggs are increased. The usual fats for these cakes are whipped-up fats which are also called 'easy-cream'. For the most satisfactory results, all the ingredients should be at kitchen temperature.

WRONGS AND REASONS

Rubbed-in Cakes

Heavy
1 Plain flour used with insufficient baking powder.
2 Insufficient fat used and/or it was soft and oily before being rubbed in.
3 Too much liquid added.
4 Oven not hot enough.

Texture full of holes
1 Fat rubbed in coarsely.
2 Mixture over-stirred or beaten after liquid was added.

Crust hard, shiny and/or sugary-looking
1 Too much sugar added.
2 Cake overcooked.
3 Oven temperature too high.

Creamed Cakes

Heavy and texture close
1 Insufficient creaming of fat and sugar.
2 Eggs added too quickly and/or not beaten into creamed ingredients thoroughly enough.
3 Eggs taken straight from the refrigerator.
4 Not enough baking powder used with plain flour.
5 Oven set too high or too low.

Texture peppered with large holes
Dry ingredients beaten into creamed ingredients instead of being folded in.

Plain and Rich Cakes

Cake peaked in centre or badly cracked
1 Oven too high.
2 Cake too near top of oven.
3 Cake tin too small for quantity of mixture.

Fruit sunk
1 If fruit washed, not properly dried.
2 Mixture too wet.
3 Oven not hot enough.

Cake sunk
1 Too much baking powder used with plain flour, or self-raising flour used where plain flour was recommended.
2 Whipped-up or 'easy-cream' margarine substituted for recommended amount of butter.
3 Mixture too wet.
4 Oven door opened and closed quickly during the early stages of baking.
5 Oven not hot enough.

Sponge Cakes

Poorly risen and biscuit-like in texture
1 Eggs and sugar under-whisked. Each egg and 1oz (25g) caster sugar should yield 6 fluid oz (175ml).
2 Flour stirred in heavily or beaten into whisked eggs and sugar.
3 Oven too hot.

Heavy and tacky
1 Too much sugar added.
2 Oven too hot or too cool.
3 Undercooked.

Deep sponge sunk
1 Self-raising flour used.
2 Oven too high.
3 Cake removed from oven too soon.

Swiss Roll Breaks
1 Too biscuity (see previous reasons).
2 Overcooked.
3 Too thin; too little mixture for size of tin.
4 Left too long before rolling and/or crisp edges not cut off.

'Melted' Method Cakes (Gingerbreads)

Middle sunk
1 Too much raising agent used (usually soda bicarbonate).
2 Too much syrup and/or treacle added.
3 Oven too hot.
4 Cake baked too high up in oven.

Top shiny and texture close and heavy
1 Overbeaten.

Top cracked and texture dry
1 Insufficient liquid used in proportion to dry ingredients.
2 Too much or too little raising agent added.
3 Oven too hot.
4 Cake baked too high up in oven.

All-Together Cakes

If these do go wrong, it is generally due to the addition of very cold, hard fat and overbeating.

General Hints and Tips for all cakes
1 Unless otherwise stated, bake cakes in oven centre. If using a fan oven when temperature is uniform throughout, any position is suitable.
2 It is best to grease and line cake tins with greaseproof paper and then brush the paper with melted fat. If using non-stick parchment paper, it is unnecessary to grease the tins or paper. For safety, lightly grease non-stick tins and line base with paper.
3 To test if cake is cooked sufficiently, push a wooden cocktail stick or thin skewer gently into the centre. If it comes out absolutely clean with no uncooked pieces of mixture sticking to it, then the cake is ready.
4 Leave large cakes between 10 and 15 minutes before turning out of the tin to prevent breakage; shallow cakes about 5 to 7 minutes.
5 ALWAYS cool cakes on wire racks, otherwise the texture will be heavy.
6 Store cakes in an airtight tin, separately from biscuits. If kept together, the biscuits will soften rapidly.
7 Except for sponges and other very plain mixtures, cakes improve if left about 8 hours before cutting.
8 Most cakes can be deep-frozen up to 2 months. For heavily-decorated cakes covered with whipped cream or butter cream, freeze uncovered until hard. Afterwards wrap securely and store in a box. Open up before defrosting or the wrapping will stick to the cream etc and destroy the appearance.
9 If a round tin of a certain diameter — say 7in or 17½cm — is recommended in a recipe and you want to use a square tin, choose one which is 1in (2½cm) smaller; 6in or 15cm. The same applies for all sizes.

ICINGS (BASIC)

Glacé Icing

▲●●

This is used to cover tops of cakes such as Victoria Sandwiches and pastries. It can also be used to cover a fancy cake completely but has a tendency to crack. It can be coloured and flavoured according to taste.

8oz (225g) icing sugar
6 to 8tsp warm water

1 Sift icing sugar into bowl. Stir in sufficient water to form an icing which is thick enough to coat the back of a spoon without running off.
2 Use immediately, spreading icing over top and sides of cake with a knife. Leave until set before moving.
3 This amount will cover the top of a 7 to 8in (17½ to 20cm) round cake or oblong cake baked in 2lb (1kg) loaf tin. For sides as well, double the amount.

Note Add flavourings to the sugar (such as essences, coffee powder or grated fruit peel) and colourings with the water. If preferred, mix sugar to an icing with fruit juice (strained), tea or coffee.

135

Chocolate Glacé Icing

▲▲●●●

2oz (50g) plain chocolate
1 rounded tsp butter or margarine
2tsp warm water
¼tsp flavouring essence (almond, vanilla, rum, sherry etc)
6oz (175g) icing sugar, sifted

1 Break chocolate into basin standing over saucepan of hot water. Add butter or margarine. Leave until melted.
2 Stir until smooth then gradually mix in water, essence and icing sugar. Use straightaway, spreading over top of 7 to 8in (17½ to 20cm) cake.

Whipped Cream Icing

▲●●

¼pt (150ml) double cream
1 rounded tblsp icing sugar, sifted
1tblsp cold milk

1 Place all ingredients into bowl. Whip until thick. Use to fill centre and cover top of 7in (17½cm) 2-layer sponge or sandwich cake.
2 For filling only, halve the above amount. If covering sides as well, double above amount.

Note It is not usual to colour Whipped Cream Icing, though it may be flavoured with essence to taste.

Butter Cream

▲▲●●●

This is one of the most popular fillings and icings worldwide because it takes well to colouring and flavouring, is easy to pipe and sets firmly without damage. Its flavour is completely ruined if made with margarine though for economy, one-third margarine to two-thirds butter may be used. The amount below is sufficient to fill and cover top of a 7 to 8in (17½ to 20cm) 2-layer sponge or sandwich cake. For filling only, halve the amounts. If covering the sides as well, double the amounts.

4oz (125g) unsalted butter, softened but not oily
8oz (225g) icing sugar, sifted
2tblsp cold milk

1 Beat butter until light. Gradually work in sugar alternately with milk. Cream with electric beaters or wooden spoon until very light in colour, pale in texture and fluffy.
2 Leave in the refrigerator to firm up slightly before using.

Butter Cream (flavoured and/or coloured)

▲▲●●●

Follow above recipe but add grated fruit peel to the butter and sugar mixture, or flavouring essences with the milk. Colour by adding a few drops of liquid edible food colour when the Butter Cream is made.

Chocolate Butter Cream

▲▲●●●

Follow recipe for *Butter Cream* but reduce milk to 2 teaspoons and add 2oz (50g) melted and cooled plain, dark chocolate and ½ teaspoon vanilla essence to the beaten butter alternately with the sugar.

Almond Paste

▲▲●●●

The amount below will generously cover top and sides of an 8 to 9in (20 to 22½cm) round cake.

8oz (225g) ground almonds
8oz (225g) caster sugar
8oz (225g) icing sugar, sifted
yolks of 2 Grade 3 eggs
1tsp almond essence
¼tsp vanilla essence
1tsp lemon juice

1 Tip almonds and both sugars into a bowl. Run the fingers through as though it were sand so that ingredients are well mixed.
2 Add egg yolks, essences and lemon juice. Fork-mix to a paste.
3 Turn out on to a surface dusted with sifted icing sugar and knead lightly, with sugared fingers, until almond paste is smooth and crack-free. Use as required.

Marzipan

Marzipan is made from equal quantities of ground almonds and sugar, and mixed with egg whites and flavourings to taste. Because it is now so costly to prepare, no recipe has been included. Almond paste makes an admirable substitute and has been used throughout this book in place of Marzipan.

Royal Icing

▲▲▲●●

This is the traditional icing used for covering all celebratory cakes, whether they be for Christmas or weddings. The addition of a little glycerine (tasteless and harmless) prevents the icing from becoming rock hard and almost impossible to cut. The amount below is sufficient to cover top and sides of an 8 to 9in (20 to 22½cm) cake. For top only, halve the amounts.

whites from 3 Grade 3 eggs
1tsp lemon juice
1½lb (675g) icing sugar, sifted
1½tsp glycerine (available from chemists)

1 Put whites into a clean, dry bowl. Add lemon juice. Beat until foamy.
2 Gradually beat in icing sugar and continue beating until icing is snow-like in appearance and stands in peaks when beaters are lifted out of bowl. Beat in glycerine.
3 Transfer to a plastic container with airtight lid. Seal securely and leave to stand about 6 hours at kitchen temperature to give air bubbles an opportunity of dispersing and prevent a pin hole effect in the icing. (Essential if the icing is to be spread smoothly.)
4 For speed, cover bowl with a damp cloth and leave to stand for 1 to 2 hours.

American Snow Frosting

▲▲▲●●

This is an unusual icing which is crisp on the outside and soft and a bit marshmallowy underneath. Although sweet, its lack of fat makes it non-rich and ideal for walnut and chocolate cakes. The amount below will fill and cover top and sides of 3 × 7in (17½cm) sandwich cakes, 2 × 8in (20cm) sandwich cakes, or 1 × 7 to 8in (17½ to 20cm) deep cake cut into 2 or 3 layers.

136

1lb (450g) granulated sugar
6tblsp water
whites of 2 Grade 3 eggs
½tsp lemon juice
1tsp vanilla essence

1 Tip sugar into a saucepan. Add water. Melt over low heat, stirring. Bring to boil. Lower heat. Cover. Boil gently 1 minute. Uncover.
2 Boil briskly 5 to 6 minutes or until a little of the mixture, poured into a cup of very cold water, forms a soft ball when rolled between finger and thumb. If no ball forms, boil a minute or two longer.
3 While the mixture is boiling, beat egg whites and lemon juice to a very stiff snow. As soon as syrup has boiled for long enough, pour it on to egg white mixture in a slow, steady stream, beating continuously all the time.
4 Stir in vanilla. Check for consistency and beat on until Frosting is cool and is thick enough to spread without running.
5 Fill and ice cakes or cake fairly smartly as icing sets quickly when it is cold. Leave to stand about 1 hour before cutting.

PLAIN CAKES

Everyday Fruit Cake

MAKES A 6IN (15CM) ROUND OR 1LB (450G) LOAF CAKE
▲▲●●

8oz (225g) self-raising flour
pinch of salt
4oz (125g) butter, block margarine, white cooking fat or lard (or mixture)
4oz (125g) caster sugar
3oz (75g) mixed dried fruit (currants, sultanas and raisins)
1 level tsp finely-grated lemon peel
1 Grade 3 egg
5tblsp cold milk to mix

1 Grease and paper-line a 6in (15cm) round cake tin or 1lb (450g) oblong loaf tin.
2 Sift flour and salt into bowl. Rub in fat or fats finely with fingertips. Toss in sugar and fruit.
3 Add lemon peel. Using a fork, mix to a fairly soft consistency with unbeaten egg (broken into a cup

Everyday Fruit Cake

first to check for freshness) and the milk, stirring briskly without beating.
4 Transfer to prepared tin, tap gently up and down to release air bubbles, then bake cake for 1¼ to 1½ hours in oven set to 180°C (350°F), Gas 4, when cake should be well risen and golden brown.
5 Check for doneness with wooden cocktail stick or skewer (see General Hints and Tips on page 135) and leave to stand 10 to 15 minutes before turning out on to a wire cooling rack.
6 Store in an airtight tin when completely cold and remove lining paper just before cutting.

Date and Cinnamon Cake

▲▲●●

Follow recipe and method for *Everyday Fruit Cake* but sift flour and salt with 2 level teaspoons cinnamon. Add 3oz (75g) chopped, stoned dates instead of mixed fruit.

Spicy Walnut and Raisin Cake

▲▲●●

Follow recipe and method for *Everyday Fruit Cake* but sift flour and salt with 1 level teaspoon mixed spice. Add 2oz (50g) chopped walnuts and 2oz (50g) seedless raisins instead of mixed fruit.

Coconut Cake

▲▲●●

Follow recipe and method for *Everyday Fruit Cake* but omit fruit and add 2oz (50g) desiccated coconut instead. Increase milk to 7 tablespoons (as dried coconut absorbs moisture) and with it add 1 teaspoon vanilla essence.

Rock Buns

MAKES 10
▲●●

8oz (225g) self-raising flour
pinch of salt
4oz (125g) butter or margarine
3oz (75g) caster sugar
4oz (125g) mixed dried fruit
1 Grade 3 egg, beaten
1tsp vanilla essence
about 3tsp cold milk to mix

1 Sift flour and salt into bowl. Rub in butter or margarine finely. Toss in sugar and fruit.
2 Using a fork, mix to STIFF consistency with egg, essence and milk.
3 Spoon 10 rocky mounds of mixture on to lightly-greased and floured tray, leaving room between each for slight spreading.
4 Bake until well risen and golden brown; 15 to 20 minutes in oven set to 200°C (400°F), Gas 6.
5 Cool on a wire rack and store in an airtight tin when completely cold.

137

Orange Cake

Cherry Cake

MAKES 1 × 7IN (17½CM)
ROUND CAKE ▲▲●●●

As most Cherry Cakes end up with sunken fruit, this is the best of what I can only describe as a bad bunch, tried and tried again over many years! It is ESSENTIAL to wash and dry the cherries thoroughly in order to remove some of the heavy syrup which makes them drop to the bottom.

4oz (125g) glacé cherries
8oz (225g) plain flour
2oz (50g) semolina
2½ level tsp baking powder
¼ level tsp salt
5oz (150g) butter or block
    margarine
4oz (125g) caster sugar
½tsp vanilla essence
½tsp almond essence
½ level tsp finely-grated lemon peel
2 Grade 3 eggs
2 to 3tblsp cold milk

1 Quarter cherries and tip into bowl. Cover with warm water and leave to soak for 10 minutes. Drain. Dry THOROUGHLY in clean teatowel. Toss with 2 level tablespoons plain flour, taken from measured amount.
2 Sift rest of flour, semolina, baking powder and salt into a bowl. Rub in butter or margarine until mixture looks like a mass of breadcrumbs.

3 Toss in sugar and cherries. Beat rest of ingredients well together. Stir into cake mixture with a wooden spoon and mix to a semi-stiff consistency, stirring gently until all ingredients are evenly combined.
4 Transfer to a 7in (17½cm) greased and lined cake tin (see General Hints and Tips on page 135) and bake until well risen and golden brown, allowing about 1¼ to 1½ hours in oven set to 180°C (350°F), Gas 4.
5 Leave in the tin about 15 minutes then turn out and cool on a wire rack. Store in airtight tin and re-move lining paper before cutting.

RICH CAKES

Madeira Cake

MAKES 1 × 7IN ROUND CAKE
OR 1 OBLONG CAKE, BAKED IN
2LB (1KG) LOAF TIN ▲▲▲●●●

8oz (225g) plain flour
1 level tsp baking powder
¼ level tsp salt
6oz (175g) butter or block
    margarine, kitchen temperature
6oz (175g) caster sugar
4 Grade 3 eggs, kitchen
    temperature
finely-grated peel of 1 medium
    washed and dried lemon
2 strips citron peel (optional)

1 Sift flour, baking powder and salt on to a plate. In large bowl, cream butter and sugar together until light, fluffy and the consistency of whipped cream.
2 Break eggs, one at a time, into a cup to check for freshness. Beat individually into creamed mixture with all the lemon peel and 1 rounded tablespoon dry ingredients with each egg to prevent curdling (which in turn can make the cake heavy).
3 Using a large metal spoon, gently and lightly fold dry ingredients into creamed mixture, flipping mixture over and over on itself and NOT BEATING.
4 When smooth and evenly combined, transfer to greased and lined tin (see General Hints and Tips on page 135) and tap gently up and down to disperse air bubbles.
5 Bake ¾ hour in oven set to 160°C (325°F), Gas 3. Place citron peel on top. Continue to bake a further hour when cake should be well risen and golden brown.
6 Leave in tin ¼ hour then turn out and cool on a wire rack. Store in an airtight tin when completely cold. Remove paper before cutting.

Orange Cake

▲▲▲●●●

Make exactly as *Madeira Cake*, but add the finely-grated peel of 1 large washed and dried orange instead of the lemon. Omit citron peel.

Ginger Cake

▲▲▲●●●

Make exactly as *Madeira Cake*, but sift 2 to 3 level teaspoons powdered ginger (depending on taste) with the flour, baking powder and salt. Omit lemon and citron peel.

Almond Cake

▲▲▲●●●

Make exactly as *Madeira Cake* but cream fat and sugar with ½ teaspoon almond essence, and add 2oz (50g) ground almonds AFTER beating in eggs. Add also 1 tablespoon milk. Omit citron peel.

Ginger Cake

Marble Cake

Christmas Cake

MAKES 1 × 8IN (20CM) ROUND
CAKE OR 1 × 7IN (17½CM)
SQUARE ▲▲▲●●●

8oz (225g) plain flour
1 level tblsp chocolate blancmange
  powder
3 level tsp mixed spice
6oz (175g) butter or block
  margarine, kitchen temperature
6oz (175g) soft brown sugar (dark
  variety)
1 level tblsp black treacle
1tsp vanilla essence
½tsp almond essence
4 Grade 3 eggs, kitchen
  temperature
1½lb (675g) mixed dried fruit,
  including chopped peel
4oz (125g) chopped dates
4oz (125g) brazil nuts, walnuts or
  blanched almonds, coarsely
  chopped
1tblsp strong coffee or cold,
  strained tea for mixing
brandy, whisky or rum
melted apricot jam
Almond Paste for top of cake (page
  136)
Royal Icing for top of cake (page
  136)

Marble Cake

▲▲▲●●●

Make exactly as *Madeira Cake* but
cream fat and sugar with 1 teaspoon
vanilla and divide into 2 portions
after beating in eggs. Add 2 level
tablespoons sifted cocoa powder to
1 portion with 2 tablespoons cold
milk. Afterwards fold in half flour
mixture to each portion. Drop tablespoons of both alternately into 8 or
9in (20 to 22½cm) well-greased and
floured fluted tin. Bake as Madeira
Cake.

Tip
If liked, flavour plain portion with ½
teaspoon almond essence.

Hazelnut Chocolate Loaf

▲▲▲●●●

Make exactly as *Madeira Cake* but
stir in 3oz (75g) chopped hazelnuts
after beating in egg and bake in loaf
tin. When cold, brush top of cake
with 3oz (75g) melted milk chocolate or Chocolate Glacé Icing (page
136). Slice when chocolate or icing
has set.

Festive Fruit and Nut Cake

▲▲▲●●●

Make exactly as *Madeira Cake* but
after beating in eggs, add 6oz (175g)
coarsely-chopped brazil nuts, 4oz
(125g) chopped dates, 3oz (75g)
raisins, 2oz (50g) paper-dried maras-
chino-flavoured cocktail cherries,
and 4oz (125g) dried apricots, well
washed then snipped into small
pieces with scissors. Coat top with
white Glacé Icing (page 135) when
cold, and leave until set before slicing. If preferred, leave cake uniced
and keep at least a week before
cutting.

Dundee Cake

▲▲▲●●●

Make exactly as *Madeira Cake* but
add 2 level teaspoons finely-grated
orange peel with the lemon. After
beating in eggs, stir in 1lb (450g)
mixed dried fruits (including chopped
peel). After transferring to prepared
tin, cover top with 1oz (25g)
blanched and split almonds. Bake
2½ to 3 hours in oven set to 150°C
(300°F), Gas 2. Leave in tin ½ hour
before turning out on to wire cooling
rack. Store in an airtight tin when
cold and leave to mature for at least
a week before removing paper and
slicing.

Hazelnut Chocolate Loaf

1 Sift flour, blancmange powder and spice on to a plate.
2 In large bowl, cream fat and sugar together until light, fluffy and consistency of whipped cream. Add treacle and essences then beat in eggs, one at a time, adding a tablespoon of dry ingredients with each.
3 Stir in mixed fruit and peel, dates, nuts (use mixture if preferred, rather than one variety) and the coffee or tea.
4 Using a large metal spoon, fold in dry ingredients then transfer mixture to greased and paper-lined tin. Tie a double thickness of brown paper round the outside to prevent sides from burning.
5 Bake 4 to 4½ hours in centre of oven (any position in fan oven) set to 150°C (300°F), Gas 2. Leave in tin ¾ hour. Turn out on to wire cooling rack.
6 Peel away paper then make holes all over base of hot cake with thin skewer. Pour brandy, whisky or rum, in tablespoons, over surface until no more alcohol is absorbed. I usually allow 4 to 6 tablespoons. Leave to cool completely then turn right way up.
7 Wrap in greaseproof paper, tie in a clean teatowel and store about 2 weeks in a cool, DRY and airy cupboard or, if space permits, in the refrigerator.
8 Before icing, spread top with melted apricot jam then cover top with Almond Paste. Leave uncovered overnight then re-wrap and store for a further week. One or two days before required, cover top thickly with Royal Icing.
9 Make snow effect by pressing icing all over with back of a teaspoon and then lifting spoon up sharply. Add appropriate Christmas decorations and tie a cake frill round sides when icing has set.

Birthday or Anniversary Cake

▲▲▲●●

Make exactly as above but brush top AND sides with apricot jam and cover with Almond Paste. Royal Ice all over and decorate to taste.

Victoria Sandwich

MAKES 1 × 7IN (17½CM)
SANDWICH CAKE ▲▲▲●●

4oz (125g) self-raising flour
pinch of salt
4oz (125g) butter or block
*   margarine (kitchen temperature)*
4oz (125g) caster sugar
2 Grade 3 eggs (kitchen
*   temperature)*
red jam
a little icing sugar for the top

1 Sift flour and salt on to a plate. Place butter or margarine and sugar into mixing bowl. Cream until light, fluffy and consistency of whipped cream.
2 Beat in eggs, one at a time, adding 2 teaspoons of flour with each. Fold in flour smoothly with a large metal spoon, flipping mixture over and over on itself until well mixed.
3 Divide equally between two 7in (17½cm) greased sandwich tins, base-lined with greased greaseproof paper.

Festive Fruit and Nut Cake

4 Bake 20 to 25 minutes in oven set to 180°C (350°F), Gas 4, or until well risen, golden and firm to the touch. Leave tins 5 minutes then turn out on to wire cooling rack. Remove lining paper.
5 When cakes are completely cold, sandwich together with jam and sift icing sugar over the top. If liked, fill with 4 rounded tablespoons whipped cream in addition to the jam.

Christmas Cake. Photograph by Brown and Polson Cornflour

141

Chocolate Walnut Layer Cake

Chocolate Sandwich Cake

MAKES 1 × 8IN (20CM)
SANDWICH ▲▲▲●●●

4oz (125g) self-raising flour
1oz (25g) cornflour
1oz (25g) cocoa powder
pinch of salt
6oz (175g) butter or block
    margarine, kitchen temperature
6oz (175g) caster sugar
1tsp vanilla essence
4 Grade 3 eggs

1 Make exactly as *Victoria Sandwich*, sifting together dry ingredients, and creaming butter or margarine and sugar with vanilla. Bake in 2 × 8in (20cm) tins. When cold, fill cakes with either 4 heaped tablespoons lightly-sweetened whipped cream or Chocolate Butter Cream (page 136). Dust top either with sifted icing sugar or cover with more Butter Cream. Leave 1 hour before cutting.

Chocolate Walnut Layer Cake

10 PORTIONS ▲▲▲●●

Make *Chocolate Sandwich Cake* as directed previously. When cold, slice each layer in half horizontally and sandwich together with Chocolate Butter Cream (page 136). Coat completely with Chocolate Glacé Icing (page 136) and leave until set.

Decorate top with walnuts. Leave until icing has set before cutting.

American Style Walnut Gateau

10 PORTIONS ▲▲▲●●●

6oz (175g) self-raising flour
pinch of salt
6oz (175g) butter or block
    margarine (kitchen temperature)
6oz (175g) caster sugar
1tsp vanilla essence
3 Grade 3 eggs (kitchen
    temperature)
3oz (75g) walnuts, finely chopped
American Snow Frosting

Make exactly as *Victoria Sandwich* (page 141), creaming fat and sugar with the vanilla essence and add walnuts after beating in eggs. Bake in 2 × 8in (20cm) sandwich tins. When cold, slice each layer in half horizontally and sandwich together with about one-third of the Frosting. Spread remainder over top and sides then stud top with walnuts. Leave until Frosting has set completely before cutting.

Coffee Layer Cake

8 PORTIONS ▲▲▲●●●

Make exactly as *Victoria Sandwich* (page 141). When cold sandwich together and cover top with Coffee Butter Cream (page 136).

Mocha Layer Cake

8 PORTIONS ▲▲▲●●●

Make exactly as *Chocolate Layer Cake*. When cold, sandwich together and cover top with Coffee Butter Cream (page 136).

Note The Coffee Butter Cream may be flavoured with liquid coffee essence or instant coffee powder.

Fairy Cakes

MAKES 18 ▲▲▲●●

Make exactly as *Victoria Sandwich* (page 141) but add 2oz (50g) currants after beating in eggs. Divide equally between 18 fluted paper cases standing in 18 bun tins. Bake until well risen and golden; 20 to 25 minutes in oven set to 180°C (375°F), Gas 5. Leave to stand 5 minutes then turn out and cool on a wire rack. Store in an airtight tin when cold.

Butterfly Cakes

MAKES 18 ▲▲▲●●

Make exactly as *Victoria Sandwich* (page 141) and divide mixture equally between 18 fluted paper cases standing in 18 bun tins. Bake as *Fairy Cakes*. When cold, cut tops off each and halve (for wings). Pipe or spoon Butter Cream (page 136) over top of each then add halved tops, at an angle, to form wings. Dust with sifted icing sugar.

ALL-TOGETHER CAKES

Victoria Sandwich (2)

▲●●

Use same ingredients as previous *Victoria Sandwich* but sift self-raising flour and salt with 1 level teaspoon baking powder. Make sure butter or margarine is soft but not runny and eggs are at kitchen temperature. Put all ingredients into bowl and beat thoroughly for 3 minutes. Bake, cool and sandwich together as directed.

To Vary

1 Add 1 rounded teaspoon grated lemon or orange peel.
2 Add 1 tablespoon liquid coffee essence.
3 For chocolate sandwich, use 3½oz (115g) self-raising flour, pinch of salt, ½oz (15g) cocoa powder, 1 level teaspoon baking powder, 1 teaspoon vanilla essence and 1 tablespoon cold milk. All other ingredients stay the same.

Quick Fruit Cake

MAKES 1 × 7IN (17½CM) CAKE
▲●●●

8oz (225g) plain flour
pinch of salt
¼ level tsp baking powder
1 level tsp mixed spice
6oz (175g) butter or margarine, soft but not runny
6oz (175g) soft brown sugar, light variety
4 Grade 3 eggs, kitchen temperature
1lb (450g) mixed dried fruit

1 Place all ingredients into large bowl. Beat 3 to 4 minutes or until thoroughly mixed. Transfer to greased and lined 7in (17½cm) round cake tin or 2lb (1kg) loaf tin. Bake 2 to 2¼ hours in oven set to 150°C (300°F), Gas 2.
2 Leave in tin about ½ hour then turn out on to wire cooling rack and leave until completely cold. Store in an airtight tin and remove paper before cutting.

Mandarin Party Cake (page 144)

SPONGE CAKES

Sponge Sandwich

MAKES 1 × 7IN (17½CM) CAKE
▲▲▲●●

3 Grade 3 eggs, kitchen temperature
3oz (75g) caster sugar
3oz (75g) plain or self-raising flour, sifted twice on to plate
jam for filling
caster sugar for sprinkling over the top

1 Break eggs individually into a cup to check for freshness then tip into a large bowl. Beat until very frothy.
2 Add sugar. Whisk until mixture foams up and looks like a bowl of softly whipped cream and yields almost a pint (575ml) in volume.
3 Add ALL the flour, then fold in with a metal spoon by cutting it across base of bowl and flipping mixture over on itself.
4 Continue in this way, gently, until no more flour can be seen but under no circumstances beat the mixture or the cakes will be heavy.
5 Divide equally between 2 × 7in (17½cm) sandwich tins, base-lined with greased greaseproof paper.

6 Bake until well risen and golden; 20 minutes in oven set to 180°C (350°F), Gas 4.
7 Meanwhile, cover a wire rack with a damp teatowel then top with a sheet of greaseproof paper or foil. Dust with caster sugar.
8 Remove cakes from oven, leave to stand 3 or 4 minutes then turn out on to prepared rack. Leave until cold then sandwich together with jam. Dust top with a little extra caster sugar. Eat freshly made.

Tip
The reason the cakes are not turned out directly on to racks is because the wires would cut into and dent the delicate surfaces.

Deep Sponge Cake

MAKES 1 × 7IN (17½CM)
DEEP CAKE ▲▲▲●●

Make exactly as *Sponge Sandwich* but use plain flour ONLY. Transfer mixture to greased and paper-lined 7in (17½cm) deep cake tin. Bake until well risen and golden; about ¾ hour in oven set to 180°C (350°F), Gas 4. DO NOT OPEN OVEN DOOR during first ½ hour of baking or cake will fall. Cool in tin ¼ hour then turn out on to rack prepared as for the Sponge Sandwich. When cold, slice into 3 or 4 layers and sandwich together with filling to taste.

Chocolate Crumble Sponge

Mandarin Party Cake

ABOUT 10 PORTIONS ▲▲▲●●

Make *Deep Sponge Cake* as above. When cold, cut into 3 layers and sandwich together with Butter Cream (page 136) flavoured with

Swiss Roll

about 1 level teaspoon finely-grated lemon rind. Spread remainder over sides then cover with 3oz (75g) chopped and blanched almonds as shown in picture. Spread top with orange flavoured Glacé Icing (page 135). When set, decorate with canned mandarin oranges and small whirls of remaining Butter Cream. Refrigerate about 1 hour before cutting.

Chocolate Crumble Sponge

MAKES 1 × 7IN (17½CM)
SPONGE SANDWICH   ▲▲▲●●●

Make exactly as *Sponge Sandwich* (page 143) but use only 2oz (50g) flour and 1oz (25g) sifted cocoa powder. When cold, sandwich together with equal quantities of Butter Cream (page 136) mixed with chocolate hazelnut spread (such as Nutch or Nutella) and darkened with 1 or 2 teaspoons black treacle. Spread remainder over top and sides then cover thickly with 3 milk flake bars, crushed. Refrigerate ½ hour before serving.

Variation

For a simpler cake, fill with melted apricot jam then spread more jam fairly thickly over top and sides. Cover with crushed milk flake bars as above.

Swiss Roll

MAKES 1   ▲▲▲●●

Make exactly as *Sponge Sandwich* (page 143) but spread mixture into a greased and paper-lined Swiss roll tin measuring 12 × 8in (30 × 20cm). Bake 10 to 12 minutes in oven set to 200°C (400°F), Gas 6. Turn out on to piece of sugared greaseproof paper standing on damp teatowel. Remove lining paper and trim away crusty edges of cake. Spread quickly with a layer of melted red jam then roll up tightly and hold in place for 2 to 3 minutes. Leave to cool completely before slicing.

Note It is quite likely that the roll will crack but the sugar coating will hide most of the damage.

Chocolate Log

MAKES 1   ▲▲▲●●●

Make exactly as *Sponge Sandwich* (page 143) but use only 2oz (50g) flour and 1oz (25g) cocoa powder. Spread on to a greased and paper-lined Swiss roll tin measuring 12 × 8in (30 × 20cm). Bake 10 to 12 minutes in oven set to 200°C (400°F), Gas 6. Turn out on to a damp teatowel, trim away crusty edges then roll up with lining paper inside so that cake does not stick to itself. Wrap in the damp teatowel and leave until cold. Unroll carefully, remove paper and spread with plain Butter Cream (page 136). Make up extra Chocolate Butter Cream (page 136) for the outside. Cut a 1½in (3¾cm) diagonal piece off the end of the roll for a small log and stand on top of large log, holding it in place with a little jam. Cover completely and fairly thickly with Chocolate Butter Cream and ridge with a fork. Dust with a little sifted icing sugar and sprinkle with 1 rounded tablespoon chopped nuts to decorate; either walnuts or blanched and skinned pistachios which are bright green. Refrigerate 1 hour before slicing and serving.

Chocolate Log

'MELTED' METHOD CAKES

Gingerbread

12 PORTIONS ▲▲●●

> 4oz (125g) white cooking fat or lard
> 6oz (150g) black treacle
> 2oz (50g) golden syrup
> 2oz (50g) soft brown sugar, light variety
> ¼pt (150ml) cold milk
> 2 Grade 3 eggs
> 8oz (225g) plain flour
> 1 level tsp soda bicarbonate
> 3 level tsp powder ginger
> 1 level tsp mixed spice

1 Place first 4 ingredients into a saucepan and leave over a low heat until fat, treacle and syrup melt. Cool slightly.
2 Beat milk and eggs well together. Sift flour, soda bicarbonate, ginger and spice into large bowl. Make a well in the centre.
3 Pour in melted ingredients with the milk and eggs. Using a fork, stir briskly to a smooth fairly soft consistency but DO NOT beat.
4 Pour into a greased and paper-lined 7in (17½cm) square cake tin and bake 1¼ to 1½ hours in oven set to 150°C (300°F), Gas 2. When ready, the Gingerbread should be well risen and firm to the touch.
5 Leave in tin ¼ hour then turn out and cool on a wire rack. Transfer to an airtight tin when cold and leave at least 1 day before removing paper and cutting.

Fruited Gingerbread

12 PORTIONS ▲▲●●●

Make exactly as *Gingerbread* but add 2oz (50g) sultanas with the milk and eggs.

Raisin Cheesecake

SERVES 10 ▲▲▲●●●

Make up Cheesecake mixture as given in recipe for *Baked Cheesecake* in Dessert section on page 120. Line same size tin with Shortcrust Pastry (page 186) made from 6oz (175g) flour. Line with foil to prevent pastry from rising as it cooks. Bake 20 minutes in oven set to 220°C (425°F), Gas 7. Remove foil. Sprinkle base of pastry with 2oz (50g) raisins. Add Cheesecake mixture. Continue to bake a further 1¼ hours in oven set to 150°C (300°F), Gas 2. Switch off oven heat, leave door open and allow cake to cool down for ½ hour. Remove from oven and leave until cold. Refrigerate overnight and un-clip sides before cutting into wedges and serving.

Raisin Cheesecake

Austrian Linz Cake

Doughnut Hoops

ABOUT 12 ▲▲▲●●●

Make exactly as *American Style Doughnut Rings* on page 199 but toss in sifted icing sugar instead of caster. If liked, omit spice from mixture.

Austrian Linz Cake

12 PORTIONS ▲▲▲●●●

8oz (225g) butter, softened but
   not runny
8oz (225g) plain flour
8oz (225g) caster sugar
8oz (225g) unskinned almonds,
   finely ground (use food
   processor or blender)
finely-grated peel of 1 small
   washed and dried lemon
1 Grade 3 egg, separated
about 6oz (175g) redcurrant jelly
   or raspberry jam

1 Place butter, flour, sugar, almonds and lemon peel into bowl. Add egg yolk. Knead together with fingers to form a smooth dough.
2 Wrap in foil or cling film and refrigerate 1 hour so that pastry firms up. Roll out two-thirds on well-floured surface and use to line an 8in (20cm) spring clip tin (flat base with hinged sides), building up edges to form a ½in (1¼cm) thick margin.
3 Fill with half melted redcurrant jelly or raspberry jam. Roll out remaining pastry as thinly as possible and cut into strips. (A pastry wheel gives the most authentic finish.)
4 Arrange in a criss-cross design over the filling and press well on to the pastry edges. Brush with lightly-beaten egg white.
5 Bake 1 hour in oven set to 160°C (325°F), Gas 3, when cake should be light gold. Leave until cold then unclip sides. Cut into portions for serving.

To Vary
Use ground hazelnuts instead of almonds and sift flour with 2 level teaspoons mixed spice or cinnamon.

Coffee Eclairs

MAKES 12 ▲▲▲●●●

Choux Pastry (page 196)
½pt (275ml) double cream
2 level tblsp caster sugar
1 tblsp cold milk
Coffee Glacé Icing (page 135)

1 Using a forcing bag fitted with ½in (1¼cm) plain tube, pipe 12 lengths of mixture, each 4in (10cm), on to greased baking tray.
2 Bake 10 minutes in oven set to 200°C (400°F), Gas 6. Reduce temperature to 180°C (325°F), Gas 4. Continue to bake a further 20 to 25 minutes when Eclairs should be light gold and well risen.
3 Remove from oven and make a slit in side of each. Return to oven with heat switched off and door open, and leave about 7 minutes to dry out.
4 Transfer to wire rack and leave until cold. Slit each in half and fill with cream, sugar and milk beaten together until thick. Spread top of each with Coffee Glacé Icing and leave until set before eating.

Cream Buns

MAKES ABOUT 12 ▲▲▲●●●

Pipe or spoon 12 equal mounds of Choux Pastry (page 196), well apart, on 1 or 2 greased trays. Bake, cool and cream-fill as for *Coffee Eclairs*. Sift icing sugar over each.

Chocolate Eclairs or Chocolate Cream Buns

MAKES 12 ▲▲▲●●●

Make exactly as *Coffee Eclairs* or *Cream Buns* but coat tops with Chocolate Glacé Icing.

Doughnut Hoops

Cream Horns

MAKES 12 ▲▲▲●●●

Flaky or Puff Pastry (page 192) or
*   1 large packet frozen puff*
*   pastry, thawed*
cold milk
caster sugar
red jam
½pt (275ml) double cream
3 level tblsp caster sugar

1 Roll out pastry fairly thinly if using homemade (about double the thickness of Shortcrust Pastry) and as directed on the packet if using frozen puff.
2 Cut into 12 strips each measuring 12in in length by 1-in in width (30×2½cm). Dampen one side of each strip with water then wrap round 12 lightly-greased Cream Horn tins, starting at the pointed ends. (These are cone-shaped, hollow tins, sold in sets.)
3 Make sure dampened sides are placed against tins and that the strips overlap by about ¼in (¾cm).
4 Stand on slightly wet baking tray or trays, brush with milk and sprinkle lightly with caster sugar. Leave to 'relax' for 1 hour in the refrigerator.
5 Bake 15 to 20 minutes in oven set to 230°C (450°F), Gas 8, or until deep gold and puffy. Remove from oven and allow to cool down for about 5 to 10 minutes.
6 Carefully take Cream Horn tins out of each and cool cases on wire rack. When completely cold, drop a rounded teaspoon of jam into each then fill with cream, beaten until thick with the caster sugar. When once filled, eat within 8 hours.

Cream Slices

MAKES ABOUT 8 ▲▲▲●●●

Roll out homemade Puff Pastry (page 193) or 1 packet frozen and thawed puff pastry into an oblong measuring 16 × 4in (40 × 10cm). Cut into 8 pieces, each 4 × 2in (10 × 5cm). Transfer to slightly wet baking tray. Leave to 'relax' for 1 hour in the refrigerator. Bake until well puffed and golden, allowing about 15 to 20 minutes in oven set to 230°C (450°F), Gas 8. Transfer to a wire

Coffee Eclairs

rack and split in half when completely cold. Fill with a light spread of red jam and ½ pint (275ml) double cream, whipped until thick. Cover tops with Glacé Icing (page 135) colouring and flavouring to taste. Make and eat on same day.

Chocolate Cream Meringues

Chocolate Cream Meringues

MAKES 8 ▲▲▲●●●

Make exactly as *Cream Meringues* on page 115), but use 2 level teaspoons sifted cocoa powder and 1 level teaspoon cornflour instead of all cornflour.

Coconut Macaroons

Almond Macaroons

MAKES 16 ▲▲●●●

  whites of 2 Grade 3 eggs
  4oz (125g) ground almonds
  8oz (225g) caster sugar
  ½oz (15g) semolina or cornflour
  1tsp almond essence
  ½tsp vanilla essence
  8 blanched almonds, split in half
  a little extra egg white for
    brushing

1 Line 2 baking trays with rice paper if available or non-stick parchment paper.
2 Beat egg whites until foamy. Work in all remaining ingredients except blanched almonds. Spoon or pipe 16 rounds of mixture on to prepared trays.
3 Top each with a half almond and brush tops lightly with beaten egg.
4 Bake until pale gold; about 20 to 25 minutes in oven set to 160°C (325°F), Gas 2. Remove from oven and leave to cool on trays about 3 minutes.
5 Carefully lift off with a flat knife (trimming away rice paper from around edges if used) and transfer to a wire cooling rack. Store in an airtight tin when cold.

Coconut Macaroons

MAKES ABOUT 20 ▲▲●●

  whites of 2 Grade 3 eggs
  squeeze of lemon
  4oz (125g) caster sugar
  6oz (150g) desiccated coconut
  ½tsp vanilla essence

1 In clean and dry bowl, beat egg whites and lemon juice to a stiff snow. Gently stir in sugar, coconut and essence.
2 Drop about 20 mounds of mixture on to 1 or 2 baking trays lined with non-stick parchment paper. Neaten with prongs of fork.
3 Bake 20 to 25 minutes in oven set to 150°C (300°F), Gas 2. When ready, the Macaroons should be pale gold.
4 Leave on trays 5 minutes then carefully remove to a wire cooling rack. Store in an airtight tin when cold.

Almond Macaroons

Afternoon Tea or Plain Biscuits

MAKES 14 TO 15 ▲▲●●

Make up Biscuit Pastry (page 187) and roll out thinly on floured surface. Cut into 14 or 15 rounds with 2in (5cm) fluted biscuit cutter, re-rolling and re-cutting trimmings to make required number of biscuits. Arrange on greased baking trays. Brush with a little milk then sprinkle with demerara or caster sugar. Bake 15 to 18 minutes in oven set to 180°C (350°F), Gas 4. Biscuits should be warm gold in colour. Leave 2 or 3 minutes then transfer to wire cooling racks. Store in an airtight tin when cold.

To Vary
1 Sift 1½ level teaspoons mixed spice or cinnamon with the flour.
2 Toss 1oz (25g) chopped nuts or dried fruit into dry ingredients before mixing with liquid.
3 Add ½ teaspoon almond or vanilla essence with the liquid.

Chocolate Biscuits

MAKES 14 TO 15 ▲▲●●

Follow recipe for *Afternoon Tea* or *Plain Biscuits* but when making up Biscuit Pastry (page 187), substitute 1oz (25g) cocoa powder for 1oz (25g) flour.

Sandwich Biscuits

MAKES 14 TO 15 ▲▲●●●

Make up *Afternoon Tea* or *Plain Biscuits* as directed but cut into 1in (2½cm) rounds with fluted or plain cutter. When cold, sandwich together in pairs with vanilla-flavoured Butter Cream (page 136), lemon curd or jam.

Teatime Fancies

MAKES 14 TO 15 ▲▲●●●

Make up *Sandwich Biscuits* as above then cover tops with Glacé Icing.

Christmas Biscuits

MAKES 14 TO 15 ▲▲●●●

Make up *Afternoon Tea* or *Plain Biscuits* as directed, but cut into assorted fancy Christmas shapes with appropriate cutters. When cold, ice by brushing either with melted chocolate or by spreading with Glacé Icing. Decorate with silver balls, pieces of glacé cherry and grated chocolate, hundreds and thousands or leaves cut from angelica.

Ginger Snaps

MAKES ABOUT 25 ▲▲●●

  4oz (125g) self-raising flour
  1 level tsp powdered ginger
  ¼ level tsp allspice or cinnamon
  1oz (25g) lard or white cooking fat
  1oz (25g) butter or block
    margarine
  1½oz (40g) soft brown sugar
    (light variety)
  1 level tblsp black treacle
  about 1 to 1½tblsp cold milk to mix

1 Sift flour and spices into bowl. Rub in fat and margarine finely. Toss in sugar.

Afternoon Tea or Plain Biscuits

2 Mix to stiff paste with treacle and milk. Turn out on to lightly-floured surface. Knead lightly until smooth.
3 Roll out thinly and cut into 25 rounds with 2in (5cm) cutter, re-rolling and re-cutting trimmings to make required amount of biscuits.

4 Transfer to greased baking trays and bake until well risen and golden, allowing 10 to 12 minutes in oven set to 180°C (350°F), Gas 4.
5 Leave on trays 1 to 3 minutes then carefully remove to wire cooling racks. Store in an airtight tin when cold.

Ginger Snaps

Refrigerator Biscuits

Flapjack

CUTS INTO ABOUT 30 PIECES ▲●●

4oz (125g) butter or margarine
4oz (125g) golden syrup
2oz (50g) soft brown sugar
* (light variety)*
8oz (225g) porridge oats

1 Melt butter or margarine with syrup and sugar in large saucepan.
2 Stir in porridge and mix well. Spread into greased tin measuring 12 × 8in (30 × 22½cm).
3 Bake 30 minutes in oven set to 180°C (350°F), Gas 4. Cool to lukewarm in tin. Cut into 30 pieces and lift carefully out of tin.
4 Transfer to a wire cooling rack and store in an airtight tin when cold.

Shortbread

MAKES 8 TO 10 TRIANGLES
▲▲●●

2oz (50g) caster sugar
4oz (125g) butter
6oz (175g) plain flour
extra caster sugar

1 Cream sugar and butter together until light and fluffy.
2 Stir in flour to make a soft paste and, with knife, spread smoothly into 7in (17½cm) sandwich tin. Ridge edges with prongs of a fork then prick all over.
3 Dust lightly with sugar and bake until very pale gold, allowing ¾ to 1 hour in oven set to 150°C (300°F), Gas 3.
4 Remove from oven and cool 10 minutes. Very carefully cut into 8 to 10 triangles and leave in the tin until cold. Transfer to an airtight tin.

Vienna Biscuits

MAKES ABOUT 16 ▲▲▲●●

6oz (175g) butter, softened but
* not runny*
2oz (50g) icing sugar, sifted
1tsp vanilla essence
6oz (175g) plain flour
8 glacé cherries, halved
icing sugar for dusting

1 Cream butter, sugar and essence together until light and fluffy. Using a fork, stir in sufficient flour to form a soft paste.
2 Transfer to icing bag filled with a star-shaped tube and pipe about 16 whirls of mixture on to 1 or 2 lightly-greased trays.
3 Top centres of each with half a cherry then bake until pale gold, allowing 20 to 25 minutes in oven set to 160°C (325°F), Gas 4.
4 Remove from oven and cool 5 minutes. Transfer carefully to wire cooling rack and dust with sifted icing sugar. Store in an airtight tin when cold.

Coffee Crisps

MAKES 16 ▲▲●●●

4oz (125g) butter, softened but
* not runny*
2oz (50g) soft brown sugar, light
* variety*
4oz (125g) plain flour
3 level tsp instant coffee powder
16 walnut halves

1 Cream butter and sugar together until light and fluffy. Stir in flour and coffee powder to form a softish paste.
2 Place 16 teaspoons of mixture, well apart as they spread, on to 2 lightly-greased baking trays.
3 Press a walnut half on to each then bake 15 to 20 minutes in oven set to 190°C (375°F), Gas 5.
4 Leave on trays about 3 minutes then transfer carefully to wire cooling rack. Store in an airtight tin when cold.

Melting Moments

MAKES 18 ▲▲●●●

4oz (125g) butter, softened but
* not runny*
3oz (75g) caster sugar
1 egg yolk
1tsp vanilla essence
4oz (125g) self-raising flour
1oz (25g) cornflour
porridge oats
9 glacé cherries, halved

1 Cream butter, sugar, egg yolk and vanilla essence together until light and fluffy.
2 Fork in flour and cornflour. Shape into 18 balls and roll in porridge oats.

150

3 Arrange on 2 greased baking trays, leaving room between each for spreading.
4 Place half a glacé cherry on top of each and bake until light gold, allowing 15 to 20 minutes in oven set to 190°C (375°F), Gas 5.
5 Cool on trays for 3 minutes then transfer to cooling racks. Store in an airtight tin when cold.

Digestive Biscuits

MAKES 12　　　　　　▲▲●●

3oz (75g) brown flour
1oz (25g) plain flour, sifted
½ level tsp baking powder
2oz (50g) butter or margarine
1½oz (40g) soft brown sugar (light variety)
2 to 2½tblsp cold milk to mix

1 Tip flours and baking powder into bowl. Rub in butter finely.
2 Toss in sugar then, using fork, mix to stiff paste with milk.
3 Turn on to floured board and knead lightly until smooth. Roll out fairly thinly. Cut into 12 rounds with 2½in (6¼cm) plain biscuit cutter, re-rolling and re-cutting trimmings to give the required amount.
4 Transfer to a greased tray and prick each biscuit all over. Bake until pale gold, allowing 15 to 20 minutes in oven set to 190°C (375°F), Gas 5.
5 Leave on trays 4 minutes then transfer biscuits to wire cooling rack. Store in an airtight tin when cold.

Refrigerator Biscuits

MAKES ABOUT 50 IF BAKED
ALL AT ONCE　　　　　　▲▲●●

8oz (225g) plain flour
1 level tsp baking powder
4oz (125g) butter or block margarine
6oz (175g) caster sugar
2oz (50g) hazelnuts, very finely ground (optional)
1tsp vanilla or almond essence
1 Grade 3 egg, beaten
about 1tblsp milk for mixing

1 Sift flour and baking powder into a bowl. Rub in butter or margarine finely.
2 Toss in sugar and nuts if used. Mix to a stiff dough with essence, beaten egg and milk.
3 Knead lightly until smooth on floured surface then shape into a roll measuring 2in (5cm) in diameter. Wrap in foil and twirl ends like a cracker.
4 Leave in the refrigerator until required then, using a sharp knife, cut off as many biscuits as you want to bake, making the slices fairly thin.
5 Transfer to lightly-greased tray or trays and bake 10 to 12 minutes in oven set to 190°C (375°F), Gas 5. Leave on trays 2 or 3 minutes then transfer to wire rack. Store in an airtight tin when completely cold.
6 Re-wrap biscuit mixture in foil, twist ends as before and store in the refrigerator until more biscuits

are required. The mixture will keep about 1 week to 9 days.

To Vary
1 Omit nuts and almond essence and add only vanilla essence.
2 Add 2oz (50g) grated chocolate instead of the nuts.
3 Sift 2 level teaspoons mixed spice, cinnamon or ginger with the flour and baking powder. Omit nuts and essences.
4 Add finely-grated peel of 1 small orange or lemon with the sugar. Omit essences.

Cheese Straws

MAKES ABOUT 36　　　　▲▲●●

Make up *Cheese Pastry* as directed (page 187). Roll out thinly and cut into about 36 sticks, each 6in (15cm) long. Transfer to greased tray or trays. Brush with beaten egg and sprinkle with about 1oz (25g) extra finely-grated cheese. Bake 7 to 10 minutes (or until golden brown) in oven set to 220°C (425°F), Gas 7. Cool on a wire rack and store in an airtight tin when cold.

Cheese Biscuits

MAKES ABOUT 30　　　　▲▲●●

Make up *Cheese Pastry* as directed (page 187). Roll out thinly and cut into about 30 rounds with a 1in (2½cm) biscuit cutter. Transfer to tray or trays and brush with egg. Bake and store as Cheese Straws.

Sandwiches

Sandwiches

Sandwiches started life as an 18th century convenience food when the Earl of Sandwich, involved in some sort of gambling exploit, was too distracted by activities at the gaming table to pay much attention to his meal and, for ease of eating, slapped a piece of cooked steak between two slices of bread. The story, as far as it goes, sounds plausible enough and since its early beginnings over 200 years ago, this entirely British 'invention' has travelled round the world in a variety of guises – closed, open, toasted and American style club, has been filled with anything and everything from meat paste to smoked salmon, and received a warm welcome at Royal garden parties, wedding and cocktail receptions, picnics, children's get-togethers, office desks via the lunch box and every kind of celebratory occasion imaginable. Sandwiches, internationally, are a way of life and even the famous French Tartine is nothing more than a jam or chocolate-filled sandwich which little children take to school for mid-morning break!

Success Tips

1 Use thin to medium-sliced white or brown bread which is 1 day old. Over-fresh bread makes soggy sandwiches and stale bread makes dry ones.
2 About 6oz (175g) butter, provided it is softened and creamed until light, should be adequate to cover 24 large slices of bread. For a more generous layer, allow 8oz (225g).
3 Allow a minimum of 1oz (25g) sliced, cooked meat, poultry or sliced cheese per round of sandwiches (2 slices of bread). Also 1 Grade 3 shelled and sliced hard-boiled egg.
4 If using soft fillings – chopped hard-boiled egg mixed with Mayonnaise, cottage or cream cheese, mashed canned fish or even sliced banana – add something crisp in the form of salad greens or other vegetables to offer contrast of texture.
5 For a meal or picnic, allow 2 sandwiches (4 slices of bread) per person, or even 3 if appetites are large. If catering for parties, 4 to 6 small squares or triangles should be enough for 1 serving.
6 To prepare sandwiches in advance, make up as many as are required. Cut each sandwich in half. Wrap securely in cling film or aluminium foil. Alternatively, store in a plastic container with airtight lid and do not wrap. Refrigerate overnight.
7 Sandwiches, well wrapped and sealed, may be frozen up to 1 month provided they do not contain any of the following: hard-boiled or scrambled egg (it becomes watery), Mayonnaise (it gets oily), salad greenery (it wilts), tomatoes (they tend to leak) or beetroot (colour runs). For ease of separation, interleave sandwiches with special sheets of film (available from stationers and freezer centres) or squares of foil. Wrap securely then seal and label.
8 I am often asked whether it is correct to leave crusts on sandwiches, and I regret I have no exact answer that relates to etiquette on how they should be served. Sturdy sandwiches, made for packed meals and picnics, keep fresher and are more substantial if the crusts are left on. Dainty afternoon tea sandwiches look more attractive if the crusts are removed, and therefore the whole subject of crusts on or off depends entirely on personal preference.
9 Open sandwiches deteriorate less rapidly if crusts are kept on, and it is also worth remembering that a thick application of butter or margarine insulates the bread and prevents moisture from the topping seeping through and making it soggy and damp.

Sandwich Round

SERVES 1   ▲ or ▲▲ ●● or ●●●

Spread 2 large slices white or brown bread with butter or margarine. Sandwich together with selected filling. Press sandwich down firmly with flat of hand so that it holds together. Cut in half or into 2 triangles. Serve straightaway or wrap and refrigerate until needed.

SANDWICH FILLINGS

Fillings may be prepared ahead of time and left, covered or wrapped, in the refrigerator until needed. For instance, wash lettuce leaves and other salad greens and dry. Slice cucumber, tomatoes, radishes, celery, meat, poultry, ham and tongue. Grate carrots. Grate cheese if necessary or use sliced. Grate hard-boiled eggs directly into a bowl (which is a much tidier method than chopping), flake up canned fish, chop nuts, and thoroughly drain any canned or bottled vegetables you might be using. Shred white cabbage or Chinese leaves finely and either wrap tightly in cling film or put into a bowl and cover securely.

Combinations

1 Ham topped with tomato chutney and shredded lettuce.
2 Corned beef and a thin spread of mustard topped with coleslaw salad.
3 Cheese spread topped with cucumber and tomato.
4 Cottage cheese mixed with a few chopped walnuts and topped with trimmed and sliced spring onions and lettuce.
5 Chopped hard-boiled eggs moistened with salad cream, Mayonnaise or soured cream and topped with mustard and cress and sliced radishes.
6 Chicken slices topped with chopped unpeeled apple and thinly-sliced celery tossed in a little Mayonnaise.
7 Luncheon meat spread with tomato ketchup and topped with grated carrots.
8 Sliced hard-boiled egg spread with Mayonnaise and covered with strips of fresh red or green pepper.
9 Dressed crab topped with watercress leaves and cucumber slices.
10 Peeled prawns and chopped avocado mixed with Mayonnaise and topped with leaves of chicory.
11 Slices of Edam or Gouda cheese topped with pickled red cabbage.
12 Cold scrambled eggs topped with sliced stuffed olives and coarsely-chopped green or red pepper.

13 Sliced banana sprinkled with lemon juice and topped with strips of crisply-fried bacon and Chinese leaves or lettuce.
14 Honey sprinkled with grated raw apple, a little lemon juice and topped with the merest dusting of cinnamon.
15 Chocolate spread sprinkled with mixed nuts and raisins.
16 Lemon curd topped with sliced strawberries and a little demerara sugar.

Flavour Tip

Wrap each type of sandwich separately so that the flavours of the various fillings keep their individuality. Strong-smelling fillings easily infiltrate milder ones and completely spoil their taste.

Earl of Sandwich's Sandwich

Earl of Sandwich's Sandwich

SERVES 1 ▲▲●●●

Spread 2 large slices white bread with butter. Sandwich together with a slightly underdone steak spread with horseradish relish or creamed horseradish sauce. Cut into 2 triangles. Arrange on a plate with lettuce and radishes.

Open Sandwiches

Historically Danish, open sandwiches (Smørrebrød) are now enjoyed worldwide and make a colourful and appetizing contribution to any buffet, lunch or supper table. And, like cocktails, they have

Open Sandwiches. Top left to right: September Sunshine; Man About Town; Beef Tartare; Threesome. Centre left to right: Sea Serenade; Country Fresh; Pretty Polly; Danish Dream. Bottom left to right: Cool Customer; Salami Special; Parma Slice; Marble Palace

names of their own which gives them a certain air of distinction!

September Sunshine

SERVES 1 ▲▲●●

Cover 1 large slice of buttered white or brown bread with 3 folded slices of luncheon meat. Top with some horseradish relish or creamed horseradish. Garnish with 2 stoned prunes and 1 orange slice, slit from centre to outside edge and shaped into twist.

155

American Style Club Sandwich

Man About Town

SERVES 1   ▲▲●●

Cover 1 slice of buttered white or brown bread with lettuce. Add a back joint of roast chicken with leg attached. Top with a folded slice of ham. Garnish with cucumber and tomato slices and a small bouquet of cress. Cover end of bone with a cutlet frill.

Beef Tartare

SERVES 1   ▲▲●●●

Cover 1 slice of buttered white or brown bread with 4oz (125g) finely-minced and uncooked lean rump or fillet steak. Make a shallow dip in the centre and drop in an egg yolk. Surround with capers then sprinkle with chopped onions and salt and pepper to taste.

Threesome

SERVES 1   ▲▲●●●

Cover 1 large slice of buttered white or brown bread with a large lettuce leaf. Top with 3 rolls of cold sliced beef. Garnish with gherkin and glacé cherries.

Sea Serenade

SERVES 1   ▲▲▲●

Cover 1 large slice of buttered white or brown bread with a large lettuce leaf. Cover with 1 band of over-lapping tomato slices and 1 band of overlapping egg slices. Spoon a band of Mayonnaise between the two and garnish with lumpfish (mock caviar from Scandinavia or Germany).

Country Fresh

SERVES 1   ▲▲●●

Cover 1 large slice buttered white or brown bread with 3 half slices of Tilsit, Emmental or Gruyère cheese (often available already sliced in packets). Top with 3 tomato wedges and add a garnish of mustard and cress.

Pretty Polly

SERVES 1   ▲▲●●

Cover 1 large slice buttered white or brown bread with 3 rolls of ham and some Russian Salad (page 231). Garnish with a slice of cucumber, tomato and hard-boiled egg. Finally add a sprig of parsley.

Danish Dream

SERVES 1

Cover 1 large slice buttered white or brown bread with very thinly sliced cold roast pork. Top with cold scrambled egg and sprinkle with chives.

Cool Customer

SERVES 1

Cover 1 large slice buttered white or brown bread with 1 large slice of liver pâté. Garnish with thinly-sliced, raw button mushrooms and very thin slices of unpeeled cucumber.

Salami Special

SERVES 1 ▲▲●●

Cover 1 large slice buttered white or brown bread with 6 slices of salami. Garnish with 3 onion rings.

Parma Slice

SERVES 1 ▲▲●●

Cover 1 large slice buttered white or brown bread with lettuce. Top with 4 egg slices, 2 strips of Parma ham, a wedge of tomato and mustard and cress.

Marble Palace

SERVES 1

Cover 1 large slice buttered white or brown bread with lettuce. Top with

a slice of Danish Blue cheese. Garnish with 4 radish slices, 1 egg yolk and a slice of onion.

Serving Tip
Serve all Open Sandwiches with a knife and fork.

TOASTED SANDWICHES

Toasted sandwiches are best made in an electric toaster which crispens and browns the outsides to perfection, seals all the edges and keeps the fillings inside moist and succulent. As not all homes are equipped with this comparatively new gadget, the following is the standard method for making a toasted sandwich.

Toasted Sandwich

SERVES 1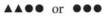

Spread 2 slices of bread thickly with butter or margarine. Sandwich together with slices of cold, cooked meat or cheese, sliced hard-boiled eggs, grilled bacon or canned flaked fish such as tuna or salmon. Spread with Mayonnaise and/or pickles. Top with either crisp lettuce, shredded Chinese leaves, cucumber or tomato slices, watercress, mustard and cress, coleslaw or grated carrots. Toast on both sides. Remove to plate. Cut in half. Serve straightaway.

Club Sandwich

SERVES 1 ▲▲●●

This is a heartier version of the Toasted Sandwich above in that it is made with 3 slices of toast instead of 2 slices. Spread 2 slices of hot toast with butter or margarine and sandwich together with salad (and Mayonnaise or salad cream to taste). Spread top with more butter or margarine. Cover with cold roast meat, poultry or canned flaked fish. Add third slice of toast with the butter or margarine side against filling. Press down firmly. Cut in half. Stand on a lettuce-lined plate.

American Style Club Sandwich

SERVES 1

This is a variation on the true American Club Sandwich which is usually made with 3 slices of toast.

Toast 2 large slices white or brown bread and spread with butter or margarine. Sandwich together with lettuce, Mayonnaise and slices of tomato and cucumber. Top with cold roast chicken and under-done cold roast beef, cut into hair-thin slices. Cut in half and serve as a main course.

Success Tip
All Toasted and Club Sandwiches should be made and eaten straightaway. Once the toast is cold, it becomes leathery.

Preserves

Preserves

Jam and chutney-making are a satisfying and colourful means of utilizing and preserving seasonal fruits and vegetables, saving money in the long run (especially if one uses garden produce) and filling cupboard shelves with a tempting display of pots and jars packed with delicious homemade produce for family eating, bring-and-buy sales – and the like – and, if prettily packaged and appropriately garlanded, for Christmas or Easter gifts.

Bottling, smoking, salting and drying have not been included as they are very much specialist subjects, requiring more detail than is possible to include in a general cookery book. For those who are keen to preserve foods by these means, I would suggest they buy an authoritative book on each or all of the methods.

JAM-MAKING

Guidelines

1 Fruit for jam-making must be in good condition and not soft, wet and squashy. The best is just ripe or slightly under-ripe as this should contain sufficient pectin and acid to produce a good set when combined with sugar.

2 Wash fruit and wipe dry when practical; raspberries and other soft berry fruits should be left to drain in a colander and not dried as they would totally disintegrate.

3 Plums and greengages (and similar hard fruits) should be halved and stoned only if the kernels are easy to remove. If not, the fruit should be split lengthwise with a sharp knife and the kernels will ease their way out of the fruit while the jam is cooking. As they inevitably float to the top, they can be skimmed off at the end of cooking.

4 Choice of pan is important and to prevent jam boiling over, it must be capacious enough to be no more than about half full AFTER the sugar has been added. Jam – and marmalade – rises up while boiling and requires room to expand. Also make sure the base of the pan is sturdy and unbuckled.

5 It is customary to stir preserves to prevent sticking and the best implement to use is a long-handled wooden spoon as it stays cool to the touch. Metal absorbs heat and can burn the hand. To save making a mess, keep a plate on the work surface near the pan so that there is somewhere to rest the spoon between stirrings.

6 Where water is recommended in a recipe, the fruit must be allowed to simmer in it until VERY SOFT before the sugar is added. This helps to extract pectin (a gel like substance which makes jam set) and softens fruit skins – vital in the case of blackcurrants for instance. If sugar is added too early, the jam etc may end up runny.

7 Sugar chosen may be granulated, caster or preserving; preserving sugar creates less scum than the other two but is slightly more expensive. It should be added in one go and stirred over a low heat until completely dissolved. Then the heat should be increased until the jam bubbles and boils briskly. Slow cooking produces dull-coloured jam which might not set satisfactorily; fast boiling ensures bright-coloured jam with a full and fruity flavour and firm consistency.

8 Though scum will collect on the top, it is inadvisable to keep skimming it off as some jam will be removed as well and go to waste. It is more practical to wait until the end, stir a knob of butter into the jam as this disperses scum and then skim it with a metal spoon. Stones can also be removed at this stage as well.

9 To test jam or marmalade for setting, spoon 1 teaspoon on to a cold saucer. Cool quickly, tilting saucer gently. If, after a minute or so, a skin forms on top which crinkles when touched, then the jam has reached setting point. If it remains runny, continue to boil and check for setting every 10 minutes.

10 The jam or marmalade should now be skimmed carefully and left for 10 to 15 minutes before being stirred round and ladled into clean, warm and dry jars. Where there are large pieces of fruit or peel, or whole fruits such as strawberries, the jam or marmalade should be left in the pan until lukewarm before being stirred round and potted. If not, fruit or peel will rise to the top of the jars, leaving a layer of jelly below.

11 The jam or marmalade should be covered with waxed discs while still warm and then topped with rounds of cellophane when completely cold. To prevent wrinkles, wipe one side of the cellophane with fingers dipped in water. Place dry side on top of jar, nearest the waxed discs. Hold in place with an elastic band and, as the cellophane dries up, it will shrink back on itself and all the wrinkles will disappear.

12 Store jam and marmalade in a cool, dry and dark cupboard. Daylight has a bleaching effect and the preserves will lose colour.

FAULTS IN JAM

Mouldy
1 Stored in damp conditions.
2 Inadequately covered.

TIP Remove about 2in (5cm) mould and jam from top of each jar and discard. Use up remaining jam fairly quickly.

Jam Crystallizes
1 Too much sugar used in proportion to fruit and water.
2 Jam boiled for too long.
3 Jam was allowed to boil briskly before sugar had completely dissolved.

Jam Ferments
1 Insufficient sugar used.
2 Jam not boiled for long enough.

FAULTS IN MARMALADE

Poor Set
1 Old fruit used.
2 Fruit and water insufficiently boiled and therefore pectin not extracted to its full extent.
3 Marmalade cooked past the gel point.
4 Marmalade cooked too slowly.
5 Insufficient sugar added.

Marmalade Ferments
See jam.

Marmalade very dark
1 Mixture boiled too long and too slowly after the addition of sugar.

Marmalade cloudy
1 Lemons, limes and sweet oranges used.
2 Too much pith in the marmalade.

TIP Cloudiness has no effect whatever on flavour and consistency but lacks the brightness of a clear marmalade.

Peel rises in jar
1 Marmalade potted while hot.

Peel tough
1 Peel insufficiently cooked before sugar was added.

Bubbles in Marmalade
1 Jars not rotated slowly while marmalade was being added.
2 Marmalade allowed to cool off too much before being bottled.

Plum Jam

MAKES ABOUT 5LB (2½KG)   ▲▲●●

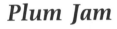

3lb (1½kg) cooking plums, well washed and dried
½pt (275ml) water
3lb (1½kg) granulated, caster or preserving sugar

1 Halve plums and remove stones. If stubborn, slit each plum lengthwise and leave stones to cook out by themselves.
2 Place in saucepan with water. Bring to boil, stirring. Lower heat. Cover. Cook until fruit is very soft and pulpy, allowing 20 to 30 minutes minimum.
3 Add sugar. Stir continuously until dissolved. Increase heat. Boil briskly, uncovered, until setting point is reached, stirring frequently and allowing 15 to 20 minutes. (See Guidelines on page 160.)

4 Stir in a knob of butter or margarine to disperse scum then skim. Leave 10 to 15 minutes. Stir round and transfer to jars. Cover and label.

Greengage Jam

MAKES ABOUT 5LB (2½KG)
▲▲●●

Follow directions for *Plum Jam*.

Damson Jam

MAKES ABOUT 5LB (2½KG)
▲▲●●

Follow directions for *Plum Jam* but do not attempt to stone the fruit. Increase the water to ¾pt (425ml) and simmer about ¾ hour or until skins are very soft. Skim off stones as they float to the surface BEFORE adding sugar. Remove remainder after jam is cooked.

Blackcurrant Jam

MAKES ABOUT 5LB (2½KG)
▲▲●●

Follow directions for *Plum Jam* but reduce fruit to 2lb (900g) instead of 3lb (1½kg). Simmer ¾ hour in 1½pt (⅞ litre) water before adding sugar so that skins are completely tenderized.

Gooseberry Jam

MAKES 5LB (2½KG)   ▲▲●●

Follow directions for *Plum Jam* but simmer topped and tailed fruit in 1pt (575ml) water for 30 to 40 minutes before adding sugar so that skins are completely tenderized. If cooked in a copper pan, the jam will remain green instead of turning its customary pink.

Gooseberry and Raspberry Jam

MAKES 5LB (2½KG)   ▲▲●●

Follow directions for *Plum Jam* but use half topped and tailed gooseberries and half raspberries. Simmer ½ hour in ½pt (275ml) water.

Gooseberry and Redcurrant Jam

MAKES 5LB (2½KG)   ▲▲●●

Follow directions for *Plum Jam* but use half topped and tailed gooseberries and half redcurrants, the latter removed from stems with a fork. Simmer ½ hour in ¾pt (425ml) water.

Pipless Raspberry Jam (page 162)

Autumn Jam

Gooseberry and Rhubarb Jam

MAKES 5LB (2½KG)　　▲▲●●

Follow directions for *Plum Jam* but use two-thirds topped and tailed gooseberries and one-third cut-up rhubarb. Simmer ½ hour in ½pt (275ml) water.

Apple and Blackberry Jam

MAKES 5LB (2½KG)　　▲▲●●

Follow directions for *Plum Jam* but use half cooking apples (weighed after peeling and coring) and half hulled blackberries. Simmer ½ hour in ½pt (275ml) water, crushing fruit with a wooden spoon periodically.

Autumn Jam

MAKES 5LB (2½KG)　　▲▲●●

Follow directions for *Plum Jam* but use 3lb (1½kg) mixed fruits to include mixed currants, plums, fresh apricots and peaches. Simmer fruits ½ hour in ½pt (275ml) water, keeping pan covered.

162

Raspberry Jam

MAKES 5LB (2½KG)　　▲▲●●

3lb (1½kg) raspberries, hulled
3lb (1½kg) granulated, caster or preserving sugar

1 Wash fruit and shake dry in colander. Tip into saucepan and crush down with wooden spoon. Stand over low heat.
2 Add sugar. Stir over low heat until dissolved. Bring to boil. Boil briskly, uncovered, for 7 to 10 minutes or until setting point is reached.
3 Stir frequently. Cool about 15 minutes. Transfer to jars. Cover and label when cold. (See Guidelines on page 160.)

Pipless Raspberry Jam

MAKES ABOUT 4LB (2KG)

　　　　　　　　　▲▲●●

Use 3lb (1½kg) raspberries and simmer gently in ¼pt (150ml) water until very soft; about ½ hour. Keep

pan covered. Strain through fine mesh sieve into measuring jug. Allow 1lb (450g) granulated, caster or preserving sugar to every 1pt (575ml) juice. Place both together in saucepan. Stir over low heat until sugar dissolves. Bring to boil. Boil briskly, uncovered, until setting point is reached, allowing about 12 to 15 minutes. Skim. Leave about ¼ hour. Ladle into jars, gently rotating each to prevent bubbles forming. Cover and label when cold.

Strawberry Jam

MAKES 5LB (2½KG)　　▲▲●●

3½lb (1¾kg) firm strawberries, hulled and washed
juice of 2 medium lemons
3lb (1½kg) granulated, caster or preserving sugar

1 Place all ingredients into pan. Heat gently, tossing fruit over and over (taking care not to break it up), until sugar dissolves.

2 Bring to boil. Boil briskly for 12 to 15 minutes, uncovered, or until setting point is reached.

3 Skim. Leave to cool in the pan until a skin forms over surface of jam. Stir round and ladle into jars. Cover and label when cold.

Dried Apricot Jam

MAKES 5LB (2½KG) ▲▲●●

1lb (450g) dried apricots
3pt (1¾ litres) water
3lb (1½kg) granulated, caster or
*   preserving sugar*
juice of 2 medium lemons
2oz (50g) split almonds

1 Wash apricots thoroughly. Cut into small pieces and tip into basin. Cover with half the measured water. Leave overnight to soak.

2 Transfer to large pan. Add rest of water. Bring to boil. Reduce heat. Cover. Simmer slowly ¾ hour. Add sugar and lemon juice. Stir over low heat until dissolved.

3 Bring to boil again and boil briskly, uncovered, until setting point is reached. Skim. Stir in almonds. Leave for ½ hour then spoon into jars. Cover and label.

MARMALADE

Guidelines

1 The best marmalade is made from winter Seville oranges with their characteristic bitterness and setting qualities.

2 Alternative citrus fruits used for this preserve are sweet oranges, lemons, grapefruits and limes. Seville oranges and grapefruits tend to produce a clearer marmalade than that made with the other types of citrus.

3 All fruit should be thoroughly washed and dried before use. This is a safety precaution against sprays and dust.

4 Marmalade — unless otherwise stated in a specific recipe — needs additional acid (in the form of extra lemon juice) to secure a good set. This is because, compared with jam, less citrus is used in proportion to water and sugar. For instance, 1½lb (675g) grapefruit is the standard amount one allows for 3pt (1¾ litres) water and 3lb (1½kg) sugar, as opposed to 3lb (1½kg) plums or gooseberries.

5 The peel must be cooked long and slowly in a generous amount of water in order to tenderize it. If the sugar is added while the peel is still hard and before some of the liquid has had the chance to boil away, the marmalade will not set satisfactorily.

Seville Orange Marmalade

MAKES 5LB (2½KG) ▲▲▲●●

1¼lb (675g) Seville oranges
3pt (1¾ litre) water
juice of 2 medium lemons
3lb (1½kg) granulated, caster or
*   preserving sugar*

1 Wash and dry fruit. Peel oranges thinly. Cut peel into thick, medium or fine shreds depending on personal preference. Leave on one side temporarily.

2 Cut fruit in half and squeeze out juice. Strain into saucepan. Keep aside all pips and put into a large piece of clean cloth.

3 Chop up orange 'shells' (now mainly pith and membrane) and add to cloth. Tie securely. Add to saucepan with water and lemon juice. Stir in peel.

4 Bring to boil. Lower heat. Cover. Simmer 1½ hours. Uncover. Continue to simmer a further hour to boil off about half the water, to extract as much pectin as possible from the pips and pith, and to tenderize the peel until it is soft enough to form a paste when rubbed between finger and thumb.

5 Lift out bag of pips and pith with kitchen tongs and stand on a large plate. Sit another plate on top and squeeze hard over the pan so that juices run back into the fruit mixture and none of the valuable pectin is lost.

6 Add sugar and stir over low heat till dissolved. Continue as for *Plum Jam* (page 161). Leave cooked marmalade in the pan until a skin forms on top. Stir round. Transfer to jars. Cover when cold and label.

Orange Marmalade

MAKES 5LB (2½KG) ▲▲▲▲●

Make exactly as *Seville Orange Marmalade*, but use 1½lb (675g) eating oranges and the juice of 3 medium lemons.

Mixed Fruit Marmalade

MAKES 5LB (2½KG) ▲▲▲●●

Make exactly as *Seville Orange Marmalade*, but use 1½lb (675g) mixture of grapefruit, eating orange, lime, clementine and the juice of 3 medium lemons.

Grapefruit Marmalade

MAKES 5LB (2½KG) ▲▲▲●●

Make exactly as *Seville Orange Marmalade*, but use 1½lb (675g) grapefruit and the juice of 3 medium lemons.

Chunky Marmalade

MAKES 5LB (2½KG) ▲▲●●

Use same ingredients as for other marmalades. Wash and dry fruit. Halve. Squeeze out juice and pour into pan. Save pips and tie in a piece of cloth. Add to pan with water and lemon juice. Coarsely mince squeezed-out fruit 'shells'. Stir into pan. Continue as directed from point 4 of method in recipe for *Seville Orange Marmalade*.

Note This is a fine-flavoured, thick marmalade which is faster to make than any of the others. It does, however, tend to look cloudy but is otherwise excellent and ideally suited to everyday eating.

Pickled Beetroot

since and eaten with curries, cold meats and cheeses. Although mango is the elite of chutneys, practically every other fruit (and some vegetables) may be used in its place, and both apple and tomato are very popular additions to a homemade chutney. Garlic and onions are used to give chutney its appetizing flavour, spices and herbs add a note of pungency, cayenne pepper a touch of fire (or not at all if omitted) and vinegar, dried fruit and sugar between them create the characteristic sweet-sour taste which makes this typically British pickle unique. For deep-toned chutneys, I advise dark brown sugar; for lighter ones granulated. The best vinegar to use is good quality malt.

Apple Chutney

MAKES 5LB (2½KG) ▲▲●●

4oz (2kg) cooking apples
2lb (900g) onions
water
1 garlic clove, peeled
1lb (450g) raisins, stoned
2pt (1¼ litre) malt vinegar
1½lb (675g) granulated or brown
 sugar, according to taste (see
 introduction to chutney)
2 to 4 level tsp salt, according to
 taste
3 level tsp ground allspice
1 bouquet garni
⅛ to ½ level tsp cayenne pepper
 (optional)

1 Peel, quarter and core apples then thickly slice. Leave aside temporarily.
2 Peel onions and chop. Place in large saucepan. Add just sufficient water to cover. Bring to boil. Lower heat. Cover. Simmer very slowly about 30 to 45 minutes or until very tender.
3 Meanwhile, coarsely mince apples (browning has no adverse effect) with garlic and raisins. Add to pan with all remaining ingredients.
4 Stir over low heat until sugar dissolves then cook, uncovered, until chutney gently bubbles and thickens to a jam-like consistency. Stir fairly often with a wooden spoon.
5 Stir round and remove bouquet garni. Cool slightly. Spoon into warm, dry jars. Cover as for jam. (See Guidelines on page 160.)

Mincemeat

MAKES ABOUT 4LB (1KG)

▲▲▲●●

8oz (225g) firm eating apples such
 as Cox (not Bramleys as they
 are too wet)
8oz (225g) seedless raisins
8oz (225g) sultanas
4oz (125g) chopped mixed peel
8oz (225g) currants
8oz (225g) molasses sugar
8oz (225g) finely-shredded suet
finely-grated peel and juice of
 2 medium washed lemons
¼ level tsp allspice
¼ level tsp cinnamon
2oz (50g) almonds, blanched and
 coarsely chopped
4tblsp spirit such as whisky, rum
 or brandy

1 Peel, quarter and core apples. Coarsely mince (or use food processor) with raisins, sultanas and mixed peel. Tip into bowl.
2 Add all remaining ingredients except spirit. Stir well to mix. Cover bowl with teatowel. Leave in the kitchen for 3 days for flavours to blend and mature, stirring 2 or 3 times a day.
3 Stir in spirit then transfer to jars. Cover as for jam (see Guidelines on page 160). Store in a cool, dry cupboard or, space permitting, in the refrigerator.

CHUTNEY

This is a sweet-sour condiment which dates back about 100 years to the time of the Raj. Britishers, who enjoyed chutneys in India, brought recipes back with them to this country and, in one form or another, they have been made ever

Green Tomato Chutney

MAKES ABOUT 6LB (2¾KG) ▲▲●●

5lb (2½kg) green tomatoes
1lb (450g) onions
water
1 garlic clove, peeled
1pt (575ml) malt vinegar
1lb (450g) light brown sugar
1 bouquet garni
¼ level tsp mixed spice
2 to 3 level tsp salt

Make exactly as *Apple Chutney*.

Red Tomato Chutney

MAKES 6LB (2¾KG) ▲▲●●●

Make exactly as *Green Tomato Chutney* but increase tomatoes to 6lb (2¾kg) and onions to 2lb (900g). To heighten colour and increase flavour, add 2 rounded tblsp tomato ketchup with the salt.

Combination Fruit Chutney

MAKES 5LB (2½KG) ▲▲●●

Follow recipe for *Apple Chutney* but instead of using only apples try:

1 Half apples and half pears.
2 Half apples and half rhubarb.
3 One-third apples, one-third pears and one-third tomatoes.

PICKLES

Piccalilli or mustard pickles, pickled walnuts, pickled red cabbage, sauerkraut and even pickled onions are fairly time-consuming to make and are best shop-bought because colour, consistency, quality and flavour will be predictable. Beetroot is worth preparing at home and here is a fairly easy recipe.

Pickled Beetroot

SUFFICIENT FOR A 2 TO 2½LB (1KG) JAR ▲▲●●

2lb (900g) cooked beetroot
2 medium dessert apples
1 medium onion
10 peppercorns
6 cloves
1 large bay leaf
¾pt (425ml) water
¾pt (425ml) wine vinegar
3oz (75g) caster sugar
2 level tsp salt

1 Peel beetroot and slice. Peel, quarter and core apples and cut into thin wedges. Peel onion and separate slices into rings.
2 Fill jar (or jars, whichever is more convenient) with layers of beetroot, apples and onions, sprinkling peppercorns, cloves and broken-up bay leaf between layers.
3 Bring rest of ingredients just up to boil. Cool slightly. Pour into jar or jars over beetroot, filling each right to the top.
4 Leave until cold before covering. Store up to 2 months in the cool and leave at least 1 week before eating.

Sauces

Sauces

The sauce family is a large one and each member – and its offspring – has its own individuality and character. This results in a wide range of assorted sauces which fall into specific groups or categories, and I think the best way of introducing you to the subject is by starting with the easiest of all; white sauces and their variations, and then progressing, in order of difficulty, through the rest of the classic repertoire to include brown sauces, egg-based sauces (Hollandaise and Mayonnaise), melted butter sauces, hard butter sauces (Brandy Butter is a typical example) and a selection of miscellaneous sauces which do not fall into any particular grouping such as the Bolognese, Neapolitan, Sweet-Sour, Bread, Cranberry, Curry, Barbecue, Chocolate, Fudge and so on.

Although not sauces in the accepted sense, salad dressings have been included in this section as they play an important rôle in moistening and/or coating all manner of foods; the ultimate object of a sauce. Similarly, I have slotted in marinades as the strained liquids are often used as foundations for classic sauces. And also savoury butters which, when placed in pats over grills of meat or fish, melt on the hot food adding richness, flavour and moisture.

Plain White Pouring Sauce

SERVES 4 TO 6   ▲●

This is a very simple, bland sauce which can be made successfully without fat and, as an added bonus for slimmers and those on low-fat or light diets, with skimmed instead of whole milk. The sauce may be of pouring or coating consistency, depending on the amount of flour or cornflour used, and also savoury or sweet according to final usage. It is worth noting here, at the very beginning, that ALL pouring sauces are fairly thin and intended to moisten food which might otherwise be dry or dull by itself. Coating sauces are thicker and are generally used to coat, enliven and add a distinctive flavour and gloss to all foods over which they are poured. To enrich a plain sauce, a knob of butter or margarine may be stirred in at the end. In all cases, flour chosen may be plain or self-raising.

> ½oz (15g) flour or cornflour
> ½pt (275ml) cold milk
> salt and pepper to taste or 1 level
>   tblsp caster sugar
> knob of butter or margarine
>   (optional)

1 Tip flour or cornflour into saucepan.
2 Gradually work to a smooth and lump-free liquid with a little of the cold milk.
3 As soon as the mixture is smooth and thin, pour in rest of milk.
4 Cover over medium heat, stirring continuously, until sauce comes to boil and thickens slightly.
5 Simmer very gently for 2 minutes. Either season to taste with salt and pepper, or add sugar and stir until dissolved. Add butter or margarine if used.

Plain White Coating Sauce

SERVES 4 TO 6   ▲●

Make exactly as the *Plain White Pouring Sauce*, but increase flour or cornflour to 1oz (25g).

Serving Tips
Serve the savoury sauces with poached or steamed poultry and white meat, poached or steamed white fish, poached eggs and freshly-boiled vegetables. Serve the sweet sauces with steamed or baked sponge puddings, hot fruit pies and tarts such as treacle or jam.

Basic White Sauce

SERVES 4 TO 6   ▲▲●

This is a richer sauce altogether than the Plain White, and is made by what is termed the roux method whereby equal amounts of fat and flour (which between them thicken and enrich) are blended together and then lightly cooked before any liquid is added. It takes fractionally longer to prepare than the Plain Sauce, but has a smoother, rounder flavour and is well worth the extra effort. All recipes in this group are of coating consistency, but pouring sauces may be made by halving the amount of flour.

> 1oz (25g) butter or margarine
> 1oz (25g) flour
> ½pt (275ml) milk
> salt and pepper to taste

1 Melt butter or margarine in saucepan. Stir in flour to form a roux.
2 Cook over low heat, stirring continually, for 2 minutes.
3 Stirring briskly all the time, gradually blend in milk.
4 Bring slowly to the boil, still stirring. When sauce has thickened smoothly, simmer gently for 2 minutes and season to taste.
5 Remove from heat and use as required.

Serving Tip
Serve over cooked vegetables, grilled or steamed fish, boiled chicken and hard-boiled eggs.

Flavour Tip
For a more pronounced flavour you can, if you like, use half cooking water (from vegetables or fish for example) and half milk.

Blender Tip
For ease of preparation, place all ingredients into blender goblet and run machine until smooth. Pour into saucepan. Cook, stirring, until sauce comes to boil and thickens. Season. Simmer 2 minutes. It is advisable to use softened fat.

Freezer Tip
Under-season as freezing develops flavours. Transfer sauce to a suitable container. Cover securely. Seal and label. Freeze up to 4 months. Defrost then reheat carefully, stirring continuously to prevent the formation of lumps. If necessary, thin down sauce with a little extra stock, milk or water.

Sweetener Tip
Instead of salt and pepper, the sauce may be sweetened to taste with 1 or 2 level tablespoons caster sugar, golden syrup or honey.

Béchamel Sauce

SERVES 4 TO 6 ▲▲●●

This is a French classic white sauce
and I am bringing it in here because
you may prefer to use this version
for the variations instead of the Basic
White Sauce (page 168). The main
difference is that the Béchamel is
made with milk which has been first
infused with vegetables, herbs and
spices to increase the flavour. To
make, pour ½pt (275ml) cold milk
into a saucepan. Add 1 small peeled
onion, 1 small peeled carrot, 1 small
broken celery stalk, 2 cloves, ¼ level
teaspoon grated nutmeg, 1 sprig of
parsley and a very small piece of bay
leaf. Bring milk to the boil, stirring
all the time. Remove from heat.
Cover at once. Leave to stand for 1
hour. Strain. Make sauce with a roux
of fat and flour, and the flavoured
milk, exactly as directed in the recipe
for Basic White Sauce.

VARIATIONS

Anchovy Sauce ▲▲●

After simmering, stir in 2 level teaspoons bottled anchovy ketchup or
essence and 2 teaspoons lemon juice.
Season to taste.

Serving Tip
Serve with fish and veal dishes.

Caper Sauce ▲▲●●

Before simmering, stir in 1½ to 2 level
tablespoons drained and chopped
capers and 2 teaspoons caper vinegar. Reheat till hot, stirring. Season
to taste.

Serving Tip
Serve with mackerel, herring and
skate dishes. Also lamb.

Chaud-Froid Sauce

▲▲▲●●●

A jellied Basic White Sauce which
literally translates into hot-cold
sauce because the hot sauce is
always allowed to get cold before use.
Make up *Basic White Sauce* using the
roux of fat and flour and flavoured
milk as in the *Béchamel Sauce* (page
169). Stir in ¼pt (150ml) unset
DOUBLE STRENGTH aspic jelly.

Basic White Sauce

Leave in the cool until sauce thickens
sufficiently to coat the back of a
spoon.

Usage/Serving Tip
Spoon evenly over portions of cold
food to form a complete and smooth
cover. The foods are usually those
intended for a buffet – cold chicken,
cutlets of fish, hard-boiled eggs and,
additionally, whole chickens and
whole fish such as skinned salmon
and salmon trout.

Cheese Sauce ▲▲●●

After simmering, stir in 3 to 4oz (75
to 125g) grated Cheddar, Edam or
Gouda cheese and ½ to 1 level teaspoon prepared English mustard.
Stir sauce, off heat, until cheese melts
otherwise prolonged cooking will
make it stringy. Season to taste.

Serving Tip
Serve with vegetables, fish, meat,
egg, poultry, ham and bacon dishes.

Dutch Sauce

Dutch Sauce (Mock Hollandaise)

▲▲●●●

After simmering, add 1 tablespoon fresh lemon juice to sauce. Beat 1 egg yolk with 3 tablespoons double cream. Pour into sauce. Cook, stirring, until sauce just reaches boiling point. Remove from heat. Season to taste.

Serving Tip
Serve with boiled vegetables, steamed or poached fish and boiled chicken.

Egg Sauce

▲▲●●

After simmering, stir in 2 medium, chopped hard-boiled eggs. Season to taste and reheat.

Serving Tip
Serve with all kinds of fish dishes and grills of veal and chicken.

Maître d'Hôtel Sauce

▲▲●●

As this is a classic sauce designed for fish, use half fish stock and half milk. After sauce has simmered, stir in juice of $\frac{1}{2}$ a fresh lemon, 2 tablespoons whipping or double cream and 2 level tablespoons finely-chopped parsley. Season to taste with salt and pepper. Reheat gently.

Serving Tip
Serve with all fish dishes from poached cod or salmon to grilled plaice and fried herrings.

Mornay Sauce

▲▲●●●

One of the most popular classics of all, this is none other than a luxury cheese sauce made with the flavoured milk used for *Béchamel* (page 169) and the standard roux of fat and flour. After sauce has simmered, remove from heat and stir in 2oz (50g) very finely-grated Parmesan or Gruyère cheese and either a large pinch of cayenne pepper or a few drops of Tabasco sauce. Season to taste with salt and pepper.

Serving Tip
Serve with exactly the same dishes as Cheese Sauce (page 169), bearing in mind the sauce is extremely good with shellfish.

Mushroom Sauce ▲▲●●●

After simmering, add 2 to 3oz (50 to 75g) thinly-sliced mushrooms and stalks, first fried in a little butter or margarine. Season to taste. Reheat before serving.

Serving Tip
Serve with all meat, poultry, offal, fish, cheese, egg and vegetable dishes. As this is such a popular and versatile sauce, it is compatible with most foods.

Mustard Sauce ▲▲●●

Before simmering, add 2 level teaspoons powder mustard smoothly mixed with 4 teaspoons vinegar. Season to taste.

Serving Tip
Serve with ham, bacon, boiled tongue, cheese dishes and grilled or fried herrings, mackerel, scallops and crab.

Normandy Sauce ▲▲●●

Make up the *Basic White Sauce* (page 168) using fish stock only and *no milk at all*. After simmering, remove from heat and whisk in 2 egg yolks. Season to taste. Do not reheat in case of curdling.

Serving Tip
Serve with all fish dishes whether grilled, fried or poached.

Onion Sauce ▲▲●●

Boil 2 onions until tender. Drain well and chop. Add to sauce before simmering. Season to taste with salt, pepper and nutmeg.

Serving Tip
Serve with tripe (in fact, if cooked tripe is reheated in the sauce this gives you traditional Tripe and Onions), lamb dishes such as grills and roasts, boiled mutton and boiled bacon or gammon steaks.

Parsley Sauce ▲▲●●

After simmering, add 2 to 3 heaped tablespoons finely-chopped parsley. Season to taste.

Serving Tip
Serve with fish and boiled bacon.

Supreme Sauce ▲▲▲●●●

A popular classic that often lends its name to a dish, ie Chicken Suprême, Sole Suprême and so forth. Make up *Basic White Sauce* (page 168) using either fish, meat, poultry or vegetable stock (depending on the dish) BUT NO MILK AT ALL. After simmering, add 3 tablespoons double cream beaten with 1 egg yolk, 3 teaspoons lemon juice and 1 tablespoon melted butter. Reheat without boiling. Season to taste.

Normandy Sauce

Serving Tip
Serve with fish, meat, poultry or vegetable dishes.

Freezer Tip for Variations
As certain flavours weaken while others intensify during freezing, I recommend that you freeze the Basic White Sauce without additions and as previously directed (page 168). After thawing, make up variations by adding ingredients and seasonings as specified under each heading. In this way the sauces will have a much fresher and more authentic taste.

WRONGS AND RIGHTS

Sauce was lumpy
1 Hot liquid added to freshly-made roux. Should be lukewarm or cold.
2 Liquid added too quickly and/or sauce not stirred enough while sauce was being brought to boil.
3 Heat under pan too high.

REMEDY Remove from heat. Whisk till smooth. Alternatively, blend till smooth in blender goblet. Return to pan. Reheat.

Sauce was too thick
1 Too much flour or cornflour used or, alternatively, insufficient liquid.

REMEDY Remove from heat. Whisk in extra liquid gradually to avoid lumps. Reheat.

Sauce was too thin
1 Sauce was not brought to the boil.
2 Too much liquid added.

REMEDY Problematic, in that adding more flour or other thickener may give rise to lumpiness. Try boiling gently for 5 or 6 minutes to evaporate off some of the liquid.

Sauce powdery-tasting and dull-looking
1 Sauce not brought up to boil.

REMEDY Cook, stirring, until sauce bubbles and begins to look glossy. Simmer 2 to 3 minutes.

Sauce speckled with brown flecks
1 Roux allowed to cook too quickly and/or too long.

REMEDY None. The only course of action is camouflage but sauce may still be thinnish and not very well flavoured.

Sauce burnt
1 Heat too high and/or inadequate stirring.

REMEDY Difficult but you can pour off the 'top' of the sauce and use, leaving the burned remains behind.

BROWN SAUCES

The most elementary of all the brown sauces is the gravy one makes after roasting a joint of meat. Next in line is richly-flavoured Brown Sauce (or Sauce Espagnole as it is sometimes called) and its variations which range from classic Orange Sauce to Madeira Sauce, Hunter's Sauce and Lyonnaise Sauce. Like the White Sauces, all the brown family are based on a roux but the fat used may be butter (unsalted for preference), margarine or meat dripping. If preferred, salad oil may be substituted for fat. True meat stock imparts the best flavour but, in its absence, stock cubes and water make a satisfactory alternative.

171

Madeira Sauce

gently until fat runs and then begins to sizzle.

2 Stir in vegetables. Cover pan. Simmer over low heat for 10 minutes. Uncover. Continue to cook until vegetables are lightly browned.

3 Add flour. Cook slowly 3 minutes, stirring continuously. Gradually blend in stock.

4 Cook, stirring, until sauce comes to boil and thickens. Add all remaining ingredients except salt and pepper.

5 Cover. Simmer over minimal heat for 1 hour, placing an asbestos mat between pan and source of heat if sauce appears to be cooking too fast.

6 At this stage it is *essential* for it to cook slowly, otherwise the liquid will evaporate too quickly and the sauce will burn.

7 To strain, remove bouquet garni and discard. Pour sauce and vegetables into a fine mesh sieve resting (or held) over a clean pan. Rub through with the back of a wooden spoon.

8 Thin down if necessary with extra stock. Season to taste.

Gravy

▲●

Pour away all but 2 tablespoons fat from roasting tin. Stand tin over medium heat. Stir in 1½ level tablespoons flour. Cook and stir for 2 or 3 minutes, working in all the brown crunchy pieces that have settled over base of tin. Gradually blend in ½ pint (250ml) beef stock (use cubes and water in the absence of the real thing) and bring to boil, stirring. Simmer 2 minutes then season to taste with salt and pepper. If necessary, heighten colour with gravy browning or mushroom ketchup.

Brown Sauce 1 (Sauce Espagnole or Spanish Sauce)

SERVES 4 TO 6 ▲▲●●

1oz (25g) fat or 1½tblsp salad oil
1oz (25g) bacon trimmings or streaky bacon, chopped (optional)
1 small onion, peeled and chopped
1 small celery stalk, scrubbed and chopped
1oz (25g) mushrooms (or stalks only), chopped
1 small carrot, peeled and thinly sliced
1oz (25g) flour
¾pt (425ml) stock (homemade or stock cube and water)
2 rounded tsp tubed or canned tomato purée
1 large blanched tomato, skinned and chopped
1 bouquet garni
salt and pepper to taste

1 Heat fat or salad oil in *heavy-based* pan. Add bacon if used. Fry

Brown Sauce 2

SERVES 4 TO 6 ▲●●

This version is not quite as orthodox in its preparation as Brown Sauce 1, or indeed as traditional. Nevertheless it is simpler to make and less likely to thicken up too much or burn.

To cook, heat fat or oil as directed in recipe for *Brown Sauce 1*. Add bacon (if used) and vegetables. Fry, covered, 10 minutes. Uncover. Fry a further 10 to 15 minutes over lowish heat when ingredients should turn a deep gold. Stir occasionally. OMIT FLOUR at this point but add all remaining ingredients. Bring to boil, stirring. Cover. Lower heat. Simmer gently 1 hour. Remove bouquet garni and discard. Strain. Measure. Allow 1oz (25g) fat (or 1½ tablespoons salad oil) and 1oz (25g) flour to every ½pt (275ml). Heat fat or oil in pan. Stir in flour to form a roux. Cook 3 to 4 minutes or until it turns a warm brown colour. Gradually blend in strained liquid. Cook, stirring, until sauce comes to boil and thickens. Simmer 5 minutes. Season.

Orange Sauce

Serving Tip

Serve with meat, game and offal dishes.

Note

1 If either of the Brown Sauces are too pale, add a little gravy browning to each. Alternatively, use Bovril or Marmite.

2 If sauces 1 or 2 look greasy, skim fat or oil off the top.

VARIATIONS

Hunter's Sauce

▲▲●●●
(for both versions)

Stir the following into every ½pt (275ml) seasoned sauce:
3oz (75g) coarsely-chopped and lightly-fried mushrooms, 1 small chopped and lightly-fried onion, 5 tablespoons white or rosé wine (or 3 tablespoons wine and 2 tablespoons brandy) and 1 rounded tablespoon tubed or canned tomato purée. Reheat, stirring, until very hot. Adjust seasoning to taste. Finally add 1 level tablespoon chopped parsley.

Serving Tip

Serve with grilled or roast meat, roast duck, grilled liver, boiled bacon and grilled or fried gammon.

Lyonnaise Sauce

▲▲ or ▲ (depending if making version 1 or 2) ●●

Stir the following into every ½pt (275ml) seasoned sauce:
1 large peeled onion, thinly sliced and then gently fried in margarine or dripping until dark gold and soft.

Serving Tip

Serve with offal dishes and roasts or grills of beef or pork. This sauce also teams well with beefburgers and sausages.

Madeira Sauce

▲▲ or ▲ (depending if making version 1 or 2) ●●●

Stir the following into every ½pt (275ml) seasoned sauce:
5 tablespoons Madeira. Reheat without boiling.

Serving Tip

Serve with hot tongue and beef dishes.

Orange Sauce

▲▲ or ▲ (depending if making version 1 or 2) ●●●

Stir the following into every ½pt (275ml) seasoned sauce:

1 tablespoon lemon juice, 4 tablespoons fresh orange juice, 2 level teaspoons finely-grated orange peel and 3 tablespoons dry red wine or port. Reheat without boiling. Adjust seasoning to taste.

Serving Tip

Serve with roast pork, roast duck, all game dishes and stuffed roast heart.

WRONGS AND RIGHTS

Sauce was greasy or oily
Inadequately skimmed.

REMEDY If all else fails, leave sauce overnight so that the fatty layer rises to the top and firms up slightly. Spoon off.

Sauce tasted acidy
This could be due to the tomato purée.

REMEDY Add ½ level teaspoon sugar or pinch of soda bicarbonate.

Sauce was too thin
1 Too much liquid added and/or vegetables themselves were more watery than usual.
2 Scant measure of flour used.

REMEDY To keep consistency smooth, thicken as required with instant potato powder or granules, adding it teaspoon by teaspoon and stirring sauce over low heat.

173

Hollandaise Sauce 1 Melt butter in a saucepan

2 Place egg yolks in a basin over a saucepan

3 Whisk until mixture thickens

EGG-BASED SAUCES

There are 3 groups of sauces under this heading: Hollandaise, Mayonnaise and Egg Custard Sauce. Accepted as tricky even by experts, they require more care, attention and skill than all the other sauces put together, and I will therefore go through each one individually and guide you through the more difficult processes.

Hollandaise Sauce

SERVES 6 ▲▲▲●●●

4oz (125g) unsalted butter
3 egg yolks
2tblsp boiling water
1tblsp mild vinegar (light malt for example)
1tblsp lemon juice
salt and white pepper to taste

1 Melt butter without allowing it to sizzle. Set aside temporarily.
2 Place egg yolks in basin standing over saucepan of gently bubbling water. Add water, vinegar and lemon juice.
3 Whisk with hand whisk until egg mixture thickens slightly and is foamy.
4 Still *whisking continuously*, add butter a teaspoon at a time. No faster or sauce will be spoiled.
5 About two-thirds of the way through, the sauce will start to thicken. Now add the butter more rapidly but *do not stop* whisking.
6 Remove basin from saucepan to stop sauce cooking any further. Season to taste with salt and pepper. Serve straightaway.

Serving Tip

Serve with poached salmon, salmon trout, trout, hake, halibut, turbot, sole, hot asparagus, hot broccoli and hot globe artichokes.

Note

1 It is not advisable to try to keep the Hollandaise Sauce hot or it will separate out, and it is one of the few sauces – and this covers the variations as well – that should be served as soon as it is made. If this is just not possible, tip sauce into a vacuum flask. Close up and leave until ready to serve. It should remain stable, but I am not prepared to give a definite guarantee.
2 There are many different ways of making Hollandaise Sauce, and although I have experimented with them all, I have found the recipe above to be the easiest and most reliable.
3 A double saucepan may be used instead of a basin over a pan of hot water.
4 Leftover, cold Hollandaise is excellent and makes a luxury substitute for Mayonnaise.
5 NEVER substitute margarine for butter.

WRONGS AND RIGHTS

Sauce looked oily and appeared to separate out
1 Allowed to overcook in basin.
2 Water in pan (or in lower part of double saucepan) was boiling too vigorously.
3 Basin was allowed to remain over hot water AFTER sauce had thickened sufficiently.

REMEDY
1 Beat in 2 tablespoons double cream.
2 Tip into blender goblet, add 1 tablespoon boiling water and blend until smooth.
3 Place egg yolk into basin or into top of double saucepan with 1 tablespoon boiling water. Whisk until foamy. *Gradually* beat in curdled Hollandaise.

Sauce looked like scrambled eggs
Overcooked and/or overheated.

REMEDY None.

Béarnaise Sauce

SERVES 6 ▲▲▲●●●

Make *exactly* as *Hollandaise Sauce* (above), but use tarragon vinegar instead of malt vinegar. Season at the end with salt, pepper and a light shake of cayenne pepper (very hot). Stir in 1 level teaspoon dried tarragon or 1 level tablespoon finely-chopped fresh tarragon.

Note True and classic Béarnaise Sauce contains shallots. If you would like to make this version, simmer 2 peeled and finely-chopped shallots in the tarragon vinegar for about 10 minutes. Make sure pan is covered throughout. Strain. If necessary, add extra vinegar to make up to 2 tablespoons as the liquid may evaporate slightly.

Blender Hollandaise

SERVES 6 TO 8 ▲▲●●●

A virtually no-fail Hollandaise that can be whizzed together in a few minutes. It is slightly more extravagant than the previous recipe in that it uses a large amount of butter, but is well worth the extra cost for the saving in time and effort.

6oz (175g) unsalted butter, melted
2tblsp lemon juice (or 1 of vinegar and 1 of lemon juice)
3 egg yolks
salt and pepper to taste

1 Melt butter in pan then heat until hot and sizzling. In separate pan, bring lemon juice (or vinegar and lemon juice) up to boil.
2 Place egg yolks in blender with boiling lemon juice. Blend 7 to 8 seconds or until frothy.
3 Remove lid. With blender set to high speed, add butter in a slow but steady stream. Replace lid.
4 Keep the blender running for 35 to 45 seconds, by which time the sauce should be thick and smooth.
5 Season to taste. Spoon out of blender and serve straightaway.

Note If too thick, thin down with 1 or 2 teaspoons boiling water.

Béarnaise Sauce

Mayonnaise

SERVES 6 TO 8 ▲▲▲●●

Mayonnaise is of Mediterranean descent with origins in the olive-growing areas of southern Europe. One could describe it as a cold version of Hollandaise, but it is more versatile and may be used either to coat cooked foods or cohere them together when cut into small pieces or shredded. The sauce is essentially an emulsion of egg yolks, oil, acid and seasonings and its production requires care, patience and good quality ingredients. I always advise people to make Mayonnaise when they have the time and inclination to do it properly without rushing, and also never to attempt it in stormy weather as it fails every time. Originally Mayonnaise was always prepared with olive oil but for those who find the taste overpowering,

groundnut or corn oil make admirable substitutes. For a touch of authenticity, half olive and half other oil may be used according to taste.

3 egg yolks (from Grade 3 eggs at kitchen temperature)
½ level tsp salt
½ level tsp prepared mustard (English or continental)
generous shake of white pepper
large pinch sugar
2tblsp light malt vinegar ⎱
1tblsp lemon juice ⎰ *kitchen temperature*
½pt (275ml) salad oil at kitchen temperature (for choice, see above)
1tblsp boiling water

1 Place egg yolks in bowl. Add salt, mustard, pepper, sugar and 1 tablespoon vinegar. Beat well.
2 Begin to add the oil, DROP BY DROP, beating vigorously all the time. When half the oil has been added, the Mayonnaise should have thickened to a buttery consistency.
3 Beat in remaining vinegar and lemon juice then add rest of oil in a slow, continuous stream, still whisking steadily all the time.
4 Stir in boiling water as this prevents Mayonnaise from separating out. Transfer to a non-metal container, cover securely with cling film and refrigerate until needed. DO NOT FREEZE.

WRONGS AND RIGHTS

Mayonnaise remained thin and looked curdled
1 The ingredients were too cold.
2 The oil was added too quickly. Drop by drop must be taken literally.

REMEDY Place another egg yolk into clean bowl. VERY GRADUALLY, beat thin and/or curdled Mayonnaise into it. As soon as sauce thickens, add rest of Mayonnaise a little more quickly.

Mayonnaise tasted oily and bland
Insufficient acid and/or seasoning added.

REMEDY Whisk in a few extra teaspoons of lemon juice and/or vinegar. Adjust seasoning to taste.

175

Blender Mayonnaise

SERVES 6 TO 8 ▲●●

A miraculous Mayonnaise that can be prepared in seconds rather than minutes. The chances of it misbehaving are remote, and it has a smooth, light and creamy consistency due to the inclusion of the whole egg, rather than yolk only. It is also more economical in that the Mayonnaise requires 1 whole egg instead of 3 yolks.

1 Grade 1 or 2 (large) egg
½ level tsp prepared English or continental mustard
½ level tsp salt
generous shake of white pepper
1tblsp vinegar
1½tblsp lemon juice
½pt (275ml) salad oil at kitchen temperature (for choice, see introduction to Mayonnaise)
1tblsp boiling water

1 Place whole egg, mustard, salt, pepper, vinegar and 5 tablespoons oil into blender. Cover. Blend about 45 seconds or until very smooth.
2 Uncover. With the blender running, add 1 tablespoon lemon juice and ¼pt (150ml) oil in slow, steady stream. By now Mayonnaise should have begun to thicken.
3 Trickle in rest of oil with blender running. Switch off, scrape down sides and spoon into bowl. Add last ½ tablespoon lemon juice and water. Adjust seasoning to taste if necessary.
4 Store Mayonnaise in a non-metal container. Cover securely with cling film. Refrigerate until ready to use.

VARIATIONS

Cocktail Sauce

▲▲▲ or ▲ ⎰ depending whether
●●● or ●● ⎱ Mayonnaise or Blender Mayonnaise

Add the following to full quantity of Mayonnaise:
2 rounded tablespoons tubed or canned tomato purée, 2 rounded teaspoons horseradish sauce, 1 teaspoon Worcester sauce, ½ level teaspoon prepared continental mustard, ½ level teaspoon paprika and either a pinch of cayenne pepper or shake of Tabasco (both fiery). Stir well to mix.

Serving Tip
Use for prawn or other seafood cocktails.

Green Mayonnaise (also called Sauce Verte)

▲▲▲ or ▲ ⎰ depending whether
●●● or ●● ⎱ Mayonnaise or Blender Mayonnaise

Add the following to full quantity of Mayonnaise:
2 level tablespoons scissor-snipped or chopped-up green part of spring onions, 2 rounded tablespoons finely-chopped parsley, 3 rounded tablespoons watercress leaves and 1 rounded teaspoon dried tarragon. Stir well to mix.

Serving Tip
This is a French classic, usually served with cold fish dishes such as salmon or salmon trout.

Tartare Sauce

▲▲▲ or ▲ ⎰ depending whether
●●● or ●● ⎱ Mayonnaise or Blender Mayonnaise

Add the following to full quantity of Mayonnaise:
3 rounded tablespoons finely-chopped gherkins, 1 to 2 level tablespoons drained and finely-chopped capers and 1 rounded tablespoon finely-chopped parsley. Stir to mix.

Serving Tip
Serve with all hot fried fish dishes.

Thousand Island Dressing

▲▲▲ or ▲ ⎰ depending whether
●●● or ●● ⎱ Mayonnaise or Blender Mayonnaise

Add the following to full quantity of Mayonnaise:
1 finely-chopped hard-boiled egg, 3 level tablespoons tomato ketchup, 2 level tablespoons finely-chopped stuffed olives, 1 small, peeled and finely-chopped or grated onion and 1 tablespoon finely-chopped parsley.

Serving Tip
Serve as a dressing for mixed salads and as a coating for hard-boiled eggs, portions of cold chicken and seafood.

Avocado 'Mayonnaise'

▲●●●

Although not a Mayonnaise in the accepted sense, this is such a superbly creamy and attractively coloured sauce that I think its inclusion is justified in this section. It cannot, however, be made without a blender or food processor.

1 large and ripe avocado (but not bruised and squashy)
4tblsp salad oil
1 Grade 1 or 2 (large) egg
strained juice of 1 medium lemon
½ to ¾ level tsp salt
large pinch sugar
2tsp vinegar
½ level tsp prepared mild mustard
1tblsp boiling water

1 Halve avocado. Remove stone and discard. Scoop avocado flesh into blender goblet or food processor.
2 Add all remaining ingredients except water. Run either machine until avocado mixture is smooth and creamy: 20 to 30 seconds.
3 Spoon into non-metal dish. Stir in water. Cover closely with cling film. Refrigerate until ready to serve.

Serving Tip
Use to coat portions of cold poultry, hard-boiled eggs and steaks or cutlets of fish. Also use as a dressing for seafood (seafood cocktail for example) and assorted salads.

Egg Custard Sauce

SERVES 4 TO 6 ▲▲●●●

This is very much a British traditional sauce which is known in France as Crème à l'Anglaise or English Cream. Dating back to the reign of Queen Elizabeth I, homemade Egg Custard Sauce is still one of the grandest and most sumptuous toppings for trifles (also a British institution) and is less complex to make than is generally supposed. The art, I suspect, is to leave the sauce to cook happily by itself, giving it a whisk round now and then and allowing it plenty of time to thicken. It dislikes being hurried.

Although many recipes for custard depend solely on the use of eggs to thicken it, I add a heaped teaspoon of cornflour. It has no adverse effect either on the flavour or consistency of the sauce and acts as a partial stabilizer; in other words, it helps to prevent the mixture from curdling and also acts as a slight thickener.

½pt (275ml) milk
2 Grade 3 (standard) eggs
1 egg yolk
1 heaped tsp cornflour
½ to 1tsp vanilla essence
1 rounded tblsp caster sugar

1 Bring milk slowly to boil, stirring. Pour into top of double saucepan or into basin standing over pan of gently simmering water. (I prefer the latter as there is more manoeuvrability.)
2 Add eggs, beaten until thoroughly mixed with the egg yolk. Whisk in cornflour, essence and sugar.
3 Cook gently, whisking now and then, until sauce thickens sufficiently to cling to the whisk or whatever other implement is used for beating. This could take anything up to 30 or 40 minutes, so be getting on with something else and turn your attention to the sauce periodically.
4 As soon as sauce has thickened to the correct consistency, pour into a clean dish or bowl to stop the cooking process. Either use straightaway or leave until cold.

Serving Tip
Serve with fruit pies and flans, syrup or jam tarts, steamed or baked puddings and stewed or canned fruits.

Note The sauce will thicken up on cooling.

Mayonnaise variations (page 175)

WRONGS AND RIGHTS

Custard curdled
Heat of water too high in base of double saucepan or under basin standing over pan of hot water. The custard consequently boiled and separated out.

REMEDY Tip custard into blender. Run machine until smooth.

Custard lumpy
Inadequate whisking.

REMEDY Beat until smooth or blend in blender goblet until custard is no longer lumpy.

Custard too thin
1 Too much milk used.
2 Eggs on the small side.

REMEDY In clean bowl, beat a whole egg until well-blended. Gradually whisk in thin custard. Return to top of double saucepan or into basin over hot water. Cook and whisk occasionally until smooth and thick.

MELTED BUTTER SAUCES

These are simple sauces based entirely, as their name suggests, on melted butter and served with poached fish dishes, brains (for those who can find them!) and vegetables such as asparagus and broccoli. Clarified butter should be used, otherwise a milky-looking sediment will be present, somewhat spoiling the appearance of a sauce which is supposed to be glassy clear. To clarify butter, place required amount into small pan and leave gently to melt over low heat. Allow to stand for 7 minutes. Pour butter carefully into a basin, leaving the sediment behind in the base of the pan. For safety, you can strain the melted butter into the basin through a piece of clean muslin or through a mesh sieve lined with muslin (sometimes called cheesecloth). The straining will obviously take longer than the pouring.

Black Butter Sauce (Beurre Noisette)

SERVES 4

3oz (75g) clarified butter
1tsp malt vinegar

1 Pour butter into saucepan. Leave over very low heat until it turns dark brown.
2 Remove from heat. Stir in vinegar.

Serving Tip
Serve over poached or steamed white fish dishes, poached eggs (which tend to be dull if left unadorned) and brains.

Brown Butter Sauce

SERVES 4

3oz (75g) clarified butter

1 Pour butter into saucepan. Leave over low heat until it turns a light brown. Remove from heat.

Serving Tip
Serve with poached vegetables to include asparagus, broccoli, poached chicory and hot celery. Also brains.

Meunière or Lemon Butter Sauce

SERVES 4

Many classic dishes take their name from this sauce, particularly grilled and poached fish dishes.

3oz (75g) clarified butter
1 rounded tblsp very finely-chopped fresh parsley
3tsp lemon juice
¼ level tsp finely-grated lemon peel
1 or 2 shakes of white pepper

1 Pour butter into saucepan. Leave over low heat until butter turns light brown.
2 Remove from heat. Stir in rest of ingredients.

Serving Tip
Serve over grilled, poached or steamed white fish dishes. Also trout.

HARD BUTTER SAUCES

These sauces are the ones most closely associated with Christmas, as they are the customary ones to serve with hot mince pies and rich plum pudding. Because they improve with keeping, they can be prepared well ahead of time, transferred to small containers, covered closely with cling film and left in the refrigerator until ready for use. The Hard Sauces may also be deep frozen for up to 6 months.

Brandy Hard Sauce (Brandy Butter)

SERVES 6

4oz (125g) unsalted butter, softened but not runny
4oz (125g) caster sugar (or mixture of caster and sifted icing)
2tblsp brandy
mixed spice for dusting over top

1 Place butter into bowl and beat until very light.
2 Gradually beat in sugar (or sugars) alternately with brandy.
3 Continue to beat until mixture is very light, fluffy and consistency of whipped cream.
4 Spoon into a small serving dish. Sprinkle with mixed spice. Leave until hard before adding, in pieces, to hot mince pies or pudding.

Rum Hard Sauce (Rum Butter)

SERVES 6

Make exactly as *Brandy Hard Sauce* but use soft brown sugar instead of caster and add a level teaspoon finely-grated lemon peel when creaming butter and sugar together. Substitute dark rum for brandy and sprinkle Hard Sauce with cinnamon instead of spice. For a smoother consistency, use half brown and half sifted icing sugar.

Cumberland Rum Butter

SERVES 6

This is a close relation of *Rum Hard Sauce*. To make, follow recipe but omit lemon peel. Instead, add a squeeze of lemon and finally beat in ¼ level teaspoon ground nutmeg. If liked, dust with a hint of extra nutmeg.

SAVOURY BUTTERS

These are the savoury versions of the *Hard Butter Sauces* (above) which I mentioned in the introduction to this section. Their aim is to add richness, flavour and a marginal amount of moisture to grilled meats and fish, but as only comparatively small amounts of the Butters are added to specific dishes they are not a direct substitute for a coating or pouring sauce. A good quality spreading margarine, or butter substitute, may replace butter.

Anchovy Butter

SERVES 4 TO 5

2oz (50g) butter
3 canned anchovy fillets, well drained
1tsp lemon juice

1 Beat butter to a cream.
2 Chop anchovies very finely. Beat into butter with lemon juice.
3 Shape into a small square block or into sausage shape.
4 Wrap in cling film. Refrigerate until hard. Cut into slices.

Serving Tip
Serve atop portions of grilled white fish.

Curry Butter

SERVES 4 TO 5

Follow recipe for *Anchovy Butter* but use 2 level teaspoons mild curry powder and a large pinch mixed spice in place of anchovies. Keep amount of lemon juice the same.

Serving Tip
Serve atop grilled chicken portions, pork chops or gammon steaks. Also shellfish.

Garlic Butter

SERVES 4 TO 5

Follow recipe for *Anchovy Butter* but use 2 medium-sized crushed garlic cloves in place of anchovies. Omit lemon juice.

Serving Tip
Serve atop grilled steaks or spread between cuts of a French loaf which is to be wrapped and oven-heated and served hot as garlic bread with soups or meat dishes.

Maître d'Hôtel Butter

SERVES 4 TO 5

Follow recipe for *Anchovy Butter* but use 1 rounded teaspoon very finely-

Bolognese Sauce (page 180)

chopped fresh parsley in place of anchovies. Increase lemon juice to 2 teaspoons.

Serving Tip
Serve atop grilled fish dishes.

Mustard Butter

SERVES 4 TO 5 ▲▲●●●

Follow recipe for *Anchovy Butter* but use 1 slightly rounded teaspoon prepared English or continental mustard in place of anchovies. Increase lemon juice to 2 teaspoons.

Serving Tip
Serve atop grilled meats, gammon, fish, shellfish and grilled mackerel.

Note These Butters can be made in a food processor but, in view of the small amounts involved, it is hardly worthwhile. However, as the Butters may be frozen up to 4 months, they can be made in bulk in a processor.

MARINADES

All Marinades serve as a 'souse' in which meats, poultry and fish are left to soak (mariné in French) for anything up to 12 hours. The object is to make foods more tender, to improve flavour and preserve colour. When strained, Marinades can be converted into coating sauces using the basic sauce proportion of ½pt (275ml) Marinade to a roux made from 1oz (25g) EACH fat and flour. Because most Marinades contain an acid, both they and the foods should be placed in non-metal containers. Small cubes of meat and fish should be marinated for about 3 to 4 hours; whole chickens and joints of meat, 8 to 12 hours. The containers should be covered and, to prevent contamination, left in the refrigerator or coldest part of a pantry or larder.

Red Wine Marinade

▲▲●●●

¼pt (150ml) dry red wine
¼pt (150ml) water
1 large onion, peeled and cut into eighths
1 large carrot, peeled and thickly sliced
2 rounded tblsp coarsely-chopped parsley
1 bouquet garni
1 small garlic clove, peeled and sliced (optional)
1 level tsp salt
¼ level tsp white or black pepper, depending on taste

1 Place all ingredients into saucepan. Bring slowly to boil. Lower heat.

2 Simmer, uncovered, until liquid is reduced by about one-third. Remove from heat. Leave until lukewarm.

3 Strain. Leave until completely cold.

Use for:
Steaks and joints of beef or lamb. Offal such as heart and kidney.

White Wine Marinade

▲▲●●●

Make exactly as *Red Wine Marinade* but use dry white wine instead of red and add 1 × 3in (7½cm) strip of well-washed orange peel and the same of lemon peel.

Use for:
Fish, meat and poultry.

Cider Marinade

▲▲●●

Make exactly as *Red Wine Marinade* but instead of wine and water, use all *dry* cider.

Use for:
Fish, poultry, pork and veal.

SALAD DRESSINGS

These are made from a base of oil and vinegar or lemon juice (or a combination of the two acids) and used for all types of mixed and green salads. To prevent vegetables from wilting, the Dressing should be added to the salad at the moment of serving and not in advance. It is also important not to drench the salad with Dressing otherwise the liquid will end up as a pool in the base of the bowl. The art is to add sufficient Dressing only to moisten and coat the foods, and a heavy hand is never the answer. As can be seen from the short selection of recipes which follow, Salad Dressings have their own basic proportion and this is 2 parts oil to 1 part vinegar and/or lemon juice.

179

French or Vinaigrette Dressing

MAKES ABOUT ¼PT (150ML) ▲●●

4tblsp salad oil
½ level tsp salt
½ level tsp powder mustard
1 or 2 shakes of white pepper
¼tsp Worcester sauce (optional)
pinch of sugar
2tblsp vinegar (or half vinegar and half lemon juice)

1 Beat oil with salt, mustard, pepper, Worcester sauce (if used) and sugar.
2 Gradually whisk in vinegar (or vinegar and lemon juice) and continue whisking until Dressing thickens and it is obvious that the oil and acid have formed an emulsion; about 1 minute maximum.

Serving Tip
Serve with all green and mixed salads and either toss Dressing with the ingredients or use as a coating – the recipe should specify. Use also for coleslaw, rice and pasta salads.

Note The emulsion quickly separates, so if the Dressing needs to stand, whisk before using. For a milder flavour, use lemon juice only. If storing Dressing, make sure it is kept well covered with either cling film or lid of container into which it was poured. Do not use a metal cover because it will react adversely with the acid in the Dressing. Do not freeze but store in the refrigerator for up to 4 to 6 weeks.

Blender Tip
Pour all ingredients into blender goblet. Cover. Run machine until Dressing has thickened; about 15 to 20 seconds.

Garlic Dressing

MAKES ¼PT (150ML) ▲●●

Follow recipe for *French* or *Vinaigrette Dressing*, adding 1 crushed garlic clove with the sugar.

Serving Tip
Serve with green and tomato salads. Also as a Marinade for whole, raw mushrooms and for coleslaw.

Blue Cheese Dressing

MAKES ¼PT (150ML) ▲●●●

Follow recipe for *French* or *Vinaigrette Dressing* but, before starting, mash 1oz (25g) blue vein cheese (Danish Blue, Italian Gorgonzola, French Roquefort or British Stilton) in small bowl. Gradually blend in oil followed by next 5 ingredients. Whisk in vinegar (or vinegar and lemon juice) as directed.

Serving Tip
Serve with green salads, especially those made with wedges of crisp lettuce.

Salad 'Cream'

▲▲●●

As I have been asked for this so often, I think its inclusion in this section is valid. This is a cooked Salad 'Cream' which is both flavoursome and economic. It is less expensive than Mayonnaise and serves a similar function. The only thing I have against this type of dressing is that it forms a skin which must be removed before using.

1 level tsp powder mustard
2 level tblsp plain flour
1 level tblsp caster sugar
½ level tsp salt
3tblsp malt vinegar
¼pt (150ml) water
1 Grade 1 or 2 egg
pepper to taste
2tblsp top of the milk or canned evaporated milk

1 Sift mustard and flour into a basin. Add sugar and salt. Gradually mix to a smooth cream with vinegar and some of the water.
2 Whisk rest of water and egg well together. Blend with ingredients already in basin. Season with pepper.
3 Stand basin over saucepan of gently boiling water. Leave to cook (as with the *Egg Custard Sauce* on page 176) until Salad 'Cream' thickens to a whipped cream consistency and clings heavily to the whisk.
4 Whisk every 5 minutes or so and allow plenty of time.
5 Remove basin from heat as soon as mixture has cooked sufficiently. Whisk in milk. Cover with a piece of damp greaseproof paper.

6 Leave until completely cold before removing paper (skin will come away with it) and using as required.

Note The Salad 'Cream' is best if used up within 48 hours of making and should be stored in the refrigerator. A secure cover is advisable as the Salad 'Cream' readily absorbs odours from stronger-smelling foods. If it thickens up too much for personal taste, thin down with a little extra vinegar or milk.

Bolognese Sauce

SERVES 4 ▲▲●●

2tblsp olive or salad oil
1 large onion, peeled and chopped
2 medium garlic cloves, peeled and chopped
8oz (225g) lean minced beef
3 rashers streaky bacon, chopped (optional)
1 medium celery stalk, washed and finely chopped
1 medium carrot, peeled and grated
4 large tomatoes, skinned and chopped
4oz (100 to 125g) trimmed mushrooms and stalks, washed and coarsely chopped
5 rounded tblsp tubed or canned tomato purée
6tblsp dry red wine
½pt (275ml) water
1 bouquet garni
1 level tsp sugar (brown or white, according to availability)
1 to 2 level tsp salt
pepper to taste

1 Heat oil in pan. Add onion and garlic. Fry over medium heat until golden brown. Add mince.
2 Increase heat. Fry fairly briskly until crumbly, fork-stirring frequently. (If pan is non-stick, use spatula.) Add bacon (if used), celery and carrot. Continue to fry a further 7 to 10 minutes or until soft.
3 Stir in rest of ingredients. Bring slowly to boil, mixing well. Lower heat. Cover. Simmer gently about 1¼ to 1¾ hours. Remove bouquet garni. Use as required.

Serving Tip
Serve with spaghetti.

Freezer Tip
Cold sauce may be deep frozen up to 3 months. To serve, thaw completely and boil gently for 15 to 20 minutes.

Neapolitan Sauce

SERVES 6　　　　▲●●

3tblsp olive or salad oil
1 large onion, peeled and chopped
2 garlic cloves, peeled and chopped
2lb (900g) ripe tomatoes skinned
　and chopped, or 1 large can
　(about 1¾lb or 800g) Italian
　tomatoes
2 rounded tsp sugar
2 rounded tblsp tubed or canned
　tomato purée
salt and pepper to taste
2 rounded tblsp fresh chopped
　parsley
1 level tsp dried basil

1　Heat oil in heavy-based pan. Add onion and garlic. Fry gently until both turn light gold.
2　Stir in tomatoes, sugar and purée. Bring to boil, mixing well. Lower heat. Season to taste. Cover.
3　Simmer ¾ hour, stirring occasionally. Uncover. Continue to bubble gently for another 20 to 30 minutes so that sauce thickens of its own accord as some of the liquid evaporates. Stir frequently as any tomato mixture has a tendency to burn.
4　Add parsley and basil and mix in well. Simmer 5 more minutes. Remove from heat.

Serving Tip
As this is a typically Italian sauce, it can be served with all kinds of pasta from spaghetti to ribbon noodles.

Freezer Tip
Sauce may be deep frozen up to 3 months.

Sauce Pizzaiola

SERVES 6　　　　▲●●

Follow recipe for *Neapolitan Sauce* but increase garlic to 3 cloves and double the amount of parsley.

Serving Tip
This is another classic Italian sauce which lends its name to a completed dish — Steak Pizzaiola for instance — and may therefore be served with meat and poultry in addition to pasta.

Freezer Tip
Sauce may be deep frozen up to 3 months.

Neapolitan Sauce

Sweet-Sour Sauce

SERVES 6 TO 8　　　　▲▲●●

1tblsp salad oil
1 small onion, peeled and thinly
　sliced
1 small celery stalk, scrubbed and
　thinly sliced
1 small carrot, peeled and thinly
　sliced
4 canned or fresh pineapple rings,
　chopped
½pt (275ml) chicken stock (use
　cube or powder and water)
1oz (25g) sultanas
¼ level tsp powder ginger
¼pt (150ml) light malt vinegar
2oz (50g) caster or soft brown
　sugar (light variety)
1tblsp Soy sauce (light for
　preference and now more
　generally available)
2 level tblsp cornflour
2tblsp cold water
salt to taste

1　Heat oil in pan. Add prepared vegetables and pineapple. Mix well. Cover. Cook very gently for about 10 minutes or until vegetables are soft but still pale in colour.
2　Pour stock into pan. Add sultanas, ginger, vinegar, sugar and Soy sauce. Bring to boil, stirring. Lower heat. Cover. Simmer 10 minutes.
3　Meanwhile, mix cornflour smoothly with water. Gradually blend into sauce. Cook, stirring continuously, until it comes to the boil and thickens. Simmer 2 minutes when sauce should be clear. Season. Use as required.

Serving Tip
Serve with pork, fish and shell-fish dishes.

Freezer Tip
Sauce may be deep frozen up to 2 months.

181

Sweet-Sour Sauce (page 181)

Tomato Sauce

SERVES 6 TO 8 ▲▲●●

2tblsp salad oil
1 medium onion, peeled and very
*   finely chopped or grated*
2oz (50g) streaky bacon, chopped
1 small carrot, peeled and grated
1oz (25g) plain flour
1lb (450g) blanched tomatoes,
*   skinned and chopped*
¼pt (150ml) water
2 rounded tblsp tubed or canned
*   tomato purée*
¼ level tsp dried mixed herbs
¼ level tsp ground nutmeg
1 level tsp salt
1 bouquet garni
white pepper to taste
1 level tblsp very finely-chopped
*   fresh parsley*

1 Heat oil in pan. Add onion. Fry gently until pale gold. Add bacon and carrot. Fry a further 5 minutes.
2 Stir in flour to form roux. Cook 1 minute. Add tomatoes and water. Cook, stirring continuously, until sauce comes to boil and thickens.
3 Blend in purée, herbs, nutmeg and salt. Stir well to mix. Add bouquet garni and pepper. Bring to boil. Lower heat. Cover.
4 Simmer very gently for ¾ hour, stirring frequently to prevent burning. Take off heat. Remove bouquet garni. Either rub sauce through fine mesh sieve or blend until smooth in blender goblet.

5 Pour into clean pan, add parsley and reheat before serving.

Serving Tip
Serve with poultry, eggs, cheese, meat, offal and fish dishes.

Freezer Tip
Sauce may be deep frozen up to 3 months.

Barbecue Sauce

FOR ABOUT 6 SERVINGS ▲●●

A barbecue sauce is more a baste than a sauce, characteristically brushed over foods which are being either barbecued, spit-roasted or grilled. Its object is to intensify flavour and increase glaze, thus making the food look and taste more appetizing and piquant.

1tblsp salad oil
1 small onion, peeled and very
*   finely chopped*
4tblsp tubed or canned tomato
*   purée*
¼pt (150ml) water
2tsp Worcester sauce
1 level tsp continental mustard
2tblsp vinegar
3tsp soft brown sugar (dark
*   variety)*
1 level tsp paprika
1tsp Soy sauce
2 or 3 drops Tabasco (very hot,
*   so can be optional)*
½ level tsp salt

1 Heat salad oil in sturdy pan. Add onion. Fry gently until light gold.
2 Add all remaining ingredients. Bring to boil, stirring. Lower heat.
3 Simmer, uncovered, until sauce is reduced by half. Strain.

Use for:
Brushing over cutlets of fish, steaks, chops, beefburgers, kebabs and poultry.

Curry Sauce

SERVES 6 TO 8 ▲▲●●

2tblsp salad oil
1 large onion, peeled and chopped
2 garlic cloves, peeled and crushed
2tblsp mild or strong curry
*   powder (depending on taste)*
1tblsp plain flour
¾pt (425ml) meat or poultry stock
*   (vegetarians can use vegetable*
*   water)*
2tblsp tubed or canned tomato
*   purée*
½ level tsp turmeric
¼ level tsp ground ginger
¼ level tsp powdered cinnamon
large pinch ground cloves or
*   ¼ level tsp ground allspice*
1 level tsp garam masala
2tblsp mango chutney
1 small Bramley apple, peeled and
*   grated*
juice of ½ small lemon
2 level tblsp desiccated coconut
2 rounded tblsp sultanas
2 to 3 level tsp salt

1 Heat oil in large pan. Add onion and garlic. Fry gently until deep gold. Stir in curry powder. Fry $\frac{1}{2}$ minute, stirring.
2 Blend in flour. Gradually add stock, cooking until sauce comes to boil and thickens. Stir frequently.
3 Add all remaining ingredients. Mix in well. Again bring to boil. Lower heat. Cover.
4 Simmer gently for $\frac{3}{4}$ hour, stirring frequently. Adjust seasoning to taste and either serve sauce as it is or rub through a fine mesh sieve if a smooth consistency is preferred. Reheat.

Serving Tip
Use as a base for reheating left-over cooked meat, poultry or nut dishes. Alternatively, spoon over hard-boiled eggs to make Egg Curry.

Freezer Tip
Sauce may be deep frozen up to 2 months.

Tomato Sauce

Cranberry Sauce

SERVES 6 ▲▲●●

6oz (175g) caster sugar
$\frac{1}{4}$pt (150ml) water
8oz (225g) fresh cranberries
(available in late autumn and winter)

1 Place sugar and water into saucepan. Heat slowly until sugar dissolves. Bring to boil.
2 Add cranberries and boil briskly until skins pop open. The popping noise is fairly audible and takes 2 to 3 minutes.
3 Reduce heat. Simmer sauce gently, uncovered, for 8 minutes. Stir occasionally. Leave until completely cold before serving. Cover leftovers and refrigerate about 2 weeks.

Serving Tip
Serve as a relish with poultry, game and pork dishes.

Bread Sauce

SERVES 6 TO 8 ▲▲●●●

4 cloves
1 large onion, peeled
1 bouquet garni
$\frac{1}{4}$ level tsp ground nutmeg
$\frac{1}{2}$pt (275ml) milk
$\frac{1}{2}$ level tsp salt
shake white pepper
3oz (75g) fresh white breadcrumbs
1oz (25g) butter
3tblsp double cream

1 Press cloves into onion. Place in saucepan with bouquet garni, nutmeg, milk, salt and pepper.
2 Very slowly bring to boil. Draw away from heat. Cover. Leave to infuse for 1 hour. Strain.
3 Pour into clean pan. Add crumbs. Cook gently, stirring, until sauce becomes thick and milk has absorbed most of the crumbs.
4 Add butter and cream. Reheat until hot, stirring constantly. Adjust seasoning. Serve hot.

Serving Tip
Serve as an accompaniment to poultry.

Horseradish Sauce

SERVES 6 TO 8 ▲▲●●●

$\frac{1}{4}$pt (150ml) double cream (or 1 carton of 5oz (142ml) soured cream)
2tblsp cold milk
3tsp mild vinegar
2 level tblsp horseradish, finely-grated (available ready-prepared in jars)
salt, pepper and a little sugar to taste

1 If using double cream whip until thick with the milk. If using sour cream, thin down with milk.
2 Stir remaining ingredients into either of the creams.
3 Transfer to a serving dish.

Serving Tip
Serve with roast beef, smoked trout and smoked mackerel. Also very good with boiled beef.

Curry Sauce (page 182)

Apple Sauce

SERVES 6 TO 8 ▲●●

1lb (450g) peeled cooking apples,
    cored and sliced
4tblsp water
2 to 3tsp sugar
1 rounded tsp butter or margarine,
    melted

1 Place apples and water into pan.
  Bring to boil. Lower heat straightaway. Cover.
2 Cook slowly until apples are very
  soft and pulpy, watching them
  carefully to see that they do not
  boil dry or burn.
3 Beat to smooth purée then beat in
  sugar and butter. Serve warm or
  cold.

Serving Tip
Serve with pork dishes, pork sausages, duck and goose.

Freezer Tip
Sauce may be deep frozen up to 6
months.

Note Consistency may be made
smoother if ingredients are blended
together in blender goblet.

Mint Sauce

SERVES 6 ▲▲●

4 rounded tblsp very finely-
    chopped fresh mint
2tblsp boiling water
2 level tsp caster sugar
2tblsp malt vinegar
¼ to ½ level tsp salt

1 Tip mint into small bowl. In small
  cup, mix together water and sugar
  and stir briskly until sugar dissolves.
2 Add to mint with vinegar and salt.
  Leave until cool.

Serving Tip
Serve with roast lamb.

Chocolate Sauce (1)

SERVES 6 TO 8 ▲▲●●●

¼pt (150ml) milk
1oz (25g) plain chocolate, broken
    or cut into small pieces
3oz (75g) soft brown sugar (light
    variety)
1½oz (40g) cocoa powder, sifted
½tsp vanilla essence
1oz (25g) butter

1 Pour milk into pan. Add all remaining ingredients. Stir over low
  heat until chocolate has melted.
2 Bring to boil. Boil briskly, without
  stirring, for 2 minutes if thinnish
  sauce is required; 3 to 4 minutes
  if fudge-like consistency is preferred.

Serving Tip
Serve over ice cream, ice cream sundaes and Profiteroles.

Mocha Sauce

SERVES 6 TO 8 ▲▲●●●

Make exactly as *Chocolate Sauce (1)*,
adding 2 rounded teaspoons instant
coffee powder or granules to milk
with rest of ingredients.

Note Cover leftovers and refrigerate.
Reheat gently before using.

Chocolate Sauce (2)

SERVES 6 ▲▲●●●

1 level tblsp cornflour
½pt (275ml) cold milk
2oz (50g) plain chocolate, broken
    into small pieces
½oz (15g) butter or margarine
2 level tblsp caster sugar
½tsp vanilla essence

1 Mix cornflour to smooth cream
  with some of the milk. Pour rest
  of milk into pan. Add chocolate.
  Stir over low heat until chocolate
  melts.
2 Whisk hot chocolate milk into
  cornflour mixture. Transfer to
  saucepan. Cook, stirring, until
  sauce comes to boil and thickens.
3 Simmer 2 minutes. Add butter,
  sugar and vanilla essence. Remove from heat. Stir until butter
  and sugar melt. Serve hot.

Serving Tip
Serve over steamed and baked sponge
puddings.

Fudge Sauce

SERVES 6 ▲▲●●●

2oz (50g) soft brown sugar (light
    variety)
2 level tblsp melted golden syrup
1oz (25g) butter or margarine
4tblsp unsweetened evaporated
    milk
2tblsp rose hip syrup

1 Place all ingredients except rose
  hip syrup into pan. Heat slowly,
  stirring, until sugar dissolves and
  butter or margarine melts.
2 Bring to boil, stirring continuously. Boil steadily for 4 minutes,
  leaving pan uncovered and mixture unstirred.
3 Remove from heat, cool to lukewarm and stir in rose hip syrup.
  Use as required.

Serving Tip
Serve over ice cream or ice cream
sundaes.

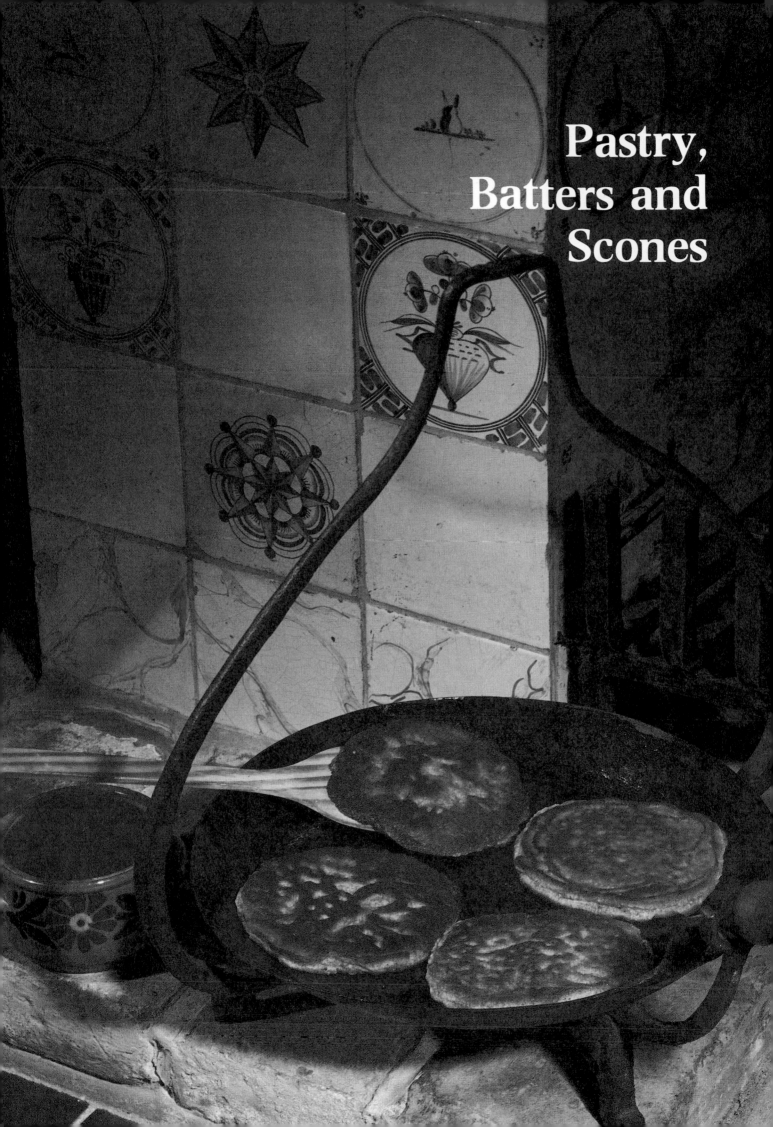

Pastry,
Batters and
Scones

Pastry, Batters and Scones

After many years of experimentation, I am now certain in my own mind that light, crisp pastry is not solely dependent on cold hands and marble slabs as was once supposed. Successful pastry results from the correct proportions of fat and water to flour, knowing how to work the ingredients together and why, and baking the various pastries in oven temperatures most suited to the nature of each. ALL pastry prefers a light hand to a heavy one; cold fingers to hot ones; cool surroundings to warm ones. But if these conditions cannot be met, one will still be able to produce highly acceptable, edible pastry, provided the recipe instructions are followed carefully and the line drawings referred to for clarity.

Whereas yeast mixtures are, in the main, good-natured and happy enough to withstand a fair amount of brusque kneading and 'knocking-about' without coming to any harm, pastry is more sensitive by far and resents too much attention in the form of over-handling. Additionally, most pastry responds best to plain flour, the exceptions being Suet Crust (the pastry used for traditional Steak and Kidney Pie, page 72) and a kind of mock Rough Puff I made up myself. For both of these, self-raising flour, or plain flour with baking powder, is generally recommended. The proportion of baking powder is 4½ level teaspoons to every 1lb (450g) flour, although please be guided by the instructions on the tin or packet of baking powder you are using.

Shortcrust Pastry

Shortcrust Pastry

MAKES ABOUT 6OZ (175G) ▲▲●

4oz (125g) plain flour
¼ level tsp salt (or generous pinch)
1oz (25g) lard or white cooking fat
1oz (25g) butter or margarine
1½ to 2tblsp COLD or chilled water
  to mix

1 Using a round-bladed knife, cut fat into flour

2 Rub fat into flour by passing it across fingertips with thumbs. Lift mixture out of bowl to incorporate air

3 After adding water, mix to a paste with a fork

186

1 Sift flour and salt into roomy bowl to give you space to move about in comfort.

2 Add both types of fat. Using a round-bladed knife, cut fat into flour until it is in pieces no larger than peas.

3 Rub fat into flour by passing it across fingertips with thumbs. At the same time, lift mixture out of bowl to incorporate air which, in turn, will lighten the pastry.

4 Continue to rub in until mixture looks like a mass of fine bread-crumbs.

5 Sprinkle ALL the water over the top in ONE go. Using a fork, mix to a paste which forms large crumbles.

6 Gather together with fingertips. Turn out on to work surface lightly dusted with flour. Knead quickly and lightly, again with fingertips, to smooth ball. Wrap in foil or cling film, then leave pastry to 'relax' for 30 minutes in the refrigerator.

7 Roll out thinly with floured rolling pin, using short, forward movements. DO NOT roll over edges of pastry and DO NOT turn it over, or you will work in too much flour and toughen the pastry.

Use for:
Large and small tarts, flans, large and small pies (tops and bottoms), pasties and turnovers.

VARIATIONS

Sweet Shortcrust Pastry

MAKES ABOUT 7OZ (200G)
▲▲●

Make exactly as *Shortcrust Pastry* but sift 1 rounded tablespoon icing sugar with flour and salt. Caster sugar may be used if preferred, but it is liable to pepper the baked pastry with tiny brown speckles.

Flan Pastry

MAKES ABOUT 7OZ (200G)
▲▲●●

This is basically Shortcrust Pastry made only with butter and enriched with egg. It turns into a warm golden colour when baked and is ideally suited to flan or tartlet cases which are to be filled with creamy

Flan Pastry 1 Shape enriched pastry into a ball

custards or whipped cream and then topped with fresh, seasonal fruits. Make exactly as *Shortcrust Pastry* but sift 1 rounded tablespoon icing sugar with flour and salt. Use butter for rubbing in. Mix with 2 tablespoons very well-beaten egg.

Brown Pastry

MAKES ABOUT 6OZ (175G)
▲▲●

A healthy, full-flavoured pastry which is best for savoury dishes. Either use half brown flour and half white or all brown flour. Make exactly as *Shortcrust Pastry* but use 4oz (125g) mixture of white and either wholemeal or wheatmeal flour. Do not sift.

Cheese Pastry

MAKES ABOUT 6OZ (175G)
▲▲●●

Full-flavoured and appetizing, Cheese Pastry may be used for all manner of savoury flans in addition to Cheese Straws (page 151) and Cheese Biscuits (page 151). Make exactly as *Shortcrust Pastry* but sift ½ level teaspoon powder mustard with flour and salt. Use only butter or margarine for rubbing in, then toss in 2oz (50g) very FINELY-GRATED Cheddar, Edam or Gouda cheese. Mix with 2 to 2½ tablespoons well-beaten egg.

Biscuit Crust Pastry

MAKES ABOUT 8OZ (225G)
▲▲●●

Usually turned into plain biscuits (page 148), this fairly rich pastry

2 Roll out and cut as required

may be substituted for Flan Pastry (this page) if a more luxurious crust is called for. Make exactly as *Shortcrust Pastry*, but use only butter or margarine and increase the amount by ½oz (15g). Toss in 2oz (50g) caster sugar. Mix with 1½ tablespoons very well-beaten egg. Leave in the refrigerator to 'relax' for about 40 minutes.

Cheese Pastry

Biscuit Crust Pastry (page 187)

Savoury Pastries

MAKES ABOUT 6OZ (175G)
▲▲●●

Make up recipe for either *Shortcrust Pastry*, *Brown Pastry* or *Cheese Pastry*. Cut out into 12 to 16 assorted shapes with fancy biscuit cutters or into finger-length rectangles of 1in (2½cm) in width. (The Cheese Pastry will yield about 20 biscuits or 30 fingers.) Transfer to baking trays (see notes below). Brush with beaten egg. Sprinkle tops with either caraway, sesame or poppy seeds and rock salt. Bake about 7–10 minutes in hot oven set to 220°C (425°F), Gas 7. Remove from oven. Transfer to wire cooling racks and leave until completely cold before storing in an air-tight container.

Cocktail Biscuits

MAKES BETWEEN 12 AND 20, DEPENDING ON RECIPE   ▲▲●●

These are identical to *Savoury Pastries* above, so follow exactly the same method of making.

Short-Cut Shortcrust Pastry

MAKES 6OZ (175G)   ▲▲●

An easily-worked pastry with no rubbing in required.

> 4oz (125g) plain flour
> ¼ level tsp salt (or generous pinch)
> 2oz (50g) whipped-up white
>   cooking fat or margarine (or
>   mixture)
> 2tblsp cold water

1 Sift flour and salt on to plate. Take a heaped tablespoon of flour mixture and put into bowl.

2 Add fat or margarine and cold water. Whisk with a fork for about ½ minute.

3 Gradually add rest of flour, stirring to form a paste that holds together.

4 Wrap in foil or cling film. Refrigerate ½ hour before rolling out as described in recipe for Short crust Pastry (page 186).

Oil Shortcrust Pastry

MAKES ABOUT 10OZ (275G)
▲▲●●

This is Shortcrust Pastry made entirely with oil. It is fairly rich, needs careful handling, but is well-suited to those who have to avoid animal fats. It should be used for savoury dishes only.

> 5tblsp salad oil (sunflower,
>   groundnut, corn etc but NOT
>   olive as it has too strong a
>   flavour)
> 2tblsp cold water
> 8oz (225g) plain flour } sifted
> ½ level tsp salt

1 Pour oil and water into bowl. Whisk briskly to blend, using fork or small hand whisk.

2 Using a fork, gradually stir in sifted flour and salt to form a dough.

3 Draw together to form a ball. Roll out between 2 sheets of lightly-floured greaseproof paper or unfloured, non-stick parchment paper.

Note Handle carefully, as this pastry has a tendency to break easily.

Success Tips

1 A combination of fats is recommended for basic Shortcrust Pastry, because the use of all lard or cooking fat would make the pastry taste too greasy, while margarine or butter would produce a fine-flavoured pastry but a somewhat tough one.

2 Fingertips are advised for rubbing in because these are the coolest part of the hands. The palms are always warmer and, if used for making pastry, could produce a heavy result.

3 Never stretch the pastry in an effort to make it fit as it will shrink back on itself while baking. If there are gaps, 'patch' up with dampened pastry trimmings, securing them to the main body of the pastry by gently pressing with fingertips.

4 Looking through recipe books you may come across the term 'bake blind'. This refers to baking a flan case with no filling in it and, to prevent the pastry from rising unevenly as it bakes, the case should be lined with a piece of foil large enough to cover the base and sides completely. The foil should be pressed very gently against the pastry so that it holds in position. In order for the pastry to brown, the foil lining should be lifted out of the flan case very carefully about two-thirds of the way through

Savoury Pastries

the baking time, and the case returned to the oven until golden brown and completely cooked. Instead of foil a piece of grease-proof paper, weighed down with uncooked haricot beans (kept especially for this purpose), can be used instead but this is a some-what old-fashioned method.

5 Do not prick an uncooked pastry case if, after baking, it is to be filled with a liquidy mixture. The holes might not close up and the filling could seep out.

6 When making a fruit pie in a pie dish or on a pie plate, make sure the top layer, immediately under the pastry, is fruit AND NOT sugar. This is because if pastry comes into direct contact with sugar it becomes soggy.

7 To keep a fruit pie a good shape, ensure that the filling is cold and well-domed up in the middle to support the pastry. Make 2 knife slits in the top to allow steam to escape and prevent sogginess. Also leave to stand for 10 min-utes in the cool before baking as this helps to prevent shrinkage during baking.

8 In general, tins used for baking Shortcrust Pastry do not need greasing as it rarely sticks. How-ever, do so if it gives you more confidence.

9 While plain flour is always recommended for purists (and I have done the same for exact-ness) self-raising flour may be used for Shortcrust Pastry if the pastry is going to be used as a pie topping where the amount of rise is not critical. If used for unfilled flan cases, the pastry would puff up too much, leaving insufficient space for the total amount of filling. Self-raising flour also produces a softer and more 'cakey' pastry which is sometimes tricky to handle. It also stales more quickly than pastry made with plain flour.

10 For success, try to ensure that all ingredients are at kitchen tem-perature. If you suddenly find you have to make pastry in a hurry and the fat is hard, grate it into the flour and salt.

11 When the weight of homemade pastry is given in a recipe, this refers to the amount of flour used to start with and NOT the total weight of made-up pastry. Thus 6oz (175g) Shortcrust Pastry means you make up a pastry mix based on 6oz (175g) flour. When the weight of shop-bought, ready-prepared pastry is given, this DOES mean total weight.

Storage Tip

To save time, pastry at the 'bread-crumb' stage should be transferred to a large polythene bag, tied securely at the top and stored up to 10 days in the refrigerator. Amounts to suit can then be made up into pastry, allowing 1 tablespoon cold water to every 3oz (75g) mix of flour and fat. If you use pastry in large quantities, it is worthwhile making up a 1lb (450g) batch of mixture using 1lb (450g) flour and $\frac{1}{2}$lb (225g) fat, and leaving it at the 'breadcrumb' stage until needed. Cooked pastry dishes containing meat, fish, poultry, offal, white sauce mixtures and eggs MUST be stored in the refrigerator to prevent contamination and should be kept no longer than 2 to 3 days. Sweet dishes such as jam tarts and mince pies can be stored in an air-tight tin.

Freezer Tip

Freeze uncooked pastry up to 3 months; cooked pastry dishes up to 6 months. Thaw completely before rolling out/reheating. If preferred, uncooked pastry may be shaped into flan cases, tartlet cases and pie lids, fast frozen until hard (uncovered), then transferred to suitable con-tainers. They should then be sealed securely, labelled and stored up to 3 months. Again, unwrap and thaw before using.

WRONGS AND REASONS

Pastry tough
1 Not enough fat used in proportion to flour.
2 Too much water used for mixing.
3 Pastry kneaded too much.
4 Too much flour used for rolling out.
5 Oven not hot enough; most Short-crust Pastry should be baked at 220°C (425°F), Gas 7.

Pastry crumbly and breaks up if rolled
1 Too much fat used in proportion to flour.
2 Insufficient water added.

Pastry heavy and/or soggy
1 Too much water used for mixing.
2 Filling very wet (in pies and turnovers for example).

Suet Crust Pastry

3 Oven too cool.
4 Pastry not cooked for long enough.

Pastry blistered
1 Fat not rubbed into flour sufficiently.
2 Water added piecemeal and not all at once.
3 Pastry not kneaded evenly.

Suet Crust Pastry

MAKES ABOUT 7OZ (200G) ▲●

4oz (125g) self-raising flour
$\frac{1}{4}$ level tsp salt
$\frac{1}{2}$ level tsp baking powder (for extra lightness)
2oz (50g) packeted shredded suet or finely-chopped beef suet
4tblsp cold water to mix

1 Sift flour, salt and baking powder into bowl. Toss in suet.
2 Using a fork, mix to soft, but not sticky, dough with the water.
3 Turn out on to floured board. Knead lightly until smooth.
4 Roll out to $\frac{1}{8}$in ($\frac{1}{4}$cm) in thickness. Use as required.

Use for:

British traditional dishes such as steamed steak pudding with either mushrooms or kidney, steamed fruit puddings and assorted steamed or baked roly polys. It is interesting to note that this is a typically British pastry and the only one used for lining and covering pudding basins.

VARIATION

Dumplings

MAKES 8

Another national institution, suet dumplings are traditionally served with Beef Stew (page 71), casseroles, soups, and also Boiled Beef and Carrots (page 73). To make, follow recipe for *Suet Crust Pastry*. Shape mixture into 8 equal-sized dumplings. Add to meat, soup etc about 25 minutes before the end of cooking time.

Storage Tip
Store goods made with suet, well-wrapped, for no longer than 1 day in the refrigerator. Reheat before serving.

Freezing Tip
Fast freeze cooked foods, uncovered, until hard. Remove from basins etc. Wrap and seal securely. Freeze up to 4 months. Thaw completely. Re-steam about 1½ to 2 hours before serving. If baked foods, wrap in foil and reheat in moderate oven set in 180°C (350°F), Gas 4.

WRONGS AND REASONS

Suet Crust Pastry close-textured and heavy
1 Water used for steaming was allowed to go off the boil.
2 Pastry was rolled too much.
3 Pastry was undercooked and/or cooked too quickly.

Suet Crust Pastry was soggy
1 Water used for steaming went off the boil.
2 Dish etc inadequately covered during steaming.

Suet Crust Pastry dotted with suet pieces
1 Suet not chopped up finely enough. (If bought in the piece from a butcher.)
2 Dish etc undercooked and so suet was unable to melt.

Note
1 If preferred, plain flour may be used with the addition of baking powder. Allow 3 level teaspoons baking powder to every 8oz (225g) flour.
2 Beef suet is the best to use. If bought from the butcher, refrigerate until firm BEFORE chopping with 1 rounded tablespoon of the weighed-out flour

which prevents fat sticking together and clinging to the knife. If the suet is hard and crisp, it can be grated on the side of the grater with medium coarse holes. Alternatively, it can be chopped, with a tablespoon of flour, in food processor or blender.

Rough Puff Pastry

MAKES ABOUT 1LB 3OZ (JUST OVER ½KG) ▲▲●●

8oz (225g) plain flour
½ level tsp salt
3oz (75g) lard or
    white cooking fat } taken from
3oz (75g) butter or } refrigerator
    block margarine
¼pt (150ml) water, iced }
1tsp lemon juice } mixed

1 Sift flour and salt into bowl. Add fats. Using a round-topped knife, cut into flour mixture until both the lard or white cooking fat and butter or margarine are the size of small dice.
2 Sprinkle all the water and lemon juice, in one go, over the flour and fat mixture. Still using a knife, lightly mix to a soft and crumbly paste, taking care not to squash the small dice of fat and/or cut it up into smaller pieces.
3 Draw quickly together with fingertips. Remove from bowl. Shape into block on floured surface.
4 Roll into a rectangle measuring 12 by 6in (30 by 15cm), using a rolling-pin well dusted with flour. Fold equally in 3, envelope style.
5 Press open edges smartly together to seal then turn pastry round (NOT OVER) so that folds are to

2 Shape into a block on floured surface

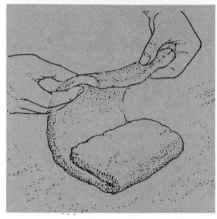
3 Fold equally in 3, envelope style

4 Press open edges smartly together to seal

1 Cut fats into the flour until the size of small dice

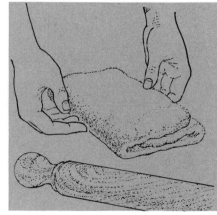
5 Turn pastry round, left to right, and roll into a rectangle as before

the left and right. Roll into rectangle as before, keeping edges straight as possible. Fold, seal and place on to floured plate.

6 Cover. Leave in the cool $\frac{1}{4}$ hour to 'relax'. Repeat rolling and folding processes twice more so that air is trapped between the folds, which in turn lightens and aerates the pastry.

7 Refrigerate, covered, a further $\frac{1}{4}$ hour. Roll out to about $\frac{1}{2}$in (1$\frac{1}{4}$cm) then used as required.

Use for:
Sweet and savoury pies, turnovers, pasties and sausage rolls.

Baking Tip
Bake turnovers, pasties and small pies etc on baking trays dampened with water, as the steam helps the pastry to rise.

Storage Tip
Provided it is wrapped in foil or cling film (or slipped into a plastic bag), uncooked pastry may be refrigerated up to 2 days. Cooked goods, especially if savoury, should be eaten freshly made. However, they may be refrigerated in a covered container up to 2 days and reheated before serving. Sweet turnovers and pies, made with fruit, jam, syrup or mincemeat, will stay perfectly fresh in an airtight container for 3 to 4 days but are greatly improved if reheated before eating.

Freezer Tip
Wrap pastry securely then seal and label. Freeze up to 3 months. Thaw, uncovered, 1 to 2 hours at kitchen temperature. Leave cooked dishes unwrapped and fast freeze until hard. Wrap securely. Seal and label. Freeze up to 4 months. Thaw 2 to 4 hours at kitchen temperature, depending on size. Reheat.

WRONGS AND REASONS

Pastry tough and heavy
1 Insufficient fats in proportion to flour and/or fat too soft.
2 Pastry handled too much.
3 Too much water added.
4 Too much flour used when rolling out.
5 Pastry not refrigerated long enough between rollings.
6 Oven too cool; unless otherwise stated in the recipe, the pastry should be baked in a hot oven set to 230°C (450°F), Gas 8.

Rough Puff Pastry

Pastry lacked flakiness
1 Fats too soft.
2 Pastry rolled too heavily.
3 Pastry not refrigerated long enough between rollings.
4 Baking tray insufficiently dampened with water.
5 Cut edges brushed with egg or milk, therefore layers were virtually glued together and unable to rise and separate out.

Pastry hard and over-cooked on outside; soft inside
1 Oven too hot.
2 Pastry placed in hottest part of oven.
3 Pastry cooked for too short a time in too high a temperature.

Pastry shrank
1 Pastry over-rolled and/or stretched to fit.
2 Pastry not refrigerated long enough between rollings.

Pastry poorly risen and soggy
1 Baking tray insufficiently dampened with water.
2 Oven too cool.
3 Pastry not baked for long enough.

Note Lemon juice is used as it gives the dough more elasticity.

Mock Rough Puff

MAKES JUST OVER 1LB ($\frac{1}{2}$KG)   ▲▲●●●

A self-styled Rough Puff which defies convention and NEVER goes wrong. It is quick and easy to make with a melt-in-the-mouth texture.

> *8oz (225g) plain flour*
> *3 level tsp baking powder*
> *$\frac{1}{2}$ level tsp salt*
> *3oz (75g) lard or*
>   *white cooking fat* ⎫ *taken from*
> *3oz (75g) butter or* ⎬ *refrigerator*
>   *block margarine* ⎭
> *6tblsp cold milk for mixing*

1 Sift flour, baking powder and salt into bowl. Add fats.

2 Using round-topped knife, cut fats into flour until they are in pea-sized pieces.
3 Add all the milk in one go. Still using a knife, work together to form a crumbly dough.
4 Shape into a ball. Put in a floured plastic bag. Refrigerate $\frac{1}{2}$ hour.
5 Roll out to $\frac{1}{4}$in (just over $\frac{1}{2}$cm) in thickness and use as required. Bake in hot oven set to 220°C (425°F), Gas 7.

Use for:
Same dishes as Rough Puff Pastry (page 190).

Note Self-raising flour, without baking powder, may be used if preferred.

Continental Rough Puff

MAKES 12OZ (325G)   ▲▲●●●

Very much part of the Astro-Hungarian scenario, this is a superbly rich pastry with a delicate puff. It is versatile enough to use for both sweet and savoury dishes, and is quite simple to make.

> *4oz (125g) plain flour*
> *4oz (125g) butter*
> *4oz (125g) cottage cheese, rubbed*
>   *through fine mesh sieve*

1 Sift flour into a bowl. Add butter. Using a round-topped knife, cut butter into flour until it is in pieces no larger than peas.
2 Fork in cheese until mixture forms a crumbly dough.
3 Draw together with fingertips. Shape into ball. Wrap in cling film or foil. Refrigerate a minimum of 4 hours.
4 Roll out to $\frac{1}{8}$in ($\frac{1}{4}$cm) in thickness and use as required. Bake in hot oven set to 230°C (450°F), Gas 8.

Use for:
Sweet and savoury pasties and turnovers.

Storage Tip
Both the Mock and Continental Rough Puff Pastries may be covered and refrigerated up to 2 days.

Freezer Tip
Wrap the Mock or Continental Rough Puff Pastries securely in cling film or foil. Seal. Deep freeze up to 2 months. Unwrap. Thaw 2 to 3 hours, at kitchen temperature, depending on the amount.

191

Flaky Pastry

Flaky Pastry

MAKES ABOUT 1LB 3OZ (JUST OVER ½KG) ▲▲▲●●

Although the ingredients are identical with those used for Rough Puff Pastry (page 190), the technique of making is completely different and requires infinitely more care and patience. The success story of Flaky Pastry lies in the way it is handled, and I always advise people to make it when they have plenty of time and enthusiasm; a half-hearted approach will not produce good results where this tricky pastry is concerned.

> *3oz (75g) lard or white cooking fat*
> *3oz (75g) butter or block*
>   *margarine*
> *8oz (225g) plain flour*
> *½ level tsp salt*
> *¼pt (150ml) water, iced* ⎫
> *2 tsp lemon juice* ⎭ *mixed*

1 Blend together both fats by mashing both together. Shape into a block. Divide into 4 equal-sized pieces. Chill 3 pieces until firm in the refrigerator.
2 Sift flour and salt into bowl. Rub in fourth (unchilled) piece of fat with fingertips.
3 Sprinkle all the water and lemon juice over the top. Using a knife, mix to a fairly soft dough. Turn on to lightly-floured board.
4 Knead thoroughly until dough is completely smooth and no longer sticky. With rolling-pin well-dusted with flour, roll into a strip measuring 18 by 6in (45 by 15cm). Keep all edges as straight as possible.

5 Using round-bladed knife, cover top two-thirds of pastry with 1 portion of fat, applying it in flakes to within 1in (2½cm) of edges. Sprinkle lightly with flour.
6 Fold in 3, envelope fashion, by lifting bottom third over centre third and bringing top third over. Seal open edges by pressing smartly together with a rolling-pin.
7 Slip pastry on to a plate and cover or wrap loosely in foil. Refrigerate ¼ hour. Remove to floured surface.
8 With folded edges to the left and right (see illustrations for Rough Puff Pastry, page 190), roll out into the same sized strip as before. Cover again with flakes of fat, using third portion. Sprinkle with flour. Fold, seal and refrigerate ¼ hour.
9 Repeat once more, using last portion of fat. After refrigerating

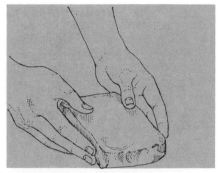

2 Shape into a block

3 Roll out kneaded dough (made by rubbing fourth piece of fat into flour and salt). Cover two-thirds of pastry with flakes of 1 portion of reserved fat

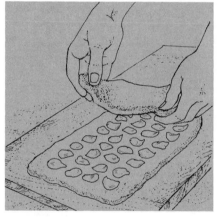

4 Fold in 3, envelope fashion. Seal edges with a rolling pin

1 Blend fats together by mashing

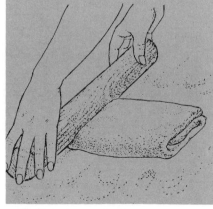

5 Refrigerate. Then, with folded edges to left and right, roll out again and repeat process

for ¼ hour, re-roll pastry into a strip. Fold as before. Refrigerate ½ hour.

10 Roll out to ¼in (½cm) in thickness and use as required. After shaping, leave to 'relax' in the cool for at least ½ hour before baking in a hot oven set to 220°C (425°F), Gas 7.

Use for:
Same dishes as Rough Puff Pastry (page 190).

Storage and Freezer Tips
See Rough Puff Pastry (page 190).

WRONGS AND REASONS

Pastry rose unevenly
1 Fat unevenly distributed over pastry.
2 Pastry rolled unevenly with too much pressure being exerted in a patchy way.
3 Sides and corners not kept straight and square while rolling.
4 Edges not cut cleanly with a sharp knife dipped in flour.
For other Wrongs and Reasons, see Rough Puff Pastry. (Page 190.)

Puff Pastry

MAKES ABOUT 1¼LB OR JUST OVER ½KG ▲▲▲●●

Probably the hardest of all to make, successful Puff Pastry should rise into a crisp, golden and light-as-air crust resembling layers of paper-thin leaves. To achieve this kind of result is no easy task, but I hope the following recipe and guidelines will inspire some measure of confidence and give you the incentive to try.

8oz (225g) unsalted butter, softened slightly
8oz (225g) plain, strong flour
½ level tsp salt
¼pt (125ml) water, iced ⎫ mixed
2tsp lemon juice ⎭

1 Cut off 2oz (50g) butter. Leave on one side temporarily. Shape remainder into block of ¾in (2cm) in thickness.
2 Sift flour and salt into bowl. Rub in 2oz (50g) butter. Add water and lemon juice in one go. Using a knife, mix to a soft dough.
3 Turn out on to floured board and knead thoroughly until smooth. Roll out into a rectangle measuring 12 by 6in (30 by 15cm).

Puff Pastry

4 Stand butter on half the rectangle, leaving a ½in (1¼cm) margin all the way round. Moisten margin with water. Fold in half, completely enclosing butter inside pastry. Press edges well together to seal.
5 Wrap loosely in foil. Refrigerate ½ hour. Transfer to floured surface. With fold on right, roll into a rectangle measuring 18 by 6in (45 by 15cm). Fold in 3, envelope fashion (see illustrations for Rough Puff Pastry, page 190).
6 Wrap again. Chill ½ hour. Re-roll and fold 6 more times, leaving wrapped pastry in refrigerator for ¼ hour each time.
7 Finally refrigerate pastry ½ hour before rolling out to ¼in (½cm) in thickness and use as required. After shaping, leave to 'relax' in the cool for at least ½ hour before baking in hot oven set to 230°C (450°F), Gas 8.

Use for:
Fancy Gateaux, Cream Horns, Cream Slices and Vol-au-Vents.

Storage and Freezer Tips
See Rough Puff Pastry (page 190).

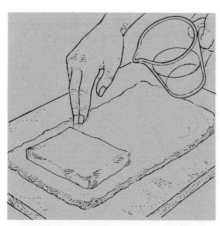

1 Stand butter on half of rectangle and moisten edges with water

2 Fold in half, enclosing butter inside pastry

193

See Rough Puff and Flaky Pastry (pages 190–193).

Vol-au-Vents

MAKES 8 ▲▲▲●●

Follow recipe for *Puff Pastry* (page 193). Roll into a rectangle just under $\frac{1}{4}$in ($\frac{1}{2}$cm) in thickness. Cut into 16 rounds with 3in ($7\frac{1}{2}$cm) biscuit cutter dipped in hot water. Remove centres from 8 rounds with a $1\frac{1}{2}$in ($3\frac{3}{4}$cm) cutter. Dampen undersides of rings with brush dipped in water. Place carefully on to 8 rounds. Transfer to dampened baking tray. Add cut-out centres which will later become lids. Brush lids and rings with beaten egg, taking CARE NOT TO LET ANY EGG MIXTURE RUN DOWN THE SIDES AS IT WILL PREVENT PASTRY FROM RISING. Rest for $\frac{1}{2}$ hour. Bake until well risen and crisp; about 10 to 15 minutes in hot oven set to 230°C (450°F), Gas 8. Use as required.

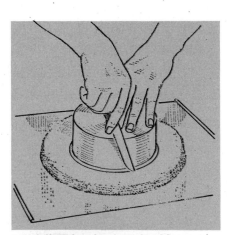

1 Cut halfway through pastry to form lid

Vol-au-Vents

Individual Vol-au-Vent

SERVES 8 ▲▲▲●●

Follow recipe for *Puff Pastry* (page 193). Roll out to $\frac{3}{4}$in (2cm) in thickness. Mark into a 7in (18cm) round using a plate as a guide. Cut out with sharp knife dipped in hot water, taking care not to drag at the pastry. Turn pastry over and stand upside down on dampened baking tray. Using a 4in (10cm) plate or round biscuit cutter as a guide, mark a circle in the centre. Cut halfway down the pastry to enable the circle to come away from the sides as it bakes, later forming a detachable lid. Bake $\frac{1}{4}$ hour in hot oven set to 230°C (450°F), Gas 8. Reduce temperature and continue to bake 20 minutes in moderately hot oven set to 190°C (375°F), Gas 5. Take out of oven. Remove lid from Vol-au-Vent and reserve. Scoop out soft and pulpy middle and discard. Return shell to oven for a further 10 to 15 minutes to dry out. Use as required.

Strudel Pastry

MAKES JUST UNDER 1 LB
(ABOUT 425G) ▲▲▲●●

Strudel Pastry takes a bit of getting to know but, having formulated a recipe that works very successfully indeed, I use it repeatedly and see no reason for a change to a new ingredient combination, even though my own version, unlike many others, contains no egg. However, this seems to give it more stretchability, enabling one to roll out the pastry to

a paper-thin, see-through sheet with much less wear and tear on the arms than one would expect. All the same, it requires infinite patience and dedication and a deep affection for Apple Strudel! Also a large cloth or piece of material with a bright and distinct pattern which should be clearly visible through the very thin pastry.

8oz (225g) plain flour
$\frac{1}{4}$ level tsp salt
4tblsp corn oil
1tsp lemon juice
$\frac{1}{4}$pt (150ml) lukewarm water

1 Sift flour and salt into bowl. Make a well in the centre. Pour in oil, lemon juice and water.

2 Using fingertips, mix to a soft dough. Lift out of bowl on to a lightly-floured surface. Knead steadily for 20 minutes. After the first 10 minutes, the best way to knead is to pass the dough from one hand to the other, pulling it this way and that until it is smooth, elastic and no longer sticky.

3 If it remains on the tacky side, work in a little extra flour and continue to knead until dough no longer sticks to the fingers.

4 Shape into a ball. Stand in an oiled bowl. Cover. Leave in a warm place to relax for a good 30 minutes. To roll out, cover a work surface or table with a patterned cloth or piece of material. Flour heavily. Stand dough on top.

5 Using a well-floured rolling-pin, roll out the pastry as thinly as possible into a square sheet. Start from the middle and work outwards and soon you will see the pattern underneath show through the centre of the pastry.

6 At this stage the edges will be considerably thicker so, with floured fingertips, pull and stretch the pastry until it is very thin all over and the pattern of the fabric underneath is clearly visible. As the pastry should be very elastic, this is less hard to do than it sounds.

7 By now you will have a square of pastry with wavy edges. DO NOT CUT OFF the edges but fold over to form a 'hem' which, in turn, will give you straight sides.

8 The pastry is now ready for its filling of apples etc to make Apple Strudel (page 110) and other variations.

Note

1 This pastry is best if made and used straightaway, and I do not recommend storing in the refrigerator or freezer.
2 Should you accidentally tear the pastry and make a hole in it, pull a piece off the edge, dampen with water and use as a patch.
3 The only thing to go wrong with the pastry is underkneading. This will result in lack of stretchability.

Strudel Pastry

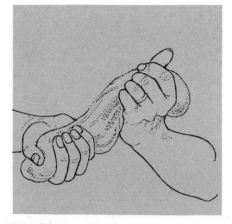

1 Knead dough with fingertips

2 Roll out pastry as thinly as possible on a patterned tablecloth until the pattern shows through

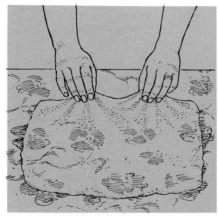

3 With floured fingertips pull the thicker edges of the pastry until it is thin all over

Pizza Pastry

MAKES 2 PIZZAS   ▲▲●

Traditional Pizza Pastry (or dough as it is frequently called) is made from bread dough. Therefore follow recipe for *White Bread* on page 241. Take one-third of the risen dough and use to make 2 Pizzas as directed on page 47.

Hot Water Crust Pastry

MAKES JUST OVER 1 LB ($\frac{1}{2}$ KG)
     ▲▲▲●●

Hot Water Crust Pastry is strong, sturdy and tough, well able to support itself and any filling it contains.

It is a curious pastry in some respects in that it is partially cooked before baking, its success depending almost entirely on warmth (as opposed to most other pastries where coolness takes top priority), and careful, deft and fairly speedy shaping before it has time to cool down and become hard and inflexible. But it enjoys being well-kneaded and handled, so the 'light touch' does not apply.

I am not sure how much Hot Water Crust Pastry is used abroad, but in the British Isles it has been the traditional pastry, since Victorian times, for 'raised' pies filled with pork, veal and ham, a melange of game and, in some instances, a cross-current of assorted meats to make ingenious and imaginative pies

Pizza Pastry

which were, and indeed still are, so popular for cold buffets and help-yourself, informal parties. The term 'raised' refers to the way in which the pastry, in the old days, was shaped by hand into containers suitable for an assortment of fillings. Today 'raising' means moulding the warm pastry over the outside of a round or oblong cake tin, or inside a loose-based cake tin or an ornamental and hinged raised pie mould, the latter being available from speciality kitchen shops.

Because Hot Water Crust is baked longer than most pastries in order that the meat filling inside be cooked through, it is moulded or rolled to a thickness of no less than $\frac{1}{4}$in ($\frac{1}{2}$cm). This not only enables it to support the filling, but also allows the pastry to withstand a baking time of several hours and, in the process, become crisp and golden brown. It responds most favourably to a moderately hot oven initially (200°C or 400°F, Gas 6), but then settles down more com-

1 Sift flour and salt into a bowl. Make a dip in the centre and drop in egg yolk. Cover with some flour in the bowl

2 Pour in melted fats, mixing with a wooden spoon

fortably in a moderate temperature (180°C or 350°F, Gas 4).

It is customary for the lid to have a small hole cut out of the middle so that steam can escape during baking. Prior to baking, however, it is usual to surround the hole with an ornamental decoration of leaves cut from trimmings. As the filling inside will shrink as it cooks, savoury jelly should be poured into the hot pie through the hole in the lid to fill up the gaps. When cold and cut open, a set layer of jelly should be clearly visible under the lid. As jelly takes time to set, and because the cooked pies need a brief spell of time to settle down and mature, they should be made at least 1 day before required and stored, wrapped, in the refrigerator. For making Raised Pork Pie, see recipe on page 84.

> *12oz (350g) plain flour*
> *1 level tsp salt*
> *1 egg yolk*
> *4oz (125g) lard or white cooking fat*
> *¼pt (150ml) water*

1 Sift flour and salt into bowl. Make a dip in the centre. Drop in egg yolk. Cover with some of the flour in the bowl.

2 Put lard or cooking fat into a saucepan with water. Melt slowly over low heat then bring to a BRISK boil.

3 Pour all at once on to the flour, mixing with a wooden spoon to form a dough. Turn out on to a lightly-floured surface. Knead firmly until dough is smooth and crack-free.

4 Continue to knead until all traces of egg yolk have gone, then shape into a ball. Transfer to a lightly-greased bowl. Stand over a pan of gently simmering water. Cover. Leave 20 minutes as this gives dough a chance to relax and keep warm at the same time.

5 Shape three-quarters of the dough into pie. Leave remainder (for lid) in the basin over simmering water until ready for use.

Use for:

Pies as described in the introduction. (See recipe for Pork Pie page 84 for moulding Hot Water Crust Pastry.)

Storage Tip

Do not store or freeze uncooked pastry. Baked pies can be deep frozen up to 3 months.

Pastry difficult to mould or 'raise'
1 Not enough fat used.
2 Liquid not boiling.
3 Too much or not enough liquid added.
4 Pastry allowed to become cold.

Pastry collapsed before baking
1 Pastry not given sufficient time to 'set' after moulding and was therefore unable to hold its shape.
2 Insufficient filling used.
3 Pastry was too thin and/or over-warm.

Cracked top and sides
1 Pastry insufficiently kneaded.
2 Not enough water added.
3 Liquid was not brought to a proper boil before being poured on to flour mixture.

Pastry hard and tough
1 Insufficient water added.
2 Pastry over-kneaded.

Lid breaks away from sides
1 Lid not properly sealed to sides through inadequate dampening.
2 Excessive amount of filling used.

Choux Pastry

MAKES ABOUT 12OZ (350G)
▲▲▲●●●

Look at a cream bun as it comes out of the oven and see how much it resembles a cabbage; hence the French name 'Choux' (pronounced shoe) meaning, in this context, a full-blown cabbage which is about to burst open. Choux Pastry has about it the sort of chic and style that makes it unmistakably French, and it is the basis of a group of widely copied French patisserie known worldwide. These include Cream Buns, Coffee and Chocolate Eclairs, Beignets, Gateau St Honoré and cream-filled Profiteroles flowing with Chocolate Sauce. On the other side of the coin, Choux Pastry has its savoury uses, and from it we get Cheese Aignettes — which were once so popular with pre-dinner drinks — and one kind of French gnocchi borrowed from the Italians!

By some quirk of culinary fate, light-as-air Choux and down-to-earth Hot Water Crust Pastries have one thing in common. They are both partially cooked BEFORE baking, though the two end results are as different from one another as chalk from cheese. Choux Pastry puffs up to at least 3 times its original size, forming hollow shells of delicate crispness. It requires more eggs and fat than any other pastry in relation to the amount of flour used. It depends entirely on air for its lightness, and this is brought about by the eggs and the way in which they are incorporated. It is the only pastry which is made in a saucepan and never rolled but piped or spooned directly on to baking trays or into a pan of hot water or oil, depending upon the requirements of the recipe. For baking, Choux Pastry favours a moderately hot temperature to start off with, 200°C (400°F), Gas 6, followed by a moderate temperature of 180°C (350°F), Gas 4.

> 2½oz (75g) plain flour
> pinch of salt
> ¼pt (150ml) water
> 4oz (125g) butter (margarine if you must!)
> 2 Grade 3 eggs, thoroughly beaten

1 Sift flour and salt together directly on to a large plate.

1 Bring butter and water to a rolling boil. Add flour and stir briskly. Cook until mixture forms a ball in the centre of the pan

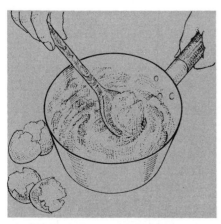

2 Draw pan away from heat. Cool slightly then add eggs gradually, beating continuously

Choux Pastry

2 Place water and butter into saucepan. Heat slowly until butter melts. Bring to a rolling boil. Lower heat.

3 Add ALL the flour in one go, stirring briskly until it has been absorbed by the liquid. Continue to cook until mixture forms ball in centre of pan, leaving sides clean. Stir all the time.

4 Draw pan away from heat. Cool pastry mixture slightly. Add eggs GRADUALLY, beating continuously until they have been thoroughly incorporated.

5 At this stage the choux paste should be smooth, shiny and firm enough to hold soft peaks when lifted up with a spoon. Use straightaway as required by the recipe.

Storage Tips
Choux Pastry responds poorly to long storage or deep freezing. If it cannot be used immediately, leave it in the pan and top lightly with a round of dampened greaseproof paper to prevent drying. As an extra precaution, cover with the saucepan lid.

Use for:
See introduction.

WRONGS AND REASONS

Mixture too slack and failed to form peaks
1 Proportions wrong. Too much liquid and/or large eggs used.
2 Insufficient flour added.
3 Mixture was not cooked for long enough before eggs were added.

Mixture did not rise and was soft after baking
1 Proportions wrong.
2 Self-raising flour used instead of plain.

3 Mixture was not cooked for long enough before eggs were added.
4 Eggs insufficiently beaten in and/or flour mixture too hot.
5 Mixture undercooked.
6 Oven not hot enough.

Mixture sank when removed from oven
1 Undercooked. Return to oven and allow extra cooking time as this sometimes helps mixture to rise.

Mixture pale and soggy after baking
1 Oven too cool. Return to oven to crispen.

Surface crazed after baking
1 Oven too hot.
2 Mixture placed too high up in oven.

Scones

Few things are simpler to make than Scones, yet they cause cooks of every calibre untold irritation because they appear to behave unpredictably for no accountable reason. They rise in a lop-sided fashion or they barely rise at all; they are tough and biscuity or stodgy and leaden; they are pale and unappetizing or burnt-looking and dry. Discouraging factors, geared to put one off Scone-making forever and a day. Hopefully the success tips below will revive confidence, and if the recipe is followed with due care and attention I can guarantee that anyone will be able to make light-hearted and tender Scones which are tall, bronzed and handsome!

Success Tip
1 Use either self-raising flour or plain flour with 4 level teaspoons baking powder to every 8oz (225g).
2 Rub in between 1 and 2oz (25 to 50g) butter or margarine to every 8oz (225g) flour. No more.
3 DO NOT USE EGG FOR MIXING unless a variation recommends it. Instead, use ¼pt (150ml) cold milk (skimmed makes for greater lightness) to every 8oz (225g) flour. This equates to 1 tablespoon to every 1oz (25g) flour.
4 Toss in any additions (sugar, fruit, grated cheese etc) LIGHTLY after rubbing in fat finely with fingertips.
5 DO NOT USE pasteurized or long-life milk which has turned sour as the quality may probably have deteriorated.
6 Add ALL the cold liquid IN ONE GO, mixing to a soft, but not sticky, dough with a fork.

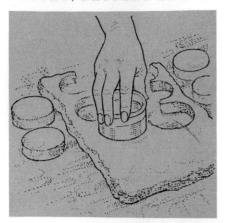

1 Using a biscuit cutter, cut straight downwards to avoid pulling the dough or cutting at an angle

2 When cooked the scones should have a central crack line which forms automatically

7 Turn out on to floured surface. Knead QUICKLY AND LIGHTLY, only just long enough to remove cracks.

8 Pat or roll out as directed in the recipe, handling as little as possible. Shape and bake. Never leave Scones to sit about in the kitchen before baking or they will be spoiled. Also make sure the oven temperature is high: 230°C or 450°F, Gas 8 for Plain Scones, but note that some of the richer variations require a slightly lower temperature.

9 After cooling, pull Scones in half to separate. Do not cut or they will immediately become doughy.

Plain Scones

MAKES ABOUT 9 ▲●●

8oz (225g) self-raising flour or plain flour plus 4 level tsp baking powder
½ level tsp salt
1oz (25g) butter or margarine

¼pt (150ml) cold milk
beaten egg or milk for brushing

1 Sift flour (or flour and baking powder) with salt into bowl.

2 Rub in butter or margarine finely with fingertips, lifting mixture out of bowl to incorporate air. (See illustrations for Shortcrust Pastry page 186.)

3 Add all the milk IN ONE GO. Quickly fork-mix together to form a soft but not sticky dough.

4 Gather together. Turn out on to floured surface. Knead lightly, and with swift movements, until dough is smooth and crack-free.

5 Pat or roll out to ½in (1¼cm) in thickness. Cut into rounds with 2½in (6cm) plain biscuit cutter dipped in flour. Plunge the cutter smartly downwards to avoid pulling the dough and cutting at an angle as this would produce misshapen scones.

6 Gather up trimmings. Quickly work together. Pat out and cut into more rounds to give a total of 9 scones.

7 Transfer to lightly-greased baking tray dusted with flour. Brush tops with egg or milk for a golden glaze.

8 Place straightaway in very hot oven set to 230°C or 450°F, Gas 8. Bake until well risen and golden brown, allowing 8 to 10 minutes.

9 Remove from oven. Cool to lukewarm on wire rack. Before serving, look for the central crack line running round each scone. (This happens automatically if scones have been properly made.)

10 Pull scones gently apart at this line. Butter and leave as halves, or put together again. Serve freshly made.

Note As these scones are so plain, they can be spread with sweet or savoury toppings.

Storage Tip
Store in an airtight tin or plastic bag up to 2 days. Warm through in a cool oven before serving. Alternatively, split, toast and butter.

Freezer Tip
Deep freeze, in well-sealed bag or container, up to 6 months. Defrost overnight in the refrigerator or 3 to 4 hours at kitchen temperature. Warm before serving.

Cheese Scones

MAKES 9 ▲●●●

Follow recipe for *Plain Scones* but sift 1 level teaspoon powder mustard into bowl with other dry ingredients. Toss in 2oz (50g) very finely-grated Cheddar cheese BEFORE mixing with milk.

Tea Scones

MAKES ABOUT 16 ▲●●●

Follow recipe for *Plain Scones* but increase butter or margarine to 2oz (50g), and toss in 1oz (25g) caster sugar BEFORE mixing with milk. Roll out to just over ½in (1¼cm) in thickness and cut into 16 rounds with 2in (5cm) biscuit cutter.

Fruit Scones

MAKES ABOUT 16 ▲●●●

Follow recipe for *Plain Scones* but increase butter or margarine to 2oz (50g), and toss in 1oz (25g) caster sugar and 2oz (50g) mixed dried fruit BEFORE mixing with milk. Roll out to just over ½in (1¼cm) in thickness and cut into 16 rounds with 2in (5cm) biscuit cutter.

Buttermilk Scones

MAKES 9 ▲●●

Follow recipe for *Plain Scones* but instead of milk only, use 4 tablespoons buttermilk and 4 tablespoons cold milk for mixing.

Scone Round

MAKES 10 WEDGES ▲▲●●

Follow recipe for *Plain Scones* but increase butter or margarine to 2oz (50g) and toss in 2oz (50g) caster sugar BEFORE mixing with milk. On floured surface, pat into a round of 1in (2½cm) in thickness. Transfer to greased and floured tray. Mark into 10 wedges with back of knife, taking care not to cut too deeply into dough. Brush with beaten egg. Bake until well-risen and golden; about 20 to 25 minutes in hot oven set to 220°C (425°F), Gas 7. Remove from oven. Transfer to wire cooling rack. Break apart into wedges when lukewarm. Split each wedge with fingers and butter.

Fruited Scone Round

MAKES 10 WEDGES ▲▲●●●

Make as *Scone Round* above but add 2oz (50g) mixed dried fruit at the same time as the sugar.

American Style Doughnut Rings

MAKES ABOUT 12 ▲▲▲●●●

Follow recipe for *Plain Scones* but sift dry ingredients with 1 level teaspoon mixed spice and increase butter or margarine to 2oz (50g). Toss in 1oz (25g) caster sugar BEFORE mixing with milk. Roll out to ½in (1¼cm) in thickness. Cut into rounds with 2in (5cm) biscuit cutter and remove centres with 1in (2cm) cutter. Re-roll and re-cut trimmings to give required number of Doughnut rings. Fry, 3 or 4 at a time, in hot (but not smoking) oil, allowing about 4 minutes and turning once. Remove from pan. Drain on crumpled paper towels. Toss in extra caster sugar. Eat while still warm.

Note These are popular for breakfast in North America with hot coffee.

American Style Fruit and Cream 'Shortcakes'

MAKES 4 ▲▲●●●

Follow recipe for *Plain Scones* but increase butter or margarine to 2oz (50g) and toss in 1oz (25g) caster sugar BEFORE mixing with milk. Roll out to 1in (2½cm) in thickness. Cut into 4 rounds with 3in (7½cm) biscuit cutter. Transfer to greased and floured tray. Bake until well-risen and golden; about 20 minutes in hot oven set to 220°C (425°F), Gas 7. Transfer to wire cooling rack. Split apart with fingers while lukewarm. Spread both sides of each scone thickly with butter. Sandwich together with canned fruit (such as drained peaches) or fresh raspberries or sliced strawberries. Top each with a mound of whipped cream. Serve as a dessert.

Wholemeal Scones

▲●●

Follow recipe for *Plain Scones*, but use half wholemeal and half white flour. Tea and Fruit Scones may also be made with the two flours.

WRONGS AND REASONS

Scones tough
1 Insufficient liquid used.
2 Liquid added gradually instead of all at once.
3 Over-kneaded.

Scones poorly risen
1 Insufficient baking powder used with plain flour.
2 Insufficient liquid added.

Scones thin
1 Mixture rolled out too thinly. It is better to err on the thick side.

Dropped Scones

MAKES 12

Also known as Flapjacks, Girdle Cakes, Griddle Cakes and Scotch Pancakes, Dropped Scones are like miniature pancakes which, served with butter and either jam, honey or golden syrup, are one of the highlights of the British afternoon teatable. Easy to make, velvety smooth and comfortably soft in texture, these little confections are packed with nourishment and, if served with cheese and salad, make a healthy and sustaining lunch, supper or high tea dish. They are different from the conventional pancake — thin, sprinkled with lemon juice and sugar and rolled up — in that they are about 2 to 3in (5 to 7½cm) in diameter, are made with self-raising flour and not plain, and are at least double the thickness of conventional pancakes.

Success Tips
1 Use a heavy-based pan with a smooth surface. If it is non-stick, so much the better.
2 If surface is NOT non-stick, brush base of pan with melted white cooking fat, using a twirl of kitchen paper dipped in fat. Avoid nylon pastry brushes as these are liable to disintegrate if in touch with the hot surface of the pan.
3 Make sure the pan, and the layer of fat, are both hot before adding scone mixture, otherwise the pancakes might stick. However, do not overheat or pancakes will scorch on the outside and be uncooked in the middle.
4 Do not add more liquid than stipulated in the recipe as this would make the batter too thin and unable to hold its shape.
5 Take care not to cook too many pancakes at once, as they might easily run into each other.

Dropped Scones (page 200)

Pancake Batter

Basic Dropped Scones

MAKES 12 ▲▲●●

> *4oz (125g) self-raising flour*
> *pinch of salt*
> *1 Grade 3 egg*
> *¼pt (150ml) cold milk*
> *2tsp melted butter, margarine or*
> *salad oil*
> *melted white cooking fat for frying*

1 Sift flour and salt into bowl. Add egg. Pour in milk gradually, beating continually with a whisk to form a thick and smooth batter.
2 Stir in melted butter. Heat pan. Brush with fat. Reheat until hot. Pour in about 3 tablespoons of mixture to form small rounds.
3 Fry until undersides are a warm gold, and the top of each pancake is covered with small bubbles. Flip over. Fry second side until light gold.
4 Stack in a clean folded teatowel to keep warm as each batch is cooked. Serve warm with the accompaniments as suggested in the introduction.

Sweet Dropped Scones

MAKES 12 ▲▲●●

Follow recipe for *Basic Dropped Scones*, adding 1 level tablespoon caster or soft brown sugar to the flour before mixing to a batter with the egg and milk.

Sweet Orange or Lemon Dropped Scones

MAKES 12 ▲▲●●

Follow recipe for *Basic Dropped Scones*, adding 1 level tablespoon caster sugar and 1 level teaspoon finely-grated orange or lemon peel before mixing to a batter with the egg and milk.

Sweet and Spicy Dropped Scones

MAKES 12 ▲▲●●

Follow recipe for *Basic Dropped Scones*, sifting 1 level teaspoon mixed spice with the flour, and add 1 level tablespoon caster sugar before mixing to a batter with the egg and milk.

Savoury Dropped Scones

MAKES 12 ▲▲●●

Follow recipe for *Basic Dropped Scones*, increasing salt to ¼ level teaspoon and sifting ½ level teaspoon powder mustard with the flour.

Dropped Scones with Cheese

MAKES 12 ▲▲●●

Follow recipe for *Basic Dropped Scones*, increasing salt to ¼ level teaspoon, sifting ½ level teaspoon powder mustard with the flour, and adding 1oz (25g) finely-grated Cheddar, Gouda or Edam cheese before mixing to a batter with the egg and milk.

Dropped Scones with Ham

MAKES 12 ▲▲●●

Follow recipe for *Basic Dropped Scones*, increasing salt to ¼ level teaspoon, sifting ½ level teaspoon powder mustard with the flour, and adding 1oz (25g) finely-chopped ham before mixing to a batter with egg and milk.

200

Blender Tip

For a speedy batter, tip all ingredients into blender goblet and run machine until smooth. Use as required.

Storage Tip

Wrap Dropped Scones in foil or film. Refrigerate 2 or 3 days. Reheat in a lightly-greased pan before serving.

Freezer Tip

Deep freeze up to 6 months. Defrost overnight in the refrigerator or about 4 hours at kitchen temperature. Reheat in a lightly-greased pan before serving.

Pancake Batter

MAKES 6 TO 8 PANCAKES ▲▲●●

Interestingly enough, a pancake batter is a variation of a Dropped Scone mixture, the main differences being in the amount of liquid which is added and the type of flour used. For the Dropped Scones, the proportion of milk is ¼pt (150ml) to every 4oz (125g) plain flour; for Pancake Batter, the milk is doubled to ½pt (275ml). Sometimes the liquid is a mixture of milk and water. Sometimes milk and stock. Sometimes skimmed milk only, which many claim makes for thinner and lighter pancakes. A flour change is also necessary which means PLAIN FLOUR and NO self-raising. In an emergency, self-raising can be used for pancakes ONLY (never a Yorkshire pudding), but they will be softer than usual and fairly difficult to handle.

There are different schools of thought on how long a batter should be beaten, or even whether it should be beaten at all. Similarly, should a batter be left to stand before being cooked, or used straightaway. I have tried out every technique in the book and my results indicate that a batter is improved if beaten hard, and the end result lighter if the batter mixture has been left to relax, covered, for at least an hour before use in the refrigerator. It gives the gluten in the flour a chance to soften and increases its 'stretchability'. You will notice that I have added 2 teaspoons melted butter, margarine or salad oil to the basic mixture as this makes the resultant pancakes more velvety in texture.

4oz (125g) plain flour
pinch of salt
1 Grade 3 egg
2tsp melted butter, margarine or salad oil
½pt (275ml) cold milk (skimmed if preferred), or half milk and water, or half milk and cold stock

1 Sift flour and salt into a bowl. Make a well in the centre. Drop in egg.
2 Gradually add half the milk (or milk mixture), beating briskly with a hand whisk to form a smooth, creamy batter. Continue to beat for 10 to 15 minutes, then add fat or oil.
3 Gently stir in rest of liquid. Cover bowl. Refrigerate for at least 1 hour. Stir round before using.

Yorkshire Pudding Batter

ENOUGH FOR 1 TIN OF
12 BY 10IN (30 BY 25CM)
▲▲●●

Follow recipe for *Pancake Batter*, but omit fat or oil. See also page 70.

Fritter Batter (page 202)

French Style Galettes

MAKES 6 TO 8 ▲▲●●

A speciality of Brittany, real Galettes require a piece of equipment called a 'galetoire' or 'galetière' and long-term experience! The nearest approach is the *Pancake Batter* recipe (page 201), made with half brown and half white flours; 2oz (50g) of EACH. Some French books recommend that the batter be left to stand for 4 to 5 hours. For how to cook, see *Traditional Pancake* recipe on page 112.

Crèpes Batter

MAKES ABOUT 10 TO 12
▲▲●●●

The French version of Pancake Batter, used for the famous Crèpes Suzette.

4oz (125g) plain white flour
1½oz (40g) icing sugar
3 Grade 3 eggs
½pt (275ml) cold milk
1oz (25g) unsalted French butter, melted

1 Sift flour and sugar into a bowl. Beat to a smooth and creamy batter with whole eggs and half the milk. Beat steadily for 15 minutes.
2 Stir in butter, followed by rest of milk. Cover. Leave in the refrigerator 1 hour. Stir round before using. For how to cook, see *Traditional Pancake* recipe on page 112.

Crèpes Batter with Orange Flower Water

MAKES ABOUT 10 TO 12
▲▲●●●

A popular version of Crèpes from Brittany, perfumed with orange flower water which is available from many pharmacies in the UK. It smells faintly of Eau de Cologne.

Follow recipe for *Crèpes Batter* but take out 2 tablespoons milk from the measured amount. Replace with orange flower water.

Savoury Crèpes Batter

MAKES ABOUT 10 TO 12
▲▲●●●

Follow recipe for *Crèpes Batter* but sift ½ level teaspoon salt with the flour and omit sugar.

Storage and Freezer Tips for ALL *Mixtures*
See under Pancakes (page 112).

Coating Batter

▲▲●●

A thick version of Pancake Batter which makes a simple but useful coating for fried fish.

Follow recipe for *Pancake Batter* but reduce liquid to ¼pt (150ml).

Fritter Batter

Light and mouth-wateringly crisp, Fritter Batter is usually used to coat foods such as pieces of cooked vegetable and fruits to make traditional savoury and sweet Fritters. Sometimes chopped-up cheese, vegetables, meat or poultry (cooked first) is folded into the batter and teaspoons are fried in hot oil. When drained, sprinkled lightly with grated Parmesan cheese or paprika and served hot, these make excellent Cocktail Fritters.

Savoury Fritter Batter

ENOUGH FOR ABOUT 4 TO 6
AVERAGED-SIZED FILLETS
OF FISH ▲▲●●●

2oz (50g) plain flour
large pinch of salt
large pinch of white pepper
4tblsp lukewarm water or vegetable stock
3tsp melted butter or salad oil
1 egg white from Grade 2 egg
¼tsp lemon juice

1 Sift flour, salt and pepper into bowl. Gradually beat in water or stock, with butter or oil, to form a smooth batter. Use a whisk or fork for beating.
2 Whisk egg white and lemon juice to a stiff snow. Gently fold into batter mixture with a large metal spoon. When batter is smooth, use as required.

Storage and Freezer Tip
The batter should be used as soon as it is made, and not stored either in the refrigerator or deep freeze.

Savoury Fritter Batter with Beer

▲▲●●●

Excellent for coating pork or beef sausages and squares of hard cheese such as Edam, Gouda, Cheddar and Caerphilly.

Follow recipe for *Savoury Fritter Batter* but use light ale instead of water or stock.

Seasoned Fritter Batter

▲▲●●●

For a more flavourful Fritter Batter, follow recipe for *Savoury Fritter Batter* but sift any of the following with the flour and seasonings:
1 level teaspoon either curry powder, Tandoori spice mix or powder mustard.

Sweet Fritter Batter

▲▲●●●

Use for coating pieces of banana, pineapple rings (well-drained if canned) and fresh apple rings to make Banana, Pineapple and Apple Fritters respectively.

Follow recipe for *Savoury Fritter Batter*, omitting salt and pepper and sifting 1 level tablespoon icing sugar with the flour. Water only, and no stock, should be used for mixing.

Fresh Vegetables

As more and more vegetables crowd into our shops, supermarkets, open markets and food halls of department stores, it is no easy task keeping up with the wide, varied and colourful selection which one sees in ever-increasing amounts, and so to prevent confusion I have concentrated on two main vegetable areas: those that are readily available throughout the UK and others which I term the 'exotics'; a few of the more elusive and cosmopolitan vegetables with a tendency to drift and concentrate in large cities all over the country, but particularly in South East England. For ease of identification, I have also divided up all vegetables into their own family groups and these are below.

Roots and Tubers
These are vegetables which grow under the ground and send up coloured leafy foliage; usually green but sometimes tinted as in the case of beetroot. Into this category fall potatoes, carrots, swedes, turnips, parsnips, celeriac, Jerusalem artichokes, salsify and, as mentioned earlier, beetroots.

Bulbous Roots
These are another group of vegetables which grow beneath ground and comprise onions, spring onions, shallots, leeks and garlic.

Stems and Bulbous Stems
These vegetables – celery, asparagus, Florence fennel and seakale – are a family of vegetables which are grown in banked-up earth in order to blanch and lighten the stems and also make them sweeter and milder.

Flowers
A large group embracing all varieties of cabbage, curly kale, Brussels sprouts, broccoli, calabrese, cauliflower and kohlrabi – in other words, what many of us know by their collective name of 'greens'!

Leaves
The vegetables which fall into this group are bright green curly endive and wide-leafed endive (escarole), lettuce, sorrel and spinach. Belgian chicory is also classed as a leafy vegetable but is very pale by comparison with the others.

Pods
Predictably, these cover peas, beans and the now popular ears of golden-yellow sweetcorn wrapped in their own 'silks'.

Squashes
A term to describe fairly liquidy vegetables packed in a hard skin such as marrow, courgettes and pumpkin.

Fungi
The best known and best loved are mushrooms, and those available in shops are generally cultivated in controlled conditions and known as button if small and tightly closed and cap if larger with more brown flesh visible. Large, flat mushrooms are sometimes about and make an excellent base for imaginative stuffings. Hand-gathered field mushrooms are in a different category altogether and, because they are often soiled and gritty, need thorough washing and peeling.

The 'Exotics'
I shall deal only with the better known vegetables such as aubergines, globe artichokes, peppers, avocados, yams (or sweet potatoes), mange tout, okra, radiccio and Chinese leaves.

The 'Extras'
These include tomatoes (also classed as fruit), cucumbers, radishes and cress.

FREEZING VEGETABLES

Because I am asked so often to give advice on the home freezing of fresh vegetables, I am going to begin this section with freezer tips rather than leave it to the end.

Guidelines
1 ALWAYS blanch vegetables before freezing to stop the action of enzymes spoiling the flavour and texture, and also to prevent loss of nutritional value.
2 To blanch, use a LARGE saucepan containing about 8 pints (5 litres) of boiling, salted water.
3 Blanch no more than 8oz (225g) vegetables at a time. Place them into a sieve or basket and submerge completely in the water.
4 Blanch for the times given later, timing the operation from when the water in the pan returns to a rapid boil.
5 Lift sieve or basket of vegetables out of pan and rinse thoroughly under cold, running water.
6 Drain thoroughly then pack, seal and label.

Asparagus
Trim so that all the stalks are the same size. Blanch slim ones for 3 minutes and thick ones for 5 minutes. Freeze 9 months.

Beans – French and Runner
Top and tail. String sides if necessary. Leave French beans whole. Slice runner beans thinly into diagonal strips. Blanch either kind for 3 minutes. Freeze up to 1 year.

Beans – Broad
Remove beans from pods. Blanch 3 minutes. Freeze up to 1 year.

Beetroot
No blanching necessary. Freeze already cooked and peeled. Slice or dice and pack into containers or plastic bags. Freeze up to 9 months.

Broccoli
Reserve all the 'flowery' heads and divide into 2in (5cm) florets with about 3in (7½cm) of stalk attached. Blanch 3 minutes. Freeze up to 1 year.

Brussels Sprouts
Choose small sprouts which are tightly closed. Remove outer leaves. Blanch 4 minutes. Store up to 1 year.

Cabbage – Dutch (or white) and green
Shred. Blanch 2 minutes. Store up to 6 months.

Carrots
For small spring carrots, top and tail then scrape off skin. For large, cold weather carrots, slice or dice. Blanch either kind for 5 minutes. Store up to 6 months.

Calabrese – see Broccoli

Cauliflower
Break head into small florets. Blanch 3 minutes. Freeze up to 6 months.

Celery
Frozen celery loses its crispness, and therefore should be used only in stews, casseroles and hot-pots. Scrub stalks and slice. Blanch 3 minutes. Freeze up to 6 months.

Corn-on-the-Cob
Remove husks and 'silks'. Blanch 6 to 8 minutes, depending on size of each cob. Cool completely. Freeze up to 1 year.

Courgettes
For small, whole courgettes, top and tail and blanch 2 minutes. For large courgettes, top and tail then either slice or cut into sticks. Blanch 1 minute. Freeze either up to 6 months.

Mange Tout
Top and tail. Blanch 2 minutes. Freeze up to 1 year.

Onions
Choose small to medium-sized onions. Peel. Blanch 1 to 2 minutes, depending on size. Slice or coarsely chop. Freeze up to 9 months.

Peas
Shell. Blanch 1½ minutes. Freeze up to 1 year.

Peppers – Red, Green and Yellow
Slice off tops. Remove inside fibres and seeds. Cut into dice or strips or leave whole. Blanch 2 minutes. Freeze up to 1 year.

Potatoes – New
Wash and scrape. Par-boil. Cool completely. Freeze up to 6 months.

Potatoes – Old
These do not freeze well as they are but are successful if creamed with butter or margarine and milk, or made into Duchesse potatoes. Freeze either type up to 6 months.

Potatoes – Chipped
Peel and chip. Blanch 4 minutes. Drain and dry thoroughly. Fry in deep fat or oil until very pale gold. Drain. Cool. Freeze up to 3 months. Re-fry before serving.

Roots – Mixed
Thickly-peel swedes, turnips and parsnips. Dice. Mix. Blanch 5 minutes. Store up to 6 months. If liked, add diced carrots and celeriac as well.

Spinach
Wash leaves thoroughly to remove grit. Remove leaves from hard stalks and shred. Blanch 2 minutes in 2oz

(50g) lots because the vegetable is so bulky. Freeze up to 1 year.

Tomatoes – Halved
Halve unblanched. Arrange on board or tray. Freeze, unwrapped, until hard. Pack in layers in box, with interleaving sheets between each layer. Freeze up to 6 months.

Tomatoes – Purée
Blanch tomatoes by covering with boiling water and leaving 3 minutes. Drain, rinse skin and de-seed. Convert to purée, adding 2 level teaspoons salt to every 1¾pt (1 litre). Freeze up to 1 year.

Tip
The following do not take kindly to deep freezing: Belgian chicory, marrow, pumpkin, mushrooms, spring onions, most of the 'exotics', cucumber, radishes, cress, lettuce and other salad greens such as endive and Chinese leaves.

PREPARATION AND COOKING OF ROOTS AND TUBERS

Beetroots

Originally from Southern latitudes, beetroots are now used mainly as a salad ingredient and are also pickled. They form the basis of Russian Beetroot Soup or Bortsch (page 34).

Boiled Beetroots

ALLOW 3OZ (75G) PER PERSON
▲●

Choose smallish beetroots and wash thoroughly. Trim, leaving on a short stub of stem. Avoid cutting off the root ends or piercing the skins as beetroots will 'bleed' in the water and become unappetizingly pallid. Cook in covered saucepan of gently boiling water for between 2 to 3 hours or until very tender. Drain. Slide off skins at once if using hot; otherwise leave till cold.

Tip
Hot sliced beetroots, coated with White or Parsley Sauce (pages 168–170), make an excellent vegetable accompaniment to egg and poultry dishes.

Baked Beetroots

ALLOW 3OZ (75G) PER PERSON
▲●

Prepare as described for *Boiled Beetroots*. Stand on lightly oiled or greased baking tray. Bake 3 to 4 hours in oven set to 160° (325°F), Gas 3. Remove from oven. Slide off skins if being used hot; otherwise leave until cold.

Pressure Cooking Tip
Cook 15 minutes at full pressure.

Sweet-Sour Beetroot

SERVES 6   ▲▲●●

1lb (450g) cooked beetroot, peeled
1oz (25g) butter or margarine
3oz (75g) onion, peeled and grated
1 medium eating apple, peeled and coarsely chopped (core removed)
2 level tsp cornflour
5tblsp orange juice
½ to 1 level tsp salt

1 Cut beetroot into medium-sized dice; about the size of sugar cubes.
2 Heat butter or margarine in frying pan. Add onions. Fry until pale gold. Add apple. Continue to fry a further 5 minutes, stirring.
3 Mix in beetroot dice then sprinkle with cornflour. Stir in orange juice and salt. Bring just up to boil over medium heat.
4 Simmer 2 minutes. Serve with meat, offal and poultry dishes.

Carrots

Prepare new, spring carrots by scraping under cold, running water; old carrots by peeling thinly and washing.

Cooked Carrots

ALLOW 3OZ (75G) PER PERSON
▲●

Boil whole new carrots in covered pan of boiling salted water for 15 to 17 minutes. Cut old carrots into slices or strips and boil, covered, 20 to 25 minutes. Drain. Return to pan. Toss either kind with butter or margarine and a touch of nutmeg. Chopped parsley adds a vivid colour contrast.

Roast Carrots

ALLOW 3OZ (75G) PER PERSON
▲●

Peel carrots (old are best) and leave whole. Boil 10 minutes. Drain. Stand round joint of meat or poultry and roast for last ¾ to 1 hour.

Pressure Cooking Tip
Cook 5 minutes at full pressure.

Spicy Lemon Carrots in Cream

SERVES 4   ▲▲●●●

Cook 1lb (450g) small, new carrots as directed. Drain. Stand pan over low heat. Add 1 level teaspoon finely-grated lemon peel, large pinch mixed spice and ¼pt (150ml) double cream. Heat through and adjust seasoning to taste. Turn into dish and sprinkle with finely-chopped watercress. Serve very hot with fish and poultry dishes.

Celeriac

Celeriac is a turnip-shaped root which tastes mildly of celery. The leaves are inedible. It is very popular in Northern Europe and is a pleasant vegetable served hot with Béchamel or even Hollandaise Sauce (page 174).

Cooked Celeriac

ALLOW 3OZ (75G) PER PERSON
▲▲●●

Choose large roots and remove a thick layer of peel as the flesh immediately underneath is coarse. Drop into bowl of cold, salted water to stop browning. Cut each bulb of celeriac into quarters, then cut quarters into slices. Alternatively, cut into chip-sized lengths or into medium-sized dice. Cook in covered pan of boiling salted water to which 2 teaspoons lemon juice have been added. Allow 25 to 45 minutes, depending on age of celeriac and size of pieces. Drain. Toss with butter or margarine or coat with sauce as suggested above.

Pressure Cooking Tip
Cook 5 minutes at full pressure.

206

Celeriac Salad

ALLOW 3OZ (75G) PER PERSON
▲▲●●

Leave celeriac to get cold in the cooking water. Drain THOROUGHLY. Toss with 1 small grated onion per 1lb (450g) celeriac and sufficient French Dressing (page 180) to moisten. Sprinkle with parsley and lightly chill.

Jerusalem Artichokes

A mildly-flavoured, easy to digest and good-tasting vegetable available during the winter. It looks like a new potato with knobs, and is therefore on the awkward side to peel.

Cooked Jerusalem Artichokes

ALLOW 3 TO 4OZ (75 TO 125G)
PER PERSON   ▲●

Peel artichokes with a potato peeler or paring knife. Wash thoroughly and drop into pan of boiling, salted water to which 2 teaspoons lemon juice have been added. Cook, covered, 30 to 35 minutes or until soft. Drain. Toss with butter or margarine or coat with White Sauce (page 168) and sprinkle with finely-chopped parsley or watercress.

Pressure Cooking Tip
Cook 7 minutes at full pressure.

Parsnips

Choose medium-sized parsnips with as few blemishes as possible if to be served as a vegetable in their own right; choose irregular specimens for stews, casseroles, hot pots and soups where appearance is not important.

Cooked Parsnips

ALLOW 3OZ (75G) PER PERSON
▲●

Peel parsnips fairly thickly (more thinly if very young) and wash under cold water. Cut into 4 lengthwise strips or into slices or dice. Cook, uncovered, in pan of boiling, salted water with 2 teaspoons lemon juice for about 30 to 40 minutes or until very tender. Drain. Return to pan.

Toss with butter or coat with Mustard or Parsley Sauce (page 170).

Mashed Parsnips

ALLOW 3OZ (75G) PER PERSON
▲●●

Cook parsnips as directed above. Drain. Return to pan. Mash until very soft, keeping pan over low heat. Beat in a large knob of butter or margarine. Serve very hot with meat and poultry dishes.

Roast Parsnips

ALLOW 3OZ (75G) PER PERSON
▲●

Peel, wash and quarter lengthwise. Boil ¼ hour. Drain. Stand round joint of meat or poultry and roast for last ¾ to 1 hour.

Pressure Cooking Tip
Cook 5 minutes at full pressure.

Potatoes

One of Europe's staples, potatoes were brought to England by Sir Walter Raleigh during the late 1500s and the cultivation of this then rare and expensive vegetable did not gather momentum in the UK until the 18th century.

Cooked Potatoes

ALLOW 3 TO 4OZ (75 TO 125G)
PER PERSON   ▲●

Scrape new potatoes under cold, running water. Peel old potatoes as thinly as possible. Halve or quarter. Drop into bowl of cold water to stop browning. Cook new potatoes in covered pan of boiling, salted water for about 15 to 20 minutes; old potatoes 20 to 30 minutes. Drain. Return to pan. Toss with butter or margarine. Sprinkle with chopped parsley if liked.

Tip
Remove stubborn 'eyes' with potato peeler.

Minted Potatoes

ALLOW 3 TO 4OZ (75 TO 125G)
PER PERSON   ▲●●

Cook as above. After draining, add 1 or 2 leaves of fresh mint, toss with

Sauté Potatoes Lyonnaise Style

butter or margarine and cover. Leave to stand 5 minutes.

Creamed Potatoes

ALLOW 3 TO 4OZ (75 TO 125G) PER PERSON ▲▲●●

Boil old potatoes as directed above. Drain. Return to saucepan. Mash. Stand over low heat. Beat in 1oz (25g) butter or margarine and 3 tablespoons warm milk to every 1lb (450g) potatoes. Continue beating until light and fluffy. Serve very hot.

Potatoes in their Skins

ALLOW 4 WHOLE PER PERSON ▲●

Also known as Potatoes 'en Chemise', these are new potatoes served in their skins. To prepare, wash as many new potatoes as required. Cook in boiling, salted water as directed above. Drain. Serve in basket or dish lined with cloth napkin and people peel their own at the table – or eat the skins, whichever they prefer!

Jacket Potatoes

ALLOW 1 MEDIUM PER PERSON ▲●●

Wash and scrub required number of potatoes. Prick skins all over with a fork to prevent potatoes from burst-

ing in oven. Stand on greased baking tray. Bake about $1\frac{3}{4}$ to $2\frac{1}{4}$ hours in oven set to 200°C (400°F), Gas 6. To serve, cut a cross on top of each potato then, holding it in a cloth, squeeze base of potato until cross opens. Fill with butter and/or soured cream.

Stuffed Jacket Potatoes

ALLOW 2 HALVES PER PERSON ▲▲●●

Bake as directed for *Jacket Potatoes*. Remove from oven. Cut in half. Scoop out potato, leaving shells on one side for time being. Mash finely. Beat in 1oz (25g) butter and 2 tablespoons milk for every 4 medium-sized potatoes. Add 3oz (75g) grated Cheddar cheese and 1 level teaspoon prepared English mustard. Pile back into potato shells and stand on lightly greased tray. Sprinkle with 1oz (25g) cheese. Heat through and brown in hot oven set to 220°C (425°F), Gas 7.

Potato Chips

ALLOW 2OZ (50G) PER PERSON ▲▲●●

Peel potatoes, removing eyes with potato peeler. Cut into chips. Tip into a bowl of cold water. Rinse. Cook 7 minutes in boiling, salted water. Drain. Fry in deep, hot fat or oil until crisp and golden brown; this should

take about 8 minutes. Remove from pan and drain on paper towels.

Tip
Chips are easier to remove from pan if placed in a chip basket.

Sauté Potatoes

ALLOW 2OZ (50G) PER PERSON ▲▲●●

Follow recipe for *Potato Chips*, but instead of cutting peeled potatoes into strips, cut into rounds. Fry in about 2in (5cm) fat or oil in large frying pan. Turn from time to time.

Sauté Potatoes Lyonnaise Style

ALLOW 2OZ (50G) POTATOES AND 1OZ (25G) ONION PER PERSON ▲▲●●●

Prepare potatoes as for *Sauté Potatoes* above. After draining, leave on one side. Peel required weight of onions (half the weight of the potatoes). Thinly slice. For 1lb (450g) potatoes and 8oz (225g) onions, heat 2oz butter or margarine in large frying pan. Heat until hot. Pour in 1 tablespoon salad oil. Add onions. Fry over medium heat until pale gold. Add potato slices. Continue to fry fairly briskly until both onions and potatoes are light brown, cooked and crisp. Sprinkle with chopped parsley.

207

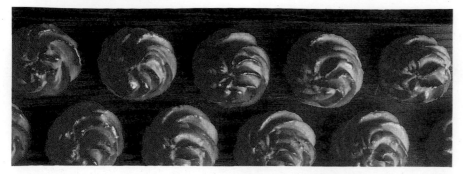

Duchesse Potatoes

Duchesse Potatoes

ALLOW 1LB (450G) POTATOES
FOR 4 SERVINGS ▲▲▲●●●

Boil old potatoes as directed on page 206. Drain. Return to pan. Stand over low heat. Mash very finely. Alternatively, mash to a purée in food processor and return to pan. Beat in 1oz (25g) butter or margarine, 2 egg yolks from Grade 3 eggs and 3 teaspoons milk. Beat over low heat until very smooth. Cool to lukewarm. Transfer to icing bag fitted with a large, star-shaped tube. Pipe mounds or rosettes on to buttered baking tray. Brush with lightly-beaten egg white. Bake ¼ hour in oven set to 200°C (400°F), Gas 6. For a border of Duchesse Potatoes, pipe potato round edge of large dish or platter and bake as above. Fill centre with, for instance, cooked seafood in a white sauce.

Pressure Cooking Tip
Cook medium, whole potatoes 5 minutes at full pressure.

Salsify

Salsify is shaped like a very slender parsnip and tastes faintly of oysters.

Cooked Salsify

ALLOW 4OZ (125G) PER PERSON ▲●●

Peel salsify thinly but leave whole. Wash thoroughly. Boil exactly as parsnips. Drain. Toss with butter.

Pressure Cooking Tip
Cook ¼ hour at full pressure.

Swedes

Large, yellow-fleshed vegetables with a distinctive flavour of their own.

Cooked Swedes

ALLOW 3OZ (75G) PER PERSON
▲●

Peel swedes thickly. Wash thoroughly. Cut into dice. Cook ½ hour in a covered pan of boiling, salted water to which 2 teaspoons lemon juice have been added. Drain. Toss with butter or margarine.

Pressure Cooking Tip
Cook 10 minutes at full pressure.

Gourmet Swedes

SERVES 6 ▲▲●●●

Cook 1½lb (675g) peeled and washed swedes as directed above. Combine with ½pt (275ml) freshly-made White Coating Sauce (page 168) then add 4 heaped tablespoons cooked peas. Turn into serving dish and scatter with 2 heaped tablespoons flaked and toasted almonds. Very good with offal, poultry and meat.

Turnips

Choose young, small turnips which are white and rotund as large, stale turnips are very woody. Peel thinly. Leave whole if small, or slice and dice if medium.

Cooked Turnips

ALLOW 3OZ (75G) PER PERSON
▲●

Cook, uncovered, for 20 to 30 minutes in pan of boiling salted water to which 2 teaspoons lemon juice and 1 level teaspoon granulated sugar have been added. Drain. Toss with butter or coat with White, Béchamel, Mustard or Cheese Sauce (pages 168–169).

Pressure Cooking Tip
Cook 5 minutes at full pressure.

Spring Turnips

SERVES 6 ▲▲●●●

Cook 6 young turnips as directed. Drain. Dice. Return to saucepan. Heat through with 4 tablespoons milk then stir in 1 carton (5oz or 142ml) soured cream and 1 bunch trimmed and coarsely-chopped spring onions. Season well to taste then transfer to greased heatproof dish. Sprinkle top with 2oz (50g) grated Cheddar cheese and brown under a hot grill. Serve with meat, poultry, offal, fish and egg dishes.

PREPARATION AND COOKING OF BULBOUS ROOTS

Garlic

Although garlic makes a significant contribution to the cuisines of Southern Europe, the Middle East and Far East, it is still used more sparingly in the northern hemisphere and rarely served as a cooked vegetable. Yet boiled garlic, tossed with butter, loses much of its potency and is pleasantly mild with a delicious flavour; an ideal partner, in fact, for lamb or veal. However, as it is doubtful whether we, in the UK, are likely to change our habits, I shall treat garlic as a flavouring only and suggest you use it crushed in salads (there are special crushers readily available from kitchen and hardware shops) and in savoury dishes where the recipe recommends that you do. A point of interest. The intensity of flavour is the same whatever size garlic clove you use. To prepare, remove one section or clove from the whole head. Peel and crush. In the absence of a crusher, chop the garlic and put into a tiny bowl. Sprinkle with salt and crush down to a pulp with the back of a teaspoon.

Leeks

Choose small to medium leeks if serving as a vegetable, although large ones are satisfactory for soups or stews.

Cooked Leeks

ALLOW 2 SMALL OR 1 MEDIUM
PER PERSON ▲●

Trim away crown from each leek and all but 3in (7½cm) of green 'skirt'. Remove one or two layers of outside leaves, depending on damage. Slit lengthwise ALMOST to top but NOT RIGHT THROUGH. Wash thoroughly to remove grit. Put into frying pan so that leeks can stay in a horizontal position. Cover with boiling water. Sprinkle with salt. Half cover with lid. Simmer gently for 20 minutes. Drain. Coat with melted butter or White Sauce (page 168).

Pressure Cooking Tip
Cook 5 minutes at full pressure.

Onions

Probably one of the most widely used vegetables in the world, the onion is a member of the lily family. Choose firm onions with a dry, flaky skin as these are fresh and crisp. For a mild flavour, the best are the large, juicy variety sometimes known as Spanish and which are relatively mild. For general cooking purposes, choose medium-sized onions which are stronger. For pickling, use baby pickling onions.

Cooked Onions

ALLOW 1 MEDIUM PER PERSON
▲●

Peel onions, starting at the top as this prevents eyes from watering. Quickly cut off hairy root ends, then drop onions into pan of gently boiling, salted water. Cook, uncovered, for about ¾ hour or until tender. Drain. Coat with melted butter or Béchamel Sauce (page 169).

Spinach Stuffed Onions

SERVES 4 ▲▲●●

4 medium onions
boiling salted water
12oz (350g) frozen chopped
    spinach, defrosted
2oz (50g) butter
salt and pepper to taste
large pinch grated nutmeg

Spinach Stuffed Onions

TOPPING
1oz (25g) lightly toasted
    breadcrumbs
2oz (50g) butter, melted
½ level tsp paprika

1 Peel onions as directed in recipe for *Boiled Onions* above. Cook in boiling, salted water for 20 minutes, keeping pan half covered.
2 Meanwhile, put spinach and butter into saucepan. Add salt and pepper to taste. Cook gently, uncovered, until most of the liquid has evaporated and spinach has thoroughly cooked down in the butter. Remove from heat.
3 Drain onions, reserving ¼pt (150ml) water. Cool. Remove most of the centres, leaving ½in (1¼cm) thick shells. Chop centres finely. Combine with spinach. Add nutmeg.
4 Return to onion shells. Transfer to baking dish. Pour in reserved water. Sprinkle tops of onions with rest of ingredients.
5 Bake ¼ hour in oven set to 220°C (425°F), Gas 7. Serve as a light lunch or supper dish or as accompaniment to meat and poultry roasts.

Deep-Fried Onion Rings

SERVES 6 ▲▲●●

These are crisp rings, cooked in the French style, and especially recommended for meat, poultry and egg dishes.

1½lb (675g) medium-sized onions
1½oz (40g) plain flour
deep fat or oil for frying

1 Peel onions and cut into medium-thick slices. Separate slices into rings. Coat each with flour.
2 Transfer to pan basket then lower into hot fat or oil. Fry, a few at a time, until golden and crisp.
3 Remove from pan, drain on paper towels and serve straightaway.

Success Tip
Do not cover or keep warm as onions will lose some of their crispness.

Pressure Cooking Tip
Cook 8 minutes at full pressure for whole onions.

Deep-Fried Onion Rings

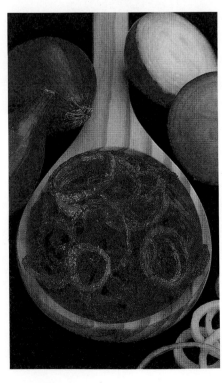

Cooked Asparagus with Hollandaise Sauce

Shallots

These are refined, delicate members of the onion family which are generally peeled and cooked whole in a variety of French classic meat and poultry dishes.

Spring Onions

More like leeks to look at than onions, spring onions are basically a salad ingredient and usually eaten raw. To prepare, remove first layer of outside leaves, then all but 3in (7½cm) of green 'skirt'. Cut off tops. Wash. Slice up and use. Alternatively, slit carefully lengthwise and use to garnish a salad.

PREPARATION AND COOKING OF STEMS AND BULBOUS STEMS

Asparagus

One of the most highly-prized and luxurious vegetables, asparagus is available fresh from May to about July and is very expensive.

210

Cooked Asparagus

ALLOW 8 STEMS PER PERSON
▲▲●●●

Trim ends then scrape skin away from each stem, avoiding the tips. Arrange in a large frying pan or oblong, flameproof dish. Add sufficient water for asparagus to float about gently. Sprinkle lightly with salt. Cover. Poach in slowly bubbling water for about 20 to 25 minutes. Drain carefully by pouring away water and tipping asparagus carefully on to a teatowel. Serve hot with Hollandaise Sauce (page 174) or melted butter. Alternatively, leave until cold and serve with French Dressing (page 180). To eat, lift up each piece of asparagus and dip the tip into sauce, butter or dressing. Eat the tip and as much of the stem as possible, stopping when it becomes tough and stringy. Accompany with finger bowls.

Etiquette Tip
In Europe, asparagus is always eaten with a knife and fork and in the UK, with the fingers.

Pressure Cooking Tip
Cook slim asparagus 2 minutes at full pressure; thicker stems for 3 minutes.

Celery

There are two kinds of celery available to us. Home-grown during the winter which is crisp, pale cream, strongly-flavoured and usually covered in earth. This one needs plenty of washing and scrubbing to get rid of grit and dirt. The second kind is imported, has been cleaned at source and is light green. All it needs is a quick rinse.

Cooked Celery

ALLOW 3 TO 4OZ (75 TO 125G) PER PERSON ▲●●

Wash and scrub celery, discarding leaves and any stalks that are badly damaged and/or bruised. Cut up into 2 to 3in (5 to 7½cm) lengths. Cook ¾ hour in covered pan of boiling, salted water to which 2 teaspoons lemon juice have been added. Drain. Toss with butter or coat with White or Cheese Sauce (pages 168–169). Alternatively, transfer to heatproof dish, sprinkle with 2oz (50g) grated Gruyère or Emmental cheese to every 1lb (450g) celery and melt under the grill. Season to taste with freshly-milled black pepper.

Pressure Cooking Tip
Cook 7 minutes at full pressure.

Florence Fennel

This is a pale, creamy-green bulbous vegetable with green side shoots which tastes very faintly of licorice. It can be sliced or grated and used in salads, or sliced and cooked in exactly the same way as celery (above). It is fairly expensive to buy.

Seakale

▲▲●●

A light and mild vegetable with a subtle taste of asparagus and appearance of slender heads of celery.

Cooked Seakale

ALLOW 8OZ (225G) PER PERSON

Cook and pressure cook exactly as celery but boil for 30 minutes only and pressure cook for 5 minutes at full pressure.

Success Tip
Wash seakale very thoroughly to remove soil and grit from between the stalks.

PREPARATION AND
COOKING OF FLOWERS

Broccoli

A vegetable that closely resembles cauliflower but instead of creamy-white, the head is green.

Cooked Broccoli

ALLOW 6 TO 8OZ
(175 TO 225G) PER PERSON
▲●●

Divide into florets (small pieces which look like miniature posies) and cut off and discard some of the stalks as they toughen towards the ends. Wash thoroughly under cold, running water. Cook in covered pan of boiling, salted water for about 20 minutes. Drain thoroughly. Coat with melted butter or Hollandaise Sauce (page 174).

Success Tip
If cooking whole head of broccoli which looks exactly like a green cauliflower, keep the flower part uppermost in pan.

Pressure Cooking Tip
Cook 3 minutes at full pressure.

Brussels Sprouts

Choose small to medium sprouts which are tightly closed, clear green and completely round.

Cooked Brussels Sprouts

ALLOW 3OZ (75G) PER PERSON
▲●●

Remove any outside leaves from each sprout which are bruised and/or damaged. Cut a cross on the base of each sprout with a sharp knife as this allows for greater heat penetration from the water. Cook, uncovered, in pan of gently boiling,

Cooked Celery

salted water about 12 to 15 minutes or until tender but still green (as opposed to yellow) and still a bit crispy in the middle. Drain. Return to saucepan. Toss with butter or margarine.

Pressure Cooking Tip
Cook 3 minutes at full pressure.

Calabrese

Also known as purple sprouting broccoli, this is sold by weight rather than by the head. Allow about 8oz (225g) per person and cook and pressure cook exactly as broccoli.

Cauliflower

To cook whole, place stalk side downwards in boiling, salted water, cover with a lid, and cook over moderate heat for about 15 minutes until stalk is tender. Drain and coat with White Sauce (page 168) or Cheese Sauce (page 169). Alternatively break up the head into florets and cook for 8 to 10 minutes until tender. Coat with sauce if desired.

Curly Kale

This is a dark green vegetable with very curly leaves and should be treated in exactly the same way as cabbage (see below).

Cabbage

Spring greens, tightly-packed heads of green cabbage and Savoy cabbage should be well-washed under cold, running water and shredded finely (minus tough stalks) before cooking.

Cooked Cabbage

ALLOW 3 TO 4OZ (75 TO 125G)
PER PERSON ▲●

Plunge cabbage into pan containing no more than about 1in (2½cm) boiling, salted water. Cook over medium heat, covered, about 8 to 10 minutes. Drain thoroughly. Return to pan. Toss with butter.

Pressure Cooking Tip
Cook 3 minutes at full pressure. White cabbage should either be shredded and cooked as green cabbage, or used in salads such as coleslaw (page 225).

Norwegian Sweet-Sour Cabbage

SERVES 4 TO 6 ▲●●

A close relation to Sauerkraut but not as sharp, this cooked cabbage dish is tasty, easy to make and partners well with pork dishes and sausages.

> 1½lb (675g) washed white
>   cabbage, shredded
> 4tblsp water
> 3tblsp malt vinegar
> 1oz (25g) caster sugar
> 2 level tsp caraway seeds
> 1 to 1½ level tsp salt

1 Place all ingredients into a pan. Bring to boil, stirring. Lower heat and cover.
2 Simmer VERY SLOWLY for about 1¼ to 1½ hours or until cabbage is completely soft and has turned a creamy gold in colour. Remove from heat.
3 Leave overnight for flavours to mature. Reheat until piping hot before serving.

Red Cabbage

Cooked Chicory

ALLOW 1 HEAD PER PERSON
▲▲●●

Prepare chicory as directed above then cook gently, covered, in about 2in (5cm) boiling, salted water with 2 teaspoons lemon juice for 20 minutes. Drain. Coat with melted butter or Béchamel or Hollandaise Sauce (pages 169–174).

Flavour Tip
If preferred, chicory may be cooked in 1in (2½cm) well-flavoured chicken stock instead of water and lemon juice, sprinkled with chopped parsley and served with pan juices.

Red Cabbage

SERVES 6   ▲▲●●●

This is rarely eaten as a vegetable by itself (except in some salads) but is cooked in the middle and northern European style, which is generally sweet-sour and mixed with onions, apples and often caraway seeds plus other herbs and spices.

> *2oz (50g) lard, dripping or margarine, or 2tblsp salad oil*
> *2lb (900g) red cabbage, washed and finely shredded*
> *8oz (225g) onions, peeled and sliced*
> *2oz (50g) soft brown sugar (dark variety)*
> *1 level tsp caraway seeds (optional)*
> *1 bouquet garni*
> *1 or 2 small bay leaves*
> *8oz (225g) cooking apples, peeled, cored and thinly sliced*
> *½pt (275ml) water*
> *4tblsp malt vinegar*
> *2 to 3 level tsp salt*
> *1 level tblsp cornflour*
> *2tblsp cold water*

1 Heat fat or oil in large, heavy-based pan. Add cabbage and onion. Fry, turning over low heat, for 30 minutes.
2 Stir in all remaining ingredients except cornflour and water. Bring to boil. Lower heat. Cover. Simmer over minimal heat about 2 hours or until cabbage becomes a deep mahogany colour. Stir periodically.
3 Remove bouquet garni and bay leaves then thicken by stirring in

cornflour mixed to smooth paste with water. Re-boil and simmer slowly 5 minutes.

Success Tip
Make one day and reheat slowly the next as cabbage matures overnight. Serve with duck, goose, ham and pork. If preferred, pressure cook ½ hour at full pressure.

Kohlrabi

An interesting vegetable and a relation of cabbage. The bulb is the part which is cooked and eaten in much the same way as other root vegetables.

Cooked Kohlrabi

ALLOW 2 SMALL BULBS
PER PERSON   ▲●

Peel and dice. Cook and pressure cook in exactly the same way as parsnips (page 206).

PREPARATION AND COOKING OF LEAVES

Chicory

This is a delicate-tasting vegetable with an appetizing crispness. It may be served raw in salads or cooked as a vegetable. To prepare, cut a slice off the base of each head (picture 1), then remove a cone-shaped segment of core (the bitter part) with a sharp knife (picture 2). Remove any damaged and/or bruised outer leaves.

The preparation of chicory

As chicory discolours in the same way as an apple, shred just before using with a stainless knife. Provided the leaves are handled carefully and left uncut, they may be used whole and look especially attractive if filled with cottage cheese and chives and garnished with red and yellow pepper strips.

Pressure Cooking Tip
Cook 4 minutes at full pressure.

Oven-Braised Chicory

SERVES 6 ▲▲●●

Prepare 6 heads of chicory as described on page 212. Place in heat-proof dish. Coat with 1in (2½cm) stock or water. Top with 4oz (125g) EACH peeled and chopped onions and chopped bacon, fried until golden in 1½oz (40g) butter or margarine. Sprinkle with 1 level tablespoon chopped parsley. Cover with lid or greased foil. Cook 40 minutes in oven set to 180°C (350°F), Gas 4. Serve with meat and poultry dishes.

Endive

This is strictly a salad vegetable, but because it tastes gritty should be very well washed and thoroughly drained. Afterwards, it should be torn into pieces and used as lettuce. Allow 1 head of endive for 4 to 6 people, and please note that it is very marginally bitter.

Lettuce

A salad ingredient of which there are 3 main varieties: elongated Cos, crisp and cabbage-like Webb and soft, round lettuces which are often from hothouses. To prepare Cos and Webb, wash and drain thoroughly then shred with a stainless knife. To prepare round lettuces, wash and dry and, because the leaves tend to be delicate, tear gently into pieces rather than shred. A glut of home grown lettuces may be cooked exactly the same way as spinach and served hot.

Spinach

A vegetable that is either liked or very much disliked, spinach is a good

Cooked Beans

source of Vitamin A and teams well with all types of main course dishes.

Cooked Spinach

ALLOW 8OZ (225G) PER PERSON ▲▲●●

Wash leaves very thoroughly under cold, running water to remove all traces of grit. Shred coarsely, discarding hard pieces of stalk. Put into large saucepan without any water as there should be enough left on the leaves from washing to provide sufficient moisture. Bring slowly to the boil, stirring. Lower heat. Half cover pan. Cook 10 to 15 minutes. Drain. Return to pan. Toss with butter and seasoning to taste.

Creamed Spinach Purée

ALLOW 8OZ (225G) PER PERSON ▲▲●●●

Cook spinach as above. Drain thoroughly. Work to purée in blender goblet or food processor. Return to saucepan. Add ½oz (15g) butter or margarine to every 1lb (450g) RAW weight of spinach. Heat until hot. Beat in 2 tablespoons double cream, a pinch of nutmeg and sugar, and salt and pepper to taste. Continue to heat, stirring, until very hot. Serve straightaway.

Pressure Cooking Tip
Bring up to full pressure and cool down straightaway, otherwise spinach will overcook.

Sorrel

A large, leafy green vegetable-cum-herb that tastes somewhat acidic and is much used in Poland and the Soviet Union. For cooking and pressure cooking, treat as spinach. For salads, shred finely before mixing with other ingredients.

PREPARATION AND COOKING OF PODS

Beans

The most common varieties are French, dwarf and runner, and make sure the beans chosen are firm and fresh green in colour. Brown specks and a wilted appearance indicate staleness.

Cooked Beans

ALLOW 4OZ (125G) PER PERSON ▲▲●●

Wash all beans. Top and tail French beans only. Top and tail dwarf beans and remove side strings if they are on the thick side. Top and tail runners, remove side strings and cut beans into diagonal strips. Cook 15 minutes in pan of boiling, salted water, keeping pan half-covered throughout. Drain. Toss with butter or margarine. Sprinkle with chopped parsley.

Pressure Cooking Tip
Cook 2 minutes at full pressure.

Mexican Style Corn

Beans Parmesan

SERVES 4 ▲▲●●●

Top and tail 1lb (450g) runner beans and cooked as directed on page 213. Meanwhile, fry 1 crushed clove of garlic in 1oz (25g) butter or margarine. Add drained beans and toss thoroughly. Transfer to a serving dish and sprinkle with 2 level tablespoons grated Parmesan cheese and a little paprika. Serve straightaway. Teams well with most main course dishes.

Broad Beans ▲▲●●

Treat as peas but allow 5 minutes longer boiling time. Toss with butter after draining or coat with Parsley Sauce (page 170). Allow 12oz (350g) raw weight per person.

Pressure Cooking Tip
Cook 3 minutes at full pressure.

American Succotash

SERVES 4 TO 6 ▲●●●

Frequently served with the Thanksgiving Day turkey, Succotash is an easily-prepared vegetable accompaniment. Combine 6oz (150g) cooked broad beans with 8oz (225g) cooked sweetcorn. Place in saucepan with 1½oz (40g) butter, 4 tablespoons single cream and salt and pepper to taste. Heat through, stirring gently with a wooden spoon, until very hot.

Peas

Choose small to medium pods and ones which are bright green and obviously fresh.

Cooked Peas

ALLOW 8oz (225g)
RAW WEIGHT PER PERSON
▲▲●●

Shell peas directly into saucepan. Add about 2in (5cm) boiling water, salt to taste and a pinch of sugar. Bring to boil. Lower heat. Half cover. Simmer 10 to 15 minutes, depending on size. Drain. Return to pan. Toss with fresh mint leaves (optional) and butter or margarine to taste.

Pressure Cooking Tip
Cook 2 minutes at full pressure.

Sweetcorn

Sweetcorn has become a very popular vegetable in the UK and is available as either whole 'ears' wrapped in their own husks and 'silks' (the silken threads nearest the cob), or frozen and canned.

Cooked Fresh Sweetcorn

ALLOW 1 PER PERSON ▲▲●●

'Unwrap' corn and put into pan containing about 2in (5cm) gently boiling water WITHOUT salt. Cover. Boil 6 minutes. Drain. Eat as a starter with butter and salt and pepper to taste.

Cooked Frozen Sweetcorn

ALLOW 2oz (50g) LOOSE CORN
PER PERSON ▲●●

Cook from frozen in covered pan of boiling water, allowing 5 to 7 minutes. Drain. Return to pan. Toss with butter or margarine and salt and pepper to taste.

Mexican Style Corn

SERVES 4 ▲▲●●

Cook 8oz (225g) sweetcorn as directed above. Drain. Combine with 6oz (175g) diced and lightly-fried red and green peppers and the same amounts of skinned and chopped tomatoes.

Pressure Cooking Tip
Cook whole corn 3 minutes at full pressure; loose corn 1 minute.

PREPARATION AND
COOKING OF SQUASHES

Courgettes

Choose small to medium-sized courgettes that are firm, deep green and shiny. Stale courgettes look dull and limp.

Cooked Courgettes

ALLOW 4OZ (125G) PER PERSON
▲●●

Top and tail washed courgettes. Slice. Drop into pan of gently boiling, salted water. Cover. Simmer 10 minutes. Drain. Return to pan. Toss with butter. Sprinkle with chopped parsley. Alternatively, slice courgettes and cook without water but with 2oz (50g) butter to every 1lb (450g). Add a little salt and pinch of sugar to taste, keep pan covered and shake periodically over medium heat. Allow about 8 minutes. Sprinkle with chopped parsley before serving.

Stuffed Courgettes

ALLOW 2 HALVES PER PERSON
▲▲●●

Top and tail washed courgettes. Halve lengthwise. Scoop out centre seeds and discard. Cook halves in boiling, salted water for 8 minutes. Drain. Leave until lukewarm. Transfer to baking dish. Top with stuffing to taste (page 234). Cover with a little tomato ketchup, a shake or two of Tabasco and 2 teaspoons melted butter for every half courgette. Reheat 15 minutes in hot oven set to 220°C (425°F), Gas 7. Serve as a starter or as a light lunch or supper dish.

Pressure Cooking Tip
Cook 1 minute at full pressure.

Marrow

Choose medium-sized marrow (as opposed to over-large ones which have outgrown their palatability) with dark green skin streaked with cream.

Cooked Marrow

ALLOW 1 MEDIUM MARROW
FOR 4 PEOPLE
▲▲●

Peel marrow then slice. Remove seeds from each slice, leaving empty marrow rings. Cut into dice. Steam 30 to 40 minutes in a covered colander over pan of gently boiling, salted water. Transfer to serving dish and toss with butter. Alternatively, coat with White, Cheese or Parsley Sauce (pages 168–170).

Stuffed Courgettes

Pressure Cooking Tip
Cook 4 minutes at full pressure.

Scarlet Marrow

SERVES 4 TO 6 ▲▲●●

> 2lb (900g) marrow, peeled and
> diced
> 1lb (450g) tomatoes, blanched
> and skinned
> 1 level tsp dried basil
> 1 level tsp salt
> 1 tsp Worcester sauce
> ½ level tsp caster sugar

1 Place marrow into pan. Coarsely chop tomatoes. Add to pan with rest of ingredients.
2 Bring to boil over medium heat. Cover. Simmer gently about 15 minutes or until marrow is tender. Serve with fish, meat, egg and poultry dishes.

Pumpkin

A winter vegetable which, because of its size, is usually sold in wedges by weight. Allow 8oz (225g) per person. Dice and cook exactly as marrow. Also pressure cook for same length of time.

PREPARATION AND COOKING OF FUNGI

Do not stock-pile mushrooms as they deteriorate fast and soon lose their freshness and resilience; the fresher the mushroom, the more cleanly and evenly it will snap if you test it. To prepare, quickly wash button mushrooms or half-opened cup mushrooms in a colander under cold, running water. Shake to remove as much water as possible then gently tip into clean teatowel and pat dry. Peel large, flat mushrooms then rinse individually and wipe dry. Trim stalks but, whenever possible, leave in the mushrooms to prevent waste and to increase flavour. Remove if mushrooms are to be stuffed.

Fried Mushrooms

ALLOW 2 TO 3OZ (50 TO 75G)
PER PERSON ▲▲●●

Leave button mushrooms whole. Slice cup mushrooms and the large 'flats'. Sizzle 2oz (50g) butter or margarine and 2 teaspoons salad oil in frying pan for every 12oz (350g) mushrooms. Add mushrooms to pan and fry 5 minutes over fairly high heat, shaking frequently. Season to taste and serve hot.

Mushroom Fritters

Mushroom Fritters

SERVES 4 TO 6 AS A STARTER
▲▲●●●

Coat 12oz (350g) button mushrooms with Fritter Batter (page 202).

Fry in deep, hot oil for about 4 minutes or until deep gold and crisp. Remove from pan with slotted fish slice and drain on paper towels. Serve very hot with a dip of Tartare Sauce (page 176).

Braised Chinese Leaves

Grilled Mushrooms

ALLOW 2 TO 3oz (50 TO 75G)
PER PERSON   ▲▲●●

Arrange button or cup mushrooms in greased grill pan, stalks upwards. Brush with 2oz (50g) melted butter or margarine for every 12oz (350g). Grill 2 minutes. Carefully turn over. Grill a further 1½ minutes. Season. Serve straightaway.

Oven-Baked Mushrooms

ALLOW 2 TO 3oz (50 TO 75G)
PER PERSON   ▲▲●●

Arrange mushrooms, stalks upwards, in buttered dish. Brush with 2oz (50g) melted butter for every 12oz (350g) mushrooms. Sprinkle with salt and pepper. Cover dish. Bake 15 to 20 minutes at 200°C (400°F), Gas 6. Serve hot.

Pressure Cooking Tip
Not recommended.

PREPARATION AND COOKING OF THE 'EXOTICS'

Aubergines

Also known as eggplants, these are a highly popular vegetable in the Balkans, Middle and Far East, North Africa and parts of Southern Europe. Choose medium-sized aubergines with deep purple skin that looks as though it has been polished to a high shine. Avoid any aubergines with wrinkled skins and brown leaves as this indicates that they are stale. As aubergines have a high water content, they should always be sliced up, arranged in a single layer on a large board, sprinkled with salt and left for ¾ hour. 'Beads' of liquid will settle on the surface indicating that some of the moisture has been drawn out. Turn each slice over, salt again and leave to stand ¾ hour. Rinse well and wipe each slice dry.

Fried Aubergines

ALLOW 2 TO 3oz (50 TO 75G)
PER PERSON   ▲▲●●

For every 12oz (350g) sliced aubergines, melt 2oz (50g) butter or margarine and 2 teaspoons oil in large frying pan. Add aubergine slices, first dusted with a little seasoned flour. Fry fairly quickly until golden brown and crisp on both sides, turning once. Drain on paper towels and serve straightaway.

Pressure Cooking Tip
Not recommended.

Avocados

Green or purple-skinned and reminiscent of a pear in shape, avocados have gathered momentum over the last decade and are now less of a luxury than they were, and a much appreciated meal starter or addition to a wide range of salads. Essentially, avocados should be eaten uncooked (although a brief application of heat does little harm and avocado soup is delicious) with a savoury filling in the cavities.

Avocados Vinaigrette

ALLOW ½ PER PERSON   ▲●●●

Halve avocados and remove stones. Brush cut sides with lemon juice straightaway to prevent discoloration. Transfer to individual plates. Fill centres with Vinaigrette Dressing (page 180).

Avocado with Seafood

ALLOW ½ PER PERSON   ▲▲●●●

Prepare avocados as directed above. Fill cavities with peeled prawns then coat with French or Seafood Dressing (page 180).

Success Tip
When preparing mashed-up avocado mixtures, bury the stone in the centre as it helps to prevent browning.

Chinese Leaves

This is a firm vegetable which is a cross between a cabbage and a long lettuce (Cos variety), and tastes a bit of both. For salad, wash quickly and remove any damaged and/or bruised outside leaves. Shred remainder and use instead of lettuce. For a cooked vegetable, treat as cabbage.

Pressure Cooking Tip
As cabbage.

Braised Chinese Leaves

SERVES 4 TO 6   ▲▲●●

> 2 medium heads of Chinese leaves
> 1oz (25g) butter or margarine or 1tblsp salad oil
> 1 medium onion, peeled and chopped
> 2oz (50g) streaky bacon, chopped
> ½pt (275ml) chicken stock (use cubes and water)
> 2tblsp Soy sauce
> 2 heaped tblsp finely-chopped parsley

1 Wash heads of Chinese leaves, cut in half centrally then cut each half into 4 lengthwise pieces.
2 Heat butter or margarine (or oil) in pan. Add onion and bacon. Fry gently until light gold. Add Chinese leaves. Fry a further 3 minutes, turning.
3 Pour in stock and Soy sauce. Bring to boil. Lower heat. Simmer, uncovered, for 20 minutes. Transfer to a serving dish. Sprinkle with parsley.

Globe Artichokes

These are large and edible thistles which are considered a delicacy. They may be served in two ways; hot with either Hollandaise Sauce (page 174) or melted butter, cold with salad dressings to taste (page 180) or assorted dips based on Mayonnaise variations as shown in the picture overleaf.

To prepare and Cook an Artichoke for Stuffing

▲▲▲●●●

Cut off stalk as close to the base of artichoke as possible then cut away tips of leaves. Neaten each leaf by cutting off pointed end with a pair of scissors. Wash thoroughly. Scoop out the central core of leaves and furry choke using a teaspoon. Brush cut surfaces with half a lemon, to avoid discoloration. Stuff as desired. Tie round with string. Stand upright in non-aluminium saucepan. Add 3in (7½cm) boiling water and 1 teaspoon salt. Simmer 45 minutes. Lift out of pan. Serve hot.

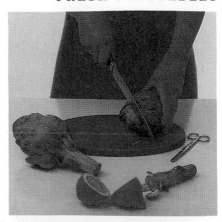

Preparing Artichokes for cooking and stuffing

217

Artichoke with Sauces

Cooked Artichokes

ALLOW 1 PER PERSON ▲▲●●●

Cut off stalk as close to the base of each artichoke as possible then remove first layer of leaves unless the vegetable is very young. Put upside down to soak in a large bowl of cold, salted water to which a dash of lemon juice has been added. Leave 30 minutes. Lift out of water. Drain. Place upright in non-aluminium pan. Add 3in (7½cm) boiling water and 1 or 2 level teaspoons salt, depending on number of artichokes. Cover pan. Simmer 45 minutes. Lift each individually out of pan. Drain thoroughly. Serve straightaway or leave until completely cold.

To Eat
Stand artichoke on individual plate with a little hot sauce or dressing in a separate bowl. Pull off a leaf at a time. Dip base ONLY into sauce or dressing. Slide through the teeth. Continue until you see a cone of leaves in the centre. Pull off then carefully remove furry choke. You will now be left with the heart which is the most delicate part. Cut into pieces, dip into sauce or dressing and eat.

Etiquette Tip
Always serve artichokes with individual finger bowls of water plus a slice of lemon floating in each.

Pressure Cooking Tip
Cook 6 minutes at full pressure for medium and 10 minutes for large.

Mange Tout

The name literally means 'eat all' and this variety of pea is merely topped and tailed and cooked, in its entirety, in boiling salted water. It comprises a flat pod with small peas inside.

Cooked Mange Tout

ALLOW 3OZ (75G) PER PERSON
▲▲●●●

Top and tail the mange tout then remove side strings. Cook briskly in boiling, salted water for about 8 minutes per pound (450g), keeping pan covered. Drain. Toss with butter. DO NOT OVERCOOK, as mange tout should be slightly crisp.

Information Tip
For those interested in Chinese cooking, mange tout are the same as Oriental snow peas.

Pressure Cooking Tip
Cook 2 minutes at full pressure.

Okra

Okra is a lightish green vegetable which looks like a cross between a runner and broad bean, except that it is 6-sided, pointed at one end and flat at the other. It is well known by its other name of 'Ladies Fingers' and is widely used in Middle and Far Eastern cookery and also American Creole. Okra is available canned in brine from Greece and the Balkans, and is also sold fresh from September to July when it is imported from East Africa. Because the insides exude a gelatinous substance, many dishes are thickened by okra without the aid of any form of starch. The best okra is firm and no longer than 4 or 5in (10 to 12½cm).

Cooked Okra

ALLOW 3OZ (75G) PER PERSON
▲▲●●

Top and tail but avoid piercing the pods as they will disintegrate and lose their characteristic sticky texture. Wash thoroughly. Cook in covered pan of boiling, salted water until tender; about 10 minutes. Drain. Toss with butter or coat with freshly-made Tomato Sauce (page 182).

Success Tip
A teaspoon of malt vinegar, added to the cooking water, enhances the flavour and texture of the okra.

Pressure Cooking Tip
Cook 3 minutes at full pressure.

American Style Okra

SERVES 4   ▲▲●●

Cook okra as directed above. Drain. Leave on one side for the time being. Heat 3 tablespoons salad oil in frying pan. Add 8oz (225g) skinned and coarsely-chopped tomatoes and 1 peeled and crushed garlic clove. Fry, uncovered, 5 minutes. Stir in okra. Season to taste with salt, pepper and a pinch of sugar. Heat through, turning over medium heat, until very hot. Serve sprinkled with chopped parsley.

Peppers

Also known as capsicums, bell peppers (in the US) and sweet peppers, the most widely available are the green variety which ultimately ripen to a vivid red or yellow and become sweeter in flavour. Peppers are rarely cooked and served as a vegetable, but are most frequently stuffed with meat and rice and either simmered or baked. Crisp, juicy and packed with Vitamin C, peppers make an attractive garnish, a colourful and healthy addition to salads, and contribute much to the flavour of the more exotic cooked dishes from Hungary's famous Goulash to Mediterranean fish soup. To prepare, wash and dry then cut off tops (which should be kept for lids if peppers are to be stuffed). Carefully remove inside fibres and seeds as these can be ferociously hot; a wise precaution is to wash the hands with soap and water after handling peppers. Use as required.

Radiccio

Becoming more available, radiccio looks like small red lettuce and should, after careful washing and draining, be used in exactly the same way. It is slightly bitter and related to chicory.

Yams

These are sweet potatoes which are much favoured in the US and also imported into the UK during the winter months. Treat exactly as potatoes, bearing in mind that yams are sweet with a distinctive, almost scented, flavour.

American Style Okra

PREPARATION AND COOKING OF THE 'EXTRAS'

Mustard and Cress

Cress, with its petite leaves, is frequently grown with mustard which also produces small green leaves. They are then used together as a decoration, sandwich filling or salad ingredient.

Cucumber

A widely-grown vegetable which is used mainly as a salad ingredient and may be either sliced or unsliced. Cucumber is invaluable for garnishing and may also be thinly sliced, wrung out in a clean teatowel to remove as much liquid as possible, then every 1lb (450g) simmered 8 minutes in a covered pan with 2oz (50g) butter. It should be well-seasoned and served as a hot vegetable with fish, poultry and veal.

Radishes

The type most widely available in the UK are either rotund or elongated, bright red and tipped with white. They should be topped and tailed, well washed and dried and either sliced or left whole. They are most frequently added to salads or cut in a decorative way and used for garnishing.

Tomatoes

Tomatoes, with onions and potatoes, are one of the most versatile vegetables available, and are used in hot dishes, cold dishes and salads. They also stand up very well as a vegetable in their own right and may be baked, fried or grilled.

Baked Tomatoes

ALLOW 3 TO 4OZ (75 TO 125G) PER PERSON   ▲▲●●

To bake whole tomatoes, make a cross cut on the base of each washed and dried tomato. Stand in greased baking dish. Top each with $1\frac{1}{2}$ teaspoon melted butter or margarine and sprinkle with seasoning to taste. Bake 15 minutes in oven set to 190°C (375°F), Gas 5. To bake halved tomatoes, stand in greased baking dish then follow method for whole tomatoes, using just over $\frac{1}{2}$ teaspoon melted butter or margarine for each half. Bake 10 minutes.

Fried Tomatoes

ALLOW 3 TO 4OZ (75 TO 125G) PER PERSON   ▲▲●●

Wash and dry tomatoes. Cut into thick slices. Heat a thin layer of butter or margarine in a frying pan. As soon as it sizzles, add tomato slices and fry until light gold on both sides, carefully turning. Sprinkle with salt and pepper and serve straightaway.

219

Baked Tomatoes with a platter of mixed vegetables (page 219)

Grilled Tomatoes

ALLOW 3 TO 4OZ (75 TO 125G)
PER PERSON ▲▲●●

Wash and dry tomatoes. Halve horizontally. Stand in grill pan. Brush with 1oz (25g) melted butter or margarine for every 8 halves. Sprinkle with salt and pepper. Grill 6 to 7 minutes. Do not turn.

Pressure Cooking Tip
Not recommended.

Tomato 'Charlotte'

SERVES 6 ▲▲●●●

1½lb (675g) tomatoes, blanched and skinned
3oz (75g) butter or margarine
2oz (50g) onion, peeled and chopped
3oz (75g) fresh brown breadcrumbs
1 level tblsp soft brown sugar
1oz (25g) salted peanuts, very finely chopped
½ level tsp celery salt

1 Slice tomatoes and leave on one side temporarily.
2 Heat butter or margarine in pan. Add onion. Fry gently until light gold. Stir in crumbs, sugar, nuts and salt.
3 Fill a greased heatproof dish with alternate layers of tomato slices and crumb mixture, beginning with tomatoes and ending with crumbs.
4 Bake 30 minutes in oven set to 180°C (350°F), Gas 4. Serve with meat, poultry and egg dishes.

Watercress

ALLOW 1 BUNCH FOR EVERY 4 PEOPLE

A dark green, leafy vegetable which is a rich source of Vitamin A. It is widely used in salads, as part of a sandwich filling and, when finely chopped, in omelets and scrambled eggs. It can also be cooked in the same way as spinach but the quantity makes it somewhat impractical.

Ratatouille

SERVES 8 ▲▲●●●

4tblsp salad oil
8oz (225g) onions, peeled and chopped
2 garlic cloves, peeled and sliced
1 large red pepper, washed and dried
1 large green pepper, washed and dried
1 large unpeeled aubergine, washed and dried
1lb (450g) courgettes, washed and dried
1lb (450g) tomatoes, blanched and skinned
1½ to 2 level tsp salt
¼ level tsp pepper
3 rounded tblsp chopped parsley

1 Heat oil in heavy-based pan. Add onions and garlic. Cover pan. Fry gently until soft but still pale, allowing about 15 minutes.
2 Meanwhile, halve peppers, remove seeds and cut flesh into strips. Thinly slice aubergine. Top and tail courgettes and slice. Cut tomatoes into quarters.

3 Add all vegetables to pan with salt and pepper. Bring to boil, stirring. Lower heat. Cover. Simmer slowly 1 hour.

4 Uncover. Continue to cook a further 20 to 30 minutes or until Ratatouille is thick and most of the liquid has evaporated. Stir in parsley. Serve with meat and poultry.

Stir-Fry Vegetable Mix

SERVES 6 ▲▲●●●

Chinese in character, Stir-Fry vegetables have an appetizing crispness and, because they are cooked quickly, retain their colour and full flavour.

1 medium carrot, peeled
1 medium onion, peeled
3oz (75g) mushrooms and stalks, peeled
1 small washed red pepper, dried and de-seeded
2tblsp salad oil
1 level tblsp cornflour
4tblsp stock
1tblsp Soy sauce
1tblsp medium sherry
¼ level tsp caster sugar
1 garlic clove, peeled and crushed (optional)

1 Cut all vegetables into strips the size of matchsticks but double in thickness.

2 Heat oil in large, heavy-based frying pan or Chinese wok if you happen to have one. Add prepared vegetables.

3 Fry briskly for 5 minutes, turning frequently to ensure even cooking.

4 Sprinkle with cornflour (which glazes vegetables) then stir in all remaining ingredients.

5 Bring to boil, stirring continuously. Simmer 2 minutes. Serve with any main course dish.

Success Tips

1 Always wash and scrub very earthy vegetables thoroughly before peeling.

2 Unless otherwise stated, peel thinly to prevent waste and loss of vitamins. For the latter reason, NEVER leave vegetables soaking in water for too long before cooking. Salad greens which have wilted are the exception, but even these should be left in water only long enough to crispen.

3 Even-sized pieces all cook at the same rate, so bear this in mind when cutting up roots, peppers and so on.

4 NEVER add bicarbonate of soda to green vegetables as it destroys all the Vitamin C and, additionally, makes them slushy.

5 NEVER overcook green vegetables and others such as cauliflower and peas. They will lose essential nutrients and the appearance will suffer. From a flavour point of view, slightly crisp vegetables are more appealing than soft and soggy ones. (This obviously does not apply to vegetables to be mashed.)

6 When cooking any vegetable, keep water to a minimum and the heat low. This way they will steam rather than boil in the water and taste AND look better.

7 NEVER cover chips and other fried vegetables as they will lose their crispness rapidly.

8 If it is essential for you to keep green vegetables of any kind warm, then be prepared to accept a change of colour; they will inevitably dull down.

9 Whenever possible, buy sufficient fresh vegetables for day to day needs rather than stock-pile. This way you will avoid stale, bedraggled vegetables with minimal flavour and a coarse texture.

10 To prevent the smell of cabbage and cauliflower drifting through the house, add a small, peeled onion to the cooking water.

Salads

Salads

When I delved into Cassell's *Dictionary of Cooking*, published in 1899, I came across the following advice on salad making which is just as appropriate today as it was at the turn of the century and phrased with charm, dry humour and the sort of sound common sense one would expect from one's learned grandmother! Here is the abridged version.

'A salad well prepared is a charming compound, and, when taken with plenty of oil, very wholesome, attractive and agreeable; badly prepared it is an abomination. A Spanish proverb says that four persons are needed to make a good salad – a spend-thrift to throw in the oil, a miser to drop in the vinegar, a lawyer to administer the seasoning, and a madman to stir the whole thing together. Lettuce is generally supposed to form the foundation of a salad, but there are few fresh vegetables that may not be used: and on the Continent every known vegetable is, when plainly dressed, used cold for salads; and cold meat, fish and game are served in the same way. Though a variety in salads is easily secured, great care is necessary in the preparation of the dish, and three or four rules must be closely observed if the salad is to be a success. First, the vegetables must be young, freshly cut, in season and in good condition. Secondly, the vegetables should not be allowed to lie long in water. If withered, they may be put in for a short time to render them a little crisp, but if fresh, they should be simply rinsed through the water and dried immediately. Thirdly – and this point requires most careful attention – the vegetables must be rendered perfectly dry after washing. The best way of doing this is to drain the salad and shake it first in a colander, or salad-basket, and afterwards in a clean napkin held by the corners and shaken lightly till the salad is dry. Fourthly, do not prepare it until a short time before it is wanted, and on no account mix the salad-dressing with it until the last moment. It is a very usual and excellent plan to pour the liquid into the bottom of the bowl, lay the shred vegetables upon it, and mix the salad at table. A wooden fork and spoon are best for this purpose. Salads may be garnished in various ways, and afford ample opportunity for the display of artistic taste.'

Andalusian Salad

Green Salad

SERVES 4 TO 6   ▲●●

1 Webb, Cos or round lettuce, medium-sized
1 garlic clove, peeled and halved (optional)
French Dressing (page 180)

1 Separate lettuce leaves and wash gently under running water.
2 Shake and/or gently pat dry with clean cloth or paper towels, but to make doubly sure most of the water drains away, leave lettuce to stand in large colander for about 30 to 40 minutes.
3 Before serving, rub cut sides of garlic over salad bowl though this is not essential and can be omitted by those who dislike garlic.
4 Tear lettuce leaves into pieces rather than cut as knives have a bruising effect on delicate greenery and tend to cause discoloration.
5 Add just sufficient French Dressing to moisten, but err on the cautious side to prevent it forming a surplus pool in the base of the bowl. Toss with a wooden spoon and fork and serve straightaway.

Coleslaw Salad

Coleslaw salad literally comes in all shapes and sizes and the European version, fairly plain and coated with French Dressing or Mayonnaise, is less copious than its American cousin which is melded together with soured cream AND Mayonnaise and often enhanced with fruit, other vegetables and nuts.

Coleslaw (Basic)

SERVES 8

1½lb (675g) firm white cabbage, usually known as Dutch
1 small onion, peeled and finely grated
about ¼pt (150ml) French Dressing (page 180)
salt and pepper to taste

1 Very finely shred cabbage, using a sharp knife. Alternatively, shred cabbage in food processor or shredder attachment of food mixer.
2 Transfer to bowl. Toss with onion, dressing and salt and pepper to taste.
3 Cover. Refrigerate until cold before serving, allowing a minimum of 1 hour.

Coleslaw with Mayonnaise

SERVES 8

Make exactly as *Coleslaw (Basic)*, but toss with about ½pt (275ml) Mayonnaise (page 175) instead of French Dressing.

Coleslaw with Carrots

SERVES 8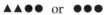

Make exactly as *Coleslaw (Basic)*, but include 4oz (125g) peeled and finely-grated carrots. Toss with either French Dressing or Mayonnaise.

Coleslaw American Style

SERVES 8

Make exactly as *Coleslaw (Basic)*, but toss with 1 carton (5 fluid oz or 142ml) soured cream and ¼pt (150ml) Mayonnaise. For a less rich version, use yogurt instead of the cream.

Mixed Salad

SERVES 6 ▲▲●●●

A few lettuce leaves, a wedge or two of tomato, a sliced-up radish, spray of watercress and a spring onion, minus dressing, are an apology for a full-blown mixed salad which should fill a large bowl to the brim and be generous to a fault. This is my version.

1 small lettuce, washed and dried
½ small cucumber, peeled and thinly sliced
12 spring onions, trimmed and halved lengthwise
12 trimmed radishes, washed and sliced
3 medium tomatoes, each cut into 8 wedges
1 bunch watercress, stalks removed and well washed
1 small green pepper, de-seeded and fairly finely chopped
French Dressing (page 180)

1 Tear lettuce into pieces. Put into large salad bowl. Add all remaining vegetables.
2 Just before serving, toss with sufficient French Dressing to moisten.

Greek Salad

SERVES 6 ▲▲●●●

Well known and well loved by those who have fond memories of Grecian holidays, this is basically a mixed salad topped with cheese. It can be served as a meal by itself or used to accompany fish or lamb dishes. Make as the *Mixed Salad* above, omitting spring onions, radishes and watercress and adding 2 peeled and sliced onions (medium size), 4oz (125g) small black olives and 1 crushed garlic clove. Toss with about 5 tablespoons French Dressing then top with 6oz (175g) Greek Feta cheese or Caerphilly cheese, cut into wedges. Trickle a little oil over the top.

Waldorf Salad

SERVES 6

An American special which has a distinctive crunch and mellow sweetness. It is at its most companionable with poultry dishes.

8oz (225g) celery
8oz (225g) dessert apples (try for bright red if possible)
4oz (125g) green grapes (optional)
3oz (75g) walnuts, coarsely chopped
about 6 rounded tblsp Mayonnaise

1 Wash then scrub celery and wipe dry. Slice fairly thinly. Tip into bowl.
2 Wash and dry apples. Quarter and core but do not peel. Dice and add to celery.
3 Halve grapes (if used) and remove seeds. Add to bowl with rest of ingredients. Toss lightly. Spoon into glass serving bowl before serving.

Andalusian Salad

SERVES 6

1 small to medium round lettuce, washed and dried
1 large green pepper, washed and dried
1 large Spanish onion, peeled
4 large tomatoes, washed and dried
3 Grade 4 hard-boiled eggs
20 stuffed olives
about ¼pt (150ml) French Dressing (page 180)
1 garlic clove, peeled and crushed
1 level tblsp chopped parsley

1 Tear lettuce into small pieces, directly into salad bowl. Leave on one side temporarily.
2 Halve pepper and remove inside fibres and seeds then cut flesh into strips. Slice onion as thinly as possible and separate slices into rings. Slice tomatoes, eggs and olives.
3 Add all prepared ingredients to lettuce in bowl. Sprinkle with dressing, first mixed with garlic and parsley. Toss gently to mix.

Chicory Salads

Creamy-white heads of chicory, born and bred in Belgium, are cool, crisp customers which add a distinctive note of subtlety to a variety of salads.

225

Chicory Salads. Left: Chicory Salad Mix;
Bottom Left: Chicory and Prawn Salad;
Bottom right: Chicory and Walnut Salad;
Right: Chicory Mandarin Salad

Chicory Salad Mix

SERVES 6　　　　▲▲●●●

4 heads chicory
1 medium cooking apple
2 medium tomatoes
1 small onion
2 Grade 3 hard-boiled eggs

DRESSING
¼pt (150ml) single cream
2 level tsp continental mustard
1 level tsp (scant) salt
2tsp cider vinegar

GARNISH
1 Grade 3 hard-boiled egg
1 medium tomato
paprika

1　Wash chicory, removing any bruised outer leaves. Cut out a cone-shaped piece from base of each as this is unpleasantly bitter. Using a stainless knife, cut chicory into slices. Tip into bowl.
2　Peel and quarter apple. Remove core and dice flesh. Slice tomatoes.

Peel onion and chop. Cut shelled eggs into wedges. Add all to chicory.
3　For dressing, beat ingredients well together. Pour over salad. Toss lightly. Transfer to serving bowl.
4　For garnish, cut shelled egg into wedges and slice tomato. Arrange attractively on top of salad then dust with paprika.

Chicory and Prawn Salad

SERVES 6　　　　▲▲●●●

4 heads chicory
8oz (225g) peeled prawns
2 large pickled cucumbers

DRESSING
4tblsp Mayonnaise
4tblsp yogurt
2tblsp cold milk
1tblsp lemon juice
¼ level tsp garlic powder
1 level tsp salt
white pepper to taste

1　Wash chicory, removing any bruised outer leaves. Cut a cone-shaped piece from base of each as

this is unpleasantly bitter. Using a stainless knife, cut chicory into slices.
2　Put into bowl with two-thirds of the prawns. Cut 1 cucumber in half centrally and leave one piece aside for garnish. Chop remainder coarsely.
3　Add to chicory and prawns. Beat all dressing ingredients well together. Toss with salad ingredients. Transfer to serving bowl.
4　Slice remaining half cucumber lengthwise into 4 slices. Use to garnish salad with last third of prawns.

Chicory Mandarin Salad

SERVES 4 TO 6　　　　▲▲●●

4 heads chicory
1 small can mandarin oranges, drained
6tblsp French Dressing or other dressing to taste (page 180)

GARNISH
1 small washed orange, dried and sliced
about 1tblsp mustard and cress

1 Wash chicory, removing any bruised outer leaves. Cut a cone-shaped piece from base of each as this is unpleasantly bitter. Using a stainless knife, cut chicory into slices.
2 Tip into salad bowl. Add mandarins and dressing. Toss. Garnish with orange slices and mustard and cress.

Note Reserve mandarin syrup and use for jellies or drinks.

Chicory and Walnut Salad

SERVES 4 TO 6   ▲▲●●●

4 heads chicory
1 small onion, peeled and grated
2oz (50g) walnut halves
6tblsp French Dressing (page 180)

1 Wash chicory, removing any bruised outer leaves. Cut a cone-shaped piece from base of each as this is unpleasantly bitter. Using a stainless knife, cut chicory into slices. Tip into salad bowl with onion.
2 Toss with 1½oz (40g) walnuts and dressing. Garnish with rest of walnuts.

Italian Style Summer Salad

SERVES 6 TO 8   ▲▲●●●

Delicious with grills of meat, poultry and offal and also with pasta dishes.

1 cucumber of about 1lb (450g) in weight
1 large red pepper, washed and dried
1 large green pepper, washed and dried
3 large tomatoes, washed and dried
1 large onion, peeled and sliced
¼pt (150ml) French Dressing (page 180)
1 rounded tblsp chopped parsley

1 Peel cucumber and thinly slice. Halve peppers, remove seeds and cut flesh into strips.
2 Thinly slice tomatoes. Repeat with onion, then separate onion into rings.
3 Tip all ingredients into bowl and toss with dressing. Arrange attractively on a plate and sprinkle with parsley.

Italian Style Summer Salad

Hawaiian Salad

SERVES 6 TO 8   ▲▲●●●

Exotic in character, this is a particularly interesting fruit and vegetable combination which teams well with poultry, egg and fried fish dishes.

4 medium celery stalks, well washed and scrubbed
2 medium peeled dessert apples, quartered and cored
1 large orange, peeled
3 large canned pineapple rings
2oz (50g) blanched almonds, cut into slivers
4 rounded tblsp thick Mayonnaise
1tblsp lemon juice
¼ medium round lettuce, washed and dried
12 radishes

1 Cut celery into medium slices. Dice apples. Slice orange, then cut slices into segments. Drain pineapple thoroughly and divide into small pieces.
2 Lightly toast almonds and leave on one side temporarily. Tip celery and fruits into bowl. Mix with Mayonnaise, beaten smoothly with lemon juice. Cover and refrigerate 1 hour.
3 Meanwhile, line a platter or shallow dish with lettuce. Slice down each radish to make petals and drop into bowl of iced water. Refrigerate.
4 To assemble, stir two-thirds of the almonds into salad then transfer to platter or dish. Sprinkle rest of almonds on top then surround with drained radishes.

Hawaiian Salad

227

1 Finely shred cabbage and tip into bowl. Slice bananas and toss with lemon juice. Slice oranges then cut each slice into small pieces.
2 Add bananas (with lemon juice), oranges and raisins to bowl. Toss with cabbage and dressing. Transfer to serving dish.
3 Slice orange thinly. Slit each slice from centre to outside edge and shape into twist. Arrange on top of salad.

Californian Vitamin Salad

Californian Vitamin Salad

SERVES 6 ▲▲●●●

Packed with vitamins and freshness, this salad can be served as a light lunch or supper dish in its own right, or served with cold roast poultry or a mixed cheese platter.

8oz (225g) white cabbage
2 medium bananas
juice of 1 medium lemon
2 medium oranges, peeled
1oz (25g) seedless raisins
6tblsp French Dressing (page 180)

GARNISH
1 large orange, washed and dried

Golden Summer Salad

SERVES 8 ▲▲▲●●●

A glorious mixed fruit and vegetable salad which makes perfect summer eating either by itself or with an assortment of cold meats. Slimmers can enjoy this feast of a salad with a topping of nothing more fattening than natural yogurt.

1 medium round lettuce, washed and dried
$\frac{1}{3}$ medium cucumber, peeled
3 medium tomatoes, washed and dried
1 medium green pepper, washed and dried
1 small, ripe avocado
1tblsp lemon juice
about 12 radishes, trimmed and washed
2 ripe peaches
1 large canned pineapple ring, drained and coarsely chopped
2 heaped tblsp canned, drained mandarins
4oz (125g) strawberries, washed and halved

DRESSING
1 small onion, peeled and finely grated
4 tblsp salad oil
1 level tsp salt
$\frac{1}{2}$ level tsp powder mustard
1 heaped tblsp chopped parsley
1 heaped tblsp chopped chives
$\frac{1}{4}$ level tsp dried tarragon
$\frac{1}{4}$ level tsp dried basil
2tblsp lemon juice

1 Tear lettuce into pieces. Thinly slice cucumber and tomatoes. Halve green pepper and remove seeds. Cut flesh into strips. Tip all prepared ingredients into large bowl.

Golden Summer Salad

2 Peel avocado as you would peel a pear, starting from the pointed end. Halve and remove stone. Cut flesh lengthwise into strips. Brush with ½ tablespoon lemon juice.

3 Cut radishes into slices. Peel peaches and halve. Remove stones. Thinly slice flesh and sprinkle with ½ tablespoon lemon juice. Add avocado, radishes and peach slices to other ingredients in bowl with pineapple, mandarins and strawberries.

4 To make dressing, mix together onion and oil then beat in all remaining ingredients. Continue to beat until dressing thickens, then toss with salad. Transfer to a large dish and serve straightaway.

French Chef's Salad

French Chef's Salad

SERVES 6 ▲▲●●●

An elegant centrepiece, ideally suited to more formal occasions.

> 8oz (225g) red cabbage, washed and dried
> 8oz (225g) white cabbage, washed and dried
> 8oz (225g) carrots, peeled
> 8oz (225g) celeriac, thickly peeled as flesh immediately beneath skin is tough
> 8oz (225g) tomatoes, washed and dried
> 1 small round lettuce, washed and dried
> ¼pt (150ml) Garlic Dressing (page 180)
> 1 level tblsp drained and chopped capers
> ½ level tsp dried tarragon

GARNISH
4 Grade 3 hard-boiled eggs
1 small onion, peeled and sliced
2 wedges of lemon

1 Shred both red and white cabbage but do not mix. Grate carrots and celeriac. Slice tomatoes.

2 Arrange all vegetables in separate mounds, on large platter, placing the odd lettuce leaf here and there.

3 Mix dressing with capers and tarragon. Pour half over the salad. Pour rest into sauce boat.

4 Shell and slice eggs. Pile in middle of salad then garnish with onion rings and lemon wedges. Pass remaining dressing separately.

Palm Heart Salad

SERVES 4 TO 6 ▲▲●●●

A pretty, young-at-heart salad which is companionable with an assortment of hot and cold meat and poultry dishes.

> 1 can (about 12oz or 350g) palm hearts, drained
> 2 heaped tblsp white cocktail onions
> 2 large oranges, peeled
> 2 canned red peppers, drained
> 4tblsp French Dressing (page 180)
> 1 rounded tsp chopped parsley

1 Cut palm hearts into ½in (1¼cm) pieces. Tip into bowl with onions.

2 Using a sharp and non-serrated knife, 'fillet' out segments of orange by cutting in between skin holding each piece together. Cut red pepper into finger width strips of about 1in (2½cm) in length. Add orange segments and red pepper to bowl.

3 Toss with dressing, transfer to a serving bowl and sprinkle with chopped parsley. Cover and refrigerate about 1 hour before serving.

Palm Heart Salad

Sweetcorn Salad

Sweetcorn Salad

SERVES 6 ▲▲●●●

A light and attractively-coloured salad which I especially recommend for egg dishes.

Fruited Red Cabbage and Nut Salad

12oz (350g) cooked sweetcorn, drained
1 large green pepper
8oz (225g) tomatoes, blanched and skinned
12 stuffed olives
¼pt (150ml) French Dressing (page 180)
about 8 washed and dried lettuce leaves for garnish

1 Tip sweetcorn into bowl. Halve pepper and remove seeds. Cut flesh into strips. Slice tomatoes into thin wedges.
2 Add both pepper and tomatoes to bowl with thinly sliced olives. Toss with dressing and spoon into serving dish. Add a garnish of lettuce leaves as shown in picture.

Fruited Red Cabbage and Nut Salad

SERVES 6 TO 8 ▲▲●●●

Appropriate with rich meats such as duck, goose and pork, this original salad looks decorative and tastes festive.

8oz (225g) red cabbage, washed and dried
1 small onion, peeled
2 medium oranges, peeled
1 large banana
1tblsp lemon juice
2oz (50g) sultanas
5tblsp French Dressing (page 180)
12 walnut halves

1 Finely shred cabbage. Grate onion. Slice oranges and cut into small pieces.
2 Peel banana and slice directly into bowl. Gently stir with lemon juice.
3 Tip all ingredients, except walnuts, into bowl. Toss with dressing. Transfer to serving dish and garnish with walnuts.

Party Buffet Salad

SERVES 6 ▲▲●●●

A few platters of this salad, dotted about a cold buffet, add a lively touch of colour and have sufficient flavour contrast to be interesting.

1 head curly green endive (about 8oz or 225g)
12oz (350g) tomatoes, washed and dried
1 large green pepper
1 can (about 7oz or 200g) artichoke hearts, drained and quartered
1 small onion, peeled and grated
¼pt (150ml) French Dressing (page 180)
2 Grade 3 hard-boiled eggs for garnish

1 Soak endive in cold, salted water for 10 minutes. Drain thoroughly and tear into large pieces.
2 Use to line a shallow serving platter. Slice tomatoes. Halve green pepper, remove seeds and cut flesh into strips. Tip both into bowl. Add artichoke hearts and onion.
3 Pour dressing over salad. Toss gently. Pile over endive. Shell eggs and slice and use to garnish as shown in the picture.

Potato Salad

SERVES 4 TO 6 ▲▲●●

1lb (450g) potatoes, peeled
¼pt (150ml) Mayonnaise
1 rounded tblsp chopped chives or parsley

1 Halve potatoes and cook in boiling, salted water until tender. Drain. Leave until lukewarm. Dice.
2 Tip into bowl. Toss gently with Mayonnaise and half the chives or parsley. Transfer to a serving dish and sprinkle with remainder.

Russian Salad

SERVES 6

▲▲ or ▲▲▲ ●● or ●●●

Always popular with cold meats, Russian salad can be made in 3 ways; with canned macedoine of vegetables, with frozen and cooked macedoine, or with a mixture of vegetables which are prepared from fresh vegetables. I shall give the authentic recipe and adjustments can be made to suit personal requirements.

8oz (225g) peeled carrots, halved lengthwise and washed
8oz (225g) peeled potatoes, halved lengthwise and washed
4oz (125g) frozen peas (fresh can be used but take longer to cook)
4oz (125g) frozen green beans (fresh can be used but take longer to cook)
¼pt (150ml) Mayonnaise
½ a smallish round lettuce, washed and dried

1 Cook carrots and potatoes until tender in boiling, salted water. If using fresh peas and beans, add straightaway. If frozen, add about

Party Buffet Salad

10 minutes before carrots and potatoes are ready. Drain.
2 Leave until lukewarm. Dice carrots and potatoes. Tip into bowl with peas and beans. Toss with Mayonnaise. Spoon on to lettuce-lined plate.

Cucumber Salad

SERVES 4 TO 6 ▲▲●●

Refreshing and gloriously cooling in the height of summer, delicately green cucumber salad is recommended for serving with poached fish dishes such as salmon and salmon trout.

1 large cucumber (about 1½lb or 675g), peeled
French Dressing (page 180)
about 1tblsp very finely-chopped parsley

1 Peel cucumber and cut flesh into wafer-thin slices. Wrap tightly in a tea towel and squeeze dry.
2 Tip into bowl and chill, covered, in refrigerator about 1 hour. Moisten with French Dressing. Toss. Transfer to serving dish and sprinkle with parsley.

Middle Eastern and Cucumber Salad

SERVES 4 TO 6 ▲▲●●

Prepare cucumber exactly as given in recipe for Cucumber Salad. In-

stead of French Dressing, mix with 1 carton (142ml or 5 fluid oz) yogurt, 1 crushed garlic clove and salt to taste.

Salad Niçoise

SERVES 6 ▲▲●●●

Colourful and vivacious, Salad Niçoise is a delicious Mediterranean salad packed full of bright vegetables and tasty tuna fish.

1 small round lettuce, washed and dried
12oz (350g) cold, cooked potatoes
8oz (225g) green sliced beans, cooked and cooled
1 can (about 7oz or 198g) tuna, drained and flaked
12 canned anchovy fillets, drained
16 black olives
3 Grade 3 hard-boiled eggs, shelled and sliced
3 medium tomatoes, washed and dried
¼pt (150ml) French Dressing (page 180)

1 Line a serving dish with lettuce leaves. Dice potatoes. Spoon into dish over lettuce.
2 Add beans then stud with flakes of tuna. Garnish with a criss-cross of anchovy fillets.
3 Finally add olives, sliced egg and quartered tomatoes. Sprinkle with dressing and serve with crusty rolls and butter.

Stuffings

Stuffings

Known also as Forcemeat and Farces, stuffings make excellent and flavoursome 'extenders', add nutritional value and texture contrast and, in some instances, help a bird or boned joint of meat retain a full and buxom appearance. A stuffing base is usually of breadcrumbs although sausagemeat, rice and chestnuts can be used either with, or in place of, the crumbs. Milk, stock, melted fat or beaten egg (or a combination) should be added to bind the stuffing together, but care must be taken not to allow the mixture to be made too wet as the resultant stuffing will be heavy and stodgy; it should be just moist enough to hold its shape when gathered together with fingers, fork or spoon. Allow 2oz (50g) prepared stuffing to every 1lb (450g) meat, fish or poultry. Pack loosely as it swells during cooking and, for reasons of hygiene, DO NOT stuff any food, and poultry in particular, ahead of time. It is worth noting 2 factors. (1) Egg as a binder produces a more firm stuffing than milk or stock. (2) Surplus stuffing should be baked separately in a small, greased dish, or rolled into balls and placed round a joint of meat or chicken. About 1 hour's baking time should be adequate. All stuffings may be deep frozen up to 3 months, but must be *completely defrosted* before use.

Giblet Stuffing

Lemon, Parsley and Thyme Stuffing

▲●●

6oz (175g) fresh white
  breadcrumbs
1 level tblsp finely-chopped
  parsley
½ level tsp finely-grated lemon
  peel
½ level tsp dried thyme
½ level tsp salt
shake of white pepper
1oz (25g) butter or margarine,
  melted
1 Grade 4 egg, well beaten
milk or stock if necessary

1 Place crumbs, parsley, lemon peel, thyme, salt and pepper into bowl.
2 Bind with butter or margarine, egg and milk or stock ONLY if stuffing remains on the dry side.

Use for:
Poultry, fish and veal.

Giblet Stuffing

▲●●

Make exactly as *Lemon, Parsley and Thyme Stuffing*, adding *cooked* giblet meat (chopped-up heart, gizzard and liver) to the breadcrumb mix before binding with butter or margarine etc.
Use for:
Poultry.

Kidney and Mushroom Stuffing

▲▲●●

4oz (125g) lamb kidney
4oz (125g) trimmed mushrooms
  and stalks
1 small onion, peeled and grated
1½oz (40g) butter or margarine
5oz (150g) fresh brown
  breadcrumbs
½ to 1 level tsp salt
1 level tsp mixed herbs
stock to bind if necessary

1 Cut kidney into thin pieces. Slice mushrooms and stalks. Grate onion.
2 Fry quickly in the butter or margarine until golden brown, then continue to cook another 5 minutes or until kidney is cooked through.

3 Stir in crumbs, salt and herbs, adding a little stock if stuffing does not bind together readily. Leave until cold before using.

Use for:
Poultry and boned leg of lamb.

Note Moisture content will vary according to kidney and vegetables, so if stuffing seems on the wet side, work in some extra crumbs.

Sage and Onion Stuffing

▲●

8oz (225g) onions, peeled and
    quartered
½ level tsp dried sage
½ level tsp salt
good shake pepper
1oz (25g) butter or margarine,
    melted
5oz (150g) fresh white
    breadcrumbs
beaten egg or stock if necessary

1 Cook onions in boiling salted water, in covered pan, until very soft. Drain thoroughly. Chop.
2 Spoon into basin. Add sage, salt, pepper and butter. Work in breadcrumbs until stuffing forms a fairly loose and crumbly mixture which holds its shape when pressed between finger and thumb.
3 If too dry, add a little egg or stock; if too wet, a few more crumbs. Leave until cold before using.

Use for:
Duck, goose and pork.

Sausagemeat Stuffing (1)

▲●●

8oz (225g) pork or beef
    sausagemeat (or mixture)
4oz (125g) fresh white or brown
    breadcrumbs (or mixture)
¼ level tsp mixed spice
½ level tsp powder mustard
1 garlic clove, peeled and chopped
    (optional)
1 level tblsp finely-chopped
    parsley
½ level tsp finely-grated lemon
    peel
salt and pepper to taste
3tblsp milk

Kidney and Mushroom Stuffing

1 Place all ingredients into large bowl and knead together until well mixed.
2 Use as required.

Use for:
Poultry, veal and beef.

Sausagemeat Stuffing (2)

▲▲●●

1oz (25g) margarine or dripping
1 medium onion, peeled and
    finely chopped
8oz (225g) pork sausagemeat
4oz (125g) fresh white or brown
    breadcrumbs
½ level tsp prepared English
    mustard
½ level tsp mixed herbs
salt and pepper to taste

1 Heat margarine or dripping in pan. Add onion. Fry gently until golden. Stir in sausagemeat. Stir and fry until light gold and crumbly.

2 Stir in rest of ingredients. Leave until cold before using.

Use for:
Poultry and pork.

Sausagemeat and Apple Stuffing

▲▲●●

8oz (225g) pork sausagemeat
8oz (225g) peeled cooking apples,
    coarsely grated
½ level tsp thyme
½ level tsp finely-grated lemon
    peel
1 level tsp prepared English
    mustard
6oz (175g) fresh white
    breadcrumbs
salt and pepper to taste

1 Place all ingredients into bowl. Knead well together with fork, fingertips or spoon.

Use for:
Poultry and pork.

Chestnut Stuffing

Chestnut Stuffing

▲▲●●●

8oz (225g) dried chestnuts (see note below)
1 large onion, peeled and quartered
1 to 2 level tsp salt
1 Grade 3 egg, well beaten
4oz (125g) fresh brown or white breadcrumbs (or mixture)
2oz (50g) butter or margarine, melted
freshly-milled black or white pepper to taste

1 Soak chestnuts overnight in cold water. Drain. Place in clean pan. Cover with boiling water. Add onion.
2 Bring to boil. Lower heat. Add salt. Cover. Simmer until very soft. Drain.
3 Tip chestnuts and onion into bowl. Mash finely. Stir in egg, crumbs and butter or margarine. Season to taste with pepper and extra salt if necessary. Leave until completely cold before using.

Use for:
Poultry.

Note The shelling and skinning of chestnuts is such a prolonged exercise that I now always use either dried (available from many delicatessens and Italian food shops) or about 1lb (450g) can of unsweetened chestnut purée. If using the latter, boil the onion as directed then drain and mash. Work into chestnuts with rest of ingredients listed. Those who prefer and know how to cope with fresh chestnuts should cook a minimum of 1lb (450g).

Rice Stuffing

▲●●

1tblsp salad oil or 1oz (25g) butter or margarine
1 small onion, peeled and chopped
1 small celery stalk, scrubbed and very thinly sliced
4oz (125g) long grain rice (American 'easy-cook' gives best results)
½pt (275ml) boiling stock or water
½ to 1 level tsp salt

1 Heat oil or butter or margarine in saucepan. Add onion and celery. Fry gently until pale gold.
2 Stir in rice. Cook 2 minutes, turning. Pour in stock or water. Add salt.
3 Bring to boil. Stir round. Lower heat. Cover. Simmer 15 to 20 minutes or until rice grains are tender and have absorbed all the moisture.
4 Leave until completely cold before using.

Use for:
Poultry.

Note This is a basic stuffing mix, but any of the following (or a combination) may be added with the stock or water:
1 2 rounded tablespoons sultanas.
2 4 heaped tablespoons cooked sweetcorn.
3 Fried and chopped-up poultry liver.
4 About 2oz (50g) sliced mushrooms.
5 2 heaped tablespoons finely-chopped parsley.
6 1oz (25g) chopped walnuts with 1 unpeeled and coarsely-grated dessert apple.

Mushroom Stuffing
▲▲●●

2oz (50g) butter or margarine
6oz (175g) trimmed mushrooms and stalks, rinsed and chopped
1 small onion, peeled and finely chopped
½ level tsp dried basil or marjoram
6oz (175g) fresh white breadcrumbs
salt and pepper to taste
2tblsp stock or water

1 Heat butter or margarine in pan. Add mushrooms and onion. Fry over moderate heat for 7 minutes, stirring from time to time.
2 Remove from heat. Stir in herbs and crumbs. Season to taste. Work in stock or water if stuffing is on the dry side. Leave until cold before using.

Use for:
Poultry, beef, lamb and whole fish.

Cranberry Nut Stuffing
▲●●●

4oz (125g) fresh white breadcrumbs
1 level tsp finely-grated orange peel
2oz (50g) walnuts, finely chopped
1 small onion, peeled and grated
¼ level tsp salt
about 6 rounded tblsp bottled cranberry sauce

1 Place crumbs, peel, nuts, onion and salt into bowl. Toss well together to mix.
2 Add sufficient cranberry sauce to bind ingredients loosely together.

Use for:
Chicken, turkey, duck and goose.

Fresh Cranberry Stuffing
▲▲●●

3 level tblsp caster sugar
3tblsp water
4oz (125g) fresh cranberries
4oz (125g) fresh breadcrumbs
1 small onion, very finely grated
½ level tsp grated orange peel
½ level tsp grated lemon peel
1 rounded tblsp finely-chopped parsley
½ level tsp salt
½ level tsp powder mustard

1 Dissolve sugar slowly in the water. Bring to boil. Add cranberries. Simmer 2 minutes or until skins pop open.
2 Simmer 5 minutes. Remove from heat. Stir in rest of ingredients. Leave until completely cold before using.

Use for:
Poultry, game and pork.

Mixed Nut Stuffing
▲▲●●●

3oz (75g) brazil nuts
3oz (75g) cashews
3oz (75g) hazelnuts
3oz (75g) salted peanuts
1 medium onion, peeled and grated
¼ level tsp dried basil or marjoram
salt and pepper to taste
1 Grade 3 egg, beaten

1 Grind nuts in blender or food processor. Tip into bowl.
2 Stir in all remaining ingredients. Mix well.

Use for:
Poultry, veal and lamb.

Veal and Lemon Stuffing
▲▲●●●

12oz (350g) pie veal, minced
1 level tsp finely-grated lemon peel
2 level tsp very finely-grated onion
1 level tsp dried thyme
2 level tsp finely-chopped fresh parsley
salt and pepper to taste
1 Grade 3 egg, beaten

1 Place all ingredients into bowl. Mix well together.

Use for:
Poultry.

Tutti-Frutti Stuffing
▲●●●

4oz (125g) trimmed mushrooms and stalks, finely chopped
3oz (75g) celery, scrubbed and thinly sliced
1 large onion, peeled and finely grated
1 large banana, peeled and thinly sliced
1 Grade 3 egg, beaten
salt and pepper to taste

1 In large bowl, toss all ingredients well together to mix.

Use for:
Body cavity of chicken, poultry and duck.

Note This is a loose stuffing which should be spooned out of bird at the time of serving. It is unusual and fragrant, but does not firm up in the same way as others with a crumb base.

237

Yeasted Goods

Yeasted Goods

The most staple of all foods, bread and its innumerable sweet and savoury variations are synonymous with the very best of home baking, evoking nostalgic memories of yesteryear and feelings of well-being and comfort. For those who still imagine or assume that the production of yeasted goods requires inordinate skill and time, I hope the following guidelines will dispel the myths and encourage wary cooks to try their hand at simple white bread and move onwards from there to bigger, if not necessarily better, things!

Guidelines

1 Dry yeast, now generally available, is just as effective as fresh yeast but needs reconstitution. For every 1oz (25g) fresh yeast, use ½oz (15g) dried yeast which equals 1 level tablespoon. Place the dried yeast, about 1 teaspoon sugar and some of the warm liquid (taken from the measured amount specified in the recipe) into a jug. Stir to mix. Leave in the warm until it froths up like a glass of beer; 15 to 20 minutes. If it fails to froth, it means the yeast is stale. Start again with new yeast. Fresh yeast SHOULD NOT be blended with sugar as the bread etc will taste very strongly of yeast. It is more satisfactory if gradually mixed to a smooth cream with some of the warm, measured liquid. As a general guide, allow 1oz (25g) fresh yeast or ½oz (15g) dried to every 3lb (just over 1¼kg) white flour; double the amount of yeast for wholemeal flour. Fresh yeast has limited keeping qualities and any that looks as if it is browning round the edges is stale. Fresh yeast should be the colour and consistency of putty.

2 Self-raising flour should be avoided for yeasted goods. Instead use flour which is clearly marked as being plain or, better still, strong plain. This contains more 'stretchable' gluten and, in consequence, the finished product will be able to expand as it bakes without collapsing. Thus the bread or cake will be well risen and attractively light in texture. Strong flours are milled from hard wheat grown in North America and the Soviet Union; softer flours are milled from European wheat. It is important to know that flours milled from other cereals such as oats, barley and rye contain minimal gluten, and goods baked with these will be close in texture, heavy and lacking in what I call 'spring'. For a more satisfactory result, it is advisable to mix any of these flours with strong plain, using half of each i.e. 8oz (225g) rye flour and 8oz (225g) strong plain.

3 Never add extra sugar or salt 'for luck'. Stick to what the recipe says as too much of either kills the yeast (which is actually a living substance) and stops it from working efficiently as a raising agent. If preferred, honey or golden syrup may be used instead of sugar.

4 Liquid used for mixing can be either water or milk or a combination of the two. As yeast grows more happily in a warm environment than a cool one, the liquid should be lukewarm or tepid. This can readily be made by mixing one-third boiling liquid with two-thirds cold. Unless otherwise specified, the most usual proportion is ½pt (275ml) liquid to 1lb (450g) flour. It is useful to know that milk gives bread a softer texture and browner crust. It also adds to the nutritional value.

5 The dough will shape up more readily and be more manageable if *all* the liquid is added in one go rather than in dribs and drabs. As soon as a dough is formed, take out of the bowl and transfer to a work surface well dusted with plain flour. Knead by hand until dough is smooth and elastic and no longer sticky; 15 to 20 minutes for white dough; 10 for brown dough. If using the dough hook attachment of a mixer or food processor, be guided by the instruction manual but still give the dough a final 2 minutes knead by hand.

6 For what I term a standard rise – about 1 hour – return dough to a clean bowl which has been lightly oiled or brushed with melted butter or margarine. Cover with a greased plate and leave in a warm place until dough doubles in size. I usually place bowl in sink half filled with hand-hot water or leave the bowl in the linen cupboard. The temperature should be no higher than 32°C (90°F). For a slower rise, leave the dough for about 1½ to 2 hours at kitchen temperature. For a very slow rise, leave dough in a cool place for about 4 hours. For an overnight rise, *halve quantity of yeast* given in the recipe (otherwise it will rise too much), place dough in a well-oiled polythene bag and tie loosely AT THE TOP. Refrigerate overnight. Allow dough to reach kitchen temperature before handling.

7 After the initial rise, most recipes tell you to 'punch down' or 'knock back' dough before going any further. What these curious terms mean is that you must punch or re-knead the risen dough in order to deflate it and so eliminate air bubbles produced by the yeast. If this is not done (bearing in mind there are exceptions where this stage is omitted) the texture of the dough will be uneven and dotted with large holes. Also it may not rise as one would like. The process of 'punching down' or 'knocking back' is quicker than the initial kneading process and takes just a few minutes, or until the dough is once again firm and no longer sticky.

8 The next stage is shaping, and each specific recipe will give details. Afterwards 'prove' the dough by covering with greased greaseproof paper or greased polythene and leaving it to rise again in a warm place until it doubles in size and looks light and puffy; about 45 minutes to 1 hour for a large loaf, and half

that for rolls. Please remember that fruited mixtures tend to be heavier than plain ones and take longer to rise.

9 Although baking times are given with each recipe, it may be useful to know that a very hot oven is needed for plain dough and a moderately hot oven for richer doughs. This is in order to kill off the yeast and prevent the dough from over-rising. A very hot oven means a temperature of 230°C (450°F), Gas 8; a moderately hot oven, 200°C (400°F), Gas 6. Leave bread etc for about 5 minutes in its tin and then turn out on to a wire cooling rack. To test if bread etc is cooked through, tap base with fingertips and you should hear a hollow sound. If not, stand on baking tray and return to oven for a further 5 to 10 minutes. Similarly, if you want the sides of the loaf to crispen, take out of tin 5 minutes before it is ready. Stand on baking tray and return to oven. For a crusty finish, stand a small roasting tin of hot water in the bottom of the oven and remove 10 minutes before the end of baking time.

10 For those who want to make dough in quantity, freezing is the most satisfactory means of storage. The kneaded but UN-RISEN dough should be divided up into manageable amounts (1lb or 450g batches), slipped into oiled polythene bags, tied at the top and frozen up to 1 month for plain dough; up to 3 months for rich dough. To thaw, the bags should be opened and left overnight in the refrigerator (and then removed and brought to kitchen temperature) or 5 to 6 hours at kitchen temperature.

11 Yeast itself can be frozen without harm. Wrap 1oz (25g) amounts securely in cling film and deep freeze no longer than 6 weeks. Thaw 20 to 30 minutes at kitchen temperature before using.

12 Baked breads, if well wrapped, can be deep frozen for 6 months. Loaves and rolls with a crackly crust should be deep frozen no longer than a week as the crusts have a tendency to break away from the bread fairly quickly after freezing.

Dinner Rolls

White Bread

MAKES 3 LOAVES ▲▲●

READ INTRODUCTION

½oz or 15g (1 level tblsp) dried yeast plus 2 level tsp caster sugar OR 1oz (25g) fresh yeast
1½pt (⅞ litre) lukewarm water
1 bag (3lb or 1.4kg) strong, plain flour
3 level tsp salt
1 level tblsp caster sugar
2oz (50g) butter, lard, margarine or cooking fat

1 Mix dried yeast and sugar with warm water and leave in a warm place for about 15 to 20 minutes or until frothy. Alternately, mix fresh yeast smoothly with some of the water then add the remainder.

2 Sift flour and salt into bowl. Toss in sugar. Rub in fat finely with fingertips. Mix to soft dough with yeast liquid.

3 Turn out on to a floured surface. Knead about 15 to 20 minutes or until dough is smooth and elastic and no longer sticky. Shape into ball.

4 Transfer to greased bowl. Cover with greased plate. Leave in warm place (kitchen sink half filled with hand-hot water or linen cupboard) until dough doubles in size; about 1 hour.

5 Scoop out on to floured surface and 'knock-back' to remove air bubbles. Knead briefly until smooth. Cut into 3 equal portions.

6 Shape to fit 3 × 2lb (1kg) well greased loaf tins. (Use melted white cooking fat or lard for greasing.) Dust tops lightly with flour.

7 Cover with greased greaseproof paper or greased polythene and leave to rise in warm place for about 45 minutes to 1 hour, or until loaves double in size and look puffy.

8 Bake 45 to 50 minutes in very hot oven set to 230°C (450°F), Gas 8. Leave in tins about 5 minutes. Turn out and cool on wire rack.

Dinner Rolls

MAKES 36 ▲▲●

Follow recipe for *White Bread* (above) but divide risen dough into 36 even-sized pieces and knead into balls. Make a cross cut on top of each with scissors. Transfer to greased baking trays. Cover with greased greaseproof paper or polythene. Leave to rise in warm place until rolls have doubled in size and cuts have opened out as shown in photograph above. Bake 25 to 30 minutes in very hot oven set to 230°C (450°F), Gas 8, when rolls should be deep golden. Remove from oven. At once brush with water which, when dry, produces a light glaze.

Note For 12 or 24 rolls, follow instructions for *Dinner Rolls* (above) but use ⅓ or ⅔ dough. Bake remainder as loaves or loaf.

241

Fruit Bread

Milk Bread

MAKES 3 LOAVES ▲▲●●

READ INTRODUCTION

Follow recipe for *White Bread* (page 241) but increase fat to 6oz (175g) and choose either butter or margarine. Make yeast liquid from half warm milk and half warm water. Brush tops of loaves with milk or beaten egg. Bake 50 to 55 minutes in moderately hot oven set to 200°C (400°F), Gas 6.

Breakfast Rolls or Flat Baps

MAKES 30 ▲▲●●

Follow recipe for *Milk Bread* (above). Divide risen dough into 30 equal-sized pieces. Shape into balls then flatten each into circle of ½in (1¼cm) in depth. Place well apart on greased and floured baking trays. Cover with greased greaseproof paper or polythene. Leave to rise in warm place about 35 minutes or until double in size. Dust fairly thickly with flour. Bake as *Milk Bread*, allowing 15 minutes. Remove from oven. Transfer to wire cooling racks. Cover with teatowel, to ensure a soft crust.

Fruit Bread

MAKES 3 LOAVES ▲▲●●

Follow recipe for *White Bread* (page 241) but toss 3 rounded tablespoons sugar instead of 1 level into sifted flour and salt. Increase fat by 1oz (25g). Add 12oz (350g) sultanas or seedless raisins before mixing to dough with yeast liquid. Bake 45 minutes in hot oven set to 225°C (425°F), Gas 7. Leave in tins 5 minutes. Turn out on to wire cooling racks. Brush tops with melted syrup for golden glaze. Alternatively, leave plain.

Pitta Bread

MAKES 8 ▲▲●

This is classic Greek and Middle Eastern bread usually made with a very basic dough mix which frequently contains no fat at all. Therefore, either follow recipe for *White Bread* (page 241) as it stands or omit

fat altogether. Divide one-third risen dough into 8 equal-size pieces. Roll out thinly into ovals measuring 10 by 5in (25cm by 13cm). Transfer to greased trays. LEAVE UNCOVERED FOR 5 MINUTES ONLY. Bake in a very hot oven, 240°C (475°F), Gas 9, for 6 to 8 minutes or until just beginning to colour. Watch carefully to ensure Pittas do not darken too much. Remove from oven. Split each to allow steam to escape and form characteristic pockets. Wrap while still hot in damp teatowel to give a soft crust. Unwrap when cold. Before serving, reheat for a few minutes under a hot grill, again taking care not to let the bread darken.

Note Pitta bread is either filled with lamb kebabs (taken off the kebab spears first) or used to 'scoop' up Taramosalata and Hummus.

Bake remaining dough as loaves or make extra Pittas which deep freeze extremely well (see Introduction).

Bridge Rolls

MAKES 40 ▲▲●●

Follow recipe for *Milk Bread* (above). Divide risen dough into 40 equal-sized pieces. Shape into 'cigars', the length of an index finger. Stand close together on greased baking trays so that they link up as they rise. Cover with greased greaseproof paper or polythene. Leave to rise in warm place about 30 minutes. Brush with beaten egg. Bake as Milk Bread, allowing 15 minutes. Remove from oven. Transfer to wire cooling racks. Cover with teatowel to ensure a soft crust.

Plaited Bread

MAKES 3 LOAVES ▲▲●●

Follow recipe for *Milk Bread* (above). Divide risen dough into 3 equal pieces. Divide each piece into a further 3 pieces. Roll each into a

16in (40cm) long sausage. Plait the 3 pieces together, forming 3 plaited loaves. Transfer to greased baking trays. Cover with greased grease-proof paper or polythene. Leave to rise in warm place about 45 minutes or until loaves double in size. Brush tops with well-beaten egg or milk. Sprinkle with poppy seeds. Bake as Milk Bread, allowing 50 to 55 minutes. Remove from oven. Transfer to wire cooling racks.

Bun Round

MAKES 8

Follow recipe for *Milk Bread* (page 242). Divide one-third of the risen dough into 8 equal-sized pieces. Shape into round buns. Place in a well-greased, 8in (20cm) round cake tin. Cover with greased greaseproof paper or polythene. Leave to rise in warm place about 20 minutes or until buns have doubled in size and joined together. Bake 15 to 20 minutes (or until golden brown) in hot oven set to 220°C (425°), Gas 7. Remove from oven. Transfer to wire cooling rack. Leave until cold. Cover top with plain Glacé Icing, made by mixing 6oz (175g) sifted icing sugar to a stiff but spreadable paste with 6 to 7 teaspoons of warm water. If liked, the icing may be tinted pale pink with edible food colouring. Split apart before serving.

Note The remaining dough may be made into 2 loaves or extra Bun Rounds.

Swiss Buns

MAKES 8

Follow recipe for *Milk Bread* (page 242). Divide one-third of the risen dough into 8 equal-sized pieces. Form into 5in (12cm) cigar shapes. Transfer to greased baking tray. Cover with greased greaseproof paper or polythene. Leave to rise in warm place about 20 minutes or until buns have doubled in size. Bake until golden brown; about 15 minutes in hot oven set to 220°C (425°F), Gas 7. Remove from oven. Transfer to wire cooling rack. Leave until cold. Cover top with plain Glacé Icing, made by mixing 6oz (175g) sifted icing sugar to a stiff but spreadable paste with 6 to 7 teaspoons of warm water. If liked, the

Currant Buns

icing may be tinted pale pink with edible food colouring.

Note The remaining dough may be made into 2 loaves or extra Swiss Buns.

Cornish Splits

MAKES 8

Follow recipe for *Milk Bread* (page 242). Divide one-third of the risen dough into 8 equal-sized pieces. Shape into round buns. Transfer to greased baking tray. Cover with greased greaseproof paper or polythene. Leave to rise in warm place about 20 minutes or until buns have doubled in size. Bake 15 to 20 minutes in hot oven set to 220°C (425°F), Gas 7. Remove from oven. Transfer to wire cooling rack. Split in half when cold and fill with raspberry or strawberry jam and whipped or clotted cream. Dust tops fairly thickly with sifted icing sugar.

Devonshire Chudleighs

MAKES 8

These are exactly the same as *Cornish Splits* above, but are split open while still hot and filled with clotted cream and strawberry or raspberry jam.

'Thunder and Lightning'

MAKES 8

These, too, are the same as *Cornish Splits* but are split open while still hot and filled with black treacle and clotted cream.

Note The remaining dough, left over from any of the 3 recipes above, may be made into loaves or extra Cornish Splits, Chudleighs etc.

Currant Buns

MAKES 8

Follow recipe for *Milk Bread*. Cut off one-third of risen dough and work in 4oz (125g) currants. When evenly distributed, divide dough into 8 equal-sized pieces. Shape into buns. Stand on greased baking tray. Cover with greased greaseproof paper or polythene. Leave to rise in warm place about 20 minutes or until buns have doubled in size. Bake 20 minutes in hot oven set to 220°C (425°F), Gas 7. Remove from oven. Transfer to wire cooling rack. Either leave plain or, for 'sticky' buns, brush tops with melted honey or golden syrup.

Note The remaining dough may be made into 2 loaves or extra Currant Buns.

243

Chelsea Buns

Chelsea Buns

MAKES 8 ▲▲▲●●●

Follow recipe for *Milk Bread* (page 242). Cut off one-third of risen dough and roll into an oblong 12 by 9in (30 by 23cm). Brush all over with about 1 level tablespoon melted butter. Sprinkle with 3oz (75g) mixed dried fruit, 1oz (25g) chopped mixed peel, 2oz (50g) soft brown sugar and 1 level teaspoon finely-grated lemon peel. Roll up like a Swiss roll, starting from one of the longer sides. Cut into 8 slices of equal thickness. Place close together, cut sides down, in 7in (18cm) well greased square cake tin. Alternatively, stand on greased baking tray. Cover with greased grease-proof paper or polythene. Leave to rise in a warm place about 35 to 40 minutes or until buns have doubled in size and joined together. Bake 25 minutes in hot oven set to 220°C (425°F), Gas 7. Remove from oven. Transfer to wire cooling rack. Leave until cold. If liked, brush with plain

Glacé Icing made by mixing 4oz (100 to 125g) sifted icing sugar to a thin paste with cold water. Separate before eating.

Note These were a favourite of King George III and his wife, Queen Charlotte, so one assumes Chelsea Buns date back to the 18th century and to London's Old Chelsea Bun House where the royal couple would sometimes take tea and buns on a Sunday afternoon.

The remaining dough may be made into 2 loaves or extra Chelsea Buns.

Yorkshire Teacakes

MAKES 15 ▲▲●●●

Follow recipe for *Milk Bread* (page 242) but, when making dough, increase sugar to a total of 3oz (75g). Work 6oz (175g) currants into all the risen dough then divide into 15 equal-sized pieces. Roll each into a round of ½in (1½cm) in thickness and 5in (12½cm) in diameter.

Transfer to greased baking trays. Cover with greased greaseproof paper or polythene. Leave to rise in warm place about 50 minutes or until double in size. Brush with milk. Bake until golden brown; about 15 to 20 minutes in hot oven set to 220°C (425°F), Gas 7. Remove from oven. Cool on wire rack. To serve, split open and spread with butter. Alternatively, split, toast and butter. Serve hot.

Note Fruit may be omitted if preferred.

Speedy White Bread

MAKES 2 LOAVES ▲●●

This heralds a movement away from tradition and introduces us to white bread made with the addition of a small amount of absorbic acid (Vitamin C) which eliminates the first rising and shortens the whole breadmaking procedure. It is advisable to use fresh yeast as dried takes longer to work. It is also recommended that double the amount of yeast be used.

> 1oz (25g) fresh yeast
> ¾pt (425ml) lukewarm water
> 1 × 25mg Vitamin C tablet, very finely crushed
> 1½lb (675g) strong plain flour
> 2 level tsp salt
> 1 level tblsp caster sugar
> 1oz (25g) cooking fat (white vegetable type) or lard

1 Mix yeast to a smooth cream with some of the water. Blend in rest of water. Add crushed Vitamin C tablet.
2 Sift flour and salt into bowl. Toss in sugar. Rub in fat. Mix to soft dough with yeast liquid.
3 Turn on to floured surface. Knead about 15 to 20 minutes or until dough is smooth and elastic and no longer sticky. Cut into 2 equal-sized pieces and shape to fit 2 × 1lb (450g) well-greased loaf tins.
4 Cover with greased greaseproof paper or polythene. Leave to rise in warm place until loaves double in size; about 50 minutes.
5 Bake 35 minutes in very hot oven set to 230°C (450°F), Gas 8. Remove from oven. Turn out on to wire cooling rack.

244

Lovers Knot Rolls

MAKES 18 ▲▲●●

Divide kneaded dough (Speedy White Bread) equally into 18 pieces. Roll each into a 6in (20cm) long strip. Tie each into a knot. Transfer to greased baking trays. Cover with greased greaseproof paper or polythene. Leave to rise in a warm place about 15 minutes or until rolls double in size. Brush with beaten egg. Leave plain or sprinkle with poppy seeds or cracked wheat. Bake as *Speedy White Bread*, allowing 10 to 15 minutes or until rolls are golden brown. Remove from oven. Transfer to wire cooling racks.

Hamburger Buns

MAKES 18 ▲▲●●

Divide kneaded dough (Speedy White Bread) equally into 18 pieces. Roll each into a ball. Roll each into a $\frac{1}{2}$in ($1\frac{1}{4}$cm) thick circle. Transfer to greased baking trays. Cover with greased greaseproof paper or polythene. Leave to rise in warm place about 15 minutes or until buns double in size. Brush with beaten egg. If liked, sprinkle with sesame seeds. Bake as *Speedy White Bread*, allowing 10 to 15 minutes or until buns are golden brown. Remove from oven. Transfer to wire cooling racks.

Note For extra large buns, divide mixture into 12 pieces instead of 18.

Wheatmeal Bread

MAKES 3 LOAVES ▲▲●

READ INTRODUCTION

1oz or 25g (2 level tblsp) dried yeast plus 2 level tsp caster sugar OR 2oz (50g) fresh yeast
$1\frac{1}{2}$pt ($\frac{7}{8}$ litre) lukewarm water
1 bag (3lb or 1.2kg) wheatmeal flour
3 level tsp salt
1 level tblsp caster sugar
2oz (50g) butter, margarine, lard or cooking fat

1 Mix dried yeast and sugar with warm water and leave in a warm place 15 to 20 minutes or until frothy. Alternatively, mix fresh yeast smoothly with some of the water then add remainder.

2 Tip flour into bowl. Toss in salt and sugar. Rub in fat finely with fingertips. Mix to soft dough with yeast liquid.

3 Turn out on to floured surface. Knead about 10 to 12 minutes or until dough is smooth and elastic and no longer sticky. Shape into ball.

4 Transfer to greased bowl. Cover with greased plate. Leave in warm place (kitchen sink half filled with hand-hot water or linen cupboard) until dough doubles in size; about $1\frac{1}{4}$ to $1\frac{1}{2}$ hours.

5 Scoop out on to floured surface and 'knock-back' to remove air bubbles. Knead briefly until smooth. Cut into 3 equal pieces.

6 Shape to fit 3×2lb (1kg) well-greased loaf tins. (Use melted white cooking fat or lard for greasing.)

7 Cover with greased greaseproof paper or polythene and leave to rise in warm place for about 45 minutes to 1 hour or until loaves double in size and look puffy.

8 Glaze by brushing with milk or salted water. If liked, sprinkle with cracked wheat. Bake 45 to 50 minutes in very hot oven set to 230°C (450°F), Gas 8. Leave in tins about 5 minutes. Turn out and cool on wire rack.

Half and Half Bread

MAKES 3 LOAVES ▲▲●

Follow recipe for *Wheatmeal Bread* but use half wheatmeal flour and half strong white. Reduce yeast to half quantity.

Granary Bread

MAKES 3 LOAVES ▲▲●●

Follow recipe for either *Wheatmeal* or *Half and Half Bread*, substituting granary flour for the wheatmeal. Reduce yeast to half quantity if using white flour.

Rye Bread

MAKES 3 LOAVES ▲▲●

Follow recipe for either *Wheatmeal* or *Half and Half Bread*, substituting rye flour for the wheatmeal. Reduce yeast to half quantity if using white flour.

Wholemeal Bread

MAKES 3 LOAVES ▲▲●

Follow recipe for *Wheatmeal Bread*, substituting wholemeal flour for wheatmeal.

Brown Rolls

MAKES 36 ▲▲●

Follow any of the recipes above. Divide risen dough into 36 equal-sized pieces. Shape into round rolls. Place on greased baking trays. Cover with greased greaseproof paper or polythene. Leave to rise in warm place about 25 minutes or until rolls double in size. Brush with milk or salted water. Bake as the breads, allowing about 20 minutes. Remove from oven. Transfer to wire cooling rack.

Quick Brown Bread

MAKES 1 LOAF ▲●

READ INTRODUCTION

$\frac{1}{4}$oz or 8g (2 level tsp) dried yeast plus 1 level tsp sugar OR $\frac{1}{2}$oz (15g) fresh yeast
$\frac{1}{2}$pt (275ml) lukewarm water
1lb (450g) wheatmeal flour (or $\frac{1}{2}$ wholemeal and $\frac{1}{2}$ strong plain)
1 to $1\frac{1}{2}$ level tsp salt
$\frac{1}{2}$oz (15g) white cooking fat or lard

1 Mix dried yeast and sugar with warm water and leave in a warm place about 15 to 20 minutes or until frothy. Alternatively, mix fresh yeast smoothly with some of the water then add remainder.

2 Sift flour and salt into bowl. Rub in fat finely with fingertips. Mix to soft dough with yeast liquid.

3 Turn on to a floured surface. Knead about 10 to 12 minutes or until dough is smooth and elastic and no longer sticky.

4 Shape to fit a 2lb (1kg) well-greased loaf tin. Place inside. Cover with greased greaseproof paper or polythene. Leave to rise in warm place for 45 minutes to 1 hour or until dough doubles in size.

5 Bake 45 to 50 minutes in hot oven set to 220°C (425°F), Gas 7. Remove from oven. Turn out on to a wire cooling rack.

Note This bread is left to rise only once, hence the saving in time.

245

Brown Cob Loaf

MAKES 1 LOAF　　　　▲●

Shape dough into a large ball. Stand on greased baking tray. Flatten slightly. Make a cross cut on top with a sharp knife. Continue as for *Quick Brown Bread*, but immediately before baking brush with salted water and sprinkle with cracked wheat.

Hot Cross Buns

MAKES 12　　　　▲▲●●●

READ INTRODUCTION

> ½oz or 15g (1 level tblsp) dried yeast plus 1 level tsp caster sugar OR 1oz (25g) fresh yeast
> 8 fluid oz (225ml) lukewarm milk and water mixed
> 1lb (450g) strong plain flour
> 1 level tsp salt
> 1½ level tsp mixed spice
> ½ level tsp cinnamon
> 2oz (50g) butter or margarine
> 2oz (50g) caster sugar
> 6oz (175g) mixed dried fruit
> 1 Grade 3 egg, beaten

> GLAZE
> 1½oz (40g) caster sugar
> 2tblsp milk
> 2tblsp water

1　Mix dried yeast and sugar with warm water and leave in a warm place about 15 to 20 minutes or until frothy. Alternatively, mix fresh yeast smoothly with some of the water then add remainder.
2　Sift dry ingredients into a bowl. Rub in butter or margarine. Toss in sugar and fruit. Mix to a soft dough with beaten egg and yeast liquid.
3　Turn out on to a floured surface. Knead about 15 to 20 minutes until dough is smooth and elastic and no longer sticky. Shape into ball.
4　Transfer to greased bowl. Cover with greased plate. Leave to rise in a warm place (kitchen sink half filled with hand-hot water or linen cupboard) until dough doubles in size; about 1 hour.
5　Scoop out on to floured surface and 'knock-back' dough to remove air bubbles. Knead briefly until smooth. Divide into 12 equal-sized pieces.
6　Shape each into a round bun. Place well apart on greased bak-

ing trays. Cut a deep cross on top of each with a sharp knife.
7　Cover with greased greaseproof paper or greased polythene. Leave to rise in a warm place about 40 minutes or until buns double in size and are light and puffy.
8　Bake about 20 minutes in hot oven set to 220°C (425°F), Gas 7 when buns should be golden brown. Remove from oven. Transfer to wire cooling rack.
9　To make glaze, place all ingredients into pan. Heat slowly until sugar dissolves. Bring to boil. Boil fairly briskly 4 to 5 minutes or until syrupy. Remove from heat. Brush over buns.

Note If preferred, pipe crosses on to each bun using a paste made from 2 level tablespoons plain flour mixed with 2 tablespoons cold water. Alternatively, make crosses from thin strips of Shortcrust Pastry (page 186).

Bath Buns

MAKES 12　　　　▲▲●●●

Follow recipe for *Hot Cross Buns* but omit spices, reduce sugar to 1oz (25g) and instead of mixed dried fruit use 3oz (75g) sultanas and 1oz (25g) chopped mixed peel. Beat risen dough in its bowl for 1 minute instead of kneading. Afterwards spoon 12 heaps of dough on to greased baking trays. Brush with a little egg beaten with water, then sprinkle with 1oz (25g) coarsely-crushed cube sugar. Leave to rise and bake as Hot Cross Buns.

Jam Doughnuts

MAKES 12　　　　▲▲▲●●●

READ INTRODUCTION

> ½oz or 15g (1 level tblsp) dried yeast plus 1 level tsp caster sugar OR 1oz (25g) fresh yeast
> 3tblsp lukewarm water
> 8oz (225g) strong, plain flour
> ½ level tsp salt
> ½oz (15g) butter or margarine
> 1 Grade 3 egg, well beaten
> 3tblsp lukewarm milk
> about 6 level tsp red jam
> deep oil for frying

> FOR TOSSING
> caster sugar

1　Mix dried yeast and sugar with warm water and leave in a warm place about 10 to 15 minutes or until frothy. Alternatively, mix fresh yeast smoothly with some of the water then add remainder.
2　Sift flour and salt into a bowl. Rub in butter or margarine finely with fingertips.
3　Mix to a dough with yeast liquid, egg and milk. Turn out on to a floured surface. Knead until smooth and elastic and no longer sticky. Shape into ball.
4　Transfer to greased bowl. Cover with greased plate. Leave to rise in warm place (kitchen sink half filled with hand-hot water or linen cupboard) until dough doubles in size; about 45 minutes.
5　Scoop out on to floured surface and 'knock-back' dough to remove air bubbles. Knead briefly until smooth. Divide into 12 equal-sized pieces and roll into balls.
6　Press a hole in each with finger. Insert ½ teaspoon jam. Pinch together dough around jam so that it is completely enclosed.
7　Stand doughnuts on 2 greased plates. Cover with greased greaseproof paper or greased polythene. Leave to rise in warm place about 20 minutes or until light and almost double in size.
8　Deep fry doughnuts in hot (but NOT smoking) oil for about 4 minutes or until well puffed and golden brown.
9　Remove from pan and drain thoroughly on paper towels. Roll in caster sugar while still slightly warm.

Ring Doughnuts

MAKES 12　　　　▲▲▲●●

Follow recipe for *Jam Doughnuts*. After 'knocking-back' risen dough, roll out to ½in (1¼cm) in thickness. Cut into rounds with a 2¾in (7cm) round biscuit cutter, removing centres with a 1½in (4cm) cutter. Re-roll and re-cut trimmings to make 12 doughnuts in total. Fry and toss in sugar as directed.

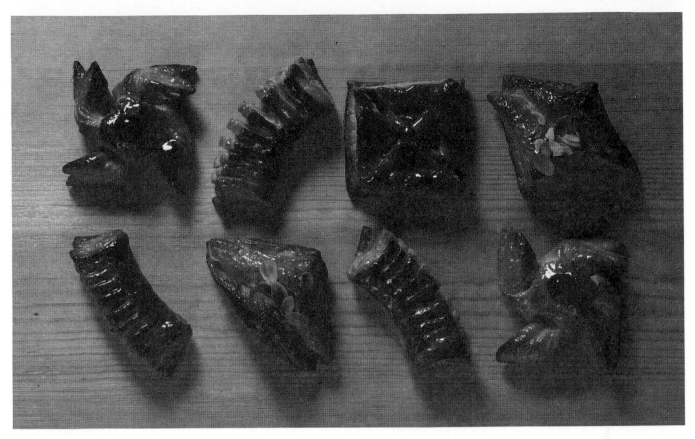

Danish Pastries

Danish Pastries

MAKES 14 ▲▲▲●●●

READ INTRODUCTION

> ¼oz or 8g (2 level tsp) dried yeast
>   plus 1 level tsp caster sugar OR
>   ½oz (15g) fresh yeast
> 5tblsp warm milk
> 8oz (225g) plain flour (not strong)
> pinch salt
> 1 level tblsp caster sugar
> 1 Grade 3 egg, beaten
> 6oz (175g) Danish butter (slightly
>   salted)
> beaten egg for brushing

EXTRAS

> double amount of Glaze as for Hot
>   Cross Buns (page 246)
> Windmills: 2 glacé cherries
> Cocks' Combs: about 2oz (50g)
>   Almond Paste, shop-bought or
>   homemade (page 136)
> Turnovers: 4 level tsp red jam and
>   1 rounded tblsp flaked almonds
> Crossovers: 2 small canned
>   apricot halves

1 Mix dried yeast and sugar with warm milk and leave in a warm place about 15 to 20 minutes or until frothy. Alternatively, mix fresh yeast smoothly with the milk.

2 Sift flour and salt into a bowl. Toss in sugar. Mix to a soft dough with yeast liquid and beaten egg.

3 Turn out on to floured surface. Knead until smooth and elastic and no longer sticky; about 15 to 20 minutes. Transfer to greased bowl and leave to relax for 10 minutes.

4 Meanwhile, press butter into a 9 by 3in oblong (23 by 7½cm). Stand on a piece of foil and refrigerate about 10 minutes.

5 Roll out dough into a 10in (25cm) square. Stand butter in middle. Bring the 2 pieces of dough on either side of the butter to the centre, overlapping them slightly so that butter is completely enclosed.

6 Press top and bottom edges together firmly with a rolling-pin to seal, then roll into a long strip measuring 18 by 6in (45 by 15 cm). Fold in 3, envelope fashion.

7 Cover. Rest 10 minutes in the refrigerator. Repeat the rolling, folding and resting processes twice more. Cut dough into 4 equal-sized pieces.

Windmills

MAKES 4

Roll 1 portion of dough into an 8in (20cm) square. Cut into 4 × 2in (5cm) squares. Make 1in (2½cm) diagonal cuts from each corner towards centre. Bring alternate corners to middle, overlapping slightly and pinching firmly together. Top with a small round of pastry as shown in picture. Brush with egg.

Cocks' Combs

MAKES 4

Roll 1 portion of dough into a 12in (30cm) square. Cut into 4 × 3in (7½cm) squares. Place a strip of Almond Paste along the centre of each. Fold in half and press dough well together to seal. Make slits in the opposite sides of the fold. Brush with egg.

Turnovers

MAKES 4

Cut out as Cocks' Combs above. Place a teaspoon of jam on centre of each. Fold each in half to form a triangle. Brush with egg and sprinkle with nuts.

Fruit and Nut Stollen

Crossovers

MAKES 2

Roll last portion of dough into a 12in (30cm) square. Cut into 4 × 3in (7½cm) squares. Remove centres from 2 of the squares. Knead together, roll out and cut into 4 long strips. Moisten edges of uncut squares with water. Top with cut out squares. Fill centres with apricot halves, cut sides down. Arrange criss-cross of strips on top of each. Brush with egg.

To Finish

Transfer Pastries to greased baking trays. Cover with greased grease-proof paper or greased polythene. Leave to rise in warm place for 30 minutes or until double in size and puffy. Bake 15 minutes in hot oven set to 220°C (425°F), Gas 7. Remove from oven. Transfer to wire cooling racks. Brush with glaze. Decorate Windmills with ½ glacé cherries. Allow to cool before serving. If possible, eat freshly made.

Fruit and Nut Stollen

MAKES 1 LARGE CAKE

▲▲▲●●

READ INTRODUCTION

YEAST BATTER
¼oz or 8g (2 level tsp) dried yeast
  OR ½oz (15g) fresh yeast
½ level tsp caster sugar
3 fluid oz (75ml) lukewarm milk
2oz (50g) strong, plain flour

REST OF MIXTURE
6oz (175g) strong, plain flour
½ level tsp salt
1 rounded tblsp caster sugar
1oz (25g) butter
1 Grade 2 egg, well beaten

ADDITIONS
2oz (50g) blanched and chopped
  almonds
finely-grated peel of 1 small lemon
4oz (125g) sultanas
1oz (25g) chopped mixed peel
1oz (25g) butter, melted

DECORATION
icing sugar

1 To make batter, stir yeast and sugar into milk. If using dried yeast, leave to stand for 5 minutes.
2 Mix in flour. Leave in a warm place for 20 minutes or until frothy.
3 Sift flour and salt into bowl. Toss in sugar. Rub in butter finely with fingertips. Mix to dough with yeast liquid and egg.
4 Turn out on to floured surface. Knead until smooth and no longer sticky; about 15 minutes.
5 Transfer to greased bowl. Cover with greased plate. Leave in warm place to rise (sink half filled with hand-hot water or linen cupboard) for about 1 hour or until dough doubles in size.
6 Scoop on to floured surface and knead in all the additions except butter.
7 Roll out into a circle of about 10in (25cm) in diameter. Brush surface of dough heavily with melted butter. Fold in 3 like an omelet.
8 Transfer to greased baking tray. Cover with greased greaseproof paper or polythene. Leave to rise in warm place about 45 minutes or until double in size.
9 Brush with melted butter. Bake until golden brown; about 30 to 40 minutes in moderately hot oven set to 200°C (400°F), Gas 6.
10 Remove from oven. Transfer to wire cooling rack. Sift icing sugar over the top when cold.

Serve cut into slices and buttered.

Note Stollen is German Christmas Cake, now enjoying great seasonal popularity in the UK.

Brioche

MAKES 12   ▲▲▲●●●

READ INTRODUCTION

¼oz or 8g (2 level tsp) dried yeast
  OR ½oz (15g) fresh yeast
½ level tsp caster sugar
6tsp lukewarm water
8oz (225g) strong, plain flour
pinch of salt
2 extra level tsp caster sugar
2oz (50g) butter, melted
2 Grade 3 eggs, well beaten
a little extra beaten egg for brushing

1 Mix dried yeast with ½ level teaspoon sugar and water. Leave in a warm place about 10 to 15 minutes or until frothy. Alternatively, mix fresh yeast smoothly with the water.
2 Sift flour and salt into bowl. Toss in sugar. Mix to a soft dough with yeast liquid, butter and eggs. Turn out on to a floured surface. Knead about 10 minutes or until dough is smooth, elastic and no longer sticky.
3 Transfer to greased bowl. Cover with greased plate. Leave in warm place to rise (sink half filled with hand-hot water or linen cupboard) until dough doubles in size; about 1 to 1½ hours.
4 Scoop out on to floured surface. 'Knock-back' to remove air bubbles by kneading quickly and lightly.
5 Divide two-thirds of the dough into 12 equal-sized pieces. Shape into balls. Drop into very well-greased fluted or plain bun tins.
6 Using a rolling-pin handle, press deep holes in centres of each. Roll remaining dough into 12 small balls. Stand on top of holes.
7 Cover with greased greaseproof paper or greased polythene. Leave to rise in warm place about 1 hour or until Brioche have doubled in size.
8 Brush with egg. Bake 12 to 15 minutes in very hot oven set to 230°C (450°F), Gas 8.
9 Remove from oven. Take out of tins. Cool on a wire rack. Serve fresh.

Croissants

MAKES 12 ▲▲▲●●●

READ INTRODUCTION

*½oz or 15g (1 level tblsp) dried
   yeast plus 2 level tsp caster
   sugar OR 1oz (25g) fresh yeast
8 fluid oz (225ml) lukewarm
   water
1lb (450g) strong, plain flour
1 level tsp salt
1oz (25g) white cooking fat or
   margarine
1 Grade 3 egg, beaten
6oz (175g) butter, lightly chilled
   and divided into 3
beaten egg for brushing
a very small amount of extra sugar*

Brioche

1 Mix dried yeast and sugar with warm water and leave in a warm place about 15 to 20 minutes or until frothy. Alternatively, mix fresh yeast smoothly with some of the water then stir in remainder.

2 Sift flour and salt into bowl. Rub in fat or margarine. Mix to dough with yeast liquid and egg. Turn out on to floured surface. Knead about 15 to 20 minutes or until dough is smooth and elastic and no longer sticky.

3 Roll into an oblong measuring 20 by 8in (50cm by 20cm). Cover top two-thirds of oblong with flakes cut from 1 portion of butter.

4 Fold in 3, envelope fashion, by bringing bottom third (without fat) over centre third and folding top third over. Press edges with rolling-pin to seal.

5 Turn dough so that folded edges are to the left and right then re-roll and re-fold twice more, using up last 2 portions of butter.

6 Cover dough with greased greaseproof paper or greased polythene and refrigerate 30 minutes. Roll and fold 3 times more, without any more butter, resting dough 10 minutes in the refrigerator each time.

7 Roll out dough into an oblong measuring 18 by 12in (45cm by 30cm). Trim away rough edges. Cut dough into 6 squares then cut each square into 2 triangles.

8 Brush surfaces with beaten egg to which a large pinch of sugar has been added. Loosely roll each triangle towards the point, finish-

Croissants

ing with the tip underneath. Curve into crescents. Transfer to greased trays, leaving plenty of room between each.

9 Cover with greased greaseproof paper or greased polythene.

Leave to rise in a warm place until double in size; about 35 to 40 minutes.

10 Brush with beaten egg. Bake until golden brown, allowing about 20 minutes in hot oven set to 220°C (425°F), Gas 7. Remove from oven. Cool on a wire rack. Serve fresh.

Blinis

Texture uneven and full of large holes
1 Dough inadequately 'knocked-back'.
2 Dough was not covered while rising.

Coarse, open texture
1 Too much liquid was used.
2 Dough was over-proved either the first or second time or both.
3 Oven not hot enough.

Close, heavy texture
1 Soft flour used instead of plain strong.
2 Too much salt added.
3 Insufficient kneading and/or proving.
4 Liquid used for mixing too hot and some of the yeast was killed.
5 Dough left to rise in too hot a place and some of the yeast was killed.

Loaf etc collapses on itself during baking
1 Dough over-proved by being left to rise for too long a time.

Top crust breaks away from loaf of bread
1 Dough was not left to rise long enough and was therefore under proved.
2 Dough was inadequately covered while rising and dried out.
3 Oven too hot.

Crust splits on one side of loaf
1 Loaf baked too close to side of oven.

Loaf has flat instead of domed top
1 Soft flour used instead of strong plain.
2 Insufficient salt added.
3 Too much liquid used and therefore dough too wet.
4 Dough badly shaped.

Crust starts cracking after loaf etc has been removed from oven
1 Dough over-proved by being left to rise too long.
2 Oven too hot.
3 Baked goods left to cool in a draught.

Bread etc very crumbly and stales rapidly
1 Too much yeast.
2 Soft flour used instead of strong plain.
3 Dough was allowed to rise too quickly in too hot a place.
4 Dough was either left to rise for too long a time and was over-proved, or for too short a time and did not rise sufficiently.

Yeasted goods smell very strongly of yeast
1 Yeast was creamed with sugar.
2 Too much yeast used.
3 Yeast was stale (particularly applies to fresh yeast).
4 Dough was over-proved.

Blinis or Russian Yeasted Pancakes

MAKES ABOUT 15   ▲▲●●

8oz (225g) strong, plain flour
½ level tsp salt
1 level tsp caster sugar
½oz (15g) fresh yeast or 2 level tsp dried yeast
½pt (275ml) warm milk
1 Grade 3 egg, separated (kitchen temperature)
melted lard or oil for frying

1 Sift flour and salt into bowl. Add sugar and yeast. Stir in milk. Cover. Leave in warm place 30 minutes or until foamy.

2 Stir round briskly with egg yolk. Beat white to stiff snow. Fold into yeasted mixture.

3 Brush heavy-based frying pan with lard or oil. Heat until hot. Add a tablespoon of batter mixture. Fry until golden. Turn over. Fry underside until golden. Continue until all the batter is used, making about 15 Blinis.

4 Stick one on top of the other as they are cooked, then serve in traditional fashion with soured cream, melted butter (for pouring over top) and smoked salmon or mock caviar. For sweet Blinis, accompany with vanilla ice cream and honey.

Index